THE OTHER COLD WAR

CANADA'S MILITARY ASSISTANCE TO THE DEVELOPING WORLD 1945-1975

THE OTHER COLD WAR

CANADA'S MILITARY ASSISTANCE TO THE DEVELOPING WORLD 1945-1975

CHRISTOPHER R. KILFORD

CANADIAN DEFENCE ACADEMY PRESS

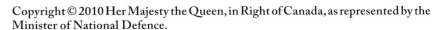

Canadian Defence Academy Press
PO Box 17000 Stn Forces
Kingston, Ontario   K7K 7B4

Produced for the Canadian Defence Academy Press
by 17 Wing Winnipeg Publishing Office.
WPO 30527

Library and Archives Canada Cataloguing in Publication

Kilford, Christopher R., 1961-
The other cold war : Canada's military assistance to the developing
world, 1945-1975 / written by Christopher Kilford.

Produced for the Canadian Defence Academy Press by 17 Wing Winnipeg
Publishing Office.
Includes bibliographical references and index.
Issued by: Canadian Defence Academy.
ISBN 978-1-100-14337-8 (bound)
ISBN 978-1-100-14338-5 (pbk.)
Cat. no.: D2-257/1-2010E (bound)
Cat. no.: D2-257/2-2010E (pbk.)

1. Military assistance, Canadian--Developing countries--History--20th
century. 2. Canada--Foreign relations--Developing countries. 3. Developing
countries--Foreign relations--Canada. 4. Canada--Foreign relations--1945-.
5. Canada--Armed Forces--History--20th century. I. Canadian Defence Academy
II. Canada. Canadian Armed Forces. Wing, 17 III. Title. IV. Title: Canada's military assistance to the developing world, 1945-1975.

UA600 K54 2010   355'.0320971091724   C2010-980137-7

Printed in Canada.

1 3 5 7 9 10 8 6 4 2

ACKNOWLEDGEMENTS

The book that you have in your hands is the outcome of my Ph.D. work at Queen's University in Kingston, Ontario. The subject is military assistance to the developing world and more specifically, Canada's role in this field during the post-war period up until 1975. It was an area of study to which, as a military officer with a wider interest in general development efforts, I took to right away and throughout my time at Queen's I was greatly encouraged by Dr. Allan English, my thesis supervisor. Dr. David Parker and Dr. Robert Shenton, as co-supervisors, also provided outstanding advice and direction, and the course work in development studies I completed under the guidance of Dr. Shenton was of great benefit to my thesis work. I was, in addition, helped immensely by staff from Library and Archives Canada who assisted me in unearthing many files never before accessed.

I must also add that during my thesis work I was most fortunate to meet Major-General (retired) John Sharpe, who served in Ghana from 1966-68 with Canada's military training assistance team. With the information he provided, I was able to make contact with many former veterans of Canada's military assistance efforts in the 1960s. Therefore, it is important that I take the time to recognize the following individuals who helped bring meaning and life to the many files and documents I was working with: Donald Atkinson, Grahame Baskerville, Robert Dallison, Desmond (Des) Deane-Freeman, Clair Donnelly, Robert Edwards, Douglas Fraser, Robert Frost, Norman Graham, Peter Harrison, Garry Hunt, George Logan, Alexander (Sandy) MacDonald, Joe Mantin, Harry Marston, William (Bill) McAndrew, Paul Robison, William (Bill) Smith, Murray Stewart, and William (Punchy) Westfall. Last, but certainly not least, I must also thank former Canadian Ambassadors Arthur Menzies and Michael Shenstone. Arthur Menzies was the first Chair of the Interdepartmental Military Assistance Committee in 1964, while Michael Shenstone became Chair in 1968. Both provided me with a great deal of insight regarding the period and the Committee's work.

FOREWORD

I am delighted to introduce *The Other Cold War – Canada's Military Assistance to the Developing World 1945-1975*. Written by Lieutenant-Colonel Christopher Kilford, an experienced and well-respected military officer with first hand development experience, the book represents an important addition to the Canadian Defence Academy Press. Indeed, the book offers valuable insights regarding the "Whole of Government" pillars of Defence, Development and Diplomacy, but from a historical perspective. It is, in essence, the early history of our current Military Training Assistance Program.

But, as in any historical work, there is much more to be gleaned. As Lieutenant-Colonel Kilford notes, historically, armed forces in developing countries were seen by many as the best means to drive political, economic and social development and, at times, reforms. That was certainly the thinking in the post-colonial period amongst many prominent political scientists in the United States who, in turn, influenced opinion within External Affairs and the Department of National Defence in Ottawa. Besides thinking that military assistance would generally advance overall development efforts, the Canadian government also realized that offering such assistance, from time-to-time and to specific developing countries, served its domestic and foreign policy interests very well.

From a more contemporary perspective, the focus of military assistance to Afghanistan has taken the form of both assisting the Afghan government in its fight against an insurgency, as well as providing advice on broader social-political issues in Kabul. Importantly, military assistance in the training of Afghan police and the Afghan National Army (ANA) contributes to national modernization. As the ANA continues to expand and develop as a true "national institution", its presence and influence in Afghan society is also increasing. It is becoming a key component of nation-building in that country. Thus I believe this book will be of considerable value for current and future Canadian policy-makers as it allows one to better appreciate, based on past experience, the political, economic and social consequences of building up military forces in developing countries, especially when other institutions of government are weak.

In closing, I wish to restate the importance of this book for those involved with the provision of military assistance to developing countries or in providing general development expertise to countries in need. At the Canadian Defence Academy Press, we also hope that it will both enlighten and educate those who serve in, and who interact with, the profession of arms in Canada.

Major-General J.P.Y.D. Gosselin
Commander
Canadian Defence Academy

TABLE OF CONTENTS

LIST OF FIGURES AND TABLES

CHAPTER 1

INTRODUCTION

The purpose of this book is to discuss how Canada, and the Canadian Forces, became involved with the delivery of military assistance to the developing world from the post-war period until the election of Pierre Trudeau as prime minister in 1968.[1] Military assistance, in effect the provision of equipment, advice or training to the armed forces of a recipient country, was an area in which Canada and the Canadian Forces became significantly, if somewhat haphazardly, involved after 1945.

Why did Canada become involved with the delivery of military assistance to the post-war developing world? The answer is that offering military assistance, from time-to-time and to specific countries, served Canada's domestic and foreign policy interests. From a domestic standpoint, sales of aircraft, arms, and ammunition helped preserve Canadian jobs. Internationally, military assistance allowed Canada to play an active role in furthering development activities. In particular, academics writing in the early 1960s on the positive role that militaries could play in modernizing developing countries had convinced many in Ottawa that military assistance would be a catalyst for wider economic and political development in the receiving countries. However and perhaps most importantly, providing military assistance to developing countries demonstrated to Canada's allies that Ottawa was also willing, when asked, to play an active role in preventing the Soviet Union and China from expanding their influence.

As it would also turn out, many developing countries were eager to distance themselves from Great Britain and the United States in particular, and they enthusiastically sought out Canada to provide them with military assistance. Yet, the Canadian military, with commitments at home, on the continent, with the North Atlantic Treaty Organization (NATO) in Europe and the United Nations (UN), were not at all eager to send personnel overseas to train foreign military forces in developing countries.

In fact, Canada's armed forces proved very successful in side stepping non-NATO requests for military assistance in the 1950s, much to the annoyance of External Affairs. As far as the senior officers were concerned, NATO was the priority, not assisting External Affairs in some hazy effort to prevent communist penetration into Asia and Africa or to increase Canada's overall presence in distant places. To turn matters around, it would take a combination of Ghanaian President Kwame Nkrumah asking for Canadian military assistance and Prime Minister John Diefenbaker wanting to help. For Canada, its military assistance contributions in the developing world would become part of the larger drama played out in Europe during the Cold War.

While Canada's military leadership did succeed in avoiding military assistance missions in the 1950s, the situation had completely changed a decade later. Indeed, Great Britain and the United States regarded Canada as a useful ally – an ally they could count on to take the lead in offering military assistance to developing countries where, for historical and political reasons, they could not. As a result, countries such as Ghana and Tanzania would eventually come to rely heavily on Canadian military assistance, and both of these countries were comfortable in doing so. Canada, as was so often mentioned in External Affairs and Department of National Defence correspondence at the time, was regarded by developing countries as having no colonial baggage and a genuine desire to lend a hand. However, while there was in Ottawa a desire to help developing countries through the provision of military assistance, more often than not, the need to counter or check Russian and Chinese influence in the developing world really determined who would and would not obtain Canada's military support.

Given the number of military assistance requests arriving in Ottawa in the early 1960s, the government established the Interdepartmental Military Assistance Committee in August 1964. Chaired by External Affairs, the Committee included members from the Departments of National Defence, Defence Production and Finance. Their role was to bring order to disorder as up until 1964 military assistance requests had been handled by External Affairs on an *ad hoc* basis. The Committee soon found out that the difficulty, from a foreign policy perspective, was what to say to those countries whose requests for military assistance were turned down.

Then again, foreign requests for Canadian arms were seldom denied as it was well understood in Cabinet that if Canada did not sell arms to the developing world there were plenty of other countries, including the British, French and the United States, that certainly would. The Department of Finance, however, was always wary of the Committee making military assistance commitments of any kind, believing that costs would eventually spiral out of control. Finance officials also believed that Canada's arms manufacturers, always in search of new markets, had far too much influence in Ottawa.

The Committee also found that providing military assistance to developing countries had its political challenges. In the case of Ghana, the Canadian-trained Ghana Army staged two coups, the first in 1966 that resulted in the overthrow of Kwame Nkrumah. Meanwhile, in Tanzania, the Canadian-trained and mentored military was actively engaged in supporting guerillas fighting Portuguese forces in Mozambique. While the 1966 coup in Ghana, to the delight of Ottawa and Washington, put an end to Russian and Chinese influence in that country, the same situation did not occur in Tanzania. Despite the presence of some 90 Canadian military advisors, their Chinese counterparts would slowly gain ground, replacing the Canadians almost entirely when Ottawa, at the request of the Tanzanian government, ended military assistance to that country in 1970.

Commenting on the early years following Trudeau's election in 1968, Sean Maloney wrote that Trudeau, unlike his predecessors Louis St. Laurent, John Diefenbaker and Lester Pearson, had been "committed to making Canada the largest of the small nations rather than maintaining Canada as the smallest of the large nations."[2] As a result of this thinking the new prime minister would go on to question almost every aspect of Canada's defence relations, from participation in NATO to why the Canadian Forces were involved in the delivery of military assistance to the developing world. In particular, Trudeau believed that any sort of military assistance was ill-advised, and he would ultimately attempt to put an end to Canada's military assistance program soon after his election. The fact was that at the beginning of his term in office he was very reluctant to spend any money on defence given the "need to make good on the Pearson government's commitments to the Canadian people regarding social programmes administered and paid for by the federal government."³ Thus, in July 1969, Cabinet decided to end Canada's military assistance program over a three-year period. The decision might have seemed short-sighted at the time, but Trudeau did have, it must be said, good grounds for wanting to end to the program and it was only through a last ditch effort by External Affairs that a small military assistance program was kept alive.

From examining Canada's military assistance to the post-war developing world, three conclusions are apparent. First, Canada became engaged in the business of military assistance on an *ad hoc* basis. There was no master plan to offer military assistance to foreign countries as a means to boost domestic armaments production, spur on wider development activities in the receiving countries or to gain greater international political influence for Canada. Second, when Ottawa began sending military advisors around the globe in the 1960s, the need to check communist influence often determined which countries received Canadian military help. Finally, Trudeau's decision to end Canada's military assistance efforts was a sound one given the domestic and international political situation at the time.

Of course, for those Canadian Forces personnel who were sent overseas on military assistance missions, the experience was one of the main highlights of their military careers. Far away from the normal routine of garrison life in Canada, or with NATO in Europe, officers and non-commissioned officers (NCO) were thrust into unfamiliar territory, given extraordinary responsibility and simply told to get on with the job. They joined, as a result of their efforts, an unofficial but influential club of military advisors whose modern history can be traced back several centuries. As Donald Stoker wrote in *Military Advising and Assistance – From Mercenaries to Privatization, 1815-2007*, "nations seeking to develop and improve their military forces have often sought the advice of foreigners."⁴

Unquestionably, many developing countries in the post-war period sought the advice of the Canadian Forces, yet there was no comprehensive study of Canada's military assistance efforts in the post-war period available. There are, in fact, only three journal articles and one chapter in a self-published autobiography that directly address the issue. The first journal article to be published was Garry Hunt's "Recollections of the Canadian Armed Forces Training Team in Ghana, 1961-1968," that appeared in the *Canadian Defence Quarterly* in 1989. Twelve years later, *Canadian Military History* published Andrew Godefroy's observations on "The Canadian Armed Forces Advisory and Training Team Tanzania 1965-1970." Both articles, as their titles imply, dealt with very specific Canadian military assistance missions. Then, in 1995, Greg Donaghy wrote a more wide-ranging work: "The Rise and Fall of Canadian Military Assistance in the Developing World, 1952-1971." His article was also published in *Canadian Military History*. Lastly, in 2007, Norman Graham's book *From The Barrack Room To The Boardroom: The Memoirs Of A Self-Made Man* was published. Graham, a retired Major, had served in Ghana for two years and a chapter of his book was dedicated to his time spent assisting the Ghana Army in the early 1970s.

Besides the references noted above, few other secondary sources mention Canada's military assistance to the developing world and when they do, it is only in passing. Ivan Head and Pierre Trudeau briefly mentioned the desire by Trudeau to end military assistance as soon as he took office in their book, *The Canadian Way: Shaping Canada's Foreign Policy, 1968-1984*. Peyton Lyon also addressed some of the requests for military assistance that flowed into Ottawa after the Second World War in *Canada and the Third World*. Finally, in *The Department of External Affairs, Volume 2: Coming of Age, 1946-1968*, John Hilliker and Donald Barry provided background on the efforts of External Affairs to address general aid requests from the developing world in the post-war period including those for military assistance.

It would, therefore, be an understatement to say that secondary sources on the subject of Canada's military assistance efforts in the post-war developing world were scarce. Indeed, the entire subject was in need of a thorough history based on serious analysis. That is the purpose of this book, which has been largely based on, but not limited to, archival material from Library and Archives Canada, the Directorate of History and Heritage in the Department of National Defence and the State Department in the United States. In addition to the primary sources, I was also able to obtain the assistance of retired military and diplomatic officers, who had served overseas on military assistance missions or as chairs of the Interdepartmental

Military Assistance Committee in the 1960s. Lastly, I profited from having over 30 years of military experience and considerable first-hand knowledge of Canada's contemporary military assistance efforts including a one-year tour in Kabul, Afghanistan as the Deputy Military Attaché – a role that allowed me to spend considerable time writing on issues related to the expansion of the Afghan National Army and observing, up-close, our more contemporary efforts in training and mentoring a foreign military force.

By utilizing primary sources, many of which had never been accessed before, the book also provides a deeper understanding of the military assistance role that Canada took on in the post-war developing world and addresses several significant gaps. There was, for example, no in-depth study of why and how Canada became involved with the selling of arms to a number of developing countries in the post-war period – countries that included Israel, India, Malaysia, Nationalist China, and Pakistan. Nor was there any scholarly research on the origins and outcomes of Canada's military assistance to Ghana and Nigeria. On the other hand, Godefroy's article provided an excellent overview of Canada's military assistance in Tanzania, but likely due to space limitations, could not tell the entire story of why the mission came about and what eventually transpired.

In addition, no in-depth study on the formation of the Interdepartmental Military Assistance Committee, its membership, overall function, thinking and decision-making had been written. Nor had there been any research conducted on the substantial and successful efforts undertaken by the Committee, supported by the Canadian Forces, to maintain a modest program of military assistance following Cabinet's decision to end all such programs no later than 1974. Moreover, no investigation had been conducted as to why the Canadian Forces had been reluctant, in the 1950s, to keep away from military assistance requests coming from the developing world. While Donaghy's article undoubtedly provided a superb overview of Canada's military assistance efforts, at nine pages, including pictures, only certain aspects of this story could be told.

To provide the foundation and proof to support the three specific conclusions stemming from the new research that has been conducted, requires the reader to embark on a journey that commences in the initial chapters of this book – a journey that begins by obtaining a fundamental understanding of the historical origins of military assistance, the need for, and creation of, armed forces in post-war and post-colonial developing countries and the initial attempts by countries such as the United States, the Soviet Union and Canada to meet the rising demands in the developing world for military assistance after 1945. Given this context, the reader is in a much better position to appreciate the situation in which Canada found itself in the post-war period and why, for example, the leadership of the Canadian Forces were almost always reluctant to support military assistance missions.

With the above roadmap in mind, Chapter 2 explains why, primarily using Egypt, Madagascar and Japan as examples, the establishment of armed forces was seen as being crucial to state-building and national development. The leaders of these three countries recognized that the selective importation of European military technology and military assistance would act as a catalyst for overall economic growth. The lesson for observers of 19th century Egypt and Japan, for example, was that modernization through militarization created rapid economic growth and allowed both countries to become, in their own spheres, regional military powers.

While the path to modernization through militarization did produce some spectacular economic results, chiefly in Egypt and Japan, stimulating economic growth through the creation of permanent armies and the production of armaments often had disastrous consequences. At best, military forces were often an economic burden. At their worst, they were a source of political instability – and when economies faltered, as they tended to do in the developing world, military establishments were loath to see their share of the national budget decrease. Coups or the establishment of civilian governments principally controlled by the military were often the result of government-inspired economic austerity programs.

Picking up from the last chapter, Chapter 3 argues that academics in the early 1960s, chiefly in the United States, were instrumental in convincing governments that armed forces in post-colonial developing countries also had a central, modernizing role to play. However, academics who believed militaries in the developing world could be the leaders of change and modernization in their respective countries were wrong in their assumptions. Military forces in the developing world, it would eventually become clear, were not agents of change and modernization at all – and once even the smallest military woke up to the fact that they were the most powerful national institution, the temptation to take over the government was frequently irresistible. Of course, there were good reasons, as Chapter 3 emphasizes, for newly independent countries to have armed forces, even if the military was not going to be a tool for modernization. Besides threats to their existence, some colonies were not granted independence until demonstrating they possessed sufficient armed forces to uphold internal security and guard their borders. Having armed forces was also often seen by the leaders of developing countries as a basic requirement of a modern state.

Whatever the case might have been for establishing armed forces, arms and training assistance, as Chapter 4 explains, were soon offered to most militaries in the developing world by developed countries eager to gain or maintain influence and ultimately sell weapons. Indeed, military assistance to the developing world was a key foreign policy tool for many governments. The United States was unquestionably keen to use military assistance, certainly after the Second World War, to cultivate new friends and contain the spread of communism. Economically, arms sales equated to jobs in developed countries and the market for arms sales was highly competitive. How military equipment sold to developing countries might be used in the end or whether it was used at all, was of little concern in Washington, Moscow, Beijing, Paris or London.

Canada, it is also argued in Chapter 4, was not exempt from the demands of countries in the developing world to sell them arms and/or provide military assistance. Nor was Canada immune to the demands of its allies and its own industries to become engaged, militarily, in developing countries by selling weapons and providing military assistance. In time, the Canadian government would find itself selling military equipment to dozens of developing countries and providing major military assistance training teams to several countries in sub-Saharan Africa.

The purpose of Chapter 5 is to provide an overview of the Canadian Forces in the post-war period and to argue that the provision of military assistance was a task that the Canadian Forces were not at all eager to participate in given their already significant commitments to NATO and the UN. The reality was, however, that Canada's armed forces were too small to support armaments and aircraft manufacturing industries at home and so new customers had to be found. Arms exports, particularly tied with military training assistance, as Chapter 6 then argues, would become a very valuable tool in this regard. Of course, countries requesting military arms and assistance in the developing world were often either at war or on the brink of war. Helping them out meant having to negotiate a political minefield at home and internationally. However, protecting jobs at home was important and although successive Canadian governments were always wary about being seen taking sides or promoting regional arms races, more often than not, arms sales would be approved.

Returning to the Canadian Forces, Chapter 7 maintains that military leaders were undoubtedly successful in side-stepping requests from the developing world in the early 1950s and requests from External Affairs to the Canadian Forces to provide military assistance to several developing countries were almost always turned down. However, it was apparent to the Canadian government that many newly independent states, especially in sub-Saharan Africa, were eager to distance themselves from their former colonial masters when it came to military assistance. There was, most importantly, also pressure on Canada from Great Britain and the United States to take an active role in stemming the growing communist influence in Africa. The result of this pressure was that the Canadian military, with little to no experience training African militaries, would soon find itself heavily involved on the continent, commencing in the early 1960s with military assistance to Ghana.

The decision to provide Ghana with military assistance opened the door for other countries to ask Canada for similar levels of support. As a result, the Canadian government took the decision to form an Interdepartmental Military Assistance Committee in 1964 as External Affairs could no longer manage the growing number of requests for military help through the *ad hoc* arrangements then in place. By 1965, major Canadian military assistance missions were underway in Ghana and Tanzania and the Finance Department was arguing that the entire military assistance program, at least from a fiscal perspective, was out of control.

The purpose of Chapter 8 and Chapter 9 is to discuss the important contribution Canada played in offering military assistance to Ghana and Tanzania respectively. Each chapter argues that the Canadian Forces had a major role in the development of armed forces in both countries, but both the Ghanaian and Tanzanian militaries were far too small to have any influence on wider development efforts in their particular countries. Each chapter further argues that the Canadian Forces did play an important role in preventing the Soviet Union and China from expanding their influence. Certainly, this was the case in regards to Ghana, where the Canadian-trained Ghana Army overthrew the government in 1966, which resulted in the subsequent expulsion of Soviet and Chinese advisors. Events in Tanzania would not turn out so favourably, at least from the perspective of Ottawa, London and Washington.

Trudeau, Chapter 10 argues, was adamant that Canada would not become entangled in Cold War intrigues in the developing world or anywhere else for that matter and the substantial Canadian military assistance missions in Ghana and Tanzania left plenty of cause for concern in Ottawa. Indeed, Canada's military assistance was almost completely terminated in July 1969, when Cabinet decided that military assistance to developing countries would be phased out over a three-year period beginning in fiscal year 1970-71. As the chapter argues, there were several reasons behind the decision to stop providing military assistance to the developing world. For one, Trudeau did not want developing countries to squander their meager resources buying weapons. He was also very concerned that Canada might become mixed up in a proxy conflict in the developing world between the United States and the Soviet Union or even China. Moreover, Trudeau was not convinced that a developing country asking the Soviets or Chinese for economic or military help was really of strategic importance.

Chapter 10 also explains how the Interdepartmental Military Assistance Committee went to great effort to convince the government to maintain a modest military assistance program. To this end, in 1969, the Committee went to work on a review of military assistance efforts so far, suggesting in their final report that military assistance would help support Canadian policy in the developing world, in particular by promoting economic and social progress – an argument first espoused in the early

1960s by academics in the United States that had already been proven false. However, as Chapter 10 claims, Trudeau quickly realized in 1968 that the country could barely afford the social programs introduced by his predecessor. Secondly, domestic security issues were at the forefront when he came to power, and if matters had deteriorated, a large part of the Canadian Forces was overseas and not immediately available. It was also likely difficult to justify in his mind the expense of sustaining troops in Europe, on UN missions and carrying out military assistance work in light of the economic and political situation at home.

Then again, the work of the Interdepartmental Military Assistance Committee did not go entirely unrewarded and in 1970, a Memorandum to Cabinet on the importance of continuing Canada's military assistance efforts did achieve its desired effect – the securing of a small amount of funds to keep some military assistance programs alive. Yet, as Chapter 10 concludes, there was no escaping the fact that Canada was giving up on any serious attempt to keep its military assistance efforts going. And while a modest program would continue, its funding was never certain. Moreover, thirty years would need to pass before the funds allocated for military assistance equaled the amounts spent in the 1960s.

CHAPTER 2

HISTORICAL LESSONS: MILITARIZATION AND MODERNIZATION

War or the very possibility of war makes the establishment of a manufacturing power an indispensable requirement for any nation of first rank.

Friedrich List, 1837

Powerful war machines, much as they may be desired by some nations, are not, however, brought into being by sleight-of-hand or wishful thinking. They are the developments of long years of work, experiment, and expense and are rooted in the infinitely complex national life of a people.

Hyman Kublin, 1949

In the mid-20th century, in particular amongst several prominent political scientists in the United States, there was a definite belief that armed forces in developing countries would help drive economic development by unifying diverse populations, stimulating literacy and creating a group of technically trained personnel – personnel who, upon leaving the military, would enter into civilian life equipped with a wide variety of skills useful for public and state-run industrial pursuits. However, these academics, writing in the early 1960s were eventually proved wrong in their calculations and the creation of military forces in the 20th century developing world did not have the same economic impact as it had had in previous centuries. In reality, post-war developing countries remained largely dependent on the developed world for military advice and support, and given the ready supply of cheap arms, for example, had little chance of stimulating economic growth through the creation of their own armament factories.

Nevertheless, as will be argued through an analysis of several historical examples, the theory that economic and societal modernization, particularly in the post-colonial developing world, could be achieved through militarization was not drawn out of thin air. There was substantive historical evidence underpinning the argument of why building up military strength in the short-term was essential to modernizing and achieving economic strength in the long-term. For example, in Egypt, Madagascar and Japan, leaders soon recognized that establishing modern armed forces was going to be an absolute necessity to keep European powers from gaining control of their economies. These three countries also recognized that the selective importation of European military technology and military assistance would act as a catalyst for overall economic growth. The lesson for observers of 19th century Egypt and Japan, and to a lesser extent, Madagascar, was that modernization through militarization resulted in rapid economic growth in all three countries.

To begin, the interrelationship between military strength and economic strength, and arguably the foundations of academic reasoning in the mid-20th century on the importance of armed forces, Edward Earle suggested, could be traced to Europe of the 1500s with the rise of "beliefs and practices" generally known as mercantilism.[5] The mercantilist system sought to overturn the last vestiges of the Middle Ages through unification and the development of insular national economic and military institutions resistant to outside intervention and influence. Moreover, said Earle, war was "inherent to the mercantilist system," in which a nation's economic strength was more so derived through weakening others economically than developing harmonious trading relations.[6] In Europe, therefore, achieving military supremacy was the path to economic success and by 1763, with "her fleets and admiralty...at the service of the economic interests of the nation," England had crushed her Spanish, Dutch and French rivals.[7]

In England, Adam Smith, well known as an anti-mercantilist and an ardent proponent of free trade, was, on the other hand, an advocate of protective duties when it came to issues of military security. "It is of importance," he wrote in the *Wealth of Nations*, "that the kingdom depend as little as possible upon its neighbours for the manufactures necessary for its defense."[8] When the first Secretary of the United States Treasury, Alexander Hamilton, submitted his *Report on Manufactures* to Congress in December 1791, he was, in essence, emulating Smith. In fact, noted

Earle, Hamilton had the *Wealth of Nations* open before him, when writing his own work.

The *Report on Manufactures* had been requested in January 1790 by a Congress eager to have "a proper plan or plans for the encouragement of manufactures" in the United States.[9] Hamilton had become Secretary of the Treasury in 1779, and as M.P. Cowen and Robert Shenton commented, he was well aware that the United States had emerged "from a revolution in which the American inability to manufacture the sinews of war had become painfully obvious."[10] Hamilton also understood that if the United States did not establish its own manufacturing sector, and simply relied on its agricultural trade, it would eternally be at an economic disadvantage. Europe would vigorously and eagerly supply the United States with manufactured exports he concluded, with no reciprocal assurance that Europeans would be willing to import American agricultural products. In such a situation, America would remain weak and no match, militarily, for its rivals.

To a large degree, the Assistant Secretary, Tench Coxe, previously Secretary of the Manufacturing Society in Philadelphia gathered much of the information contained in the *Report on Manufactures*. Coxe concentrated his efforts on explaining which economic practices and particular industries European countries had traditionally sought to be self-sufficient in – industries vital to the economic health of a country and important for military preparedness. On Coxe's list, noted Jacob Cooke, was the manufacture of gunpowder, brass, iron, wood, sailcloth, cotton goods, and linen articles.[11] Hamilton, utilizing much of the information provided by Coxe, argued that becoming self-sufficient in key industries was the best means to achieve national power and, in time, American pre-eminence. In particular, said Karl Walling, in an article comparing Hamilton to Machiavelli, Hamilton was essentially calling for a "strong national government headed by an energetic executive who could enable Americans to depend upon their own arms and virtue in time of war."[12]

Hamilton, it should be noted, had extensive military experience. A lieutenant-colonel in General Washington's field headquarters during the War for Independence, he was, by 1798, a major-general and inspector general of the army. Given the task of preparing the United States for a possible war with France, he eventually concluded that a citizen militia was not an effective means to ensure the future security of the United States. He recommended, instead, the establishment of a professional, peace-time military of just over 3,000 officers and men that would be available, when required, to quickly organize and train the militia. A military academy, he also suggested, would be necessary to ensure future officers had a good understanding of technology and the principles of war.[13] Certainly, what he did not wish to see was the United States, in its desire to preserve freedom, dominated by a large, self-serving and ultimately expensive standing army.

Like Hamilton, other leaders such as Muhammad Ali, ruler of Egypt from 1805 to 1848, also understood the important relationship between military and economic power. "Egypt's ruler," said John Dunn, "had witnessed, first-hand, the value of modern weaponry, during the French invasion of Egypt in 1798-1801."[14] As a result, in 1815, Ali set out to establish a western-style military with the best quality and mix of modern weapons possible and he was eventually supported by the arrival, in 1824, of a French military mission led by General Pierre Boyer. Boyer, with fourteen officers under his command, attached his personnel to schools and field units of the Egyptian army and had a direct, lasting influence on the education of the Egyptian military.[15] Ali, like Hamilton, also sought to create a robust, independent Egyptian military-industrial complex whose self-sufficiency would free Egypt from outside influence, high prices and possible arms embargoes. Through tax reform, a system of government monopolies and improved agricultural production, Ali was able to increase government revenues 9.5 times between 1805-1847 and anywhere from 33 to 60 per cent of this new money was allocated for military spending.[16]

To ensure his plan for a modern military would meet with success, Ali also sent Egyptians to Europe to study Western gun-making techniques. On their return, new arsenals in Cairo and Alexandria were set-up producing good quality copies of English and French weapons. Ali's efforts, wrote Dunn, represented "Africa's first military-industrial complex." By the 1820s, he added, a considerable range of armaments was flowing out of arsenals employing almost 40,000 workers. The need for uniforms was not forgotten either and Egyptian textile mills produced white cotton uniforms that "soon became the trademark of Egyptian soldiers."[17]

Creating a national arms production capability, however, did come at a price. "The Manufactories," wrote Colonel Patrick Campbell to London in 1840, "have cost enormous sums, for it has been necessary to have everything, (even to the instructors) brought from Europe and the receipts are in some cases less than the expenses."[18] Still, as the Colonel went on to say, Ali wished to give a "certain impulse to the Arab Nation by giving it a new sort of education."[19] Ali's successors continued with plans to modernize the country and build their armament production capability despite the cost. Efforts were given a boost at the commencement of the American Civil War in 1861 and the disruption of cotton supplies to the rest of the world. The resulting demand for Egyptian cotton pushed its price up 1,200 percent, and Egypt's ruler, Ismail Pasha and his government profited immensely from monies obtained through taxes.

With the end of the American Civil War, however, the price for cotton fell dramatically, yet Ismail Pasha continued spending money, embarking on an ambitious program of territorial expansion, which brought military defeat at the hands of Ethiopia in 1875-1876. By 1876, said Dunn, "Egypt faced a staggering debt burden of £68,000,000 and a predatory collection of loan sharks who could call on London, Paris, or Berlin for help."[20] Overextended and unable to pay its debts, Egypt would eventually default to its European creditors and its military-industrial complex soon declined, largely coming to an end in 1882 following the British occupation.

The attempted grafting of a modern arms industry onto what was a pre-industrial society in order to drive modernization was not unique to Egypt. Other like-minded rulers also sought to import western technology in the hope that creating a domestic arms industry and their own "manufactories" would offer a means to deter European aggression and potentially modernize their countries at the same time. So, as Ali strove to modernize Egypt in the early 1800s, at the other end of Africa on the island of Madagascar, a similar experiment was also taking place.

"The period 1820-61," noted Gwyn Campbell, "witnessed an industrial experiment in the Merina empire, Madagascar, which is possibly unique in tropical Africa for four main reasons: It occurred in the pre-colonial era, was contemporaneous with industrial experiments in Western Europe and North America, it was a result of indigenous enterprise, and it involved large scale factory machine-based production."[21] The dream of becoming self-sufficient in arms production, and modernizing Madagascar had begun with King Radama 1 (1793-1828) and continued with Queen Ranavalona 1, to a certain extent, upon his death. Radama had sought, through an alliance with the British, to conquer the entire island of Madagascar, and given enough time, he believed his kingdom would become the equal of Britain and France.

Ranavalona concentrated her efforts on fostering the domestic arms industry begun by Radama by establishing a new gunpowder mill, a sword and bayonet factory, a musket factory and a cannon foundry. Three tanneries built in 1828 continued the manufacture of military boots, belts, saddles and pouches. Efforts to build a domestic arms industry, in turn, spurred development of a new industrial centre in 1849 – a centre that eventually comprised five large factories with 5,000 workers capable of manufacturing a wide range of items. Besides muskets and cannon, noted Campbell, "copper, steel, lightening-conductors, glass, pottery, bricks, tiles, silk, a variety of cloths, candles, lime, dye, white soap, paper potassium, processed sugar for sweets and alcohol, and tanned leather were produced."[22]

When in power, Radama, at the urging of the British, had embarked upon a road and bridge building program. However, economic progress, he concluded, would require more than just factories and roads, especially since slavery, an important source of income, had been outlawed in 1820, also at the urging of the British. To stimulate growth in the absence of slave-related profits, he rejected, in 1825-26, a free-trade alliance concluded earlier with the British. Imports were restricted, for control purposes, to just twelve ports, and to discourage imports, duties increased from five to between twenty and twenty-five per cent.[23] In the long-term, Radama believed continued and self-sustaining economic growth would come through exports from a growing national economy. His government encouraged textile mills to focus on exports and farmers to cultivate cash crops, exploit forest products like wax and rubber and to boost production of traditional exports, specifically bullocks, meat and rice.

Radama also recognized the important role that education would play if the economy of Madagascar were to take off and Welsh missionaries established a formal education system in 1822. By 1828, the number of schools had increased from just three to 100 and the student body had grown from 200 to 5,000. The King "fashioned the schools into the chief institution for the recruitment and rudimentary education of soldiers, administrators and master artisans," and large numbers, noted Campbell, of "young military conscripts attended."[24]

However, Ranavalona was not interested in fostering closer relations with the British or French, preferring to rely on an undeveloped terrain with its natural obstacles to act as a barrier to European invasion. In addition, a mass expulsion of foreigners in 1835 and again in 1857 created a "near paralysis of foreign trade," and took away skilled European workers from key industries.[25] Then, in November 1853, the gunpowder mill exploded, killing several workers and creating another set back. Revolts amongst the population, opposed to expanding Government forced labour schemes, also undermined economic progress. Thus, the policies adopted by Madagascar caused the country to lose ground and enter a period of de-industrialization that Campbell remarked, continued into modern times. The policies adopted by Ranavalona and her successors also brought the country into direct confrontation with the British and French. Like Egypt, the leadership of the country had overestimated their own military strength and underestimated the will of their enemies. Madagascar would eventually fall to the French, becoming a colony in August 1896.

A fate similar to that of Egypt and Madagascar could have happened to Japan but it did not. However, when Commodore Matthew Perry cast anchor at Edo Bay on 8 July 1853, the Japanese, said L.S. Stavrianos, "seemed to have slight chance of escaping the fate of Third World status that had befallen other non-Western countries. After more than two centuries of self-imposed isolation, Japan lagged as far behind Europe in industrial and military technology as had the Ottoman, Mogul and Manchu empires."[26] The arrival of Perry in Japan meant an end to almost three centuries of isolation and on 31 March 1854, the Japanese were compelled to sign the Treaty of Kanagawa with the United States, opening the way for the increasingly detrimental penetration of their domestic markets. In fact, from 1863 to 1870, imports increased from 34 per cent to 71 per cent, irreparably damaging local industries and wiping out the tax base.[27] Resentment amongst the Japanese soon led to anti-foreign unrest and a military crackdown by western powers. However, the death of the Japanese Emperor in 1866 and the forced replacement of the Tokugawa leadership by rival clans paved the way for what became known as the Meiji Restoration. Central to the Meiji Restoration was a decision by the new Japanese leaders to acquire a western style military and more importantly, western armaments. Furthermore, the principal driver of the overall modernization of Japan would be a policy of "weapons independence."[28] Their decision, Stavrianos wrote:

> …pointed to the contrast between the Japanese and the Chinese ruling elite. The latter, consisting of literati, were ignorant and contemptuous of Western military technology, whereas the Japanese clan leaders, because of their martial background and interests, were very sensitive and responsive to the spectacle of foreign warships shelling their homeland with impunity. Thus, whereas the literati allowed their country to drift into a hopeless and disastrous war with the despised Western barbarians, the Japanese leaders instead set out to learn from the barbarians in order to better resist them.[29]

For Barton Hacker, the Chinese were in fact not so much contemptuous of Western military technology as they were Western culture. During a period of Chinese restoration in the 1860s, he wrote, the concept of "self-strengthening" was adopted, which centered on the adoption of Western armaments and the creation of a modest arms industry. However, the Chinese failed to address fundamental issues of military organization, command and control and general administration, resulting in defeat by the better organized Japanese during the Sino-Japanese war of 1894-95. "China's defeat," he noted, "was rooted in a fundamental miscalculation. Self-strengthening assumed that China could defend its traditional society against the West with Western weapons, that the West's military technology could be detached from Western culture as a whole."[30]

The Japanese, however, recognized that equipping themselves with Western armaments was only part of the equation and if an efficient, capable military was to be fielded then its organizational and fighting techniques would have to be adopted from Europe. As a result, a French military assistance mission arrived in 1873 to help create a new Japanese Army and a similar British mission undertook a mentoring role with the Japanese Navy. Modernization of the economy, principally heavy industry, was also carried out, often driven by the needs of the military in areas such a steel production and shipbuilding. Thus, and by the turn of the century, "four major arsenals with satellite plants and three government shipyards were fully engaged in supplying the needs of a modern military force."[31] However, the real breakthrough from an overall modernization perspective was that the government-sponsored armaments industry fueled the economic development of the private sector – something that did not occur in Egypt or Madagascar on the same scale. The weapons arsenal in Osaka for example, produced steam engines, lathes, grinding machines and gears for a developing private sector. The Yokosuka arsenal, observed Yamamura, became heavily in-volved with the construction of government buildings, private factories, roads, and harbours:

> Though rarely noted by economic historians, six of the ten private cotton textile firms, which began operation in the early 1880s using spindles imported by the government, relied on steam engines produced at the arsenal. Many of the satellite, specialized plants of the arsenal produced numerous simple machine tools and more explosives for mining than for military use. Akabane and other factories, under the jurisdiction of the Ministry of Construction, were even more actively engaged in aiding the private sector by producing boilers, steam engines, and several dozen other types of machinery used in the mining, tex-tile, machine-tool industry and others, as well as by the railroads.[32]

"One great lesson of Japanese history," said Hyman Kublin, "was that imperial political power had almost always been a mockery because of the absence of imperial military power."[33] The new regime in Japan would ensure this did not happen in future and plans called for a peace-time army of 31,680 personnel, a wartime force of 46,350 and an Imperial Guard of 3,880 men.[34]

CHAPTER 2

While the economic growth of Japan had been noteworthy, a lack of raw materials to fuel new industries was a constant cause for concern. To alleviate matters the Japanese turned their attention to Korea, which resulted in war between China, the historical guarantor of Korean independence, and Japan in August 1894. The Chinese armies, as it transpired, could not match Japan's modern military forces and in April 1895, the Chinese government surrendered. As a result, the Japanese gained the upper hand in Korea, annexing the country in 1910. Japan's new military capabilities were on display once more in 1904 and 1905 when the Japanese army and navy handily defeated the Russians in the Russo-Japanese War.

The political and economic situation in Korea was in stark contrast to Japan and even China. Taking the unusual step of sealing its borders in 1637, Korea's leaders regarded their country as a "tributary to China and thus encased in a vast protective cocoon that the controlled, limited, and indirect trade with Japan did not pierce. She saw first aid to the shipwrecked as her only legitimate point of contact with foreigners."[35] However, the loss of Chinese support following the Sino-Japanese War left Korea at the mercy of the western powers and above all Japan. The country and its leaders, preferring isolationism, had failed to modernize in any significant way – Korean military forces, such as there were, proved no match for the Japanese. The source of Korea's weakness had, as its root, the decision to remain remote and cut-off from the rest of the world.

As Mary Wright wrote, many of the foreign policy pillars embraced by the government in Seoul had been jettisoned by Japan very quickly after 1866. Whereas the Japanese were disposed to westernization as quickly as possible, the Korean government purged the entire country of foreigners that same year. Korea, noted Wright, was determined:

> To refuse even to discuss maritime trade or missionary work; To fight valiantly and without hesitation where local pressure threatened, blissfully ignorant of the ultimate power behind the small foreign forces that appeared in her waters; To prevent the importation of any ideas, the learning of any languages or any skills; To execute the purveyors of ideas whenever this seemed desirable. To keep the

northern frontier sealed; to fire without inquiry on anyone – Korean, Russian, or Chinese – found near the border; to refuse all discussion.[36]

In 1895, the Japanese, eager to promote reform in Korea and remove the current leadership, took the bold step of raiding the Korean palace, murdering the Queen and establishing a puppet regime. The King, held under guard, eventually managed to escape, finding refuge in the Russian legation.[37] Fearing a Japanese occupied Korea would become a strategic handicap, the Russians took action, providing military assistance and training to the Korean forces and taking charge of their limited military industry. However, both Great Britain and Japan opposed the aggressive inroads of the Russians, forcing the Korean government to request Russia remove its military advisors, which they did in 1898, thus paving the way for the complete domination of Korea by Japan.[38] From 1910 onwards, noted Hilary Conroy, Korea would be governed by a "succession of benevolent looking Japanese generals ruling Korea in brutally repressive fashion, while mouthing reforms in wordy annual reports published in English."[39]

As Stavrianos observed in *Global Rift*, "Japanese industrialization was stimulated by war but was also responsible for war."[40] Major industrial advances came about as a result of the Russo-Japanese War and later, the First World War. While, in 1900, only 500,000 Japanese were employed in industry, this number increased to 854,000 by 1914 and 1,817,000 by 1919. Through the exclusion of foreign investments but the adoption of western ways, Japanese society was militarized, modernized and able to compete with the west.

It was Dunn who remarked on how Egypt, like the Ottoman Empire and China were unable or unwilling "to incorporate significant political, cultural, and social changes, [which] doomed otherwise sound strategies" for the modernization of their countries.[41] The policy of isolation, maintained in Korea and Madagascar, would prove extremely detrimental, ensuring others would eventually dominate these two countries for failing to modernize. In 1885, Friedrich List remarked how he could now clearly see:

> That free competition between two nations which are highly civilized can only be mutually beneficial in case both of

> them are in a nearly equal position of industrial develop-
> ment, and that any nation which owing to misfortune is
> behind others in industry, commerce, and navigation…
> must first of all strengthen her own individual powers, in
> order to fit herself to enter into free competition with more
> advanced nations.[42]

The economy of a country, List added, was not only important for the production of individual wealth. Instead, an economy, foremost, was important, or needed to be considered important, for the production of national power. Individuals in a country may be very wealthy, List continued, "but if the nation possesses no power to protect them, it and they may lose in one day the wealth they gathered during the ages, and their rights, freedom and independence too."[43] Productive power, summarized Earle, was the key then to national security and the source of diplomatic, economic and military power a state could employ in the furtherance of its own interests. State power, continued Cowen and Shenton, was, in fact, both the product and the source of productive powers. Indeed, they concluded that the powers a state might have at its disposal would ultimately depend "upon both the extent to which armaments, and the capacity to produce military arms, had been developed."[44]

Given the experiential evidence of events in Egypt, Madagascar and Japan, the relationship between military strength and economic power was apparently not lost on developing nations in the 18th and 19th centuries. Beginning with Alexander Hamilton's *Report on Manufactures*, delivered to Congress in 1791, to the development of national economies through militarization around the globe in the 1800s, the importance of establishing an armaments industry and modern armed forces was recognized as an important first step towards overall modernization. In particular, an indigenous arms industry and western-trained armed forces, from countries as far and wide as Egypt, Madagascar and Japan was seen as the only means of resisting the economic overtures of European powers interested in finding new markets for their exports – more often than not at the economic expense of the importer.

In the 20th century, academics such as John Johnson and Lucian Pye, writing in the 1960s, genuinely believed that well-trained, professional militaries would act as the catalyst for national unity and economic development along the lines of what had been achieved in Egypt, Madagascar and Japan. In particular, they had been influenced by efforts to modernize the Turkish armed forces following the Second World War. However, as the following chapter will explain, post-colonial countries in the developing world either had or created armed forces to meet immediate regional threats or, quite often, simply for reasons of prestige – seldom, if ever, did leaders in the post-colonial period regard their armed forces as a tool for national modernization.

CHAPTER 3

MILITARIES AND MODERNIZATION IN THE POST-COLONIAL PERIOD

A proper role for military forces is particularly difficult to achieve in underdeveloped countries which, lacking an educated populace and democratic political institutions, find their politics resting inevitably on force.

Charles Windle, 1962

Aid to specific military regimes may be justified, but we ought not spuriously to hope that development and modernization are going to be inevitable or even probable outcomes. The mistakes of American military aid programs in Latin America and Asia ought not be repeated in Africa in this regard at least.

Henry Bienen, 1971

As the previous chapter noted, there was a belief amongst many academics in the early 1960s that military forces in the developing world might be a key instrument by which a nation could quickly modernize. "During the early history of the United States," wrote Charles Windle in 1962, "our armed services were used to assist in economic development by providing engineering skills, conducting explorations, constructing roads, canals, and railroads, assisting flood control and maintaining internal security."[45] In his view, military assistance to newly independent countries was a practical way to promote economic, political, and social modernization throughout the developing world.[46]

Edward Shils, also writing in 1962, observed that there were, indeed, very few new states that did not "aspire to modernity."[47] To be modern, he continued, meant a state would embrace democracy, focus on public education, meet the economic needs of citizens through industrialization, look after its own sovereignty and become an independent actor on the world stage. However, and even though he understood militaries had an important role to play in developing societies, he could not account for why so many states believed that to be modern required the maintenance of armed forces. In particular, he was surprised that having a modern military was such a high priority in Africa, the Middle East and Asia when, "on the whole, martial accomplishments have not headed the list of public virtues and where, with a few exceptions, the military has not distinguished itself on the battlefield."[48] In response to Shils' observation regarding the desire of newly independent countries to form armed forces, Janowitz simply replied that it appeared to be a "universal political conception that a new state requires an army."[49] Sylvanus Olympio, President of Togo from 1960 until 1963, had said as much upon becoming President. "We cannot be an independent country," he told his listeners, "without an army of some sort."[50]

The belief in the early 1960s that military assistance could play an important role in modernizing developing countries, besides the historical examples outlined in the previous chapter, had been strongly influenced by events in Turkey after the arrival of the Joint American Military Mission for Aid to Turkey in 1949. The work of the Mission would eventually result in revolutionary changes within the Turkish military and eventually spur on development activities nation-wide. Indeed, as an American military advisor noted in 1949, "the most complicated piece of machinery [Turkish conscripts] may have seen before coming into the service is a wooden stick plough. They hardly know the difference between a hammer and a screwdriver." In order to address the issue of illiteracy, uneducated draftees were sent to one of sixteen specially constructed army education centres located throughout the country – a considerable effort as usually 50% or approximately 120,000 men of the annual draft intake were classed as illiterate on entry. Once inside one of the new centres, soldiers faced a seven-week curriculum that included how to read and write, understand basic mathematics and personal hygiene.[51]

Undoubtedly, however, it was the 1959 *Report of the President's Committee to Study the United States Military Assistance Program* (known as the *Draper Report*) that introduced the idea that armed forces in developing countries would have an important role in stimulating wider modernization efforts. In particular, the *Draper Report* suggested that armed forces were often the only national institution able to take a leading role in economic and social development activities.[52] In 1962, John Johnson, writing in *The Role of the Military in Underdeveloped Countries* also surmised that militaries in developing countries "would have a modernizing effect on society and therefore an indirect, positive impact on the economy." Optimistically, he continued:

> In many of the new states that have emerged in the recent era of de-colonization the military play a vital role. As a revolutionary force they have contributed to the disintegration of traditional political order; as a stabilizing force they have kept some countries from falling prey to Communist rule; as a modernizing force they have been the champions of middle class aspirations or of popular demands for social change and have provided administrative and technological skills to the civilian sector of countries in which such skills are scarce.[53]

Military assistance in Asia, in particular American military assistance was also regarded as a force for modernization. Professors John Lovell and Eugene Kim, in their 1967 article "The Military and Political Change in Asia" suggested the relationship between indigenous military elites and the processes of socialization and political communication was "worthy of systematic investigation."[54] They further postulated that Asian militaries had a key role in rejecting old values and beliefs and introducing Western values instead. Military officers receiving training from the United States, they wrote, could be viewed as one of the key means available for disseminating "signals" such as "ideas, values, skills, techniques, and strategies of political change," from the external environment.[55] As Lovell and Kim pointed out, the Soviet Union and China also believed that training and supplying indigenous military elites and their forces was a means to introduce change and modernization.

Conferences and studies, most pointing to the modernizing role that militaries in developing countries could play, were popular events in the early 1960s and in 1962, for example, James Coleman and Belmont Brice both concluded that:

> The mobilization and training of nearly one-half million Africans during World War II was unquestionably one of

the major developments in launching the great transforma-
tion that is currently in process. The new recruits learned
how to speak, read, and write a *lingua franca*; they became
habituated to modern sanitation and health practices; they
had experience beyond their own territory – indeed, beyond Africa – which served to broaden their horizons of
interest and knowledge; and above all, they learned a wide
variety of skills appropriate for participation in a modern
society. As the colonial armies from 1945 onwards could
not absorb so many veterans, former soldiers drifted back
into civilian life and their towns and villages and due to
their wartime experiences, directly and indirectly, acted as
agents of change and modernity.[56]

Militaries in the developing world were also regarded, often inaccurate-
ly, as being the only "unifying institution wherein diverse ethnic groups
come together in a common bond."[57] In 1962, it was Shils who suggested
that the military in a developing country would be capable of teaching
"skills useful in economic development; it can widen horizons beyond vil-
lage and locality; it can keep young men from being infected by nationalis-
tic demagogy and give them a greater concern for the nation as a whole."[58]

However, those academics who assumed the military would lead wider
modernization efforts, said Olatunde Odetola in 1982, were working in
an "empirical vacuum" in which they wrongly believed that militaries in
the developing world were professional, disciplined and responsible, or
at least could be made so through foreign military assistance.[59] Bienen
had concluded as much a decade earlier. Researchers, he wrote, who
believed military organizations were best placed to undertake economic
and social reforms in their countries and act as a vehicle for national in-
tegration were basing their theories on the "proposition that the military
[was] at least relatively the most modernized group in a society." However, how a military in the developing world actually became "rational,
universalistic and industry oriented" and therefore the most modernized
group in society, he noted, was seldom explained.[60] As a matter of fact,
his research had begun casting doubt "on the proposition that the military is the most modern organization in certain underdeveloped countries." However, since 1959, he continued:

Those who have argued that the military is the organization best able to bring about development in non-Western countries have not been arguing a minority position. A bandwagon effect operated in the controversy over the role of the military in developing areas and academic opponents of the conception of militaries as modernizing institutions largely left the field between 1960 and 1965. During this period, insofar as doubt was cast on the role of the military as a nation-builder it came less from the universities than from Congress and the editorial pages of the *New York Times*. It was in the Congressional hearings [May 1961] on military assistance that the value of direct military rule for economic growth and political stability were questioned.[61]

Commenting on the spate of "speculative essays" in the early 1960s regarding the importance of armed forces in the developing world, Morris Janowitz pointed out that most authors had "grossly exaggerated" the capacities of the military as agents of change and modernization.[62] Moreover, he added, "the propositions and generalizations about the political behaviour of military leaders that have been entered into the literature must be used with extreme caution… there can be no doubt that much of the writing of this period has disappeared with appropriate dispatch."[63]

The truth was that militaries in the developing world, particularly in sub-Saharan Africa, were based around infantry battalions that lacked armoured vehicles or logistics support of any kind. In particular, in the post-colonial period few, if any, newly independent countries had the technical ability or wherewithal in their militaries to operate modern equipment. While the arrival of new rifles, trucks and artillery might on the surface have appeared an improvement in overall capability, these improvements were on the whole very basic. Jet fighter fleets, at least initially, were non-existent. Furthermore, the militaries in sub-Saharan Africa notably, as a percentage of the overall population and as Table 1 shows, were really quite small and did not have reservoirs of highly skilled leaders, organizers and technical people. There was no form of conscription either and given the small numbers involved, "the influence on the labour market of the organization of armed forces [was] practically negligible compared with the percentage of unemployment."[64]

Country	Population (millions)	Armed Forces Personnel	Percentage of Population
Benin	2.4	1,000	0.0
Cameroon	5.2	3,000	0.1
Ghana	7.7	10,000	0.1
Kenya	9.4	3,000	0.0
Nigeria	42.7	9,000	0.0
Tanzania	10.5	1,000	0.0
Togo	1.6	1,000	0.1
Uganda	7.6	2,000	0.0
Zambia	3.7	3,000	0.1

Table 1 – Armed Forces as a Percentage of Population (1965) in Select Sub-Saharan African Countries[65]

In reality, post-war developing world leaders, when deciding to establish militaries, did not do so on the grounds that their armed forces would eventually lead wider modernization efforts. In fact, they had far more immediate reasons for wanting to build up their armed forces with the help of foreign military assistance and hardware. Chief among these reasons was the actual or perceived threat from hostile neighbours, as, while the end of the Second World War might have created a sense of hope that the world would soon enter a period of peace and stability, the truth was far different. In Africa, the Middle East and Asia, the desire for independence would lead to violence and upheaval. European powers, believing their colonies would not become independent for many more decades, were to be unpleasantly surprised by the rapidity of events.

Besides threats to their existence, developing countries were often required to form armed forces for other reasons. For example, some countries upon independence had to absorb guerrilla fighters and revolutionaries into the regular armed forces. Turning these young men into soldiers within a professional armed force probably appeared, at least for the politicians, the most expedient route to avoid future unrest. In addition, William Gutteridge had suggested in 1961 that "the real internal danger to developing states in Africa today, [was] the emergence of new and rootless generations with little sense of service to the nation and no self-discipline."[66] The success of a state, he surmised, would hinge on keeping young men occupied and in his view, creating armed forces was a suitable means to do so. For other countries though, there were also strong psychological reasons to develop modern armed forces on par with militaries in Europe, if only to demonstrate they were just as capable of having and operating up to date weapons.

The need to create armed forces in the post-war developing world, therefore, can be traced back to one or more of the reasons noted above and based on the country in question. In the case of India, Great Britain, faced with either using military force to keep its hold on the sub-continent or allowing the Congress Party to lead the country to independence, chose the latter course in 1947. However, the partition of India led to huge unrest and eventually fighting between India and Pakistan – both newly independent countries soon asking Ottawa to supply their armed forces with arms and ammunition. For example, the Secretary of State for External Affairs discussed arms shipments to India and Pakistan with his Cabinet colleagues in September 1948. The Indian government, noted the Minister, had expressed interest in purchasing 100,000 rifles and 100 million rounds of ammunition (.303) from Canadian Arsenals Limited.[67] Two months later, it was the turn of the prime minister to tell his Cabinet colleagues that Pakistan now wished to purchase 20,000 rifles and 30 million rounds of ammunition. These requests for arms and ammunition were the first of many.[68]

Newly independent African countries bordering Rhodesia, South Africa and Portugal's African colonies also had cause for concern as the region became very volatile following the Rhodesian government's Unilateral Declaration of Independence in November 1965. In particular, the Tanzanian government regarded itself as "naturally and inevitably allies of freedom fighters," and therefore directly in opposition to the regimes in Salisbury, Pretoria and Lisbon.[69] Determinedly, President Nyerere set out to host several African liberation movements leaving his country open to incursions by Portuguese forces on the hunt for freedom fighters. For politicians in Dar es Salaam, having armed forces of their own to protect their sovereignty, unsurprisingly, became a top priority. The need for armed forces in Kenya, Uganda, and Zambia was also paramount for similar reasons. These three countries, along with Tanzania, were the only regular contributors to a fund set up in 1963 by the Organization of African Unity (OAU) to finance liberation movements across the continent. Thus, they too were potentially open to attack and this provided justification for increasing military expenditures.

CHAPTER 3

As Tim Shaw wrote in 1969:

> The regional arms race [between southern Africa and free Africa] is…leading to a diversion of Zambia's and Tanzania's resources away from development and towards more sophisticated deterrents. Zambia is buying a 6 million Rapier ground-to-air missile system from Britain, which will be operational in 1970 to deter border incursions by Rhodesian and Portuguese planes; it is the largest ever single military purchase by a black African state.[70]

Canada's Interdepartmental Military Assistance Committee concluded in 1969 that such expenditures would likely become the norm in future. A high degree of military strength, the Committee agreed, seemed to be considered an "essential attribute" of sovereignty. Indeed, they recognized that most newly independent nations, would likely "consider it an overriding national necessity to expend a significant portion of their pitifully slim financial resources on the maintenance of armed forces."[71] The Committee also recognized that countries like Zambia would continue to spend money on weapons that would "be used wastefully or for equipment which the countries in question do not know how to operate or maintain efficiently."[72]

Across the Atlantic Ocean, the British also imposed the requirement to establish defence forces as a prerequisite for the granting of independence. Therefore, Jamaica, Trinidad and Tobago and Guyana were all obliged to divert resources to the formation of armed forces.[73] While an outside threat to Jamaica did not exist, the British were ever mindful that the internal political situation was fragile and they did not want their military forces engaged in internal security efforts after independence in 1962.

While the threat from neighbours or internal security matters provided good grounds to have and maintain armed forces there were other reasons as well. In his 1968 article *Military Expenditures and African Economic Development*, J.D.C Boulakia remarked on how African countries had been eager upon independence to create military forces, not only because of threats from inside and out, but for institutional and political needs and most importantly, psychological reasons. From an institutional standpoint, he wrote, when a country became independent, it was obliged to take on the task of national defence previously assumed by the colonizing country. Politically, an army was also an important element of power and when African countries became independent after a struggle with the colonizing country, the national liberation army had to be converted into a regular force. Psychologically, he concluded, an army was an important "symbol of political independence. It can be seen by the crowd and stimulates its sense of power."[74] A modern military force, wrote Coleman and Brice in *The Role of the Military in Sub-Saharan Africa*, would mean, in the minds of the elite in a developing country, "the extinction of the stigma of primitiveness and backwardness."[75]

Nevertheless, as most colonial powers did not anticipate such a quick end to their presence in much of Asia and Africa they had not foreseen the need to put in place programs to groom their colonies for eventual independence, especially when it came to preparing individuals for key leadership positions in the military. Even relatively generous military assistance programs after independence only served to aggravate matters as the presence of foreign officers in developing countries simply reinforced the notion that new states were incapable of managing their own affairs. As Claude Welch wrote in *Praetorianism in Commonwealth West Africa*:

> Only as the Union Jack came fluttering down were reserved powers – including internal security and control of the armed services – transferred to full African control. The late transfer of responsibility, and the slow pace of Africanisation of the officer corps, encouraged both apathy and ignorance about the armed forces among the emerging African elite. Several factors help explain this lack of awareness. The military played no direct role during the thrust towards independence. Self-government in Commonwealth West Africa came through constitutional negotiation rather than force of arms. Political leaders, seeking the 'political kingdom,' neglected the under-pinning of force, and saw little reason – at least initially – to question the arrangements bequeathed them by the British. Defence expenditures remained relatively small. None of the leading political figures – Nkrumah in Ghana; Azikiwe, Awolowo, and Sardauna in Nigeria; the Margai brothers

and Siaka Stevens in Sierra Leone – had ever served in the armed forces, and they apparently had few close acquaintances with any military experience. The relatively peaceful paths the three states followed towards independence made the armies less conspicuous – and the breakdown of public order in the Congo, the key event in drawing attention to the role of the military, had not become apparent by early 1960.[76]

As far as the new armies in sub-Saharan Africa were concerned, many observers assumed the very idea of them turning on the governments that had authorized their creation could be "thoroughly discounted."[77] "None of the African states has an army," noted Gabriel Almond and James Coleman in *The Politics of Developing Areas* published in 1960, "capable of exerting a political role."[78] This assumption, said Simon Baynham was not uncommon, as "at independence armies were not generally considered to be key elements in the political equation of African states and a military career looked one of the least promising avenues to political influence."[79] Even Lucien Pye, added Baynham, had concluded that "Westernized intellectuals, socialistically-inclined bureaucrats, nationalist ruling parties and menacing communist parties," would determine the future of Black Africa, not African militaries that had been largely indoctrinated in the Western model of military-civilian relations in which the military was subservient to the governing party.[80]

Thus, the arrival and frequency of military coups in Africa, said Welch, had obviously caught "academics off guard...and revealed the shallowness of scholarly knowledge about African armed forces."[81] Even the smallest of African military forces, as it turned out, were able to coerce or replace governments. Because, remarked Welch, "most sub-Saharan states had received self-government through negotiation, scholars had focused attention on nationalist movements that had mobilized anti-colonial sentiments, and on the leaders and institutions that seemed best suited to transforming African societies; the armed forces, as relics of the colonial era, appeared to be politically inconsequential."[82] "In retrospect," said Baynham, it was "surprising that the political significance of the armed forces was not more fully anticipated."[83]

For an indication of what might happen if post-colonial developing countries did elect to build up their own militaries and invite in outside military assistance, Latin America presented a very good example of the problems that could occur. As Johnson noted in 1964, "military intrusions into civilian politics [had] long been a fact of life in Latin America." Civilian governments on the continent, he added, had been "unable to devise workable systems for permanently keeping officers in check and military machines subordinate to policy objectives." The result was that South American armies, in his opinion, fast became the most modern and developed sectors of society with officers who were politically motivated, elitist in outlook, and eager, at the first sign of trouble amongst their civilian political counterparts to "assume responsibility for the conduct of national affairs."[84] Brian Loveman also observed that "as Latin American military leaders became more attuned to European professional norms and expectations, they more vociferously and vigorously denounced inept, short-sighted civilian politicians who shamelessly fought like pigs over slop in the public trough while failing to create political stability or promote economic development."[85] As Edwin Lieuwen would observe, however, the promotion of economic development by civilian governments in most Latin American countries was, in fact, often impeded by the exaggerated demands Latin American military leaders made upon government revenues in the first place.[86]

In Latin America and many African, Middle Eastern and Asian post-colonial developing countries indigenous military forces would often challenge the existing political order.[87] As Table 2 notes, military coups were frequent because, more often than not, the establishment of military forces in developing countries also created a new elite – the military officer. Indeed, entry into the military at whatever stage of modernization, even at the lowest level, was a social step up, especially if one became an officer. In Ghana, Gutteridge observed, "a peasant cocoa farmer or a post office clerk is more likely to be the father of an army officer at present than a member of one of the professions who will probably have educated his son for the Bar of the Civil Service or similar occupation of established prestige."[88] In the Middle East, wrote, Shils, armies recruited into their officer ranks:

> The brightest and most ambitious young men of the small
> towns and countryside. These young men often come from

the families of petty traders, small craftsmen, and cultivators of small holdings. Like their fathers, they are aware of the distance separating them from the rich and the political elite. Thus, there is brought into a potentially powerful position a body of intelligent, ambitious young men, equipped with a modicum of modern technical education but with little sense of identity with politicians and big businessmen.[89]

In 1969, the Canadian Interdepartmental Military Assistance Committee, in their report: *Canadian Military Assistance to Developing Countries* also noted that military officers were often drawn from lower and middle classes and not from the families of the political elite. Military education, often carried out in the developed world, coupled with an introduction to advanced technology contributed, in their opinion, to "an innovating outlook in the context of a tradition-oriented society." In many countries, the report continued, "the military are also less concerned by traditional forms of religion and therefore less likely to let religious conservation serve as a barrier to change."[90] Notably, the Committee also concluded that "as development proceeds, the chances of a military oligarchy taking power seem to increase rather than decrease. Even in countries where the military do not aspire to or attain political control, they are apt to form one of the 'core institutions' of national life to a degree unknown in the majority of modern developed countries."[91]

Five-year period	Middle East	Asia	Sub-Saharan Africa	South America	Central America	Total Number of Coups in the five-year period
1945-49	3	1	0	8	5	17
1950-54	5	0	0	6	4	15
1955-59	2	2	0	5	6	15
1960-64	8	3	3	6	6	26
1965-69	8	1	18	5	1	33
1970-74	1	2	9	5	0	17
1975-	0	1	2	1	1	5
Total Number of Coups	27	10	32	36	23	
Number of Nations Affected	17	15	26	10	10	

Table 2 – Frequency of Successful Military Coups in the Developing Nations in the Post-World War II Period (Tabulated by Five-Year Periods)[92]

What then were the overriding reasons as to why governments in the post-colonial developing world were so eager to create armed forces other than it being "universally accepted" that a modern state needed to have an army? In the case of India, Pakistan and Israel, for example, the answer was relatively simple. The security situation on the Indian sub-continent in 1947, and in the case of Israel, simple national survival, provided ample reason enough to establish armed forces as quickly as possible. On the other hand, in sub-Saharan Africa the need to create armed forces was not so readily apparent. The threat of boundary disputes had been greatly diminished by a decision taken by the Organization of African States in 1961 to respect the borders decided upon in 1885 in Berlin. Internal unrest, such as in the Congo and later Nigeria suggested the need for military forces to maintain internal control but there was little justification for high-end military capabilities such as frigates, jet aircraft and tanks. If there had been, of course, a genuine attempt to unseat white-led governments in Southern Africa through conventional military operations these capabilities would have been necessary. However, such operations were never seriously considered by black African leaders. Gutteridge, based on research carried out over an eight-month period in West and East Africa, suggested that in reality, newly independent countries in Sub-Saharan Africa would likely have been better to form armed mobile police forces to meet their security needs and not spend money on a Western style military. But, as he concluded, nationalist leaders regarded "armed forces of some sort simply as part of the essential paraphernalia of a new state without which independence would not be seen to have been achieved."[93]

However, the establishment of military forces was only the beginning of future trouble for most African leaders, as Aristide R. Zolberg would write in *Military Intervention in the New States of Tropical Africa:*

> As African regimes came to rely increasingly on force to deal with challenges to their authority, the military rapidly learned how much weaker were the African rulers than their predecessors. Called upon repeatedly to put down strikes or to deal with disorder in a dissident region, being asked to support one faction of the government against another in a showdown, participating in similar operations in

> a country other than their own (as in the case of the Ghana-
> ian and Nigerian forces in the Congo), or merely acquiring
> information about the involvement of other military units
> in the events of this sort, officers and men at all levels be-
> came acquainted more intimately than many others with
> the seamy side of political life in their own country and
> on the continent as a whole. They also learned that con-
> trol over even a small, ill-equipped, poorly trained body of
> men was crucial…by virtue of their organizational charac-
> teristics [they became] the best-organized "trade union" in
> the country.[94]

Those countries that decided to offer military assistance to the developing world in the post-colonial period did not likely envision the rapid
appearance of so many military-led governments. At the outset, the aim
in training, equipping and advising militaries in the newly independent
countries had generally been to preserve the colonial *status quo* and retain
a degree of influence with whatever form the civilian government took
on. There was also a belief, certainly amongst Western governments and
Western academics, that military organizations in developing countries
could lead overall development and modernization efforts in their respective countries. Regardless of the reason or reasons behind wanting to
have military forces, it was apparent that, compared to building other institutions of government or expanding the economy, military forces were
just easier to create. There were plenty of former colonial powers and
other countries eager to sell weapons and provide military training assistance. There were also plenty of former colonial powers who believed
that building a robust military in their former colonies was one way of
continuing, indirectly to influence the politics in their former holdings.
Military assistance, even for non-colonial countries such as Canada, was
also good for business and, as the following chapters will reveal, Ottawa
would eventually become a major provider of arms and military training
throughout the developing world.

CHAPTER 4

MILITARY ASSISTANCE TO THE POST-COLONIAL DEVELOPING WORLD

The question is not whether armies will participate in politics but to what extent and by what means.

William Gutteridge, 1985

Since the end of World War II, checking the spread of Soviet influence had been an important objective of American military assistance programs; by mid-1948 it was the overriding purpose.

Chester Pach, 1991

After the Second World War, it was readily apparent that new and developing countries were in a hurry to build up their armed forces. However, in the late 1950s and early 1960s, previously colonized countries that arguably faced no direct threat to their existence were just as eager, as the previous chapter explained, to create armed forces. As a result and whether a consequence of the threat or not, arms and training assistance were soon offered to most militaries in the developing world by developed countries eager to gain or maintain influence and ultimately sell weapons. Certainly, the former colonial powers were keen to engage their new colleagues but they did so in an increasingly crowded market place as China, the Soviet Union and the United States, in particular, vied for allies, profits or both.

Canada was also not immune to home-grown economic pressures from companies wanting to capture a portion of the emerging arms market. Nor could the Canadian government easily avoid their allies who wanted Ottawa to take an active part in containing communism, above all in sub-Saharan Africa. In fact, the Secretary of State for External Affairs had been advised by his staff in August 1964 that the Canadian government had already "been strongly pressed by the U.S. and U.K. to do everything possible to provide promptly some military assistance to Tanganyika, however slight. The Chinese are sending a mission for this purpose."[95]

This pressure from the United States and the United Kingdom on the Canadian government to engage in military assistance work in Tanganyika was difficult to avoid. Ottawa had already committed itself to supporting the Ghanaian government with a similar program three years earlier, a program that appeared to be having some success, so why not have a similar Canadian led effort in Eastern Africa? If the Secretary of State had any reservations about becoming more engaged militarily in Africa, his staff simply noted that Canada was and would "probably continue to be, in the business of providing military assistance."[96]

In June 1970, and during a period when Canada's military assistance efforts were coming under ever increasing scrutiny by the prime minister, a definition of the term *military assistance* and an explanation of its importance was given to Cabinet:

> Military assistance, in the context of this document, is defined as the provision of advice, training or equipment to the armed forces of a recipient country. It seems incompatible with the sort of image Canada should project abroad, unnecessary for the promotion of our international interests, and unrealistic in terms of financial and military priorities, for the government to envisage military assistance as a major constituent of Canada's policy in its relations with the developing world. But equally, there is solid evidence for the view argued above that a modest programme of such assistance, judiciously and selectively applied, can and does serve important Canadian interests.[97]

As already alluded to, the provision of military assistance to developing countries not only served the interests of Canada. Many other countries also regarded military assistance as a vital tool of foreign policy. In the case of the United States, at least initially, military assistance efforts were designed to protect American economic and strategic interests, especially in the Caribbean. In the 1920s, for example, surplus American arms and munitions were sent to Mexico, Cuba, Honduras and Nicaragua. Meanwhile, military advisors were deployed to Cuba, Haiti, the Dominican

Republic, Nicaragua and Panama while military and naval missions began operations in Brazil, Guatemala and Peru. American military assistance in Latin America, as a means to combat growing German influence in the late 1930s also grew in importance and magnitude.[98]

For the United States, military assistance emerged as a key strategic tool of American foreign policy in the late 1940s. Yet arms aid was largely uncoordinated with money flowing into developing countries based on a combination of "securing customers for American armaments industries, checking the spread of Soviet influence, and cultivating foreign goodwill."[99] Indeed, in early 1946, President Harry S. Truman asked Congress to approve plans to provide military assistance to the Philippines, the Nationalist Chinese, and several countries in Latin America. Authority was also requested to send military advisors overseas whenever it was believed in the national interest to do so.

The decision to commence wide-scale military assistance to the developing world can be traced to President Truman's speech on 12 March 1947 before a joint session of Congress. The speech, according to Chester Pach, was the most famous of his presidency. Concerned about growing Communist influence, Truman requested approval for $400 million of military and economic aid for Greece and Turkey, telling Congress and the American people how he believed:

> That it must be the policy of the United States to support free peoples who are resisting attempted subjugation by armed minorities or by outside pressures. In addition to funds, I ask the Congress to authorize the detail of American civilian and military personnel to Greece and Turkey, at the request of those countries, to assist in the tasks of reconstruction, and for the purpose of supervising the use of such financial and material assistance as may be furnished. I recommend that authority also be provided for the instruction and training of selected Greek and Turkish personnel.[100]

The result of Truman's speech was the approval by Congress of the *Mutual Defense Assistance Act* (MDAA) of 6 October 1949. The product of a two-year effort to institute a "unified, cohesive military aid program," the MDAA was designed to coordinate military assistance efforts to better contain communist expansion throughout the developing world. Essentially replacing the *Lend-Lease Act* that had been approved by Congress in March 1941, the new Act authorized the outlay of $1.314 billion to arm thirteen countries. The Act also provided the President with the extraordinary power to "sell, lend, lease, exchange, or otherwise transfer virtually any item to any country whose defense he deemed vital to the security of the United States."[101]

Notably, the passage of the MDAA did not imply that the entire government apparatus in the United States was in agreement with providing arms and training assistance to foreign governments. The military had certainly been the leading proponent of providing assistance immediately after 1945 as "military aid, advisory groups, and foreign training programs were powerful instruments not only for building American influence abroad but also for providing defense officials with a major voice in postwar foreign policy. War Department authorities thus urged programs of military assistance to advance their own interests both abroad and at home."[102] However, by 1949, Pentagon planners were beginning to worry that they lacked the necessary funds to support their own rearmament efforts. On the other hand, the State Department, not fully engaged with military assistance efforts in the beginning, was convinced by the late 1940s that military assistance efforts were in fact having a positive impact on containing the spread of communism. The State Department, as a result, soon became the lead promoter in Washington of supplying arms and aid to foreign governments. For example, the Department was an advocate of military assistance for Saudi Arabia so that country could effectively protect American oil interests while military aid for France, it was believed, would ensure the country would became a barrier to communist expansion in Europe. In fact, for many in Washington, military aid "was no longer an unfamiliar or unusual device but a tested instrument for securing American objectives overseas."[103]

By 1962, almost $2 billion had been set aside by the United States for military assistance, including $125 million specifically for the training of foreign military personnel. As Windle noted, the training offered to foreign military personnel constituted "by far the largest effort the world has known on the part of one country to educate and train citizens of others."[104] From 1946 to 1960 alone, about 120,000 students from approximately 60 countries received military training of varying kinds in the United States. In 1960, Windle reported that of the non-European trainees in the United States, 1,870 were from Latin America, 3,730 came from the Middle East and South Asia, 6,950 from the Far East and 130 were African. In total, 73 per cent were officers. "Through this extensive and growing involvement with foreign military forces," added Windle, "our own armed forces have come to assume, more or less inadvertently and inevitably, major political responsibilities in the underdeveloped nations."[105]

That the military assistance program was growing at an alarming rate was a concern recognized by some in Washington right from the beginning of post-war military assistance efforts. Paul G. Hoffman, the Economic Cooperation administrator in the State Department wondered whether America's military assistance efforts were the "beginning of an enormously costly program that will go first to Europe and then perhaps to Asia and then to South America and where does it stop." John O. Bell, assistant director of the State Department's military assistance program added that "if we indulge in either starting or continuing programs without having pretty clearly in mind where we want to stop and when we want to stop and what we are trying to do, then we can very easily get into a large series of ratholes which are both costly and dangerous."[106] Still, in Washington, there was a high degree of optimism that offering military assistance was an important tool of foreign policy. "No doubt," said Bienen:

> American government officials, military leaders, and academicians believe that the military in the developing areas is the best counterforce against both internal and external disruption. Some rather pessimistic observers believe that at least the armed forces provide something of a guarantee against the sort of chaos which would ultimately make development, hard as it is now, almost impossible. Others have higher hopes for the military regimes, believing that they can and will be more effective than political parties in modernizing their societies.[107]

Pach wrote in 1951 that American military assistance had initially been justified as "a means of deterring aggression, containing Communist expansion, [and] protecting overseas interests short of the dispatch of combat troops." Nevertheless, he observed, military assistance efforts had often been driven by parochial interests and only vague notions of combating communism and had "continued even after they ceased serving useful purposes, if indeed they had ever done so."[108] Critics of American arms aid, he went on to say, were convinced that military assistance really only "exacerbated local and regional hostilities, assisted more often in the suppression of legitimate opposition than in the repulsion of external aggression, and burdened the United States with new obligations to defend foreign countries."[109]

However, in the West, and certainly by the early 1970s, increasing arms exports had become an important source of revenue. The United States, the United Kingdom and France witnessed an increase in defence exports of 208 per cent, 97 per cent and 156 per cent respectively from 1974-1977 as compared to the 1970-1972 period. German arms sales also went up by 481 per cent while Italian military exports climbed by 191 per cent.[110] Defence sales were becoming a big business and an economic driver. In the United Kingdom, the dependency of the shipbuilding industry on foreign military sales grew from just 10 per cent in 1971 to 38 per cent in 1974. In France, overall arms sales in 1970 accounted for 20 per cent of total national armaments production. The French aerospace industry was particularly reliant on overseas markets with 70 per cent of their aircraft heading to foreign markets.[111] Between 1969 and 1978, arms exports from communist countries also gained a major foothold, climbing from 25.9 per cent of the world total to 43.1 per cent in this period.[112]

The competition amongst countries (primarily NATO countries) to supply arms to the developing world was intense. The United States, depending on which party occupied the White House, could often be an unreliable partner, especially if Congress took issue with plans to supply certain countries with arms. This was the case in Latin America where total military sales declined from $421 million (1963-1967) to $316 million (1968-1972).[113] The French, on the other hand, were the most pragmatic about defence exports and had few political restrictions in place. Despite a UN arms embargo against South Africa, for example, Paris continued to supply sophisticated weapons to the apartheid regime ignoring the complaints of its former sub-Saharan colonies. Other African states were equally irritated.   Julius Nyerere, speaking publicly in New York at the 25th United Nations Assembly was prompted to say in 1970 how "it is noticeable that to France the obligations of friendship and peace go only one way."[114] Commenting on French market penetration in the 1960s and early 1970s, Augusto Varas wrote:

> France has acquired all the markets orphaned by the politi-
> cal restrictions of other suppliers. France became a major
> supplier to South Africa after the British embargo in 1964,
> and to Pakistan after the U.S. embargo to India and Paki-
> stan in 1965. France also received orders from Greece for
> major weapons after the U.S. embargo, and provided Por-
> tugal with counterinsurgency weapons to be used in Af-
> rica. In South America, France began to supply the *Mirage*
> to several countries, including Pinochet's Chile, after the
> United States refused sales in 1968 and in the 1970s.[115]

For the United States, military assistance for countries in sub-Saharan Africa represented a real challenge. The decision to intervene in the Congo after the election of Patrice Lumumba in May 1960, by orchestrat-ing his removal and replacement by General Joseph Mobutu, caused tre-mendous backlash around the world. African leaders, noted Odd Arne Westad in *The Global Cold War*, were, moreover, "shocked at the brazen-ness of the intervention" and denounced American objectives in Africa. Furthermore, Africans had "watched the African American struggle for civil rights and saw little for Africans to admire in the response of white America."[116] Nevertheless, the United States was eager to prevent the Soviet Union or China from gaining ground in Africa. As President Ken-nedy told an audience in 1961:

> We live in a hazardous and dangerous time. We live in a
> world which has changed tremendously in our lifetime –
> history only will secure a full perspective of this change.
> But there is Africa, which was held by Western European
> powers for several centuries, now independent – which
> holds within its countries masses of people, many of them
> illiterate, who live on average incomes of 50 or 60 or 75
> dollars a year, who want change, who now are the masters

of their own house but who lack the means of building a viable economy, who are impressed by the examples of the Soviet Union and the Chinese, who – not knowing the meaning of freedom in their lives – wonder if the Communist system holds the secrets of organizing the resources of the state in order to bring them a better life.[117]

As Kennedy feared, the Soviet Union was definitely eager to expand its presence in the developing world as a means to counter American and Chinese influence, expand its network of global military facilities and to help the Soviet economy in general.[118] However, as Table 3 portrays, the total amount of Soviet arms exports reaching sub-Saharan Africa was often small in comparison to the military assistance sent by Moscow to Middle Eastern and South Asian countries.

Country	From the Soviet Union	Total arms imported	Soviet percentage of total
Egypt	2,365	2,801	84.4
Iraq	1,795	2,451	73.0
Syria	2,015	2,261	89.1
Afghanistan	100	131	76.3
India	1,365	1,680	81.3
Angola	190	315	60.3
Nigeria	70	221	31.7
Tanzania	30	125	24.0
Zambia	10	81	12.3

Table 3 – Deliveries of Soviet Arms to Non-Communist Developing Countries from 1967-1976 (in millions of United States dollars based on an exchange comparison in 1983)[119]

Still, the Soviet presence in Africa did grow considerably in the early 1960s. So much so that the Assistant Secretary of State for African Affairs, G. Mennen Williams was prompted to write in a 1963 State Department Bulletin that "the principal thrust of Communist activities, at the present time and for the near future, continues to be destruction of the Western position in Africa and insinuating their way into African good graces by the establishment of an identity of Communist bloc-African positions on major international issues."[120] Kwame Nkrumah had visited several Eastern European countries in 1961 and a Soviet trade mission stood-up in Accra soon after. Then, in late 1962, air service between Moscow and Ghana commenced. The Soviet Union was also far more eager to help developing countries with cash, disregarding the strict financial conditions the West often insisted on before loaning money or beginning a project. However, Soviet assistance often came with indirect consequences. For example, in Ghana, "six out of eight *Ilyushin* 18's had to be withdrawn from West African air routes because they were too expensive to operate. They were replaced with [Western] *Viscount* Aircraft."[121]

Nevertheless, Western countries found it difficult to escape Russian criticism for their role in not supporting African nationalism. The United Kingdom and the United States, Moscow frequently pointed out, continued to trade with Rhodesia and South Africa. Portugal's refusal to give up its African colonies was not lost on the Soviets either and they enthusiastically went about implicating NATO as having a hand in helping Lisbon hang on in Angola and Mozambique. The growing Russian presence in Western Africa had been aided in great part by the actions of France towards Guinea in 1958. President Sekou Touré, much to the annoyance of French President Charles de Gaulle, decided on complete independence for Guinea, relinquishing entry into a proposed federation of former French colonies forever, it seemed, tied to France. The decision taken by Touré essentially led to the total abandonment of the country by France. All French government, technical and military advisors returned home immediately. Records were destroyed and moveable capital equipment smashed. "What could not be burned," noted Robert Legvold, "was dumped into the ocean."[122]

The French departure led the Soviets to quickly fill the vacuum. Opening moves began almost immediately after Guinea obtained its independence on 2 October 1958. Two days later the Soviet Union recognized the new state and "in March 1959 two shiploads of arms and armoured cars arrived in Conakry, accompanied by an eighteen-member Czech military mission."[123] Trade relations between Guinea and the Soviet Union rose rapidly as well. Before Guinea's independence the two countries had no trade relations whatsoever. By 1959, the Soviet bloc was providing 9.3 per cent of Guinea's imports and purchasing 16.2 per cent of its exports. Just one year later, 44.2 per cent of Guinea's total foreign imports were now coming from the Soviet Union.

Still, not everything went as planned for the Russians. Several key projects, including a state rice farm in Guinea and the construction of an atomic research reactor in 1964-65 in Ghana proved to be failures. The Guinean government then expelled the Soviet ambassador, claiming that the Russians were planning on overthrowing the government of Sekou Touré. The establishment of Communist parties in Africa did not go well either and "by 1963 all Communist Parties in Africa were illegal, and none seemed to be faring well."[124] By the mid-1960s, Melady noted, it had become clear "that the role of irresponsible adventurer in African affairs was being played by the Red Chinese, not the Russians."[125]

While the Soviet Union failed to have a major influence in the immediate post-colonial period in sub-Saharan Africa, the same could not be said of China whose leaders provided "arms, supplies and moral support to insurgency and guerilla groups fighting wars of national liberation in more countries and regions of the world than any other nation."[126] As Peter A. Poole pointed out in 1966:

> Foreign aid has been one of the chief forms of contact between the Peking-regime and the non-Communist world. Between 1956 and the end of 1965, China pledged the equivalent of $942 million in economic aid to some 18 non-Communist countries. Moreover, China's military aid, in relatively small but lethal doses, has gone to at least two non-Communist governments and to numerous insurgent groups. Chinese personnel have almost invariably been stationed in large numbers wherever Chinese economic or military aid programs are active.[127]

Achieving even the smallest amount of political influence in non-Communist countries was of huge strategic importance to the Chinese. As a result economic and military aid flowed to Burma, Cambodia, Egypt, Indonesia, Nepal, Sri Lanka, Syria and Yemen. Chinese efforts to obtain political influence in Africa found success in 1959, with rice shipments to the newly independent Republic of Guinea. Additional aid and loans were then made available to the Central African Republic, Congo-Brazzaville, Ghana, Kenya, Mali and Tanzania. However, the Chinese presence in Africa was not always entirely welcome. In May 1965, for example, a convoy of Chinese small arms destined for Uganda was intercepted in Kenya, which led to a "poor atmosphere" when Chinese leader Chou en Lai arrived in Tanzania for a state visit that June. When he did arrive, Chou told his audience that Africa was "ripe for revolution." President Nyerere simply replied that Tanzania was "not for sale."[128]

Although the Chinese lacked the military and economic resources of the United States and Soviet Union, what resources were available were largely spent convincing African countries to recognize the communist government in Beijing instead of the Nationalist Chinese government based on the island of Taiwan. The first African country to extend recognition was the United Arab Republic in 1956. By the end of 1960, Morocco, Sudan, Guinea, Ghana, Mali and Somalia had joined the list. Four years later another eight African countries, including Tanzania, now recognized the communist Chinese government. In essence, the communist Chinese were successful in playing the racial card said Melady in *Western Policy and the Third World*, noting that they had "become increasingly blunt in aligning themselves with the Afro-Asian peoples against all whites, Russians included."[129]

Still, the efforts put forth by China to gain influence in Africa had mixed results. Although Mao had once described China and Africa as being "one and the same," amongst Africans there was a deep suspicion of the Chinese simply because most African leaders knew little or nothing about China in the 1950s and 1960s. Overt Chinese support for liberation movements had caused six pro-Western African governments to break or freeze relations with China while journalists from the *New China News Agency* were eventually expelled from seven countries. The support offered by Beijing to Haile Selassie in Ethiopia and Mobutu in Zaire was also a disappointment to many African leaders. As Phillip Snow remarked in *China and Africa*:

> African leaders had never been any more interested in learning Communism from China than the Chinese had been in teaching it to them. In the first place they had no wish to import doctrine wholesale. Having just escaped a Western tutelage, they had no desire to submit themselves to an Eastern one. And Communism was off-putting in certain

important ways. It was an atheistic creed, whereas most leaders in Africa were Christians or Muslims. It was based on a concept of social division and class struggle, while African leaders were endeavouring to solidify fragile new states in the face of ethnic tensions and conflicting tribal loyalties.[130]

Indonesia also proved to be a battleground for influence amongst the United States, the Soviet Union and China. Thwarted in their attempts to obtain heavy weapons from the West and unable to win control of Western New Guinea through diplomatic means, the Indonesian government decided to approach the Soviet Union and China for military assistance. This led to a series of reciprocal visits between high-ranking government and military officials beginning in 1956. President Sukarno, for example, traveled to Moscow and Beijing while President Khrushchev arrived in Djakarta in February 1960 offering a $250 million dollar loan on top of another $100 million that had been provided in 1956. Although publicly this money was to be used for economic projects, it was later determined that much of it was used to purchase arms from Czechoslovakia and Poland that included 4,000 Soviet half-ton military scout cars along with 60 MiG-15 jet fighters, 32 Il-28 jet bombers and 11 Czech AVIA-14 cargo planes.[131]

Marshal Tito also paid a visit to Djakarta in 1958 in an effort to sell arms to the Indonesians and in due course Yugoslavia sold six *Kraljevica*-class submarine chasers and three landing craft to the Indonesian government while providing their navy with military advisors. Concern in the West that Indonesia was falling into the communist sphere of influence, however, soon resulted in a change of policy and by 1958, the United States and other Western countries began supplying arms to Jakarta. The Indonesian navy was a major recipient of this aid, with Italy providing four frigates and the British selling naval aircraft. What with Yugoslavian ships, two Polish built submarines, four Polish *Skoryi*-class destroyers and a host of other naval vessels in Indonesian ports, it was clear by 1959 that the Indonesian government was eager to play East against West in the search for arms.[132]

One fundamental problem with all the arms flowing into the developing world was that more often than not the receiving militaries did not possess the means to either operate the equipment they obtained, or if they could, to carry out the necessary repairs when needed. Heavy tanks or sophisticated fighter jets, often supplied to developing countries, were usually a waste of money – most roads and bridges in sub-Saharan Africa were simply not robust enough to withstand the passage of several tanks and there were few security issues that demanded a fighter fleet. Thus pre-industrial militaries, that organizationally resembled their Western counter-parts, completely lacked the infrastructure and trained person-nel to operate the weapons they acquired. As Sunday Ochoche noted, developing countries that imported arms also imported an industrial model of warfare, which required "plenty of technical staff, heavy infra-structures, large logistical machinery and so on."[133] The result was that military equipment supplied to many newly independent countries was more often than not simply abandoned.

All the same, military assistance to the developing world was a tool of foreign policy for governments from the West and East. The Germans, French and Italians had all used training assistance and arms sales to gain influence in Latin America prior to 1939. The United States was also keen to use military assistance, certainly after the Second World War, to cultivate new friends and contain the spread of communism. Economi-cally, arms sales equated to jobs in developed countries and the market for arms sales was highly competitive even amongst Western powers. How military equipment sold to developing countries might be used in the end or whether it was used at all, was of little concern in Washington, Moscow, Beijing, Paris or London.

Certainly, both Moscow and Beijing were prepared to provide military as-sistance to developing countries as an important tool for the furtherance of their respective foreign policies. Yet, they did not cooperate together, in particular when providing support to sub-Saharan Africa. Without a doubt, wrote Legvold in 1970, the Chinese had moved "into Africa as a rival of the Soviet Union rather than a collaborator."[134] Still, none of the superpowers, the former colonial powers or China found that the going was easy, and influence gained could easily be influence lost if the leader-ship in a developing country did not get their way.

Canada was not immune to the demands of countries in the developing world to sell them arms and/or provide military assistance either. Nor was Canada immune to the demands of its allies and its own industries to become engaged, militarily, in developing countries by selling weapons and providing military support. In fact, at the urging of the United States, the United Kingdom and Canadian arms manufacturers, Ottawa soon found itself training armed forces from Ghana to Malaysia. Both the Indian and Pakistani governments, following partition, also bombarded the Canadian government with requests for arms and ammunition. Once these orders were approved, more demands for even heavier weaponry, such as field and air defence artillery began to arrive. In time, the Canadian government would find itself selling military equipment to dozens of developing countries and providing major military assistance training teams to several countries in sub-Saharan Africa. It might have seemed "incompatible with the sort of image Canada should project abroad," noted External Affairs in 1970, but the fact was that Canada had also become a major player in the military assistance market.

CHAPTER 5

CANADA'S MILITARY IN THE POST-WAR PERIOD

The Soviet Union has flouted...war-won friendships, obstinately obstructed every move to arrive at understanding, and promoted chaos and disorder and the darkness of the iron curtain. It has produced an attitude in Canada towards defence which is quite different from any that we ever had before in peacetime.

Brooke Claxton, June 1948

Any nation must be concerned that its obligations do not outrun its capabilities. A middle power such as Canada must be particularly careful to ration its commitments.

Canadian Defence White Paper, 1964

Before discussing Canada's post-war military assistance efforts it is important to understand why Canada's military leadership were so reluctant to become engaged in assisting developing countries given the circumstances they found themselves in after 1945. Without doubt, Canada emerged from the Second World War with one of the largest militaries in the world. But the maintenance of a modern military force, following the end of hostilities, was not at all a priority for Prime Minister Mackenzie King, convinced as he was that the country needed to "get back to the old Liberal principles of economy, reduction of taxation, anti-militarism, etc."[135] Thus, for the post-war period, only 32,610 military personnel were authorized – a tremendous difference from the 1,086,771 serving during the war.[136]

Initially, the Canadian government sought to guarantee Canada's security through participation in the UN. However, it soon became clear to Ottawa that the UN would not live up to expectations, and therefore Canada helped establish NATO in 1949 and the North American Air Defence Command (NORAD) in 1958. For the military, participation in NATO provided plenty of justification for maintaining a wide range of capabilities and therefore funding. A large Soviet ground, sea and air threat meant that by the early 1950s the Canadian government had deployed a brigade in Germany with two more brigades in Canada, an air division split between bases in France and Germany while the navy took on responsibility for anti-submarine warfare in the North Atlantic. Certainly, wrote Dan Middlemiss and Joel Sokolsky, "without NATO, it would have been difficult at best to justify the maintenance of modern conventional armed forces, equipped with tanks, artillery, fighter aircraft, and a wide range of anti-submarine warfare (ASW) forces."[137]

But, as much as the Canadian government was prepared to enter into collective arrangements such as NATO to ensure Canada's security, there nevertheless remained a desire in Ottawa to promote international security by other means. To this end, working through and hoping to improve the UN security apparatus appeared to be the right solution. Accordingly, small numbers of Canadian peacekeepers deployed to Palestine and the India-Pakistan border in 1948 and to Indochina in 1954. Canadian troops would also fight in Korea, deploy to the Suez in 1956, the Congo in 1960 and later Cyprus. In addition to providing much needed support to the UN, post-war Canadian governments also found themselves, often reluctantly, supplying substantial military arms and assistance to many developing countries in Africa, the Middle East and Asia. While arms transfers and sales to NATO countries might have been non-controversial, countries requesting military arms and assistance in the developing world were often either at war or on the brink of war. Helping them out meant having to negotiate a political minefield at home and internationally. To be sure, providing arms to developing countries was upsetting for many inside and outside of government, yet military-related sales were good for the sizeable post-war Canadian armament and aviation industries regardless of the buyer.

For Canada's military leadership, UN peacekeeping missions and increasing military assistance deployments after the war took the attention of Canadian politicians and the public away from what they perceived to be their main role in NATO. Indeed, peacekeeping missions would eventually prove a major drain on manpower and resources, taking "time away from the important task of preparing to fight the Russians."[138] The first steps on the path to NATO's formation had begun in March 1948 when the United Kingdom, France, Belgium and Luxembourg signed the Treaty of Brussels, pledging to defend each other if attacked. This agreement was followed by the determination of 10 European states, with Canada and the United States, to band together in 1949 under the umbrella of NATO with each agreeing:

> That an armed attack against one or more of them in Europe or North America shall be considered an attack against all of them; and consequently, they agree that, if such an armed attack occurs, each of them, in the exercise of the right of individual or collective self-defence recognized by Article 51 of the Charter of the United Nations, will assist the Party or Parties so attacked by taking forthwith, individually and in concert with the other Parties such action as it deems necessary, including the use of armed force, to restore and maintain the security of the North Atlantic area.[139]

The problem for Canada was that not much in the way of an armed force existed in April 1949 and there was no desire in Ottawa to see defence expenditures increase. Douglas Abbott, Brooke Claxton's predecessor as Minister of National Defence, had called for a defence budget of $365 million for 1947-1948. However, after moving from Defence to the Finance portfolio he quickly revised his thinking, telling Claxton that a defence budget of $150 to $160 million was more in order. "I would not, I could not, agree to that," said Claxton.[140] As a result, Cabinet agreed to apportion $200 million for the military in 1947-1948, or approximately 12 per cent of the national budget. However, in order to remain within budget, "the three services had been told that they should recruit only up to 75 per cent of the force levels approved by the Cabinet Defence Committee in September 1945.[141] Claxton was also hopeful that joining NATO would help reduce costs. "By pooling resources," he wrote in 1949, "the effect of the pact [would] be to reduce the total expenditures which each of the 12 countries would have found necessary [to spend otherwise]."[142]

A lack of funding, and tardiness in arriving at a force structure for the post-war period, provided plenty of fodder in Ottawa for the Conservative opposition. E.D. Fulton was moved enough to say, in his view, that "the belief in the minds of the [Government is] that we shall again have an opportunity for leisurely preparation…leisurely mobilization, leisurely assembling of our forces and leisurely direction of our forces to those places where we wish to send them, and that we shall be able to conduct the war as the last one was conducted in its early stages."[143] Presciently, he added, Canada was "making no effective plans to meet the next war, which, whenever it comes, I am certain will be characterized by a totally new, much more rapid, and in many respects totally unexpected, form of attack."[144]

Indeed, it was the Korean War that helped focus the Canadian government's re-armament plans and put an end to any thoughts of Canada remaining isolated, militarily, from global security issues.[145] The Navy began exercising on a regular basis with its NATO partners and from 16 September to 4 October 1953, five Canadian warships, including the light aircraft carrier *Magnificent*, deployed in the largest gathering of NATO warships and aircraft ever assembled. The 1ˢᵗ Canadian Brigade Group then replaced the 27ᵗʰ Canadian Infantry Brigade Group that had been in Germany since November 1951. In addition, a Canadian air division with four wings totalling 12 squadrons had fully deployed to Europe by the last week of August 1953.[146] But, maintaining such a force was going to be costly. In December 1953, the North Atlantic Council agreed that its first priority would be keeping its forces at the highest level of readiness possible and armed with the most up-to-date equipment. This meant, noted the Council, that:

> Defence programmes of the nations concerned must be organized to maintain adequate defences for an indefinite period. Such long term commitments as are now envisaged raise important military and financial problems, and considerable effort will be required to continue the maintenance of NATO forces with modern equipment and to keep these forces at an adequate state of readiness.[147]

The result, noted the 1954-1955 official government publication *Canada's Defence Programme*, was that any meaningful defence activity would most certainly have to be directed towards NATO in future and the "collective efforts of all NATO members to reduce the probability of a major war."[148] In 1956, *Canada's Defence Programme* reinforced this position, adding:

"almost everything Canada is now doing in the military field relates quite naturally to our participation in NATO."[149] Of course, this was true and NORAD, which came under NATO as part of the North America Region Planning Group, also proved to be a drain on what resources were available – as the *1964 White Paper on Defence* made clear, the threat to North America continued to be from the air and therefore the three squadrons of CF-101 aircraft and the two BOMARC ground-based air defence squadrons dedicated to NORAD since at least 1959 would remain necessary for the foreseeable future. There were not that many Army Reserve personnel to tap into for overseas missions either as the Army Reserve, or Militia, had been given national survival responsibilities. As a result, much of the Militia switched from their regular military training to conducting casualty evacuation and doing damage assessments following a Soviet nuclear missile attack.

Though the Canadian government might have been convinced in 1956 that NATO would be the main focus of Canada's defence policy in future, a change in emphasis was about to occur with events that began innocently enough on 29 October 1956, when Israel launched a surprise attack on Egypt. The next day, and by pre-arrangement with Israel, the British and French governments issued an ultimatum to both sides to stop fighting and withdraw 10 miles from either side of the Suez Canal. British and French troops then entered the region in order to separate the two parties, but the real aim was to secure the Suez Canal after President Nasser of Egypt nationalized the waterway – much to the anger of the British government.

Kept in the dark and caught by surprise, both the Soviet Union and the United States were outraged at the British and French for invading Egypt and the Soviet government announced it would take military action against both countries. Fortunately, Lester B. Pearson, Secretary of State for External Affairs at the time, broke the impasse, suggesting in New York that the UN deploy a "force large enough to keep these borders at peace while a political statement is being worked out."[150] The initiative would later earn him the Nobel Prize for Peace. On 7 November 1956, the Canadian government, having supported a call for a UN peacekeeping force, detailed what they would in fact do to support the mission: "It is proposed to offer a Canadian contingent of battalion strength, augmented by ordnance, army service corps, medical and dental detachments, to en-sure that the battalion group is self-contained and can operate indepen-dently from a Canadian base. The size of the contingent is expected to be 1000 men."[151]

The intent, at first, was to deploy an infantry battalion, The Queen's Own Rifles of Canada. However, the Egyptian government was not pleased and neither was Pearson, who noted that the Egyptians "had just been fighting the Queen's Own." When he made his objections known to the Minister of National Defence, the only alternative, he was told, was to deploy the Black Watch. Not a great choice either noted Pearson; writ-ing that what was really needed was the "First East Kootenay Anti-Imperialistic Rifles."[152]

The Canadian contingent that eventually deployed as part of the United Nations Emergency Force (UNEF) consisted of some 900 Army personnel stationed in Abu Suweir and El Ballah in Egypt. Their task was to pro-vide communications, transport, engineer and administrative support to the entire contingent. The infantry battalion that stood by in Halifax for several weeks never deployed. In addition, 220 members of the Royal Canadian Air Force (RCAF) were sent to Capodichino, Italy. Using four C-119 Flying *Boxcar* aircraft, they ferried supplies for UNEF while anoth-er 80 RCAF personnel in Abu Suweir provided general support with four *Otter* and one *Dakota* aircraft.[153] This deployment would last until 1967.

The UNEF mission came at a difficult time for the military, who were already watching the money allocated to defence decrease slowly but surely. Certainly, this had not been the case when NATO was created and Canadian troops deployed to Korea – defence spending had in-creased nearly five-fold from 1949-1950 to 1952-1953 or from $385 million to $1.814 billion. But, after 1952-1953, defence expenditures had begun to slip and by 1962-1963 the amount allotted to defence was $1.575 billion. Little relief was possible, as increased social spending by the government had led to large deficits beginning in 1958-1959.[154]

The full impact of this decline in defence funding was outlined in the then secret *Report of the Ad Hoc Committee on Defence Policy* published on 30 Sep-tember 1963. In this foundation document for the 1964 White Paper, the Committee noted that expenditures in 1962-1963 represented a decrease over those for 1952-1953 by: 13% measured in dollars; 38% measured in real purchasing power; 45% measured as a percentage of federal budgetary expenditures; 49% measured as a percentage of GNP at current prices; and 57% measured as a percentage of GNP at constant prices.[155] As R.J. Sutherland, Chairman of the Ad Hoc Committee on Defence Policy wrote in August 1963, if the defence budget was to be held at the planned level of $1.6 billion, a substantial reduction of manpower would prove essential in order to make funds available for the purchase of new equipment.[156] However, in September 1963 he became even blunter, noting that:

> Defence manpower is already substantially below establishments, that is the number of personnel regarded as necessary by the services in order to meet approved commitments. There is accordingly a *prima facie* case that reductions in manpower must be accompanied by reductions in commitments if the latter are not to become a façade. If present trends continue – a fixed or declining defence budget and increasing running costs owing to inflation – the day is not far off when there will be no funds available for equipment. The trend would then be for Canada to acquire a South American style military establishment: a substantial number of uniformed personnel, no modern equipment and no significant capability.[157]

In fact, it was only through a reduction in manpower from 120,781 in 1963 to 110,000 in 1967 that the military remained on budget, yet even then the expenditures on capital spending had fallen by $39 million to just $212 million in 1967.[158]

If Lester Pearson had thought the Suez deployment would result in a political win for the Liberal Party in the run-up to the 1957 election he was to be sadly mistaken. Although the Liberals, under Louis St. Laurent had governed the country since 15 November 1948, their time in office was coming to an end. After 21 June 1957 the Conservatives were in power and John Diefenbaker, the new prime minister, was eager to seek a counterweight to the United States through closer relations with the United Kingdom and the Commonwealth.[159] Indeed, in his memoirs he wrote that, "throughout my life, I have had a deep and abiding emotional attachment to the Commonwealth," and had viewed "the Common-wealth as a tremendous force for good in the world: for peace, progress and stability in a world fraught with tension and on the brink of nuclear cataclysm."[160] He was also ready to continue using the military as a tool for foreign policy – and ready, if need be, to deploy more Canadian military personnel to support UN peacekeeping operations.

However, not wanting to upset senior military leadership too much, Mr. G.B. Summers from External Affairs sought to calm the fears of the military during an address to the National Defence College in 1957. He made it clear "that the current emphasis on the UN by the government did not in any way affect how Canada would do business in NATO." The real issue affecting the small shift in focus to the UN, Summers explained, was the decolonization process currently underway.[161] A 1957 External Affairs briefing note summed up the new thinking in Ottawa:

> One can say immediately that Canadian policy in the UN is, like that of other countries, firmly based on grounds of national self-interest... Consider for example such a basic interest as the preservation of our national security...it does not take much argument to show that insecurity far from our own borders can endanger our own security; that any serious threat to the peace in another part of the world contains danger for us.[162]

The next major opportunity to deploy Canadian troops with the UN came just three years after Summers' talk in Kingston after the newly elected government of the Congo, led by Patrice Lumumba, took office in June 1960. Within weeks of receiving independence from Belgium, the mineral rich province of Katanga declared its independence from the rest of the Congo, prompting Lumumba to ask the UN for help. By mid-August some 15,000 UN troops from 24 countries were deployed in the southwest of the country helping to prevent the Congo from falling apart. At first, the Canadian government was not keen on taking part in the operation at all – there were too many domestic issues on-going and the military, given its large-scale Suez deployment, was short of troops and specialists.[163] Africa, at the time, was also a bit of a mystery – Canada's diplomatic representation on the continent was limited to just Egypt,

Ghana and South Africa. There was no African Division in External Affairs. Nevertheless, the Canadian contingent consisting of mostly army signalers and air force personnel eventually reached 421 all ranks and the commitment lasted until 30 June 1964.[164] It was an important mission; John Diefenbaker was adamant "that should the Congo operation fail, the future effectiveness of the United Nations in dealing with emergency situations involving peace and security would be jeopardized."[165]

As Canadian troops went about keeping the peace in Egypt and the Congo, yet another major UN commitment was looming, this time on the island of Cyprus. The British colony of Cyprus gained its independence in 1959. However, Greece, Turkey and Great Britain were each given the right to take unilateral action if they believed their interests were at stake. Matters came to a head in 1963 when the Cypriot president, Archbishop Makarios, seemed ready to introduce constitutional changes that would favour the majority Greek-Cypriot population – a move that upset the Turkish government who appeared eager to intervene. The result was a decision by the Security Council to deploy a peacekeeping force on the island, designed to head off a conflict between two NATO partners. In Canada, the Canadian Forces had to move quickly to meet a demand by the Canadian government to send troops. A battalion of infantry and a squadron of armoured cars were sent by air and sea – the main party arriving on 17 March 1963. The Canadian contribution was not small either – some 1,150 troops out of a UN force numbering 6,500.[166] The period between 1962 and 1963 was also marked by trouble in New Guinea and Yemen. In the case of New Guinea, Canada provided two *Otter* aircraft with pilots and maintenance personnel to the United Nations Temporary Executive Administration (UNTEA) from 1 October 1962 until 1 May 1963. In Yemen, the RCAF established an Air Transport Unit with about 50 personnel from 4 July 1963 until 4 September 1964 as part of the United Nations Yemen Observer Mission (UNYOM).[167]

All this activity was a great drain of manpower and resources for all three services. In 1963, the Navy had 21,439 personnel, the Army 49,515 and the Air Force 52,383 all ranks. By all accounts, each one was under-strength, with the Army estimating that given current and forecasted commitments they would require 61,833 personnel in 1967-1968. As R.J. Sutherland noted in his report, there was "a substantial gap between the manpower currently being provided to the Services and the manpower which they state as their requirement to carry out their present commitments."[168] Certainly, the deployment to Cyprus was telling in this regard. General Charles Foulkes had reminded the NATO Military Committee in 1956 that the nuclear-conventional hybrid force structure in Europe had kept the peace so far. As far as he could see, this was the main effort for NATO and "mindful that there are brushfires on the periphery of NATO which cannot be ignored…we want to ensure that in dealing with such situations nothing is done to in any way weaken the determination to defend the NATO area."[169]

Although the Cyprus deployment was not expected to last more than several months, its mandate was constantly extended while political negotiations continued. In Ottawa a sense of frustration over a lack of progress in resolving matters was clearly apparent and in June 1967, the prime minister announced that: "the purpose of the force in Cyprus is to help keep the peace while political negotiations are going on. If these negotiations are postponed indefinitely, then the reason for the force being there indefinitely has been eliminated." Word was that the Canadians might come home in 1968.[170] This, as we now know, was an overly optimistic assessment as the last Canadian battalion did not leave until 1993.

By 1966, it was clear to Canada's military leadership that UN deployments were the source of ever increasing personnel shortfalls. The Army was running out of trained infantry personnel, which had resulted in the conversion of artillerymen into infantry for the spring 1966 Cyprus rotation. Even infantry battalions sent following the initial deployment were lacking personnel; when the 1st Battalion of the Royal Canadian Regiment deployed to Cyprus in late 1966 it did so with just 600 personnel not the planned 700.[171] This shortage of personnel was somewhat surprising as in 1964 the new Liberal government had actually established new priorities for defence, the first focusing on achieving collective security through the UN, for which the deployment to Cyprus was a prime example. Collective defence within NATO was relegated to second place while defending Canada and North America came last.

The re-orientation of Canadian defence priorities would have a significant impact on the commitment to provide a division for NATO, considering that the Army only had four brigade groups and of them, noted then Minister of National Defence, Paul Hellyer, only "one was up to strength and even it was ill-equipped."[172] To meet the demands of UN missions the Department of National Defence had no choice but to use the brigade group allocated for the defence of Canada. The two remaining brigade groups, it was determined by the military, could still prepare to round out the division in Europe. But as Hellyer noted, they were not adequately equipped and the sea and air lift to move them to Europe in an emergency simply did not exist. Besides, as UN missions and eventually military assistance tasks increased, even these two brigade groups could not escape the mounting demands that would siphon off their personnel, principally specialists, in ever increasing numbers as noted in Table 5. Yet, despite the number of missions, author Jack Granatstein concluded in 1986 that:

> Peacekeeping at no time was a very important role for the country. At most perhaps 2200 servicemen were employed at any one time on UN operations. More men supported NORAD in Canada and the United States. More troops were stationed in Europe with NATO. More were on anti-submarine patrols off the coasts. Peacekeeping was only a minor role performed by the military forces of a minor power.[173]

Having some 2,200 personnel deployed on UN peacekeeping and military assistance missions, however, was actually a major effort. Once a series of six-month deployments were underway, while 2,200 troops were overseas, 2,200 would just be returning and 2,200 more would be getting ready to go. At a minimum, over 6,000 personnel would be involved – almost as many as the entire Canadian brigade in NATO that had a peak strength in 1965 of 6,719 personnel.[174]

As Table 4 and Figure 1 further illustrate, in 1964, for example, approximately 2,500 Canadian personnel were overseas on UN or military assistance missions. With tour lengths varying between six months and up to two years in duration, it is possible to conclude that by 1965 that at least 6,000 personnel were directly supporting non-NATO overseas missions. Furthermore, indirect support is difficult to quantify, but administrative and training preparations in Canada would have been sizeable.

Year	Mission	Personnel	Remarks
1948	United Nations Military Observer Group India-Pakistan (UNMOGIP)	Maximum was 19 observers and 8 aircrew	Until 1979. Aim was to supervise the cease-fire agreement between India and Pakistan within Kashmir.
1950	United Nations Command, Korea	8,000 at the height of operations	Navy – 3 destroyers. Army – Infantry Brigade Group. Air Force – transport squadron plus 21 fighter pilots with the 5th USAF.
1953	The United Nations Command Military Armistice Commission (UNCMAC)	1 officer, 1 other rank	Aim was to supervise the armistice agreement.
1954	United Nations Truce Supervisory Organization (UNTSO)	20 observers	Aim was to observe and maintain the cease-fire in Palestine.
1954	International Commission for Supervision and Control Vietnam (ICSC)	150 all ranks in the 1950s	Until December 1967 (not a UN mission). Aim was to control, observe, inspect, and investigate the execution of the 1954 Geneva Agreement with particular reference to the importation of war material and military personnel and the establishment of military bases.
1956	United Nations Emergency Force, Egypt (UNEF)	Maximum was 1,150	November 1956 to June 1967. Aim was to maintain the cease-fire agreement between Egypt and Israel and the withdrawal of French, Israeli and British military personnel from Egyptian territory.
1958	United Nations Observer Group in Lebanon (UNOGIL)	Maximum 77	June to December 1958. Aim was to ensure no illegal infiltration of personnel or arms across the Lebanese border.
1960	United Nations Operations in Congo (UNOC)	400	Until June 1964.
1961	Ghana	27	Military Assistance until 1973.
1962	United Nations Temporary Executive Administration (UNTEA)	Maximum 13	West New Guinea. Also the United Nations Security Force in West New Guinea (UNSF) from 3 October 1962 to 30 April 1963.
1963	United Nations Observer Mission Yemen (UNYOM)	Maximum 53	July 1963 to September 1964. Aim was to observe and certify the implementation of the disengagement agreement between Saudi Arabia and the United Arab Republic.
1964	United Nations Force in Cyprus (UNFICYP)	1,000 all ranks initially then approximately 600	Until 1993 then limited numbers. The aim was to prevent a reoccurrence of fighting and maintain law and order.
1964	Tanzania	82	Military Assistance until 1970.
1965	United Nations India-Pakistan Observer Mission (UNIPOM)	112	September 1965 to March 1966. Aim was to supervise the ceasefire along the India-Pakistan border except in the State of Jammu and Kashmir.
1965	Operation Nimble	Maximum 20	Humanitarian Assistance in Zambia (air lift of supplies).
1965	Mission of the Representative of the Secretary-General in the Dominican Republic (DOMREP)	1 observer	May 1965 to October 1966. Aim was to observe the situation and to report on breaches of the ceasefire between the two *de facto* authorities in the Dominican Republic.

Table 4 – Canadian Forces United Nations and Military Assistance Missions from 1948-1965[175]

There is little doubt that the Canadian government had, in 1964, a significant number of their personnel tied-up with non-NATO deployments overseas, most on UN missions and a growing number involved with military assistance. Yet, for R.J. Sutherland, writing his covering letter to the 1963 *Report of the Ad Hoc Committee on Defence Policy*, the "future of the United Nations during the next quarter century is an invitation to rhetoric and pontification." He was not at all taken with the Commonwealth either – an organization, he noted, that by 1990, if it existed at all, would have ceased to be a significant factor in world politics.[176]

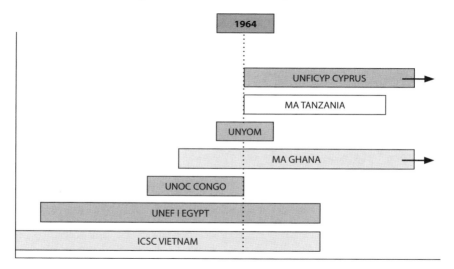

Figure 1 – Select Canadian United Nations and Military Assistance (MA) Missions 1956-1971

If anything though, the period after the Second World War was an increasingly dynamic one as Canada searched for a meaningful role in the world. And, despite Sutherland's view regarding the usefulness of the UN, the November 1964 Ottawa Peacekeeping Conference, attended by representatives from 23 major troop-contributing countries, provided a firm indication that the Canadian government was going to continue supporting the UN and whenever possible provide military assistance to new Commonwealth partners. In fact, military assistance in the form of arms sales and later, training missions and advisors would become an important economic and diplomatic tool for the Canadian government. The reality was that Canada's armed forces were too small to support armaments and aircraft manufacturing industries in Canada and so new customers had to be found. Arms exports, particularly tied with military training assistance would become a very valuable tool in this regard.

But what about the leadership of the Canadian Forces – were they convinced that dividing their dwindling resources amongst defence, diplomacy and economic pursuits in the developing world was worth the effort? "There are grounds for suspecting," said Granatstein in 1968, that some of the Chiefs of Staff likely believed peacekeeping, and one could add military assistance, to be "a waste of time and money."[177] Nevertheless, arms exports and military training assistance to foreign governments and militaries, largely unknown before 1945, were about to become major policy issues for future Canadian governments in the post-war and then the post-colonial period.

CHAPTER 6

CANADA'S ARMS SALES AND TRANSFERS IN THE POST-WAR PERIOD

Many would no doubt feel that, on moral grounds, Canada should not be in this kind of business at all.

Lester B. Pearson, 1956

There is another aspect of this, which is of very great importance to the future of the world. For, if the Eastern bloc nations make arms available to freedom fighters, and the Western bloc nations sell arms to South Africa and to Portugal, what is the likely result? Africa will become a hot front to the cold war.

Julius K. Nyerere, 1974

After 1945 and especially following the formation of NATO, there was hope in Ottawa that demands from its allies to increase defence expenditures could be mitigated by training NATO aircrew in Canada and through the contribution of surplus war equipment to its European partners. Indeed, Ottawa proposed that 1,400 NATO aircrew train in Canada each year and an entire division's worth of equipment was donated to the Netherlands, followed by similar arrangements for Belgium and Italy. In the 1950s more modern equipment was transferred to NATO members including fifty 90mm anti-aircraft guns, 17 *Tracker* aircraft and 225 *Orenda* engines.[178] Though Canada's efforts may have appeared generous in nature, Desmond Morton would later characterize the period as simply the government's way of getting rid of a "stockpile of obsolescent British-pattern equipment stored since 1945."[179]

Morton's assessment was not that far from the truth. Canada had emerged from the Second World War with its economy largely intact compared to that of Europe. Furthermore, and unlike most other NATO members, Canada had no intention of introducing conscription and maintaining large standing military forces regardless of what the Soviet Union might say or do. Nevertheless, as the Secretary of State for External Affairs was advised in November 1954, Canada's "relatively favourable economic position" had not gone unnoticed in Western Europe. "It would not be unreasonable," he was told, for other NATO members to continue "to expect a considerable amount of assistance from Canada."[180]

The provision of military assistance to NATO members was initiated in 1950 with the introduction of the Canadian Mutual Aid Programme, designed to assist in the buildup of NATO and to help develop Canada's defence production capacity. The Canadian government also instituted an aircrew-training program for NATO countries eager to achieve their NATO force goals and develop their own national training systems as quickly as possible. By 1958, when the program officially terminated, approximately 5,500 pilots and navigators from ten NATO countries had completed training.[181] A separate program was then introduced for Norway, Denmark and the Netherlands in late 1957. In June 1960, the Netherlands withdrew but training continued for Denmark and Norway with thirty-five and twenty-five places offered yearly to Danish and Norwegian student pilots respectively. However, training was not free. Both Norway and Denmark were expected to reimburse the Canadian Government $44,000 for each graduate pilot.[182]

The peak of Canada's Mutual Aid Programme occurred in 1953-1954 with the provision of $289 million worth of military equipment to NATO members. By fiscal year 1957-58, however, this amount had fallen to $118 million and it was estimated that for 1959 transfers would decrease to just $90 million. This was due to several factors including the termination of the Canadian aircrew-training program, the gradual reduction in surplus Canadian weapons and equipment available for transfer, the ability of more NATO countries to manufacture their own armaments and that, in general, equipment levels throughout the alliance were now deemed adequate.[183]

The Mutual Aid Program, as previously noted, had been initiated by Ottawa to supply NATO members with surplus military equipment. However, in some cases, new military production lines were begun in Canada to help establish modern arms industries. In 1958, as the future of the Mutual Aid Program remained in doubt, the Panel on the Economic Aspects of Defence was told that by 1952-53 it had already become apparent "that the Mutual Aid Programme could play only a small part in the overall problem of maintaining production facilities."[184] So, if Mutual Aid business was coming to an end and Canada wished to maintain a cost-effective arms industry, additional customers would need to be found. Fortunately, neither the Canadian government nor Canadian arms industries had to wait too long. As a matter of fact, new clients in the developing world, through the efforts of the War Assets Corporation, were already in receipt of Canadian arms and ammunition soon after 1945.[185]

The export of arms, ammunition and military equipment, however, was always a sensitive issue in Ottawa. The prime minister, for example, was advised in April 1946 that External Affairs had hoped "Canada could refrain from engaging in the arms traffic until the Security Council had an opportunity of considering the regulation of the traffic by international agreement."[186] As soon as the war ended though, plenty of buyers were in-line who wanted to acquire, for example, Canada's many surplus naval vessels, even if they were going to be sold in a demilitarized state and only useful, it was thought, for commercial pursuits. *River*-class frigates, at just over 2,000 tons each, were sold to Chile, the Dominican Republic, Honduras, India, Israel and Peru.[187] *Castle* and *Flower*-class corvettes, at approximately 1,000 tons, went to Argentina, Cambodia, Chile, the Dominican Republic, Honduras, Israel, Morocco, the Nationalist Chinese, Panama, Uruguay, and Venezuela.[188] Theoretically, if there were doubts about the intentions of the buyer, it was up to the War Assets Corporation, and from 1946 onwards the Canadian Commercial Corporation, to demonstrate to the Canadian government that it was unlikely owners would remilitarize them later.[189] More often than not, however, countries remilitarized their new vessels by adding guns and radar equipment.

To try and avoid Canadian military equipment ending up in the wrong hands, export permits were tightly controlled. The Export Permit Branch in the Department of Trade and Commerce had overall responsibility for the issuing of export permits but any request to sell military equipment abroad required consultation with the Department of External Affairs. While the War Assets Corporation and the Canadian Commercial Corporation had authority to export surplus military equipment after the war without obtaining export permits, they too were required to consult External Affairs for approval. With few exceptions, sales to the United States

and countries of the British Commonwealth for example, government policy required Cabinet to review each individual request on its own merits.[190]

Given the post-war security circumstances, the decision by Cabinet to review almost all export requests was a wise one. Demands for military assistance from Nationalist China, India, Pakistan and Israel were considerable,
requiring the government to often choose sides while paying careful attention not to inadvertently breech UN-sanctioned arms embargoes. In fact,
the issue of supplying other governments with Canadian military assistance
was so sensitive that Secretary of State for External Affairs, Lester B. Pearson, wrote a letter to the heads of posts abroad on 1 May 1948 noting that:

> During the past six or eight months the progressively wors-
> ening international situation has led an increasing number
> of foreign governments or their agents to evince consider-
> able interest in the purchase of Canadian arms, ammuni-
> tion and military supplies. In the circumstances, you will
> understand that such matters must be handled with con-
> siderable discretion. I suggest, therefore, that if you receive
> a direct approach, or learn indirectly of any enquiries re-
> garding Canada as a source of military supplies and mate-
> rials capable of being turned to a military use, you should
> take particular care to keep the Department promptly and
> fully informed. In this way, it should be possible to avoid
> commitments which, upon fuller examination, prove to be
> undesirable or embarrassing.[191]

Pearson's letter came just a few months after a major milestone in Canadian defence related exports was reached. In early 1948, the Netherlands
had expressed interest in purchasing 10,000 barrel assemblies from Canadian Arsenals Limited for 9mm *Sten* machine-guns. The sale was worth
$20,000 in American funds. The awkward point for Ottawa was that the
proposed sale would be sourced from a current production line and not
from war surplus stock. "It was," wrote the Assistant Under-Secretary
of State for External Affairs, Escott Reid, "clearly necessary that the matter be referred to Cabinet." If the decision was made to fill the order, he
added, "I would assume that we would make the usual condition that the
arms are not to be used in Indonesia."[192]

There were good reasons, however, to consider selling arms worldwide from current production lines. Certainly, the post-war Canadian military, by itself, was not large enough to keep the domestic armaments industry in business for long. As the *History of the Department of Munitions and Supply* in the Second World War noted, Canada's domestic armaments industry had gone from simply being a pre-war supplier of basic materials to an industrialized state in just a few short years:

> From the automotive plants came over 700,000 mechanical transport vehicles and more than 50,000 armoured fighting vehicles; field, anti-aircraft and naval guns were produced to the number of more than 40,000; more than 1,700,000 small arms were manufactured; ammunition, chemicals and explosives were produced in astronomical figures. From shipyards came escort ships, minesweepers, landing craft and cargo vessels; from aircraft factories combat, patrol and trainer aircraft.[193]

The Canadian aircraft industry, in particular, had grown appreciably from 1939-1945 and although in the immediate post-war period aircraft production had fallen, events in Korea coupled with a general buildup of Canada's military in the 1950s resulted in a significant recovery. For example, in 1950, the aircraft industry included 15 establishments employing 10,500 people with sales amounting to about $55 million. Five years later, the aircraft industry had grown threefold. There were now 52 establishments with 33,000 employees and sales of $354 million.[194]

The possibility that Canada might have to mobilize for a future war also supported the continuance of an armaments industry that could expand quickly in an emergency. Politically, Reid suggested, Canada would also be in a position, if an armaments industry were supported, to provide its friends with arms for use against the Soviet Union. On the other hand, he was well aware of the problems associated with becoming an arms supplier:

> The political argument against our manufacturing arms for export is that by so doing the Canadian Government will deliberately be creating for itself a series of new and difficult problems in foreign relations which we have

> hitherto been able to avoid: since we would presumably
> not be willing to sell to all corners, we would from time
> to time be faced with the necessity of deciding whether to
> accept or reject orders from countries A, B, C, etc. Decisions
> will be relatively easy if the countries are the Netherlands,
> Belgium, France and the members of the Commonwealth
> on the one hand, or the Soviet Union, Roumania, Bulgaria,
> etc. on the other hand. The marginal countries in Europe
> and the Latin American countries with their dangers of
> civil wars will create difficulties.[195]

Despite the potential for "new and difficult problems in foreign relations," Cabinet was advised by External Affairs that the sale of arms from
current production should be permitted, and in some cases encouraged,
on condition that sales would only be approved for countries deemed to
be democratic and potential allies; that orders for arms were clearly on
behalf of a government and not a third party engaged in black market
operations; and that arms manufacturers would not have the freedom
to build to whatever the foreign demand might be. The Canadian munitions industry, said External Affairs, would only buildup in a way "in
which the Canadian Government wishes it to develop."[196] In the same
memorandum, then-Secretary of State for External Affairs, Louis St. Laurent, recommended the sale of 10,000 *Sten* machine-gun barrel assemblies
to the Netherlands. At the same time he supported a request from the
Nationalist Chinese Government Supply Agency for 100,000 rounds of
7.92mm ammunition. Canadian Arsenals Limited, he wrote, could supply the request at a price of approximately $53.00 per thousand rounds.
Moreover, "the Chinese Government Supply Agency [was] prepared to
make payment in U.S. dollars."[197]

At first glance, the decision to support the Nationalist Chinese government in their civil war against the Communist Chinese was a bold one
considering that Ottawa wished, as previously noted, to avoid commitments which might prove undesirable or embarrassing. Yet, as early as
1946, the Canadian government had become a key ally of the Nationalist
government, selling significant amounts of surplus war stock to Chiang
Kai-shek's forces. The initial offer of aid came in February 1946 when
Canada extended a $60 million credit to the Nationalists. Of this amount,

$35 million was to be used in procuring Canadian goods and services for reconstruction and other general post-war purposes in China. The remaining $25 million was to go towards the purchase of surplus war stocks. Repayment was to be made in thirty equal annual installments including interest.[198]

The decision by Cabinet to aid the Nationalists was likely not seen to be a potential source of trouble at the time given the "sweeping victories" achieved by Nationalist Armies at the commencement of the civil war in November 1946.[199] The United States, for example, had also been quick to offer the Nationalists support at the end of the Pacific War and President Truman directed the 12.5 million Japanese troops in China remain in place to prevent the Chinese Communists from taking over large portions of northern and eastern China. In addition, American planes ferried Nationalist troops into northern cities while 50,000 Marines occupied key airfields and ports in northeastern China.[200] When it appeared likely that the Nationalists would easily retain the upper hand in China, sales of Canadian surplus military equipment quickly mounted to include 200 surplus *Mosquito* bombers with ammunition, 200 *Harvard* trainer aircraft, 100,000 rounds of 7.92mm ammunition and 125 Pratt-Whitney aircraft engines.[201] Despite extensive military assistance though, as the Communists shifted from guerilla warfare to more conventional operations they found the Nationalist forces overextended, weak and therefore easy prey. In early 1949, they were able to fight their way to and across the Yangtze River. Nanking fell in April 1949 then Shanghai the following month and Canton in October. Chiang Kai-shek, with two million troops in tow, had little choice but to flee.

Some members of the Canadian public, Cabinet was advised in 1948, had criticized the sale of *Mosquito* bombers and arms to the Nationalists, and since the sale "there has been a considerable amount of adverse comment regarding Canadian support of the National Government."[202] In fact, certain segments of the Canadian public did, as *Time Magazine* reported on 5 January 1948, their utmost to disrupt the sale of arms to the Nationalists:

> Canada's government had decided that it was in Canada's interest to sell surplus warplanes (and ammunition for their guns) to the Nationalist government of China.

> Theoretically, Ottawa's policy toward the Chinese civil war
> was still "hands off," but by selling excess war equipment
> the government saw a chance to turn an honest dollar. For
> 323 Mosquito fighter-bombers, and to put them in condi-
> tion for shipping, China spent $10,000,000 [Cabinet docu-
> ments put the number of bombers sold to China at 200]. But
> last week, Canada's Communists and fellow travelers were
> trying to overrule Canada's government. In Halifax the
> freighter *Islandside* was loading general cargo, but 600 tons
> of ammunition and six crated aircraft destined for China
> lay on the dock. Members of the Red-tinged Canadian Sea-
> men's Union would not man the winches to load ammuni-
> tion. If the ammunition were loaded, C.S.U. men would not
> take the ship out.[203]

In Vancouver, similar events took place. Picketers, many from the University of British Columbia, said *Time,* attempted to disrupt the loading
of another ship carrying 630 tons of ammunition intended for China.
Despite public opinion in Canada, Ottawa could, however, rightly point
out that Chiang Kai-shek's government was recognized as the legitimate
government and had been a wartime ally. Not selling arms to the Nationalists, External Affairs advised Cabinet, would have been tantamount to
providing indirect aid to the Communists.

Orders from the Nationalist Chinese government also required Canada
to sell armaments from current production lines to keep up with demand.
In 1948, Mr. Roy Peers, representing the Chinese Government Supply
Agency in Ottawa, enquired about the availability of 18,000 9mm *Browning* pistols, 250,000 *Sten* guns and 9,000,000 rounds of 9mm ammunition.
The quoted price was approximately $3 million (US).[204] Although the po-
litical situation in China was unsettled and the Nationalist government
appeared to be losing ground, the Canadian government still remained
willing to sell, to the extent possible, the weapons Peers requested. In
October 1948, Cabinet was then advised that the Chinese Government
Supply Agency had now asked the Canadian Commercial Corporation purchase and export to China: 2036 *Bren* guns for approximately
$412,000; 5,071,000 rounds of .30 calibre cartridges worth approximately
$50,710; and 126,000 rounds of 7.92mm ammunition for $3,780.[205] But, by

mid-1949, the Nationalists were losing the war thus jeopardizing future Canadian military sales.

The worsening situation in China, however, was not a complete surprise in Ottawa. Escott Reid advised his Minister in mid-November 1948 that the Communists were gaining ground and that the estimated 800 Canadians in China would eventually have to be evacuated. "You may wish," he added, "to make a report to Cabinet on the deterioration of the Chinese situation."[206] What optimism there might have been present in Ottawa about the possibility of the tide turning in China likely dissipated in December 1948 when the Chiefs of Staff released a Joint Intelligence Committee paper on their view of the situation. "It is considered doubtful," given the morale of the Nationalist Government and the civilian population, they concluded, "whether the Chinese National Government will remain in effective existence until 15 June, 1949."[207]

Fortunately, for the Canadian arms industry, there were other customers in Asia for Canadian arms and ammunition besides China. The Secretary of State for External Affairs first discussed arms shipments to India and Pakistan with his Cabinet colleagues in early September 1948. The Indian government, noted the Minister, had expressed interest in purchasing 100,000 rifles and 100 million rounds of ammunition (.303) from Canadian Arsenals Limited. However, the security situation in India and Pakistan following partition, and ongoing fighting in Kashmir, were cause for concern in Cabinet that Canada might in fact end up fuelling the crisis. On the other hand, refusal to supply arms might be resented in both countries. "It might be argued," noted minutes of the debate, "that if the small arms and ammunition that were requested were primarily for use in maintaining internal order; their acquisition might be differentiated from that of heavy equipment suitable for extensive military operations."[208] With this reasoning in mind Cabinet gave its approval for any orders that might be forthcoming from Pakistan and India for small arms and ammunition.

The approval of small arms sales to India was soon followed by more requests from Delhi for military equipment. In October 1948 the Indian Government asked to buy 289,000 4.2-inch mortar bombs while Pakistan was interested in purchasing 20,000 rifles and 30 million rounds of ammunition worth $3 million. However, mortar bombs and the mortars they would be launched from, were deemed by Cabinet to be offensive not defensive weapons and therefore the sale of mortar bombs to India was denied. Sales of small arms and ammunition to Pakistan, however, were permitted.[209] India and Pakistan now had their foot firmly in the Canadian armaments door, leading to increasing demands from both countries for more advanced weaponry.

On 8 December 1948, Prime Minister Louis St. Laurent broke the news in Cabinet that both India and Pakistan had requested Canada sell heavy weapons to them. While selling such weapons had been against the general policy adopted earlier to limit sales to small arms only, the prime minister was now ready to reconsider. The Acting Secretary of State for External Affairs, Brooke Claxton, noted that there were no international restrictions preventing sales of heavy weapons and if the Canadian government decided not to offer military equipment to India and Pakistan, the United Kingdom would. The Minister of Trade and Commerce added, supportively, that "acceptance of orders for military equipment from India and Pakistan would result in substantial savings in next year's estimates in connection with the procurement programmes of the Armed Services."[210] The support in Cabinet to sell arms to India and Pakistan meant that arms shipments to both countries could proceed and the sale of mortar bombs to India, earlier denied by Cabinet, was finally given the go-ahead. Immediate sales to Pakistan would be more substantive, including 20,000 *PIAT* anti-tank rounds, 36 *Bofors* 40mm anti-aircraft guns plus spares, and an unspecified number of *Oerlikon* anti-aircraft guns, artillery ammunition, small arms, mortar bombs, and various engineer explosive stores.[211]

More requests for military equipment were forthcoming in 1949. De Havilland Aircraft of Canada Limited requested permission to export 36 *Chipmunk* aircraft to India. The Canadian Commercial Company wished to sell spare parts for 25-pounder artillery guns to Pakistan. The two export contracts, both approved by Cabinet, were worth $358,000 and $100,000 respectively.[212] One year later, discussion then centred on a request from the Canadian Commercial Corporation to export ammunition valued at some $1.8 million to Pakistan. In view of the political situation in the region External Affairs determined it would be more appropriate if Cabinet members decided whether or not to proceed. Important to the discussion were several key points. Cabinet was advised that while India was able to manufacture ammunition, Pakistan did not and therefore relied on countries like Canada to meet their needs. Arming Pakistan, the Cabinet minutes noted, might also help in deterring any Soviet move to expand their power southwards. The Minister of National Defence added that foreign sales would also allow Canada to maintain a reasonable military industrial base for future needs. Lester Pearson, then Secretary of State for External Affairs, then noted that: "Canada had supplied very little in the way of arms to India, and that Pakistan, over the past year, had shown every evidence and desire to settle matters peacefully."[213] As Table 5 notes, Pakistan was an early and major recipient of Canadian military assistance.

Date	Description of Sale	Dollar Amount
24 November 1948	20,000 rifles and 30 million rounds of ammunition	$3 million (US)
8 December 1948	20,000 *PIAT* anti-tank rounds, 36 *Bofors* 40mm anti-aircraft guns plus spares, and an unspecified number of *Oerlikon* anti-aircraft guns, artillery ammunition, small arms, mortar bombs, and various engineer explosive stores	Unknown
5 January 1949	Spare parts for 25-pounder artillery guns	$100,000
4 March 1949	*Browning* machine guns and spare barrels	$93,582.50
23 June 1950	Ford military truck spare parts	$326,000
13 December 1950	Sixty-one units of "single purpose shell-making machinery" to Pakistan for the manufacture of 25-pounder artillery shells	$526,000
12 June 1951	Twenty-three million rounds of .303 Mark VII rounds	Unknown
17 March 1952	Seven, 25-pounder artillery guns	Unknown
17 June 1952	Field artillery ammunition, charges and fuses	$5 million
23 February 1956	Sale by the *Levy Auto Parts Company Limited* of tank spare parts to Pakistan. The majority of the sale involved tank treads	$444,679.62
12 April 1956	Army radars and spare parts	$1.36 million
19 May 1960	Sale by the *Levy Auto Parts Company Limited* of *Sherman* tank spare parts. In Cabinet, it was discussed if India should be informed of the planned sale. However, as the "items under consideration were merely spare parts for obsolescent equipment" permission was granted to proceed with the sale and India would not be advised.[214]	$483,000

Table 5 – Canadian Arms Sales to Pakistan 1948-1960[215]

Like India and Pakistan, the Israeli government was also eager to ensure their armed forces were well prepared for any eventuality. One source of arms was Canada, and in early 1950 the Israeli government requested Canada export four *Harvard* aircraft, valued at $26,000, to a private company in Israel training air force pilots. In addition, they wished to purchase four *Mosquito* bombers with spare parts, valued at $70,000 for the Israeli air force. The Canadian military's Joint Intelligence Bureau noted that Canada had sold, since August 1949, 27 *Harvard* aircraft and one *Chipmunk* trainer to Israel and in their view there was no military objection to the follow-on request for aircraft. However, the Deputy Minister of National Defence was not positive Cabinet would agree to sell *Mosquito* aircraft, which "could hardly be considered as purely defensive equipment."[216] The Chief of the Air Staff added that although the *Mosquito* might be regarded as obsolescent, it was still a useful fighter-bomber and night fighter. Based on the views expressed by the Deputy Minister and the Chief of the Air Staff, the Chiefs of Staff Committee agreed that an export permit for the *Mosquito* aircraft could not be recommended to Cabinet.

The role of the Joint Intelligence Bureau in screening requests for arms export permits had come about in late 1949. In a memorandum from the Under Secretary of State for External Affairs to the Chiefs of Staff Committee on 22 December 1949, the Under Secretary mentioned that export controls, as far as arms and ammunition were concerned, were a form of economic warfare that needed strict oversight. Attending a Chiefs of Staff Committee meeting in January 1950, he added:

> It was essential that a single agency with access to all available intelligence should deal with this subject [arms exports]. As the Joint Intelligence Bureau was created with the object of collecting, collating, appreciating and providing information on the economic and industrial war potential of foreign countries, it appeared to be the appropriate agency in which all relevant intelligence should be pooled.[217]

The decision taken by the Committee was that in future External Affairs would ensure all applications for arms-related export permits would be directed to the Joint Intelligence Bureau for assessment.

In 1952-53, Israel requested the Canadian government approve the export of twelve 90mm anti-aircraft guns, spare parts for M4 tanks and M10 gun carriers and, according to an External Affairs memorandum, an "excessive" amount of .50 caliber ammunition.[218] Another order followed for $110,160 worth of anti-tank ammunition and in May 1953, the Israeli Embassy in Washington, through the Canadian delegation to the UN, enquired about the possibility of Ottawa selling 12 jet aircraft, 40 anti-aircraft guns, and 40 25-pounder guns complete with ammunition. Of most concern, however, was a request by the Canadian Commercial Corporation to ship 500 tons of RDX/TNT explosives to Israel. At the time, and due to unrest along the Israeli-Jordanian border, the United Kingdom, the Pentagon and State Department were not eager to see large weapons shipments enter the region. In the opinion of the Commonwealth Relations Office "the Arab States would look upon a shipment of 500 tons [of RDX/TNT] as being a threat to their security." As it was, the order for 500 tons was reduced to 200 tons and the request approved, "partly in order to avoid cancellation charges totaling $50,000."[219]

In October 1955, the Secretary of State for External Affairs reported that Israel had recently placed an order with the Canadian Commercial Corporation for 48 25-pounder artillery guns, plus spares and fire control equipment. This, however, was a major order providing enough firepower to create a new artillery division and the United States and Great Britain were not at all supportive of Canada selling guns to Israel. The Joint Intelligence Bureau also noted that the sale "should not be approved on the grounds that Israel's artillery strength would be materially increased, and exceed her legitimate peace time needs, and that the acquisition of the guns would widen the gap in this type of equipment between the Arab States and the Israeli Army."[220]

Certainly, the Canadian government did not want to fuel an arms race in the Middle East. However, Mr. Michael S. Comay, the Israeli ambassador to Canada, had assured the Canadian government that for each gun purchased, an existing gun would be retired. This assurance, Cabinet was advised, had been followed up in a letter from the ambassador to the Secretary of State. Certainly, Cabinet was leaning towards approving the Israeli request for new guns and during the discussion, Cabinet minutes noted how "the political situation in the Near East had improved slightly in recent months," and "in general, it was desirable to support a nation setting such a good example in improving the productivity of an impoverished section of the world."[221] Following the discussion Cabinet agreed that the Canadian Commercial Corporation could accept an order for guns from Israel and the export permit would be approved.

The sensitivity of arms shipments to the Middle East arose once more in March 1956 when the Secretary of State for External Affairs reported to Cabinet that a ship had left New York on its way to Halifax to pick-up nine *Harvard* trainer aircraft, which represented the last of an uncompleted order from the Egyptian government. The question for the Canadian government was, if it did move to block the delivery based on the poor security situation in the Middle East, did it have the authority to do so? In the end, Cabinet determined that the remaining nine aircraft would be delivered to Egypt.[222]

There was, in Cabinet however, a desire to come to the aid of Israel as much as possible and not defer the sale of arms to Tel Aviv. It would be a mistake "to abandon help to Israel" noted Cabinet minutes in March 1956.[223] However, while a final shipment of 1,754 25-pounder artillery rounds was approved, Cabinet decided that given the situation developing in the region they could not sanction the sale of the 800 *Browning* machine guns that Israel had requested, nor another request for seventy 6-pounder anti-tank guns.[224] Prior to the Suez Crisis, the Israeli government had also ordered 24 F-86 *Sabre* aircraft from Canada and Cabinet decided on 21 September 1956 to "release the 24 jet aircraft in installments over a period of time on the understanding that deliveries would be suspended or cancelled if the political situation appeared to warrant such action."[225] However, when Israel attacked Egypt in October 1956, the sale was automatically suspended and a permit that had been issued allowing delivery of the first eight aircraft, worth $2.6 million, was cancelled.[226] The decision to provide Israel with jet fighters had been a courageous one for the Canadian government as in April 1956, John Holmes had advised Cabinet that the fighter decision would: "have important consequences concerning the government's general policies. If they should be released specifically to assist Israel in meeting the threat posed by Egyptian acquisition of Russian-built jet bombers, this would involve taking sides in the Arab-Israeli conflict to a degree that no western power has yet done."[227]

Even with the eventual resolution of the Suez Crisis and the arrival of UNEF 1 in Egypt, successive Canadian governments would continue to face the question of what to do when it came to arms sales in the Middle East? While Cabinet did not wish to be accused of fueling a regional arms race the future of Canadian arms and arms-related "manufactories" depended on overseas markets. For example, in December 1963 the Minister of Industry told Cabinet that denying export permits for the sale of aircraft to Middle Eastern countries was having an increasingly negative impact on De Havilland.

For example, the company was not able to offer the *Caribou* aircraft, which he noted, was mainly a transport airplane and therefore not offensive in nature. As *Caribou* orders from the United States were drying up, unemployment at the plant in Toronto would no doubt result. The Minister of Trade and Commerce added that Canada's policy of not selling aircraft to countries in the Middle East was far more rigid than that of Great Britain and France. In light of the discussion, Cabinet agreed that export permits for *Caribou* aircraft sales to the Middle East would be authorized in future. However, sales of "significant" military equipment to Israel, the United Arab Republic, Syria, Lebanon, Jordan, Iraq and Saudi Arabia would continue to be denied except in cases where Canadian equipment was already in service and Canada was the sole source of spare parts.[228]

Despite hesitation in Cabinet regarding the export of arms in general, there was certainly little indecision in Ottawa surrounding military assistance to India following Chinese border incursions in November 1962. And Canada was not alone in taking action as President Kennedy and Prime Minister Macmillan, meeting in the Bahamas in December 1962, also discussed the urgent need to provide short-term military assistance to India in the form of "military equipment of immediate operational value."[229] The resulting "Nassau Plan" envisaged the United States and the Commonwealth offering India $60 million each of grant assistance. Canada also agreed to support the plan, though the Government would not commit to a specific amount. Nevertheless, Ottawa did provide India with almost $6 million of military equipment, including eight *Dakota* aircraft valued at $646,985. Six of the eight *Dakota* aircraft were delivered to India soon after the Chinese attack as an immediate show of support.

Aircraft	Manufacturer	Role	Cruising Speed	Armament	Original Cost
Sabre	Canadair	Fighter	787 km/h	Six .50 caliber machine guns plus provision for carrying bombs and unguided rockets	$360,000
Tutor	Canadair	Trainer	782 km/h	None, but provision for under-fuselage tanks	$425,000
Harvard	North American	Trainer	225 km/h	The aircraft, although designated a trainer, could be modified to carry machine guns, rockets and practice bombs.	$27,000 (US)
Chipmunk	De Havilland	Trainer	200 km/h	None	Unknown
Caribou	De Havilland	Transport	290 km/h	None	$632,648
Dakota	Douglas	Transport	269 km/h	None	$165,000
Twin Otter	De Havilland	Utility	274 km/h	None	$670,000
Beaver	De Havilland	Utility	209 km/h	None	Unknown

Table 6 – Canadian Aircraft Sold or Provided to Foreign Countries[230]

As a result of the Chinese attacking India, Canada also supplied the Indian government with five *Otter* aircraft (total cost $744,050), 36 *Harvard* trainer aircraft (total cost $883,000), military clothing (worth $1,530,973), and a grant in connection with the sale of *Caribou* aircraft valued up to $2 million. The grant was to cover half the interest costs as a result of a $12.5 million loan to the Indian government associated with the purchase of 16 *Caribou* aircraft (the interest rate on the loan was 5½ percent). Five hundred tons of nickel, not included as part of the Nassau Plan, was also sent to India.[231] On the other hand, when the Minister of Defence Production proposed that Canada build an ammunition factory in India in March 1963 officials in the Departments of Finance and External Affairs objected on the grounds that this was going too far.[232]

Besides the major requests for arms that arrived in Ottawa from governments in China, India, Pakistan and Israel, there were other arms requests, principally from Latin America that flowed into Ottawa in the late 1950s. One of the first from a Latin American country occurred in March 1956 when Colombia enquired about purchasing *Sabre* jets – the first large order from a non-NATO, non-Commonwealth country. It would be difficult, the Secretary of State informed Cabinet, to refuse the sale to a country interested in developing its defences. The sale, he added, would also benefit Canadian industry although the Minister could "foresee criticism if the order were filled." Cabinet, therefore, decided to defer the decision although six *Sabre* jets were eventually sold to Colombia.[233]

In August 1956, the Secretary of State for External Affairs reported to Cabinet that several enquiries had now been received from other South American countries asking if Canada might sell *Sabre* jet aircraft to them. These requests, the Minister noted, had been dealt with "individually and gingerly" but in his opinion the time had come to develop a general policy as there were several good arguments in favour of sales:

> [Including] the commercial gain in selling products of a Canadian industry abroad; the desirability of maintaining the industry on as economic a basis as possible, having in mind that domestic demand was limited and that only a relatively small number could be given away; and the stability of an important defence facility. On the political side, while certain [countries] might be better advised to devote their resources to domestic development, the fact remained that many of them would buy aircraft anyway. Several South American countries, for example, had invested fairly substantially in U.S. and U.K. aircraft and some were even considering buying from Russia. In the circumstances, it would seem to be of advantage, in appropriate cases, for Canada to supply such equipment. On the other hand, many would no doubt feel that, on moral grounds, Canada should not be in this kind of business at all.[234]

During the discussion it was noted that foreign aircraft sales and the follow-on supply of spare parts was very important for the domestic aircraft industry. However, Cabinet decided that the sale of aircraft to overseas customers was still too sensitive an issue and therefore a general policy would not be implemented. On the other hand, it was agreed that sales to potential trouble spots around the world would not be automatically precluded unless they would lead to a rise in international violence or might threaten the position of another government with which Canada maintained friendly relations.

An example of Cabinet decision around the issue of aircraft sales arose in July 1959 when the Canadian Car Company Limited applied for an export permit allowing them to deliver $110,000 worth of *Harvard* aircraft spare parts to the Dominican Republic. At the time, the Dominican government operated a fleet of 40 *Harvard* aircraft that could be used to support ground combat operations. This potential use of the aircraft for combat purposes was cause for concern in Cabinet as the Dominican Republic was on External Affairs' "sensitive list" due to the repressive nature of President Hector Trujillo's government. Any decision to send aircraft spare parts, noted the Cabinet minutes, might be construed throughout the Caribbean as being tacit support for his regime. Indeed, by the end of the Cabinet discussion it was agreed that not only would the export permit for *Harvard* spare parts be denied, but also all requests for arms exports to the Caribbean would not be approved for the foreseeable future based on the deteriorating security situation at the time.[235]

Latin American countries were also eager to obtain more than just aircraft from Canadian suppliers. For example, the Levy Auto Parts Company Limited of Toronto requested the Canadian government approve the sale of $180,400 worth of truck and tank spare parts to the Venezuelan military in late 1959. The Canadian ambassador in Caracas was in favour given that Venezuela was a democracy and therefore, in his view, not a real threat in the region. However, in light of the previous decision not to supply arms to the Caribbean, Cabinet was hesitant to agree with the ambassador even if the spare parts were for Second World War equipment.[236] Faced with a difficult decision, Cabinet took up the matter on 28 September 1959. During the ensuing discussion, Ministers reflected on the fact that when they were in opposition three years earlier, they had taken a strong stand against the Liberal government and its military exports program. Now, positions were reversed. If there was an agreement in Cabinet to sell military equipment to Venezuela they would all appear to be hypocrites. Nevertheless, in the subsequent debate on what to do, the Secretary of State for External Affairs and the Minister of National Defence prevailed, convincing their colleagues to support the sale of military equipment to Venezuela.

Not unexpectedly, the Levy Company soon followed their export permit success with another request in February 1960. This time, permission from Cabinet to supply Venezuela with 40 military *Reo* 2½-ton trucks was sought. The contract, amounting to $200,000 was fairly substantial and Howard Green, the Secretary of State for External Affairs added that the Venezuelan ambassador was keen to expand economic ties between Canada and his country. Approving the export of military equipment, the Ambassador had implied, might result in Canada being in a good position to double its then $40 million a year in exports to Venezuela. In particular, noted the Cabinet minutes, the Venezuelan ambassador had made clear his nation was well behaved and "governed along democratic lines. Accordingly, there was no danger of war in that area." With little additional debate the export permit was approved.[237]

Although arms exports to Latin American countries might have been one way to foster better ties between the many countries in the region and Canada, in Ottawa the view was that closer ties with Latin America would do little to improve Canada's national or economic security. As early as 1949, Prime Minister Louis St. Laurent had determined that there was little to no advantage in joining a hemispheric security arrangement. In his view, the government considered it "much more pressing to realize the North Atlantic Treaty Organization than to add one more voice to an organization that one can consider exclusively reserved to the Western Hemisphere."[238] The desire not to become entangled in Latin American defence or political issues persisted throughout the 1950s even though C.D. Howe had led a trade delegation to the region in 1953 and four years later the Secretary of State for External Affairs, Sidney Smith, visited three Latin American countries.

Invitations to join the Organization of American States (OAS) were also rebuffed even after President Kennedy, speaking in the House of Commons on 17 May 1961, invited Canada to become a member of the organization. The reasons for not joining, however, were many: there was little advantage from a national defence point of view, there was good potential for disagreement with the United States over Latin American issues, and it was believed that OAS members would begin pestering Canada for aid when much of Ottawa's interest and attention was directed toward newly independent countries in Africa and Asia.[239] The election of Prime Minister Trudeau in 1968 did little to change matters even though his 1970 Foreign Policy White Paper had a specific volume dedicated to Latin America. In fact, Canada did not join the OAS until 1991.

The reluctance to become involved politically and economically in Latin America contrasted significantly with the position taken by the Canadian Government with regards to sub-Saharan Africa. Canadian diplomatic representation on the continent in 1960 was limited. However, as more African countries were soon to be independent, the question of how best to expand Canadian representation was raised in Cabinet in November 1961. Cabinet was informed that Tanganyika would become independent on 9 December 1961 – the first fully independent Commonwealth country in Eastern Africa. The establishment of a High Commissioner and mission in Dar es Salaam would be, it was suggested to Ministers, a good strategic move.

At the same meeting, the importance of reaching out to French-speaking African countries was raised. An embassy in Cameroon, with an ambassador accredited to the Republic of Congo (Brazzaville), the Congo (Leopoldville), Chad, the Central African Republic and Gabon was recommended, especially if Canada wished to expand trade relations.[240] During the ensuing discussion several points came out. Some Ministers said the "expansion of Canadian diplomatic representation [would result] in costly expense accounts, too rapid expansion and the assumption of responsibilities without accompanying benefits." Others around the Cabinet table disagreed, concluding that it was vital for Canada to "be represented in those countries that were reaching independence. Such missions could contribute much to the new nations and also serve as intelligence centers observing the influence of communists and others."[241] The result of the discussion was a decision by Cabinet to establish a High Commission in Dar es Salaam and an embassy in Yaoundé in fiscal year 1961-62.

The desire to increase Canada's diplomatic representation and aid in Africa was not unsurprising. Many of the new nations would become future members of the Commonwealth – an important point for Prime Minister Diefenbaker who believed the organization to be "the greatest instrument for freedom the world has ever seen."[242] However, Commonwealth issues related to South Africa and its apartheid policies would take up considerable Cabinet time. For example, in April 1960, Cabinet requested a policy be developed regarding the export of military equipment to Pretoria. The proposed policy was presented to Cabinet in September 1960 and the general consensus was that arms exports should be limited to NATO and Commonwealth countries only. Given the challenges facing several newly independent Commonwealth countries though, it was proposed that Cabinet only would approve exports to Ceylon (Sri Lanka), Ghana, India, Malaya, Pakistan and South Africa. These countries would be kept on a "sensitive list" and would be joined by the eventual addition of Cyprus, Nigeria and the Federation of the West Indies upon independence.[243] During the ensuing discussion, ministers expressed concern that the "sensitive list" could not remain secret for too long and that "South Africa, a country which at this time paid allegiance to the Crown should not be placed on the same footing as Ghana, nor in a position inferior to West Germany, a former enemy."[244] However, the use of a "sensitive list" was deemed prudent and the best means to ensure sensitive arms exports issues were brought to Cabinet.

Selling arms to South Africa was a particularly thorny problem for Ottawa following a referendum held in October 1960 in which the white South African population narrowly voted in favour of becoming a republic. Under Commonwealth rules, and normally a formality only, any country wishing to become a republic was required to re-apply for membership. The policy that Canada should adopt regarding the re-admission of South Africa, however, took up a considerable amount of Cabinet time. Most contentious, naturally, was the South African policy of apartheid that was likely to be raised during the next Commonwealth Conference in March 1961.

For most countries, the question of whether to re-admit South Africa into the Commonwealth was not easy. Australia and New Zealand, Ministers were told, would likely support South Africa even though the New Zealand Rugby team had recently been forced to leave its Maori players behind during a recent visit to South Africa. Cabinet was also advised that

Canada would be looked to by other nations, especially the "non-white" countries for guidance on what to do. Certainly, Ceylon, Ghana, India, Malaya, Nigeria and Pakistan were not supportive of re-admitting South Africa. In the course of discussion, Cabinet was also informed that a senior advisor to President Kwame Nkrumah of Ghana had warned that if strong action were not to be taken at the up-coming Commonwealth Conference, "various new African governments might be defeated and replaced by communist or pseudo-communist regimes."[245] Certainly, the Conservative government was concerned that they might be held responsible by Canadians for the break-up of the Commonwealth if they did not take a firm stand against South Africa. The prime minister needed no reminding that Canadians were very supportive of the organization and the government might "suffer severely at the polls" if the Commonwealth fell apart.[246] As it was, Diefenbaker was instrumental in ensuring South Africa would leave the Commonwealth when it officially became a republic on 31 May 1961.

However, this did not mean ties with South Africa were severed completely nor did it mean an end to Canadian arms exports to the white regime. In September 1962, the Secretary of State for External Affairs reported to Cabinet that the South African government had inquired about the possibility of Canada issuing export permits for the sale of 70 Position and Homing Indicators (PHI) for use in jet fighters and an unspecified number of high-altitude pilot pressure suits. Cabinet minutes indicated that in line with other Commonwealth countries that had decided not to sell arms to South Africa, "Canada had been refusing to license the export to South Africa of arms and military equipment which could be used for civil control or enforcement of the policy of apartheid. It would appear that the equipment under discussion was not related to operations against the native population."[247] Cabinet agreed that if South Africa wanted to purchase the said items, they would approve.

In June 1963, the Secretary of State for External Affairs, Paul Martin Sr. advised Cabinet that Canadair was aware the South African Air Force was keen to purchase 50 jet-trainer aircraft. The company wished to make a strong sales effort as likely the British and French would. Cabinet was also advised that the South Africans were interested in the CL-41G *Tutor* jet aircraft that could be used for ground strafing and carrying napalm bombs. Mr. Martin, however, was firmly against any sales to South Africa of this nature, noting a recent walk out of thirty-five African nations from the International Labour Organization over South Africa's continuing membership. The walkout, he added, was indicative of the risk Canada's reputation would suffer if offensive weapons were sold to South Africa.[248] Before the matter of aircraft sales could proceed much further, the Security Council called upon member nations to cease weapons sales to South Africa in August 1963.

Canadian arms sales to South Africa had been limited in past years to supplying spare parts for F-86 *Sabre* aircraft sold to the South Africans in 1956. In general, the policy had been to only sell arms and equipment for the external defence of South Africa and not anything that could be used for internal security.[249] To stop selling parts for equipment Canada had previously sold to South Africa, some Cabinet Ministers believed, would not be fair to the South Africans. In addition, Ministers also noted, "in Ghana and Nigeria, Canada was helping to establish armed forces, which would, if the declarations of Ghanaian and Nigerian leaders were to be believed, be used against South Africa when the time was ripe."[250] The decision, after some debate, was to have the Secretary of State for External Affairs inform the Secretary General of the UN that Canada would continue to sell spare parts to South Africa including *Sabre* spare parts, Pratt and Whitney piston engines and the 70 PHI sets. However, the Secretary General was told, Canada would respect the Security Council's desire to limit the sale of offensive weapons to South Africa.

After the Second World War, the likelihood that Canada would become involved with selling arms to South Africa or anywhere else for that matter must have seemed a very remote possibility for a government determined to downsize its military establishment as quickly as circumstances permitted. Moreover, the focus in Ottawa was to support the UN in becoming the global security arbitrator. Only later, when it was clear the Soviet Union would be a major threat to the West and the UN was unable to prevent conflict, did Canada become a founding member of NATO in 1949.

However, the Canadian government was not at all enthusiastic about investing in defence, collective or otherwise, after 1945. If training NATO aircrew in Canada and sending surplus war equipment to European allies could suffice as a form of membership dues then that would do. Yet, there was no escaping the fact in Ottawa that the Canadian economy was on very firm ground compared to Europe's in 1945 and that the alliance would expect Canada to contribute more of its resources and defence budget in sustaining NATO over the long term. In Ottawa, though, there was a certain Machiavellian quality attached to supporting the alliance with arms and ammunition sales. For one, the Canadian government wanted to have an arms industry that could expand quickly should mobilization be necessary and foreign customers would be necessary to keep defence companies in business and cost-effective.[251] Indeed, many of the discussions that took place in Cabinet focused on the need to protect jobs especially in the aviation industry.

However, as Western Europe began to recover from the war, the demand for Canadian arms exports began to fall and, therefore, new markets were needed. But, exporting arms, ammunition and military equipment to non-NATO countries was a sensitive issue in Ottawa and successive Canadian governments were always wary about becoming involved in foreign conflicts and to be seen taking sides or promoting regional arms races. Export permits, therefore, were always tightly controlled, with Cabinet playing a pivotal role in the approval process. Still, the Canadian government had set a precedent immediately after the Second World War by agreeing to supply the Nationalist Chinese government substantial arms and ammunition in their civil war against the Communist Chinese. India and Pakistan then became frequent arms customers in Ottawa and with each sale came more appeals for heavier and heavier weapons. India would also become a major recipient of Canadian-manufactured aircraft, many of them provided as gifts – but no matter if they were sold or given away, Canadian workers in Montreal and Toronto kept their jobs.

Unquestionably, arms exports to China, Pakistan and India proved controversial at times for Cabinet. The Canadian public and press had roundly criticized the sale of so many aircraft, including the *Mosquito* bomber, to the Chinese Nationalist government. However, exporting arms to Israel was also divisive in Canada, and successive governments did not wish to cause further unrest in the Middle East. Requests from Latin American countries were also problematic as Canadian politicians were eager not to be seen supporting South American dictators with military assistance. On the other hand, after South Africa left the Commonwealth, Canadian arms exports, although limited to spare parts, continued to be sold to Pretoria.

By the end of the 1950s, arms exports had become a fixture of the Canadian economy. Yet a new form of military assistance for foreign governments was on the horizon and beginning in 1961, Canadian military personnel would find themselves, often with their families in tow, stationed in several countries in sub-Saharan Africa providing military training and advice. Meanwhile, more and more non-NATO foreign military personnel were arriving in Canada for various training courses. This was a demand, alluded to earlier, which placed considerable demands on a Canadian military that continued to support NATO, NORAD, and the UN. As it was, General Foulkes had not been enamored with the training of NATO aircrew in Canada in the first place, let alone creating military assistance programs overseas for countries in the developing world. In fact, the Defence Liaison Division in External Affairs had remarked to their European desk colleagues as early as 1955 that Foulkes was examining where cuts could be made to support other priorities and the Mutual Aid Programme was one area he had his eye on. In fact, Foulkes had already concluded "the aircrew training programme in particular [should be] chopped in half."[252] The NATO aircrew-training program did indeed wind up in 1958, likely to the relief of a stretched Canadian military. Then again, the relief was only momentary. Spare billets for pilot, officer and technical trades training would soon be taken up by military personnel from non-NATO countries as Ottawa courted new friends and allies in the developing world.

CHAPTER 7

CANADA'S MILITARY ASSISTANCE TO THE POST-COLONIAL DEVELOPING WORLD

There is ample evidence of a critical need in Africa for professional military training. Developing African states are confronted with internal security problems in a climate conducive to insurgency. In most areas, military elements are emerging as the principal guardians of national sovereignty. To cope with this situation and to counter Soviet and Communist Chinese exploitation, it is desirable for the United States to contribute to the strength and authority of all pro-Western elements within state power structures, particularly the military elements.

United States Joint Chiefs of Staff, 24 December 1964

A developing country's possession of armed forces, modest in size, but still sufficient to discourage adventures by sometime ambitious neighbours, can reduce the potential for upheaval and conflict in a given area; Canadian military assistance to the right countries at the right time can in this sense be a contribution to our overall objective of maintaining world peace.

Inter-Departmental Military Assistance Committee, July 1969

The post-war Canadian military had its hands full. While the end of the war was undoubtedly a relief, initial plans to drastically reduce the size of the military and military related expenditures had, by 1950, given way to a new security situation posed by the Soviet Union. Reacting to the communist threat by joining NATO, fighting with the UN in Korea and later establishing NORAD, in fact, rejuvenated the Canadian Forces whose fortunes were on the decline immediately after 1945. However, even with the attention the military was now receiving from the Canadian government, its capabilities, given new obligations around the globe, were often stretched to the limit. Any new commitments, including military assistance to the developing world, were not likely to be welcome in military circles whatsoever. General Foulkes, for certain, was not interested in the pace of decolonization in Asia and Africa in the post-war period and the apparent need to prevent communism gaining ground. As a result, requests from External Affairs to the Canadian Forces to provide military assistance to several developing countries in the early 1950s were almost always turned down. In External Affairs the situation was exasperating, as military assistance was seen in the early 1950s as a means to "increase Canada's heightened postwar international stature."[253]

While requests from non-NATO countries for military training assistance in Canada after the war had not been that overwhelming, the Service Chiefs and the Minister of National Defence were concerned about setting any sort of precedent. A request from Pakistan in November 1948 for training spots in Canadian Staff Colleges, they concluded, would soon lead to similar requests from India and other Commonwealth countries. Besides, NATO countries had taken up what training space was available in Canadian military schools. In October 1953, for example, the Minister of National Defence could point out to Cabinet that the Navy had three Belgian cadets undergoing training at Royal Roads while the Army had ten NATO students at the Army Staff College. The Air Force was host to 1,191 aircrew trainees – all from NATO countries.[254]

As Table 7 notes, several requests for military assistance, mainly from Commonwealth countries in the developing world, were received between 1948-1953 but all were rejected by the military. The grounds for refusal were simple. Many Canadian courses, the military pointed out to External Affairs, required access to or the use of sensitive information provided by the United States, the United Kingdom or NATO. Foreign students from the developing world did not have the necessary security clearances or need to know. Training offered in Canada, more often than not, was also inappropriate for officers coming from developing countries in Asia and Africa. For example, the Army Staff College in Kingston concentrated on the study of allied forces equipped with modern weapons, vehicles and communications conducting mobile warfare in Northwest Europe against the Soviet Union. A lack of accommodation on Canadian bases was another reason the Service Chiefs were not interested in helping developing countries.

The position taken by the military was undoubtedly frustrating for those in External Affairs who wished to expand Canada's influence worldwide. Indeed, the Secretary of State had written to the Minister of National Defence in May 1952 pointing out that it "was politically desirable for Canada to give this kind of help to other members of the Commonwealth and especially to new members, such as Pakistan and India."[255] One year later, Charles Ritchie, the Deputy Under Secretary of State, advised his Minister that Canada "should not lose sight of the fact that some of these requests come from parts of the world in which western policy is often suspect. Anything we can do, however small, to offset this suspicion is an aid to our associates in both NATO and the Commonwealth, and is in our long-term interest."[256]

Country	Request	Date	Status
Pakistan	To train two officers at the Army Staff College and two at the RCAF Staff College	November 1948	Rejected
Israel	To train an unspecified number of officers	October 1951	Rejected
Mexico	To train an unspecified number of jet pilots in Canada	February 1952	Rejected
Ethiopia	Request for a vacancy at the Royal Military College	March 1952	Rejected
Pakistan	To train 90 pilots in groups of 30 spread over 1953-54-55	March 1952	Rejected
Pakistan	To train an unspecified number of medical officers	October 1952	Rejected
Burma	To train officers at training establishments in Canada	October 1952	Rejected
Pakistan	To train air force officers at the RCAF Staff College	December 1952	Rejected
India	To train a selected number of aircrew and photographic personnel in air survey techniques	May 1953	Rejected
Burma	To train officers at the Army and RCAF Staff College	August 1953	Rejected
Indonesia	Whether Canada might be agreeable to providing advanced training for a number of air force personnel	August 1953	Rejected
Israel	To discuss the possibility of obtaining vacancies in Canadian service training establishments	September 1953	Rejected

Table 7 – Non-NATO Requests For Military Training Assistance 1948-1953[257]

In spite of the ongoing pressure from External Affairs to engage the Department of National Defence in foreign military assistance, the Canadian Forces were undoubtedly successful in side-stepping requests from the developing world in the early 1950s. The military, despite an end to the fighting in Korea in 1953, could also claim to be equally as busy in 1957 with new UN and NATO commitments – reason enough to continue rebuffing requests from External Affairs. However, between 1953 and 1957, the Cold War began to fully embrace the developing world as both sides pursued new allies in Asia and Africa. In April 1955, for instance, China took on a leading role at the Bandung conference of Asian and African nations. Meanwhile, the Soviet Union concluded economic assistance agreements with a number of countries in the Middle East and Southeast Asia, including Indonesia and Burma. Both of these countries had unsuccessfully requested that Canada provide them with military assistance in 1952-1953.

In 1957-1958, Indonesia and Burma were ready to try again, but once more Foulkes was not convinced that the Canadian military could or should help. In the case of Burma, however, External Affairs was prepared to tackle the Department of National Defence. Norman Robertson pointed out to the Deputy Minister of National Defence in November 1958 that the Burmese government was fending off both Communist Burmese rebels and incursions from Communist Chinese forces. "In addition to our desire to encourage Western ties with Burma," he wrote, "we have a further interest in assisting the Burmese to improve their defence forces in order to strengthen their position against external aggression and in the maintenance of internal security."[258] Nevertheless, the Department of National Defence was not convinced or at all eager to take on responsibility for training the Burmese armed forces.

For George Glazebrook, then head of the Commonwealth Division in External Affairs, the Department of National Defence was too focused on Europe in the late 1950s. He believed that Canada might be missing out on an opportunity to combat growing communist influence in the developing world and in his view National Defence would have to accept, "as a new aspect of Canadian military policy the expansion of training facilities [for non-NATO foreign students] just as they have come to accept truce commission work as a normal part of their activities."[259] Yet, by 1957, the end was already in sight to the unwritten policy of refusal adopted by Foulkes and others in National Defence, as a wave of independence was about to sweep through sub-Saharan Africa. In this post-colonial period, new countries were about to appear almost overnight and just as quickly the East and West were ready to jockey for new friends. For the Canadian military, focused as it was on Europe as the centre of the Cold War, there was about to be a rude awakening. Canada was about to become a key player in the military assistance field, especially in sub-Saharan Africa.

In May 1958, the Canadian High Commissioner in Ghana wrote to Glazebrook about the upcoming visit to Canada by Ghana's new President, Kwame Nkrumah. The visit was to set to take place from 24-27 July 1958 and the High Commissioner wished to ensure Ottawa understood the importance of playing host to the President of the first sub-Saharan African colony to gain independence. In general, he wrote, different things from those that would normally impress Europeans would likely impress President Nkrumah. "The Africans like ceremony" he said, and "would be quick to notice if our reception falls short of what they themselves would do for a visiting dignitary. There should, in my view, be plenty of red carpet, a good deal of sabre rattling (parade ground variety) and the wailing of sirens."[260] The fact was that there was great excitement in Ottawa and Canada about becoming more engaged in Africa.

In a confidential paper prepared by External Affairs in October 1959, the authors contemplated Canada's future relations and involvement in Africa. The long-term trend, noted the report, was "unmistakably towards autonomy in all areas, with the ultimate establishment of régimes which will be at least dominated by the preponderant racial group in each." The transition to independence, the authors added, would "be long and quite possibly bloody."[261] With great perception it was also recognized that the colonial powers would likely prefer a gradual transition while growing African nationalism would demand that independence be granted as soon as possible even if government institutions were weak or nonexistent. Then there were other factors of concern for the West, including the "influence of outside powers, such as the Soviet Union, which espouse nationalist causes as a means of gaining a foothold in Africa."[262] With regard to this latter point, two years after the External Affairs paper had been prepared Walter Laqueur wrote in *Foreign Affairs* that "almost overnight Communism in Africa has become an international problem of the first magnitude… Now in 1961, Africa has replaced the Middle East as the world's trouble center, and it is likely to remain the main area of contest between West and East for many years to come."[263] In 1961, added Peter Snow, military commanders in China had begun describing Africa as the "last battlefield" on which the West and East would soon fight it out.[264]

As for a Canadian position toward the colonial powers and new African states, the thinking in External Affairs was that Canada had no reason not to support the broad trend towards independence. On the contrary, noted an External Affairs paper, "the degree of sympathy Canada may show towards African aspirations in the coming months and years will largely determine the relations this country may eventually enjoy with the African powers which emerge – and these states and groups of states will be of major economic and political importance to the world."[265] There was also recognition that the colonial powers, all NATO members, might benefit from Canada's help even if Ottawa did not have any substantial representation in sub-Saharan Africa in 1959. However, it was difficult in External Affairs to see what role a seemingly impartial Canadian government might play in the transition to independence in Africa in the early 1960s:

> With its limited resources, Canada has been forced to be satisfied with much less representation on the spot than is desirable, and has been subject to a variety of pressures in deciding where its limited resources should be concentrated. To date, the force of the Commonwealth incentive has been decisive, and south of the Sahara Canada has diplomatic missions only in two Commonwealth states, the Union of South Africa and Ghana, and plans for establishing missions in two more, Nigeria and the Federation of Rhodesia and Nyasaland. Other independent states, particularly Guinea and Liberia, and the North African states of Morocco and Tunisia, have been ignored, together with the important groupings of former French colonies in West Africa and Equatorial Africa, the rapidly evolving Belgian Congo and the British territories in East Africa. For the moment, no further expansion of Canadian representation in

> Africa is planned, but it is nonetheless useful to consider what pattern of representation would be most desirable for the future.[266]

Finally, it was recognized that Canada's economic and technical aid in the whole of Africa was very modest and concentrated in Commonwealth areas with Ghana, which obtained its independence in 1957, being the principal beneficiary. What the actual impact of the report had on the government is unknown, but Canada's aid to Ghana, Tanzania and Nigeria was fairly substantial beginning as early as 1957. In fact, the Canadian International Development Agency (CIDA) delivered over $1 billion in development aid to Ghana between 1957 and 2002. The Canadian government from 1964 to 2002 also provided Tanzania with $1 billion for a broad range of initiatives in sectors such as education, transportation, agriculture, and health.[267]

Economically, the immediate post-colonial period did result in Canada establishing an important foothold in Africa despite a lack of government representation on the ground. Major mining operations in Ghana and Nigeria plus smaller efforts in Kenya, Liberia, Namibia, Somalia, Uganda, Zambia and the former Rhodesia all commenced. Canadian companies such as the Aluminum Company of Canada, the Ford Motor Car Company of Canada, Falconbridge Nickel Mines, Massey-Ferguson, Consolidated-Bathurst and many others also maintained significant operations on the continent. Thus, contributing to the stability of the countries where Canada had interests made sense and the traditional ways and means of providing assistance through loans or technical expertise was one way of accomplishing this.

However, it was also apparent to the Canadian government that many newly independent states in sub-Saharan Africa were eager to distance themselves from their former colonial masters when it came to military assistance. There was also pressure on Canada from Great Britain and the United States to take an active role in stemming the growing communist influence in Africa. The result was that the Canadian military, with little to no experience training African militaries, would soon find itself heavily involved on the continent, commencing in the early 1960s with military assistance to Nkrumah's Ghana.

CHAPTER 7

Military assistance to Ghana had not been a topic of discussion in Ottawa during Nkrumah's visit to Canada in 1958 as the Ghanaian Armed Forces continued to receive considerable military support from the British. However, in early 1961, the situation on the ground in Accra was changing as Nkrumah, bit by bit, sought to lessen British influence in a bid to demonstrate his leadership and independence from the former colonial power. In February 1961, for example, the Secretary of State for External Affairs reported to Cabinet that de Havilland had received an order from Ghana for 8 *Caribou* and 12 *Otter* transport and utility aircraft valued at $5.7 million and $1.7 million respectively. While there was some apprehension expressed amongst Ministers about supplying Ghana with aircraft, the Minister of National Defence pointed out that the *Caribou* and *Otter* were not fighters or bombers. If Canada did not supply transport and/or utility aircraft, he added, some other country certainly would. This was justification enough for Cabinet to approve export permits for the entire order. One month later, the Minister of National Defence reported that the Ghanaian government had now asked Canada to provide four civilian professors and nine military officers for their new staff college.[268]

A reluctant Canadian military was not at all keen, however, to engage in training military forces in sub-Saharan Africa. By September 1960, several hundred Canadian Forces personnel had already deployed to the Congo, or were on their way, in support of the UN and the conditions they experienced were abysmal. Sending an unknown number of experienced military trainers to Ghana was another unwelcome diversion. Besides, the Canadian military had little to no experience training militaries in the developing world. Conditions were far different than those experienced in Canada training new recruits in training depots and battle schools. Any Canadian military training team sent to Ghana, for example, would have to work with new recruits that could not read or write as approximately 80% of the Ghanaian population was illiterate.[269]

As the prime minister was keen to support newly independent countries in the Commonwealth, the military had little choice but to send an officer to Ghana to report on conditions and what help the Canadian military might be able to provide. Therefore, in late March 1961, Colonel P.S. Cooper travelled to Accra in order to assess the feasibility of providing military assistance to Ghana. He arrived in the capital on 26 March and was met by Mr. B.M. Williams, the Canadian High Commissioner, at the airport. After a two-hour discussion with the High Commissioner, Colonel Cooper then met with Major-General Alexander, Ghana's British Chief of Defence Staff and was a guest at his residence throughout. A few days later he met President Nkrumah at the Presidential Palace but the meeting was short – just three to four minutes. Nevertheless, reported Cooper, Nkrumah had been pleased that Canada had sent an officer to Ghana to survey the situation.

Upon his return to Canada, Colonel Cooper concluded that "assistance to Ghana in building well disciplined, loyal forces under competent and reliable leadership is one of the best contributions which could be made toward ensuring the continued peace and good order of that country."[270] He suggested that tour lengths for Canadian officers could vary from 18 months to two years and surmised that military assistance would be needed for at least five to eight years but not longer. As for the mission and staff requirements, the Colonel recommended that the tri-service Military Academy at Teshie required eight officers. Two officers would be company commanders, each responsible for cadet companies of approximately 100 cadets organized into three platoons each commanded by a Ghanaian captain. Duties would include lecturing "in any or all military subjects," including survival and jungle training.[271] The other six staff would be employed as academic instructors teaching two or three different subjects at the high school level. A further five to eight officers were needed for the Ghanaian Armed Forces Training Center in Kumasi given President Nkrumah wished to double the size of the Army as quickly as possible.

Besides the requirements noted above, Major-General Alexander was also interested in having a Canadian major, who was recommended to command a battalion in future, act as the second-in-command of a Ghanaian battalion. Finally, three medical officers were needed along with ten air force personnel to help buildup the Ghana Air Force, which was "literally starting from scratch."[272] The British team assisting the Ghana Air Force was already quite substantial, comprising 45 officers and 110 non-commissioned officers. However, as President Nkrumah had decided to equip the Air Force with mainly Canadian aircraft, and expand operations, the British training team was now in need of Canadian expertise.

Based on the recommendations made by Colonel Cooper, Douglas S. Harkness, the Minister of National Defence, announced on 3 July 1961 that the Canadian government would provide up to 30 officers to assist in the training of the Ghanaian Armed Forces. A military assistant would also be appointed to the High Commissioner and the military assistance team would be known as Canadian Armed Forces Training Team Ghana (CAFTTG). However, it was clear that politicians in Ottawa remained wary of becoming caught up in foreign political issues and as a result the Ghanaian government was told that "Canada reserved the right to withdraw any and all military personnel at any time." Furthermore, the Ghanaian government agreed "not to involve Canadian officers or men directly in aid of the civil power or in any military operations outside Ghana."[273]

Despite the fact that Ghana was a developing country and in need of foreign assistance, military and otherwise, Canada's military assistance was certainly not free. The Technical Assistance agreement between Canada and Ghana was very specific on who would pay salaries and other benefits. The agreement, signed on 8 January 1962, included several key provisions. First of all, Ghana was required "to reimburse the Government of Canada quarterly one half of the salary costs for each member from the date of his arrival in Ghana to the date of his final departure." Other benefits to be paid for by the Ghanaians included leave transportation for service personnel and their families between Accra and London and "reasonable accommodation and other facilities for all members whether single, married unaccompanied or married accompanied with dependent children." Finally, free education at the best schools available was to be provided for all dependent children accompanying service personnel to Ghana.[274]

The decision to provide Ghana with military assistance opened the door for other countries to ask Canada for similar levels of support. In September 1961, the Canadian Embassy in Washington advised External Affairs that it was likely the Nigerian Defence Minister would visit Ottawa from 23-28 September to discuss military assistance for his country. For the most part, it was believed he would seek help in training the army, navy and for drawing up plans to create a new Nigerian air force.[275] External Affairs, asked to sketch out a visit plan for the Nigerians, was eager to find out more information on any specific requests the Nigerian government might have. However, it was soon apparent that the Defence Minister had not consulted the Nigerian army and navy commanders before he left the country. Fortunately, the High Commission in Lagos was able to intervene and discuss the matter of training assistance with the Nigerian military.

Generally, the requests for help were across the board from the need to have training spots in Canada, to the establishment of a military academy. The air force required the greatest amount of assistance though, and it was suggested by the High Commission that the Nigerians would seek a single Commonwealth country to help them build up a communications and transport flight. The new air force, added the High Commission, would likely be looking for up to eight *Beaver* and four *Caribou* transport aircraft.[276] Recognizing the drain on resources that this request would have, the Minister of National Defence was adamant nothing could be done. Nevertheless, once one offer of help was made, it was proving difficult in Ottawa to say no. As an External Affairs memorandum to Howard Green, then Secretary of State made clear:

> Canada has sent a full training team to Ghana a neighbouring but smaller Commonwealth country, whose government follows a neutralist and occasionally anti-Western foreign policy. We believe that from a purely political point of view, it would be inadvisable to come up with a significantly smaller proposal to the Nigerians who follow a generally friendlier line.[277]

In the end, Cabinet determined that if Ghana was getting help, so should Nigeria and the Canadian Forces were tasked with putting together a broad program of support for all three Nigerian services. With regards to its air force, Nigeria had asked for a complete training package – from pilots to aircraft technicians. However, the RCAF was not in a position to provide such extensive training support and instead focused on a program to assist the Nigerians in selecting suitable candidates for pilot training. To this end, an RCAF training team traveled to Nigeria in January 1963 and from a Nigerian government approved list of 120 candidates, 16 were found suitable for pilot training and sent to Canada for a two-year flying course.[278] As to the training and equipping of the Nigerian air force, West Germany eventually stepped in – a decision, C.M. Drury, Minister of Industry and Defence Production would write in 1964, that had had dreadful results for Canada because the West German aircraft industry sold the Nigerians 78 aircraft, plus support equipment and spares.[279]

In addition to the RCAF team, Canada also agreed to provide the Commandant and a Director of Studies for the Nigerian Military Academy. However, the two positions were unable to be filled and the British eventually stepped-in. Efforts to assist the Nigerian navy also ran into problems. In June 1962, Canada approved plans to send six navy officers to Nigeria for instructional purposes (although the initial Nigerian request had been for 15 naval officers). The five lieutenants and one lieutenant-commander were expected to teach navigation, gunnery, anti-submarine warfare, engineering duties and communications. To facilitate plans, Lieutenant-Commander J.H. Wilkes was assigned to the High Commission in Lagos in November 1962. However, when the only Nigerian frigate was declared unseaworthy, the request for naval military assistance was cancelled and the Canadian training team never left Canada.[280] However, some training spots for Nigerians were found in Canada, and in the period 1962-63 six navy officer cadets and 20 naval technicians were sent to Canada for training. Six more Nigerian army officer cadets also arrived for their initial training.[281]

Still, there were challenges associated with the Nigerian program as Brigadier R.L. Purves, Coordinator of the Joint Staff, pointed out in a letter to the Chairman, Chiefs of Staff in April 1964. Of the six Nigerians who started naval cadet training in Canada in August 1962, he wrote, one had failed and returned home and three were likely to fail. No doubt, as the training program was two and a half years in duration, a certain amount of homesickness had a role to play. Of the 16 Nigerian pilot trainees that had begun training in April 1963, only 11 were still on course. Four had been found unsuitable for flying and of these, three were transferred to air traffic control training and one was sent on a supply course. One student was returned to Nigeria.[282]

Along with the program to support Nigeria, the Secretary of State for External Affairs reported to Cabinet in January 1962 that the Acting Secretary

General of the UN had asked Canada to provide 15 French speaking officers to help train Congolese officers. The demand for military assistance was driven by a desire in New York to withdraw UN troops from the Congo in the summer of 1962. According to the UN, Canada "was one of the few acceptable sources of French speaking instructors."[283] The Cabinet minutes also remarked on how "such a contribution would boost Canada's prestige in the U.N. It would similarly be a matter of pride for Quebec to have such an important role."[284] However, Ottawa decided not to support the request as there were already 38 Canadian officers in the Congo who spoke French and the army was not in a position to supply any more. Air Commodore Morrison, the UN Air Commander in the Congo, back in Canada on leave further estimated that to be successful the training program would have to remain in effect for at least four years and probably ten.

Nonetheless, the issue of military assistance to the Congo was still a topic for discussion in 1963 when General Mobutu, the new leader of the country, attempted to arrange a series of bilateral agreements with several countries to reconstruct his armed forces. Belgium would train the army, Italy the air force and Canada would ideally agree to provide aid and assistance for the navy.[285] As it was, no Canadian assistance was forthcoming, but in the same year a new request arrived in Ottawa from three East African countries – Uganda, Kenya and then Tanganyika – to provide instructors and staff for a joint air force school. However, Paul Hellyer, the new Minister of National Defence, was preoccupied with plans to reorganize the Canadian Forces and while he laboured, this request, along with new ones from Ghana, Malaysia and the West Indies remained unactioned.[286] As it turned out, however, he would be unable to avoid the Tanganyikan (Tanganyika was renamed Tanzania in 1965) request for long, principally because Prime Minister Pearson was eager to take a more active role in international affairs.

The matter of military assistance to Tanganyika was first raised in March 1963, when the High Commissioner in Dar es Salaam advised Ottawa that the Tanganyikan Minister for External Affairs had asked to see him about the possibility of Canada providing military assistance to his country. In particular, the Minister enquired whether Canada might be willing to establish a military aviation school. The High Commissioner noted in his message that he been completely non-committal, however, he doubted "whether this would be a big project and I feel sure the RCAF would be able to handle it."[287] Furthermore, he stressed that Canada's involvement on the continent had been largely directed to Western Africa so far. Embarking on a project to provide military assistance to Tanganyika, he stressed, would reverse this trend.

One month later, Norman Robertson, the Under Secretary of State for External Affairs, wrote to Air Chief Marshal Frank Miller, the Chairman of the Chiefs of Staff, regarding the message received from the High Commission in Dar es Salaam. "The proposal," he wrote, "clearly comes within the scope of the Cabinet decision of June 1, 1961 stipulating that requests for military assistance to Commonwealth countries may be accepted on the understanding that each request would be considered on its merits and would be subject to the approval of our two Ministers."[288] As far as Robertson was concerned, External Affairs was inclined to support the sending of an RCAF officer to Tanganyika to assess the overall requirements of establishing a training program. "Our preliminary assessment," he added, "is that a Tanganyikan air force will probably be set up eventually, if only for prestige purposes."[289]

The issue of providing military assistance to Tanganyika was discussed at a Chiefs of Staff Committee meeting on 2 May 1963. The Chairman reviewed the request from External Affairs and asked the Chief of the Air Staff for his views. The air force, after studying the issue had considered several possibilities, the Vice Chief of the Air Staff noted, the most favoured being a program of training in Canada and a small advisory staff in Tanganyika. However, he added, the RCAF had its hands full and would be "unable to accept any further commitments at this time."[290] In preparation for the meeting, the army also considered what they might offer. "The capability of the Canadian army for providing training assistance to Commonwealth countries is limited," their report noted. However, if additional positions were provided in the army establishment, then matters might be different as there was recognition that such training efforts were "of considerable value to the Army in the experience and interest which they create."[291] In the end, External Affairs was advised by the Canadian Forces that the military was unable to support the Tanganyikan request – at least until the matter could be studied in further detail. If this last statement was designed to prevent the establishment of a Canadian military assistance program in Tanganyika, its effect would only be temporary.

It was eventually left to Pearson to break the impasse regarding the request from Tanganyika for military help and he promised Prime Minister Julius Nyerere military assistance when the latter visited Ottawa in July 1963. Pearson's eagerness to support Nyerere, considering the military advice he was given was surprising because the Canadian Forces were already busily engaged in Ghana and Nigeria, along with fulfilling their NATO, NORAD and UN commitments. But both London and Washington were secretly placing a fair amount of pressure on Ottawa to offer the Tanganyikan government help in building their armed forces. This pressure was typified in a private message sent by Sir Alec Douglas-Home, then Prime Minister of Great Britain, to Pearson, in August 1964:

> I expect you have heard that, in addition to other forms of communist aid, President Nyerere has agreed to accept a Chinese military mission in Tanganyika to train his army.
>
> We have been wondering whether there is anything we can do to counter this Chinese influence. We are already in touch with your Government and with the Australians about training courses for Tanganyikan officers, and are ourselves planning to make available a substantially increased number of places for Tanganyikans at Mons. But the main difficulty arises in regard to military training in Tanganyika itself.
>
> The Commonwealth Secretary offered Nyerere a British military training team when he was in Tanganyika in March, but this was turned down, and we feel it would be counter productive to press further British help of this kind on him. We understand, however (though we are uncertain of the precise nature of the request) that your Government may have been asked to provide staff or expert advice for a military academy in Dar es Salaam. If this is so, I hope you will not mind my saying how immensely valuable it would be if you were able to respond to this request. It might indeed be the only way of preventing the communists from

gaining virtual control of the local training of the United
Republic's ground forces.[292]

In early 1964, with military assistance training now underway in Ghana
and Nigeria and a request from Tanganyika that in all likelihood would
be approved, External Affairs was eager to establish a formal means of
coordinating all military assistance efforts including military arms exports. In June 1964, therefore, Leo Cadieux, the Under Secretary of State
for External Affairs, sent a letter to Air Chief Marshal Miller regarding
the possibility of establishing a military assistance coordination body of
some sort. "As you know," he began:

> The Canadian Government has in the last few years been
> receiving a considerable number of requests for military
> assistance from non-NATO countries, and particularly the
> newly-independent members of the Commonwealth. We
> have for some time been concerned that present procedures,
> which were devised for a period when the great require-
> ment for Canadian military assistance was in the NATO
> area, are not entirely suitable for dealing with many of the
> requests which are received today. An additional problem
> is that Ministerial guidance has never been obtained on the
> question of whether, in principle, requests for military as-
> sistance in the form of training and material for non-NATO
> countries could be given sympathetic consideration.[293]

In addition, Cadieux noted that similar letters had been sent to the dep-
uty ministers of National Defence, Finance and Defence Production, the
Secretary of the Cabinet, the Secretary of Treasury Board and the Director
General of the External Aid Office. He further suggested that all inter-
ested parties meet in the East Block on 18 June 1964 to discuss what to do
in order to manage the growing number of military assistance requests.
Included with the letter was a draft Memorandum to Cabinet, dated 8
June 1964, on the subject of military assistance.

Ad hoc arrangements for the provision of military assistance, noted the
authors of the Memorandum to Cabinet, could not longer suffice and the
"responsibility for all types of military assistance needs to be shared more
evenly across interested Departments."[294] The writers also expounded

upon the importance of maintaining a military assistance program of some sort – from combating the tide of growing communist influence in the developing world to paving the way for potential Canadian arms sales. Foremost, however, amongst several recommendations to Cabinet was the need to guarantee "adequate procedures and inter-departmental machinery" were established, "to ensure that the interests of all departments and agencies [would be] taken into account."[295] In the Memorandum to Cabinet it was further suggested a military assistance committee be formed with the Privy Council Office providing the Chairman and members coming from External Affairs, National Defence, Defence Production, Finance, the Treasury Board and the External Aid Office. As it would turn out, External Affairs provided the Chairman and External Aid would not participate in committee business until 1968.

It is highly likely that the effort by External Affairs to establish a formal committee of some sort to manage the increasing number of military assistance requests was supported by the Department of National Defence and the Canadian Forces. Indeed, in May 1963, one year prior to Cadieux's letter, Purves had written to the Chairman, Chiefs of Staff Committee, noting, "because requests for training assistance from various nations have been dealt with as they were received, you may find the current situation as confusing as I do."[296] Adding to Purves' concern at the time – that military training assistance commitments would soon get completely out of hand – was a new request from Malaysia that had been favourably received by the Canadian government.

The day before a Cabinet meeting that would decide on whether or not the Canadian government should create a military assistance committee, the Minister of External Affairs was given a final set of notes on the importance of why a committee was, without a doubt, essential:

> In recent years a number of requests [for military assistance] have been received, but they have often been neglected because of a lack of policy or machinery in dealing with them. This has cost us goodwill, a loss which usually could have been avoided by a prompt and polite refusal.
>
> Some requests have been approved on an *ad hoc* basis – e.g., Ghana, Nigeria, India. We are also committed to send

a survey team to Malaysia, with an implied commitment to help, and I hope we will decide to do the same for Tanganyika. Undoubtedly there will in future be other such requests to which we will wish to respond sympathetically.

Thus we are, and will probably continue to be, in the business of providing military assistance. The choice is whether we continue to operate on an *ad hoc* basis, with consequent delay and perhaps, on occasion, lack of careful examination, or whether we operate within an agreed policy directive and through efficient inter-departmental machinery. Clearly the latter course is preferable.[297]

The decision to form an Interdepartmental Military Assistance Committee was taken on 27 August 1964 and the Committee was instructed that they were to ensure Canada's future military assistance efforts would "help recipient governments maintain the internal stability necessary for political, social and economic growth."[298] In fact, Cabinet was sold on the idea of increasing military assistance based on the rationale that: "Such assistance would constitute a direct, although modest contribution to the establishment of efficient and stable military forces in friendly countries where armed forces are often the largest single group of disciplined and trained personnel, and usually a good influence for law and order. Local armed forces, if properly trained and led can contribute to stability and the preservation of peace."[299]

As for the military assistance policy Canada would adopt, the membership of the Committee, future military assistance efforts and funding levels, Cabinet instructed:

That no general policy would be adopted in relation to the granting of military assistance to non-NATO countries but that individual requests for such assistance should be considered singly and on their merits;

That an interdepartmental committee, to be known as the Military Assistance Committee, composed of officials from the Departments of External Affairs (Chairman), National Defence, Finance and Defence Production, be established to examine, individually and on their merits, requests from non-NATO countries for military assistance and make appropriate recommendations on individual requests to the Cabinet Committee on External Affairs and Defence;

That survey missions composed of representatives of the departments directly concerned be dispatched promptly to Tanganyika and Malaysia to examine their current requests for assistance and to make appropriate recommendations to the Military Assistance Committee;

That direct expenditure costs of military assistance shall not exceed $1.5 million in the case of either country prior to the end of fiscal year 1965-66, and that total loans to be made to the two countries over the same period shall be determined after the survey missions have reported but shall not in any event exceed $20 million; and

That the Prime Minister would determine, after consultations with the Ministers directly concerned, the most appropriate placement in departmental estimates of the appropriations for this purpose.[300]

While there was agreement in Cabinet about the need for a military assistance committee, there was, on the other hand, considerable disagreement amongst senior ministers as to who would have responsibility for military assistance funds. Hellyer was reluctant to fund a program he believed would eventually expand and take away resources from the defence budget. Although military assistance had been given to Ghana and India before, Hellyer noted, "the amounts involved had been insignificant." The latest proposals he remarked, while "seemingly modest in cost, would lead inevitably to much larger expenditures if the program were to have any effect at all in comparison with the programs of the Communist countries, which at present were of significant magnitude."[301] The Secretary of State was certainly not keen to have his Department directly fund military assistance efforts either. Mr. Martin noted that, "it had long been established as a matter of Canadian foreign policy that external aid was granted on the basis of need, with no political strings attached, in contrast to the kind of aid provided by the Soviet Union and communist China. To grant military assistance in connection with the Canadian external aid program would belie this aspect of our foreign policy and lead to accusations of political interference."[302]

Hellyer, however, was not convinced by Martin's position, as he believed the granting of any aid was political in nature. In reference to military aid for Tanganyika and Malaysia, he noted that the government was granting political aid through military support, which was a major departure "from Canada's established policy of granting military aid [to NATO countries] for clearly definable military purposes." Consequently, and as recorded in the Cabinet minutes, "it would be wrong in principle to charge the costs [of running a large scale military assistance effort] to the Department of National Defence, as the decision to grant funds, an overwhelmingly political decision, would have to be made by the Department of External Affairs."[303]

Although the decision as to who would be responsible for funding future military assistance efforts was to be decided later, there was agreement in Cabinet on why Canada should provide military assistance to countries such as Tanganyika and Malaysia. Primarily, the focus of Canada's contribution, it was thought, would be to assist in impeding the spread of communism in Africa and Asia, especially when "assistance from the United States and the United Kingdom was unwelcome in these areas."[304] There was also a desire in External Affairs to maintain good relations with President Nkrumah who was regarded at the time as one of the most influential statesmen in Africa. However, the prime minister noted that "there were dangers involved in contributing to the buildup of armed forces in such countries as Tanganyika, and great care would have to be exercised in determining the uses to which Canadian assistance might be put."[305] Malaysia was also another country, noted Martin, for which there were reasonable grounds to provide military assistance, "considering the present assault on her by Indonesian guerrillas, and the Communist orientation of President Sukarno's government."[306] More telling was his subsequent note that the Malaysian government was well aware of the help given to India and therefore would expect the same treatment as a fellow Commonwealth country.

The Cabinet decision to form the Military Assistance Committee was followed quickly by its first meeting in the East Block at 11:00 a.m., on Wednesday, 9 September 1964, chaired by Mr. Arthur Menzies from External Affairs. Attending were three representatives from the Department of National Defence, two each from Defence Production and Finance and five additional members from External Affairs.[307] Right at the start, the Chair noted that until External Affairs received additional monies to support new military assistance efforts, good ideas or suggestions would have to be financed with whatever Departments could spare – not necessarily an auspicious start but financial matters would improve with time. The first meeting led to several key decisions. A survey team under the direction of Brigadier H.W. Love would be sent to Dar es Salaam and report directly to the Military Assistance Committee on what military assistance efforts would be most appropriate for Tanganyika. A proposed side visit to Kenya was not approved. It was also agreed that an RCAF *Yukon* leaving Nairobi on 13 September would bring back between 12 and 15 Tanganyikan officer cadets for training in Canada. Terms of Reference for a proposed survey team visit to Malaysia were to be prepared and circulated for review by the Committee.[308]

Without doubt, the Military Assistance Committee would be fully occupied in late 1964. In July 1964, for example, the Venezuelan government requested military assistance from Canada. However, the concern in External Affairs was that offering military aid to Latin American militaries, given the historical role of militaries in South America, could lead to embarrassment for Canada. A favourable response on the part of Ottawa to support the Venezuelan military might also create a precedent leading to greater involvement. "We are inclined to take a negative view in principle of the extension to Latin American countries of military training assistance at the present time," noted a letter drafted by External Affairs to the Committee in September 1964.[309] External Affairs further suggested that the Venezuelan military attaché in Ottawa be told that Canada only offered military training assistance to its NATO partners and certain members of the Commonwealth. A change in this policy was not expected.

While the issue of military assistance to Venezuela was being dealt with, Brigadier Love led his survey team to Washington in September 1964 for briefings on the political and defence situation in Tanganyika and

Zanzibar from an American point of view. These high-level briefings were provided by the State Department, the Department of Defence and the Agency for International Development.[310] Prior to his departure, the Military Assistance Committee also provided Love with terms of reference and "confidential instructions." In the "confidential instructions" team members were told that "military training aid from Western countries was obviously most important to offset the Chinese offers," and Canada had been "strongly urged by the United States and Great Britain to provide such aid."[311]

In addition to briefings in Washington, Love and his team also went to London, immediately after, to receive briefings from the Commonwealth Relations Office and the Ministry of Defence on the security situation in Eastern Africa. The survey team was also advised of the West German presence in Tanganyika and a German offer to provide six small naval vessels for the navy. Russia, the Canadians were told, had also offered torpedo boats and a party of eleven Chinese military instructors, including three "senior colonels" and interpreters had just arrived in the country.[312]

By now, it must have become clear to the survey team that providing military assistance to Tanganyika was unlikely to be straightforward and under no circumstances did Ottawa want Nyerere to know that briefings had been provided for them in Washington and London.[313] The "confidential instructions" further impressed upon the survey team the importance of avoiding specific offers of military assistance and the Tanganyikan government, they were told, needed to be aware that Canadian personnel would only assume training roles and not become involved in operations. As discretely as possible, Love was also asked to inquire about the activities of communist training teams in Tanganyika. "It should be assumed," continued the "confidential instructions," that the Canadian government would not willingly "agree to any programme which involved collaboration between Canadian service personnel, and advisors, civilian or military, from communist countries."[314] On return to Canada, Love would provide a complete overview of the country's needs and in December 1964, a general program to support Tanganyika with military assistance was approved by Cabinet.

In November 1964, a second military assistance survey mission departed for Malaysia to determine what assistance would be necessary or welcome. Their report painted a picture of growing tension between Indonesia and Malaysia with increasing numbers of Indonesian troops crossing the border into northern Borneo. To counter the Indonesian military, the British had brought their troop levels in the area to approximately 50,000 personnel. The situation described was so grave that Hellyer was determined to quickly increase aid levels and instead of $1.5 million in direct aid the Minister now proposed $4 million over two years. The $4 million would include the provision of four *Caribou* aircraft and spares ($3,428,000), training of air and ground crew (up to $500,000) and 250 light motorcycles ($72,000). Cabinet was in agreement with the proposal and direction was given for the offer to be made to the Malaysian government. There was also a great deal of enthusiasm around the table, for "political, psychological and military reasons," to send the four aircraft as soon as possible. The Minister, as result, suggested the possibility of transferring the aircraft directly from RCAF operational stock or sending directly, from the de Havilland Company production line, new aircraft that were destined for the Canadian Forces.[315]

Part of the enthusiasm in offering support to Malaysia was likely driven by a desire to sell jet aircraft. The Minister of National Defence, speaking on behalf of Defence Production, suggested that with the proposal to deliver aircraft and motorcycles, the Malaysian government also have an opportunity to consider purchasing the Canadair CL-41 *Tutor* jet trainer/ tactical fighter. If the offer were accepted, "Canada would make available immediately four training positions for jet pilots in Canada at the expense of the Canadian government."[316] In March 1965, Cabinet duly considered the request from Canadair to sell 20 CL-41 ground-attack *Tutor* jet aircraft to Malaysia. In the event of a sale, however, Cabinet determined that "an effort should be made to limit the possible foreign policy repercussions of Canadian government involvement." Cabinet also wished that any discussion regarding the sale would focus on the economic benefits to Canada and not on military considerations. The sale was also not deemed, by Cabinet, to be part of Canada's military assistance program, nor, it was noted, should a previous offer to train Malaysian jet pilots be linked to future sales. Finally, Cabinet agreed that the aircraft could only be exported without armaments. Despite these restrictions Malaysia ordered, and Canada approved, the sale of 20 *Tutors* for use in a counter-insurgency role in March 1966.

Given the growing political and economic importance of military assistance and arms exports, Cabinet approved a set of recommendations in February 1965 pertaining to the operations of the Military Assistance Committee in future. Foremost, and beginning on 1 April 1965, funding for military assistance would now come from the Department of External Affairs and not the Department of National Defence. The Military Assistance Committee was also granted control of all present and future military assistance programs and could make minor adjustments to previously approved programs. Cabinet approval, however, was required for any new program that would lead Canada having to station troops overseas. In addition, the Military Assistance Committee was directed that any new military assistance program, or major adjustment to an existing program, would have to be presented to Cabinet and include the proposed timetable, estimated costs and political implications. The Committee was also given the authority to approve the training of non-NATO officers in Canada, provided offers for training would "not involve political considerations and subject to a limit of $300,000 for the total annual cost for all countries."[317]

By 1965, major Canadian military assistance missions were underway in Ghana and Tanganyika and additional help was on the way for several other countries. In Ottawa, the Department of National Defence was pressuring External Affairs to hold regular Committee meetings and the Privy Council Office and the Treasury Board were now seeking membership. The Finance Department was also keen to have an agreed upon fixed budget as there was concern that military assistance would expand "in all directions without limit, plan or policy."[318]

The concern about expanding military assistance efforts was well founded. Mr. Hudon, from the Finance Department, could rightly argue that the number of requests reaching Ottawa was considerable and to not have regular Committee meetings was an oversight that needed correction. For example, following approval in principle by Cabinet in March 1965 for a $10.5 million dollar program to assist the Tanganyikan air force, large scale requests had been received from Nigeria in July 1965 for air technical officers' training (turned down) and naval assistance (which remained under consideration), and from Malaysia in August 1965 asking to extend a two-year military assistance program to five years (turned down). In late 1965 requests for help arrived from India, Ghana and Jamaica for more training billets in Canada (then under consideration). With regards to Jamaica, the prime minister had been very eager to improve relations with countries in the West Indies and the diplomatic staff in Kingston had encouraged the Jamaican government to switch their military assistance requirements from Britain to Canada. The "geometric increase" in military assistance was of great concern in Ottawa with three programs: aid to the Tanganyikan army (estimated to be $4.5 million) and air force ($10.5 million) plus $4 million for the Malaysian air force – in total, $19 million dollars, which was a substantial amount that did not include military assistance provided to Ghana and Nigeria.[319]

Military assistance to developing countries was, as previously noted, good for Canadian business and there was a strong link between the sale of Canadian military equipment and the provision of military assistance. In May 1966, for example, de Havilland provided the Ministries of Industry and External Affairs with a list of countries that had purchased the *Caribou* aircraft and another list showing countries they believed might purchase the airplane in future. In their letter, the company made it clear they were "seeking the Government's support where appropriate for stimulating sales of *Caribou* aircraft and thus enabling the company to extend its production line of these aircraft up to two more years."[320] Part of the "stimulating sales" concept, the company implied, was for Canada to offer military training and general assistance to any country wishing to purchase de Havilland aircraft. In all, they noted, 82 *Caribou* had been sold to countries around the world, not counting the United States. However, the company had its sights set on selling more aircraft to Nigeria and Zambia. The Nigerian air force, said de Havilland, had a requirement for 10 aircraft but the company was encountering competition from the German government who had offered military assistance if Lagos purchased German transport aircraft. Furthermore, Zambia had four *Caribou* aircraft and wanted to purchase four more, but only on the provision that military assistance or subsidization was offered from the Canadian government.[321]

For a military not at all eager to offer training assistance to foreign militaries in the 1950s and early 1960s, the Canadian Forces policy toward supporting Canadian companies selling arms was almost the opposite. In early 1961, a sub-committee of the Vice Chiefs of Staff Committee examined the role of service attachés and where they might best be located. In addition to the report prepared by the sub-committee consideration was also given to the support attachés might render the Government in furthering arms sales. The discussion centred on a memorandum received from the Deputy Minister who requested the Committee consider having attachés engage in "periodic exchange[s] of information on potential equipment sales possibilities" with Defence Production officers.[322] The Canadian Army, however, had already instructed their attachés to do their utmost to support arms sales. In fact, they were told that they were "in an excellent position to further the aims of this programme in their countries of accreditation and should enthusiastically assist the Trade Commissioner, or the head of the commercial section of their mission, in arranging military contacts [Defence Production officers] and/or Canadian manufacturers."[323]

Certainly, critics argued that Canada's military assistance program was nothing more than a means to assist Canadian manufacturers sell arms and aircraft. For example, in 1964 the Department of Finance noted in an internal letter that there were now three memorandums regarding military assistance for consideration by the Cabinet Committee on External Affairs and Defence. The first addressed military assistance in general, and the next two concerned military assistance for Malaysia and Tanganyika. The first memorandum alone recommended that $5 million be set aside to fund efforts and a further $20 million be considered for loans to buy equipment from Canada – the writer concluding that in his opinion the push for a military assistance program originated in "the Department of Defence Production. It sees in it a way to support the Canadian aircraft industry which has been adversely affected by the reduction in our Mutual Aid Programme."[324]

This opinion of who might be driving the military assistance program was probably not far from the truth. At a meeting of the Military Assistance Committee in early 1966, Mr. Knowles, representing the Department of Defence Production asked if the Committee would be disposed to recommending loans to foreign countries for the purchase of Canadian military equipment. The Chairman could not see any reason why this sort of help might not be extended by the government, but cautioned that "it should not be assumed that military assistance funds could be used indiscriminately to stimulate the purchases of Canadian military equipment by underdeveloped countries."[325] While the Department of Finance might have been concerned about the rising costs of Canada's military assistance programs, the fact was that by 1966, Canadian arms manufacturers had found new markets in developing countries. More-over, the Canadian Forces were playing a key role in supporting the sale of Canadian arms. Most surprisingly, the military now appeared to be more interested in supporting military assistance missions than they had in earlier years likely due to the success achieved by the training team assigned to Ghana.

"Last week," wrote the High Commissioner in Accra to Ottawa in January 1964, "we had a thoroughly enjoyable and very successful visit by Major-General W.A.B. Anderson."[326] Anderson, an army officer and future commander of the army, was the most senior Canadian officer to visit the Canadians in Ghana since their arrival several years prior. During the visit, the General met with the Deputy Chief of Defence Staff, Brigadier-General Joseph Ankrah, as the Chief of Defence Staff, Major-General Stephen Otu had flown to the UN at the last minute for deliberations concerning the future presence of Ghanaian peacekeeping troops in the Congo. Brigadier-General Ankrah, Anderson reported, made it clear how pleased he was with Canada's support. In fact, he was eager to have vacancies on Canadian courses for their personnel something that Anderson was unable to commit to.[327] The High Commissioner was also eager to show his support for the work underway in Ghana by the Canadian Forces. "Why is some form of military training useful for the newly independent African countries?" he asked in a letter to External Affairs:

> The first and most important reason is to assist the new governments to maintain internal order by helping them to develop small but relatively efficient military forces. Otherwise, the conditions in which they can undertake economic and social development will not long exist. In view of

developments in a number of countries over the last year, political leaders are rightly worried lest there develop in Africa a tradition as is in the Middle East and Central and South America where the military call the tune and governments come into being, live, and are overthrown at the whim of the armed forces. Throughout the history of Ghana, there has been no evidence of a desire by the military to play an active role in politics; indeed, quite the reverse is the case.[328]

In keeping with the High Commissioner's 1964 comments on the importance of military assistance, a Chief of the Defence Staff (CDS) directed *Review of International Commitments* in 1966 had much the same to say. As part of the *Review*, led by Air Vice Marshal F.W. Ball, two papers were prepared. The first addressed Canada's military participation in UN operations while the second paper covered military assistance to non-NATO countries. Excluding commitments to NATO and NORAD, the *Review* began, there were two main areas where the Canadian Forces were engaged internationally: service with or in support of the UN and service through the provision of military assistance training in Canada or overseas. "Despite the fact that the two areas of employment are discussed separately," noted the authors, "it is important to recognize that both peacekeeping and military assistance are major military methods for maintaining peace and are therefore closely allied. It might even be argued that military assistance is part of the peacekeeping task assigned to the Canadian Armed Forces in the [1964] White Paper."[329]

The first paper on Canada's UN operations noted that at the time of writing, Canadian troops were involved in five peacekeeping missions and more personnel were deployed with the International Commission for Supervision and Control in Vietnam. All told, 1,900 Canadian military personnel were deployed overseas on UN missions and an infantry battalion was on standby in Canada for UN service if required. It was difficult to assess the overall political and military effectiveness of each peacekeeping operation according to the paper. Nevertheless, peacekeeping operations had been successful in preventing further fighting if nothing else. What is more, the paper noted "that from an operational point of view it can be argued that the efforts and funds expended on peacekeeping commitments contribute more to world peace than any of our other operational commitments."[330]

The second paper, on the other hand, was not optimistic regarding the future of Canada's military assistance efforts or if the effort would indeed have any tangible impact on promoting world peace. The authors recorded that there were 100 Canadian personnel overseas supporting military assistance missions and approximately 200 foreign military personnel from seven different countries undergoing training in Canada. In particular, the second report, given increasing requests for military assistance, projected that demand would soon outstrip capacity based on an assessment of training billets required from 1967 onwards:

- Thirty vacancies on piston engine courses for pilot trainees;

- Ten vacancies for jet engine pilot trainees;

- Fifty vacancies on aircraft technical courses;

- Fifty vacancies for officer cadet training;

- Ten vacancies on miscellaneous army technical courses;

- Five vacancies for light aircraft or helicopter pilot courses;

- Fifteen pilot vacancies for *Caribou* conversion training;

- Thirty technician vacancies for *Caribou* conversion training;

- Ten pilot vacancies for CL-41 *Tutor* conversion training; and

- Fifty technician vacancies for CL-41*Tutor* conversion training.

All told, an estimated 260 vacancies on a wide variety of generally very advanced courses would likely be necessary. But meeting such a demand, the second paper surmised, would create mounting difficulties for the Canadian Forces, and the pressure would be "felt most acutely in pilot and aircraft technician training."[331] Furthermore, the fairly significant number of officer candidate vacancies available for foreign students in past had come about as a direct result of the Canadian Forces not meeting recruitment quotas – a situation, noted the paper, likely to be only temporary in nature.

The final proposals contained in the second paper were fairly blunt. It was suggested that foreign students only be given vacancies in military training schools that could not be filled by Canadians. Additional vacancies, specifically for foreign students, were not recommended. Training for pilots and aircraft technicians, the paper suggested, should also be stopped due to a lack of capacity. Besides, there were civilian flying schools and aircraft companies who could be contracted for this work. Finally, the paper proposed that overseas commitments remain at the same level but no additional military assistance tasks be taken on. Still, despite the gloomy forecast, the second paper did have a few positive words to say on the subject of training foreign militaries:

> It is becoming increasingly evident that Canada can provide a worthwhile contribution to world security and economic stability through sensible and well-controlled military assistance programmes to newly independent countries and for this reason it is going to be difficult to refuse legitimate requests knowing that the Communist nations are both anxious and willing to pick up our fumbles and to step in while we procrastinate.[332]

With the *Review* complete, Air Marshal Sharp requested the CDS read and comment on the two papers prepared by the staff. Canada's commitments overseas, Sharp wrote, had grown like "Topsey." Now was the time, in his view, to "sit-back" and reassess.[333] If the Air Marshal was hoping for some insightful direction, however, he was going to be sadly disappointed. The CDS, General J.V. Allard, simply suggested in reply that it might now be timely "to channel our military aid to certain areas of the world where it would have the most impact and do the utmost good instead of fragmenting it in small packages all over the world."[334] Yet, Canada's military assistance, mainly centered in sub-Saharan Africa in 1966, was not that fragmented at all.

The *Review of International Commitments* may not have resulted in concrete direction from the CDS regarding the future of Canada's military assistance, but it certainly did lead the Canadian Forces to think more strategically about the programs they were running and might possibly conduct in the future. In September 1966, a study was undertaken by the

Canadian Forces, likely in parallel with the *Review*, on the subject of establishing a single military training assistance training school in Canada, or possibly overseas in a Caribbean country. The new school, the study proposed, would allow for the centralized delivery of Canadian military assistance to "in particular non-European countries."[335]

The Canadian Forces were also interested in obtaining a permanent location for jungle training in the Caribbean and some consideration in the study was given over to the potential of setting up a military assistance training school in warmer climes. A Caribbean location, it was suggested, would allow foreign military students, who did "not appreciate Canadian winters" to live and train in a climate similar to their own. A Caribbean location, the study continued, might also turn out to be a "morale booster" for staff posted to the new base.[336] However, as the study unfolded, the cost and potential political ramifications of operating a Canadian base on foreign soil worked against this option. What if, suggested the study, Canada was training Tanzanians in Barbados and then the Tanzanian and Barbadian governments had a falling out? "Taking this still one step further," the authors continued, "Canada's military assistance programmes would have to be in line with the host nation's foreign policy and this may not always be in Canada's best interests."[337]

There were, nevertheless, advantages to having a single location, either in Canada or overseas, for providing military assistance. A single location would be simpler to run and support and allow the Canadian Forces to tailor training for individual countries instead of simply offering foreign students vacancies on already scheduled Canadian courses. The belief was that a better relationship between the instructors and students might also be formed, and instructors would soon become familiar with the challenges of instructing foreign military personnel. On the other hand, the study noted there were an equal number of disadvantages to having a single school in one location. If the school was in Canada it was believed a closed based would have to be re-activated in order to handle the expected number of foreign students – no doubt an expensive proposition. If the school was located in another county, a new set of facilities would likely be required – again expensive. Additionally, new staff would be needed no matter where the school was located along with training aids and, in the case of pilot training, aircraft. Lastly, the *Review* noted that foreign students, regrettably, would not have any contact with Canadian military students if they were isolated in a separate facility. The final recommendation, therefore, was to continue training foreign military students in Canadian military schools, as had been the practice.[338]

With the prospect of Canada's military assistance efforts expanding in the 1970s, Air Marshal Sharp, now CDS, wrote to External Affairs in June 1967 regarding the military training of "foreign nationals" by Canada. Enclosed with his letter was an updated report on the entire subject of Canada's military assistance efforts to date, along with recommendations on the courses of action open should the government wish to adopt a broader military assistance policy in the period 1968-1972.[339] The report opened by noting that the Canadian Forces were becoming increasingly involved in the military training of foreign military personnel both in their respective countries and in Canada. As a result, it was now important for the Canadian Forces to understand what would be required so plans could be developed "to meet our possible future commitments in this field."[340]

The report itself concluded that Canada's military assistance efforts in Ghana and Tanzania had not gone unnoticed in the developing world. Hosting Expo 67 in Montreal, the report further suggested would allow government officials from emerging countries to see "first-hand Canada's apparent prosperity" and prompt additional requests for military aid.[341] While it was easier to train foreign military personnel in their own countries, the report did note that certain specialized training, with foreign students incorporated into the normal Canadian Forces training system, was still preferred. It was also suggested once more that Canada might want to acquire a tropical or semi-tropical training site to conduct military training assistance and as a location to train Canadian personnel preparing for UN operations or for environmental training such as jungle warfare.

As it would turn out, however, a wider Canadian Forces role in the developing world was not to be. Nor would acquiring an overseas location to conduct jungle warfare be a high priority. 1967 would be the high point of Canadian military assistance in terms of the number of military personnel deployed overseas and the funds spent to support their efforts. From 1968 onwards, financial pressures on the Canadian government, driven by new and expensive social programs, would lead to steadily declining defence budgets. There was also concern in government and the public that arms races in the developing world were spiraling out of control. For example, the Secretary of State for External Affairs, Paul Martin Sr., speaking in August 1967, remarked on the "ominous tide" of increasing conventional arms purchases in the developing world. "In some regions," he said, "the arms race is only an "arms walk"; in others it is a pell-mell scramble. In all it is a severe drain on the economic and technical resources of the poor countries and contributes to an increase of tension. We must find ways of putting an end to the renewal of this arms race."[342]

Although the election of Prime Minister Trudeau in 1968 would mark the beginning of the end of Canadian military assistance to the developing world, the Canadian Forces had succeeded in deploying fairly substantial training and advisory teams to Ghana and Tanzania while smaller numbers of Canadian officers had fanned out to other countries such as Nigeria and Malaysia. On the home front, hundreds of non-NATO students from across the globe had or were receiving military training, often of a highly advanced nature. However, the leaders of the Canadian Forces was never that interested in engaging in military assistance work and had to be pressured into offering support by the government. No doubt Foulkes was focused on ensuring that the Canadian Forces would centre its efforts on supporting NATO and he was undoubtedly successful in side-stepping requests from the developing world for military assistance prior to the 1960s precisely due to NATO commitments.

To turn matters around, it would take a combination of Kwame Nkrumah, events in Ghana and a persistent prime minister to force the military into action – much to the delight of External Affairs and the British and American governments, who had begun to place a good deal of pressure on Ottawa to step in and provide military assistance to countries in sub-Saharan Africa. Yet, when Colonel Cooper traveled to Accra in March 1961 even he did not likely realize that his trip would result in the Canadian Forces becoming a key provider of military assistance in the developing world for almost a decade to come. The eventual dispatch of Canadian Forces personnel to assist in the training of the Ghana Armed Forces, for example, opened the door for other countries to ask

Canada for similar levels of support and requests poured into Ottawa from Nigeria, the Congo, Tanzania, Malaysia and others.

The decision to form an Interdepartmental Military Assistance Committee was taken by Cabinet because External Affairs and other interested Departments could no longer manage the growing number of requests for military help through the ad hoc arrangements currently in use. There was also a realization that military assistance could be beneficial for the Canadian economy and the Committee would be one way of ensuring Canadian arms and aircraft companies could take advantage of opportunities in countries where the Canadian Forces were active. De Havilland, supported by the Department of Defence Production, was the most aggressive in this regard although there was a genuine desire amongst most Committee members not to be seen as simply a tool supporting the Canadian aircraft industry. While the Department of Defence Production and the Ministry of Industry were eager to see the Canadian Forces expand their military assistance operations for economic purposes, the reverse was true of the Finance Department who were imagining a program that would grow, as the Vice Chief of Defence Staff had remarked, like "Topsey." The Finance Department clearly did have reasons to be concerned with major Canadian military assistance missions underway in Ghana and Tanzania in 1965 and additional help on the way for several other countries.

However, funding for military assistance would fall considerably in the Trudeau era and from spending millions of dollars each year in the 1960s, the estimated outlay for 1973-1974 was only $221,000.[343] Developing countries that were desperately short of foreign exchange and the infrastructure needed to support economic activity, said Trudeau, had been unnecessarily "lured by the siren song of 'defence preparedness,' and [to] find the money to pay for this illusory state."[344] As far as his government was concerned, Ottawa would no longer support arms sales or transfers and military assistance efforts to the developing world – and, if Cabinet did relent, it would only be in the most exceptional cases. But before discussing the decline of Canada's military assistance efforts in detail, it is worth examining, at this time, the missions to Ghana and Tanzania in far greater depth. That is the purpose of the next two chapters, beginning with Canada's military assistance effort in Ghana.

CHAPTER 8

CANADA'S MILITARY ASSISTANCE TO GHANA

Here is a message just received from London. A military coup took place in Ghana today. The army has seized power. Kwame Nkrumah, President of the Republic, who is on a trip abroad, has been deposed; Ministers have been dismissed; and Parliament and the People's Convention Party, the ruling party, have been dissolved.

Moscow Radio, 24 February 1966

A very popular novel of 1960, The Ugly American, emphasized the lack of training, knowledge, and the general stupidity of American representatives abroad. But in Ghana, at least, it was the Russians and Chinese who quickly managed to offend or exasperate the Ghanaians, including those who were initially favourably disposed towards them.

Lieutenant-Colonel G.D. Hunt, 1989

In March 1961, in response to a military assistance request from President Nkrumah, Canada sent Colonel P.S. Cooper to Ghana to assess the state of their armed forces and prepare a report for Ottawa. On his return, he wrote that a military assistance team of approximately 30 personnel, working for up to eight years on-site in Ghana, would be necessary to build up the Ghanaian military to a point that it could look after itself. What he did not and could not have forecast was how tumultuous political life in Ghana was going to be while the Canadian training team were there. Nor did he ever likely imagine the central role that the Canadian trained Ghana Army would eventually play in overthrowing the civilian government, on two occasions, the first in 1966.

Why did Canada send its military personnel to Ghana in 1961 when there was certainly no compelling reason to do so? Upon independence in 1957, Ghana had been relatively wealthy, faced no external threats or internal unrest. The British had also stayed on to help Ghana's armed forces. For President Nkrumah, eager to present Ghana as a leader in African affairs, the British military presence was, however, a reminder of the country's colonial past. In his mind it would eventually have to end. Turning to countries like Canada for military and other assistance, though, was acceptable. Canadians had no colonial baggage and from a military viewpoint, given common training standards with the British, were ideal candidates to replace them.

When Nkrumah asked Canada for military assistance, Prime Minister Diefenbaker readily agreed, although in Cabinet there were questions raised about the long-term political plans of the Ghanaian President. Becoming involved militarily in Africa, some believed, was risky and best avoided. However, Diefenbaker wanted to assist a fellow Commonwealth member and many Canadians were enthusiastic about taking an active part in the overall development of the continent in the early 1960s. Reflecting on Canada's growing presence in Africa during a speech at Queen's University in 1966, Paul Martin Sr. spoke about how:

> The establishment of a trades training centre in Accra has been a noteworthy development in Ghana, along with the launching of an irrigation and land development project in the northern regions and the provision of food aid to that country for the first time. In Nigeria, a $3.5-million project involving the aerial photography, ground control and mapping of the Western region is nearing completion. A trades training centre will be established in Nigeria also and Canadians are providing training and technical advice in the operation of the Niger dam. Canadian firms are engaged in the aerial photography and mapping of Tanzania's southeast region and a development loan is being extended for transmission lines. In Kenya we are assisting in the development of a wheat-breeding programme. We have undertaken, in cooperation with Britain, a study to determine the line of route and economic feasibility of a proposed railway from Zambia to Dar-es-Salaam.[345]

Canada was, as Martin said, eager to help the new nations of sub-Saharan Africa and providing limited military assistance was simply another means of doing so. For those in government who might have worried about Canada's pending military role in Ghana, Cooper had also written in his 1961 report that while there were "considerable pressures" amongst Ghanaian Ministers to follow the Soviet bloc line in African affairs, Nkrumah had resisted many of these so far. Furthermore, Cooper noted that Nkrumah had "refused to part with his British Army officers, he seeks the advice of his [British] Chief of Defence Staff and has often taken it against that of the pro-communist members of his government."[346] In Ottawa, in early 1961, keeping Nkrumah firmly in power must have appeared to be a sensible course of action.

As for Nkrumah himself, he was unquestionably well educated and profoundly involved with pan-African affairs for a considerable amount of time before becoming President of Ghana. In 1935, he arrived in Philadelphia and commenced undergraduate work at Lincoln University, in time obtaining a bachelor's degree in Sociology. He then enrolled at the University of Pennsylvania and received, in 1941, a Master's degree from the Graduate School of Education followed by a Master's degree in Philosophy two years later.[347] In May 1945, Nkrumah moved to London, England in order to attend the London School of Economics and while in London he helped organize the 5th Pan African Congress. Later, he became Secretary of the West African National Secretariat in London.[348]

Nkrumah's path to eventual power in Ghana began in 1947 after returning home from London. Initially, he took on the role of general secretary of the United Gold Coast Convention Party but in June 1949 created his own Convention People's Party (CPP) "to express a more radical line toward the independence struggle than that of the elite-controlled, urban-based, United Gold Coast Convention."[349] As an organizer, Nkrumah worked tirelessly to establish the CPP as the main party in Ghana, and hundreds of branches were opened throughout the country. Because of his political activities, the British arrested and imprisoned him in 1950 for a period of three years. But, in February 1951 the CPP won elections and Nkrumah was released and became prime minister the following year. In 1957, Ghana became fully independent from Great Britain with Nkrumah as the Republic's new President.

Ghana's independence in 1957 was seen throughout the world as a major achievement. "African Nationalists, Pan-Africanists and their supporters in other parts of the world," said Henry L. Bretton in early 1958, "hailed the event as a milestone on the road to complete emancipation of the Africans, as proof that the "dark continent" had come of age and that all of its people were now fully capable of governing themselves."[350] There was also good reason to be optimistic about Ghana's future as economically the country was on sound footing:

> Ghana's economy and society were seen to embody char-
> acteristics that were considered advantageous for modern
> economic development. Boasting one of the highest per
> capita incomes in Africa south of the Sahara, Ghana was
> the world's largest producer of cocoa beans and possessed
> an imposing array of mineral resources, including gold,
> diamonds, manganese, and bauxite. Its potential for the
> generation of hydroelectric power was substantial, and
> the transportation network of rail and motor roads link-
> ing its capital and commercial-administrative centers with
> each other and to the territory's hinterland were the envy
> of sub-Saharan Africa of the late 1950s. With respect to the
> development of human resources, the situation was also
> encouraging by comparative African standards. A process
> of social change dating well into the nineteenth century
> had produced by the 1950s a small western-educated pro-
> fessional middle class in Ghana's coastal towns and cities,
> and the educational infrastructure and resultant strata of
> educated cadres was amongst the most extensive in sub-
> Saharan Africa. On this basis the new Ghanaian state was
> seen as blessed with an efficient and professional public
> service bureaucracy.[351]

For the West, the results of the 1956 elections that preceded independence were encouraging as well. One hundred and four seats were contested by several political parties, with the final results provided in Table 8.

Party	Number of Seats Won	Remarks
Convention People's Party	71	Led by Kwame Nkrumah
National Liberation Movement	12	Membership was primarily drawn from the Ashanti cocoa growing areas of Ghana
The Northern People's Party	15	Membership was drawn from the poorer northern region of Ghana
The Togoland Congress	2	Membership was drawn from Eastern Ghana, formerly British Togoland. British Togoland had been previously incorporated into the Gold Coast
The Moslem Association Party	1	This small, religious based political party drew its support from the Kumasi area
Federation of Youth	1	
Independents	2	

Table 8 – Ghana: 1956 Election Results[352]

Although the elections had been marred "through bribery, blackmail, economic pressure, deliberate circulation of misleading rumors, invocation of fetishes, ju-ju, and tribal sanctions," Ghana had, upon independence, a democratically elected government.[353] On the other hand, said Mazrui, "Nkrumah's popular support was not, by the standards of charismatic leaders elsewhere, quite overwhelming."[354] In fact, Ghana was a very ethnically diverse country and as the elections proved, not all Ghanaians supported Nkrumah. However, the opposition was weak and divided. The National Liberation Movement, the Togoland Congress and the other political parties, concluded Bretton, "ought [not] really to be classified as political parties, being no more than factions or loose conglomerations of tribal and other interest groups seeking autonomy. None reveal the slightest promise of democratic orientation. None could be expected to become effective carriers of a system of parliamentary democracy."[355] When, in 1957, Nkrumah introduced the "Avoidance of Discrimination Act" banning political parties formed along tribal or religious grounds, most opposition parties joined forces to become The United Party.[356] But, in reality, little could be done to prevent the CPP from consolidating power in the post-independence period.

As President, Nkrumah's main objective was to ensure rapid economic development and overall modernization by improving Ghana's infrastructure and addressing matters such as illiteracy and health care. Yet, at independence, Nkrumah was faced with two regions in near or actual revolt, and unrest was growing in other parts of the country:

> In the Ashanti Region, the National Liberation Movement had created a condition of virtual civil war in central Ghana. At the time of independence, leaders of the ruling political party, the CPP, could not travel there safely. In the Volta Region a long-established irredentist movement continued to operate. Supporters of the Togoland Congress Party established camps in the Alavanyo District of Eastern Ghana, marched about in military formation, and practiced with shotguns. When the government moved in troops to disband the camps rioting broke out in Ewe towns. In the capital city, Accra, independence was greeted by the organization of a militant movement, the Ga Standfast Association, whose purpose appeared to be the protection of the Ga inhabitants of the Accra area from domination by the "strangers" who controlled the central government. Within two years this movement would engage in various acts of violence and sabotage against central authority.[357]

No doubt Nkrumah recognized that challenges to his authority might lead to the breakup of Ghana and his own loss of power. For example, Ashanti resistance in the north of Ghana to the government in Accra, said Gutteridge, was "more significant than it seemed on the surface."[358] Thus, it was not too long before Nkrumah was ready to embark on the creation of a one-party state that would clamp down on regional unrest. In the March 1958 edition of *The American Political Science Review*, Bretton had already concluded that Nkrumah had accepted the British Parliamentary model only as a temporary measure. Nkrumah, he continued, actually viewed parliamentary democracy as too onerous and too costly and at odds with his desire to form a one-party state or as Bretton described it, a "benevolent dictatorship." "There is every reason to believe," he presciently wrote, "that election administration, once the controlling European influence has been withdrawn, will deteriorate and that genuine election results will be impossible to obtain."[359]

By 1960, the opposition in Ghana was in disarray. The United Party had lost considerable strength. Some members had crossed the floor of Parliament to join the CPP, one went into exile and three were placed in preventative detention.[360] In 1960, Welch wrote, Nkrumah also engaged in a "turn to the left," surrounding himself with a new group of advisors who strongly advocated the government become increasingly involved in the economy. Nkrumah, moreover, became less and less tolerant of opposition to his leadership and in 1964 held a national referendum on whether Ghana should become a one-party state. The vote, "marked by extensive vote tampering," resulted in a win for Nkrumah with 2,773,920 voting yes for a one-party state and only 2,452 voting no. "Thus ended the idea in Ghana of a legal opposition," said Welch.[361] Elections that were scheduled in 1965, never took place.

"Wherever one goes in Ghana," Fritz Schatten observed one year later, "it is impossible to get away from Kwame Nkrumah." There are, he continued, "Kwame Nkrumah roads, streets and avenues, Kwame Nkrumah training centres, schools and institutions – and everywhere there are his statues and pictures, many of them larger than life."[362] His photograph was displayed in offices and shops while his profile appeared on coins, banks notes and postage stamps – his birthday became a public holiday. In 1961, the government controlled *Ghanaian Evening News*, went as far to say that when Ghana's history was recorded, "the man Kwame Nkrumah will be written of as the liberator, the Messiah, the Christ of our day, whose great love for mankind wrought changes in Ghana, in Africa and in the world at large."[363] As Martin Meredith noted, referring to a Ghanaian press release issued in 1961, "Kwame Nkrumah is Africa and Africa is Kwame Nkrumah."[364]

In fairness, the personality cult building around Nkrumah, said Mazrui, was not unprecedented or unsurprising. Nkrumah had brought independence to Ghana, not unlike Washington in the United States who was "adored with the same extravagance that came to be extended to his Ghanaian counterpart two hundred years later."[365] As President, Nkrumah also worked diligently to modernize Ghana, and at least initially, met with great success. New schools, hospitals and roads linking major cities were constructed while a major hydroelectric project, harnessing the power of the Volta River, provided the country with cheap electricity. A

Young Pioneers organization was also established along with a Builders' Brigade some 12,000 strong for unemployed school leavers. The ultimate aim for Nkrumah, Gutteridge said in 1961, was to have a modern state "capable of playing a major role in the final termination of colonial rule in the continent and in the creation of some sort of association of African states."[366] In this latter drive to forge African unity, Nkrumah's profile as a leading black politician was bolstered by the international diplomatic presence in Accra – by late 1962, there were fifty embassies and high commissions in Ghana, more than in any other capital on the continent.[367]

Despite his early successes as a leader, Nkrumah had, nevertheless, positioned himself "to rule by decree, to reject decisions of parliament, to dismiss any public servant or members of the armed forces or judiciary."[368] Unofficially, government was run by the President and a small secretariat and in order to maintain his control, a KGB-trained National Security Service supervised a growing network of informers "placed everywhere – in factories, offices, drinking bars, political rallies and even in churches, not forgetting the taxi drivers, bus drivers, shop assistants, peddlers and seemingly unemployed persons who were all acting as informants."[369] Firmly in power, Nkrumah would set about to make Accra the home of a new African Union government.

In his 1957 autobiography, Nkrumah wrote how it would be the duty of Ghana, in the post-independence period, to act as a "vanguard force to offer what assistance we can to those now engaged in the battles that we ourselves have fought and won. Our task is not done and our safety is not assured until the last vestiges of colonialism have been swept from Africa."[370] For Nkrumah, a strong military was therefore a basic necessity and as he told cadets at the Ghana Military Academy in 1960, he was determined to "build the best equipped and most efficient armed forces in modern Africa."[371] Nkrumah, said Simon Baynham, viewed his armed forces as "the most visible sign of his foreign policy objectives." Moreover, he concluded, "a growing belief that change in South Africa, Rhodesia and the Portuguese colonies could only be accomplished through armed intervention lay at the heart of Ghana's military build-up."[372]

For the Canadian military assistance team assigned to Ghana in 1961, Nkrumah's political manoeuvrings were not something that was discussed before their departure. Prior to their leaving, for example, members of the training team were provided an intelligence briefing on the situation in Ghana that was described as woefully inadequate. "Apparently," added G.D. Hunt, a member of the training team, "no one in Canada knew very much about Ghana, and those who might have had some knowledge, such as the African desk in External Affairs, either were not asked, or did not wish, to enlighten the soldiery."[373] But, once in Ghana, and despite the political situation, the Canadian training team had little choice but to get on with the job they had been handed. Building up the Ghanaian military was going to be a significant, long-term effort requiring patience, skill and respect for the men in their charge.

It is important to acknowledge, however, that military service was not at all a new phenomenon in sub-Saharan Africa. Both the British and French recruited soldiers from their colonies long before the First World War. In Africa, British military forces had been organized into two commands, the Royal West African Frontier Force (RWAFF) and the King's African Rifles (KAR). Composed of volunteers, they were mainly infantry with very little in the way of logistics support.[374] While the RWAFF and KAR were not used in operations outside of Africa in the First World War, matters were significantly grave enough in 1939-1940 that by 1945, an estimated 525,000 African troops had seen service around the world. However, their experiences, vast as they were, did not translate into an Africanization plan for Britain's colonial military forces and the pool of African non-commissioned officers was never used to create commissioned officers. The result was that "virtually all British West African armies still had a majority of British officers on independence day. East Africa trailed even further behind."[375]

The supply of African officers was also limited by an absence of secondary schooling and for those who had a high school leaving certificate, civil service positions were far more attractive. An over-supply of British officers after 1945, many of whom ended up serving in colonial armed forces, further blocked promotion opportunities for Africans. Admission to Sandhurst or to shorter training courses at Mons or Eton Hall in Great Britain did not occur until after 1960 for the most part. As a result, only 12 per cent of the officer corps in Ghana, 29 officers out a total of 209 in all, was African at independence.[376] The small number of African officers was in stark contrast to the Ghanaian Civil Service of which 1,581 were Ghanaian and 1,135 expatriates.[377]

As for the Ghana Army, its modern roots began in 1879 when the British formed the Gold Coast Constabulary to carry out internal security and policing work in their Gold Coast colony. In 1901, the Gold Coast Constabulary was renamed the Gold Coast Regiment (part of the RWAFF) and during the First World War, the Regiment took part in campaigns against the Germans in West and East Africa. In fact, the Gold Coast Regiment had the distinction of being first to capture enemy territory when German Togoland was occupied in August 1914. The Regiment then fought in Cameroon from August 1914 until February 1916. By the end of the war, 397 Europeans and 9,890 Africans were serving in its ranks.[378]

During the Second World War, a total of nine battalions were raised from the Gold Coast, totaling 63,038 men. Of these, in 1945, approximately 6,000 were serving in East Africa, 5,500 in the Middle East and 3,500 in Burma.[379] Upon independence in 1957, the Gold Coast Regiment was renamed the Ghana Regiment and the military structured for internal security only. Of importance, however, was that the high command remained staffed by British Officers, with Major-General A.G. Paley, who had been appointed in 1954, in charge. Besides the almost 200 British officers supporting him, there were an additional 230 British warrant officers and senior non-commissioned officers in Ghana as well.[380]

In 1957, the Ghana Army consisted of its headquarters, a support services organization, three battalions of infantry and a reconnaissance squadron with armoured cars. Total strength was approximately 5,700 men. In 1958, a government appointed National Security Committee examined Ghana's future military requirements and based on their recommendations additional funding was forthcoming – in 1958-1959, for example, the annual defence budget totaled $9.35 million. However, by 1965, it had quadrupled to $47 million as Nkrumah sought to acquire modern weapons and double the size of the Ghana Army. In all, 8.4% of Ghana's total spending in 1965 was dedicated to defence.[381]

With the influx of money and relatively decent salaries compared to the average Ghanaian, there was no shortage of recruits. "The Ghana Armed Forces Training Center in Kumasi," noted Gutteridge, "may get as many as 1,500 applicants for 40 places in a recruit squad without any elaborate publicity."[382] Given literacy levels in the North were low, most Northerners entered the infantry. Most tradesmen and officers came from the Southern tribes – although, said A.K. Ocran, "it was thought improper or wasteful for a young school leaver of Southern Ghanaian origin to join the Army."[383] For those that did join, basic training for infantry recruits was 32 weeks and 24 weeks for tradesmen who were largely better educated and spoke passable English. In fact, the additional training period for the infantry usually commenced with language training during which new soldiers learned simple English sentences. As Gutteridge observed, "the aim of army education, in the first instance, [was] a measure of literacy in English, though the first phase is entirely oral."[384]

While the Ghana Army had substantial roots, the decision to form a navy in December 1958, against the advice of the British, took the Ghanaian government into new territory. Nevertheless, the provision of Israeli military assistance, at least in the first few years, produced good results.[385] By 1967, the navy had two new 600-ton corvettes, two seaward defence craft with 40mm guns, two inshore minesweepers with 40mm and 20mm guns, four Soviet P-class (under 100-tons) fast patrol boats, one training ship and a maintenance and repair craft.[386] Plans were also in development to purchase a frigate at a cost of $19 million plus a larger support ship. All told, the strength of the navy in 1967 was 827 all ranks.[387] Surprisingly, given the lack of any real threat, the navy was organized as an anti-submarine, anti-mine warfare force. Anti-smuggling, fisheries patrols and search and rescue were all secondary. The small force was also consuming large amounts of the military budget – a new naval port under construction by a Yugoslavian company at Sekondi was proving to be very expensive. Costs for the Sekondi naval base, noted a Canadian intelligence report, "are as far twice the original Yugoslav estimates, and are mounting monthly."[388]

In 1959 the Ghanaian government was now ready to spend money on a new air force and by the end of that year a flying school opened in Takoradi under the direction of an Indian officer supported by flying instructors from Israel. In October 1960, however, the training of the Ghana Air Force was transferred to the Royal Air Force and by 1965 the strength of the air force was 900 all ranks with a fleet of approximately 70 aircraft and helicopters. This fleet, in 1965-66, consisted of seven *Macchi* jet trainers (Italy), twelve *Chipmunks* (UK), fourteen *Beavers* (Canada), twelve *Otters* (Canada), eight *Caribous* (Canada), three *Herons* (UK), one *Hawker Siddley* 125 (UK), five *Whirlwind* (UK) helicopters, five *Hughes 269* (USA) helicopters, one *M14* (Russia) helicopter, seven *Sikorsky H-19D* (Russia) helicopters and two *Wessex* (UK) helicopters – an amazingly diverse fleet for what was a developing country.[389]

As the Ghanaian government began to grow and expand its military capabilities, the question arose as to the future of the British officers who were largely running the armed forces. When Major-General Paley left Ghana in 1959, he provided his successor, Major-General H.T. Alexander, a plan for replacing all foreign officers with Ghanaians by 1970. Under pressure from Nkrumah, Alexander had reluctantly revised this plan in August 1961, with a view to having Ghanaians occupy all key positions by 1962. However, with the abrupt dismissal of Alexander and all the British officers in September 1961, Ghanaians found themselves in charge even though they lacked leadership skills and had little to no experience as senior officers.

One of the key reasons behind Nkrumah's dismissal of Alexander and his staff was the Ghanaian deployment to the Congo in July 1960. During the initial stages of the UN operation Ghana deployed a substantial portion of its armed forces. In fact, by August 1960, 2,394 Ghanaian personnel were in the Congo and this force, rotating on a six-month basis, remained in support of the UN for three years. For Nkrumah, the Congo operation was an opportunity to demonstrate his growing desire to play a major role in African affairs. However, as white officers mostly led the Ghana Army, it did not take long for other African countries to point this out. His embarrassment, noted Maj A.K. Ocran, was shared by the soldiers: "The Congolese and the other African troops…were always pointing fingers at the white officers in the Ghana Army and wanting us to explain their presence in the ranks of the Ghana Army, whilst the Congolese were being urged to sack their Belgium officers; for they could hardly reconcile the presence of British officers in our Forces with this advice."[390] To counter his critics, Nkrumah rapidly promoted Ghanaian officers into the top positions in the Ghana Army, whether they were qualified or not.

The dismissal of British officers meant that inexperienced African officers occupied key posts. When Lieutenant-Colonel David Hansen was appointed the battalion commander of the Third Infantry Battalion deployed in the Congo he had been an officer for just under seven years compared to the more normal twenty years in most Western armies. His troops, faced with pay issues and news that the battalion would be transferred on return from Accra in the South to Tamale in the North, mutinied on 19 January 1961. Incapable of addressing their concerns, the battalion commander was "clubbed with rifle butts and left for dead."[391]

Back in Ghana, Major-General Otu replaced the outgoing Alexander. Otu had served a mere 14 years, as had his deputy, Brigadier-General Ankrah. More telling of the problems the Ghana Army would encounter in future were the rapidity of promotions to the rank of major and lieutenant-colonel. When Captain Tachie-Hansen was promoted to major in 1961, he had served a total of two and a half years in the Ghana Army. Newly promoted to lieutenant-colonel in 1961, Major J.C. Adjeitey had 31 months of commissioned service. Meanwhile, Lieutenant-Colonel Kotoka had spent just eight weeks as a major before his promotion. Although Tachie-Hansen and Adjeitey had the least amount of commissioned time, most of the officers promoted to major in September 1961 had, on average, served just over six years. Clearly, the Ghana Army was facing a potential host of problems in late 1961. However, "the wholesale shambles," said Baynham, "which surely must have resulted from simply expelling the expatriate contract and seconded officers was [only] averted by the arrival of Canadian military technicians and training officers."[392]

On their arrival in Ghana in 1961, the CAFTTG quickly took up key training and staff positions and began dealing with the situation created by the rapid departure of the British. Canadian personnel were assigned to a wide range of posts, including the Military Academy (1961-1968), the Military Hospital (1961-1968), Training Schools and as Brigade Training Officers (1961-1968), the air force (1961-1967), and later the Ministry of Defence (1963-1968), Ghana Army Headquarters (1963-1968) and finally the Airborne School (1963-1964).[393] They would, in the period they were deployed to Ghana, oversee one of the most ambitious military expansion plans on the African continent as by 1965, the Ghana Army would consist of five infantry battalions, one paratroop battalion and a reconnaissance battalion – in all, some 14,600 men commanded by 670 officers. The air force and the navy combined had another 2,000 person-nel.[394] By 1966, the Ghana Army was the largest in West Africa and eighth largest on the continent.

From mid-1965 onwards, the Ghanaian military also structured itself much like the Canadian Forces. A CDS reported directly to the President, and there were three Service Chiefs under the CDS. A common pay and records office existed for all three services along with a central bureau for equipment acquisition. Nevertheless, there were significant deficiencies. Although "well equipped by African standards," Canada's military attaché in Ghana noted, there was, nevertheless a lack of competent, well-trained officers.[395] A shortage of spare parts also hampered air force operations and the navy would not have existed without the presence of British Royal Navy officers. However, the military attaché frankly described the greatest challenge was to simply have the average Ghanaian officer "accept the responsibility that goes with his rank. They are masters at getting the expatriates from the Teams to do the work and, ipso facto, accepting the responsibility. This applies from the very top on down."[396]

Despite a lack of spare parts and motivational issues amongst the Ghanaian officers, Colonel Desmond Deane-Freeman, the Canadian military attaché to Ghana, still believed the Canadian team was having a positive impact on the Ghanaian military. His officers and men, he wrote in 1965, had been employed in the Basic Training Centre, the Infantry Training Wing and the Flying Training Centre. More recently, the team had been asked to organize and run the Junior Staff Officers course and some Canadian officers were given key appointments in the Ministry of Defence. Indeed, he added, Canadians had been placed in positions of tremendous influence, not only imparting military training but also "our way of thinking."[397] "Firstly," he continued:

> …both officers and men are under Canadian officers at their most impressionable age; the Cadets during their two years at the Military Academy; the boys (14-17 years) in the Junior Leaders' Coy at Kumasi during their three year course; and the recruits of the three services during their

Basic Training (17-28 weeks) at the GAFTC Kumasi. Secondly, our Canadians have many officers and men under them again at the Infantry wing MATS where the officers take Pl and Coy Comd courses and the men take Jr and Sr NCO courses. And thirdly, the brighter officers come under our Canadians for training at the Jr Staff Course.[398]

The training of Ghanaian officers on the Junior Staff Officers Course, according to Deane-Freeman was paying great dividends. At a recent study period, he added, graduates had "startled the senior officers, not only by their knowledge, but by the manner in which they presented their arguments. They showed up many of the more senior officers, majors and lieutenant-colonels, who have had no staff training, to such an extent that it was almost embarrassing."[399] In receipt of the Colonel's letter, the High Commissioner was also quick to add his praise when writing to the Under Secretary of State in External Affairs. He agreed with Deane-Freeman about the "considerable contribution" the team had played. In fact, the Canadian presence in 1965 was, in his opinion, even more important than it had been in 1961. "With the downgrading of the police force," he wrote, "the Army has taken on added importance as the custodian of law and order in this country. Since independence, it has changed in outlook, perhaps less than any other institution. It is still equipped with Western arms and although essentially non-political, is Western oriented."[400]

That the Ghana Army was considered to be "Western-oriented" would eventually be of importance to the political future of Ghana because an assassination attempt on Nkrumah at Kulungugu on 1 August 1962 was blamed on the United States, Britain, France and Germany in the Ghanaian press.[401] Nkrumah's relationship with the United States further deteriorated in early 1964, in part due to the assassination of President Kennedy in November 1963 – Kennedy, had worked closely with leaders in Africa and above all Nkrumah, promising the Ghanaian President in 1963 that "the CIA [would never] threaten his regime."[402] Kennedy's successor, Lyndon B. Johnson, however, was not so inclined to respect the opinions of small states such as Ghana, and as a result the relationship between Accra and Washington quickly faltered. In the United States, the *New York Times* reported that Ghana was viewed as "Going Marxist." In response, the government controlled *Ghanaian Times* retorted how, "the dopes and drunks who run the Murder Incorporated called the CIA are after the blood of Osagyefo [Nkrumah]."[403]

Seeking to exploit the political situation developing between Ghana and the United States, China increased its support for the Ghanaian government. Full diplomatic relations between China and Ghana had commenced earlier, in July 1960 and by August, seven Chinese officials were firmly established in Accra at a new embassy.[404] From October 1960 onwards the Chinese also helped run several training camps in Ghana for African revolutionaries coming from the Ivory Coast, Niger and Cameroon. For example, Chinese guerilla warfare experts conducted a twenty-day warfare course at a camp in Half Assini. When this camp closed, due to its poor location on the Ghana/Ivory Coast border, another opened in Obenemasi.[405] The Director of the Ghanaian Bureau of African Affairs, A.K. Barden, in particular, had boasted to the President that he had personally taken six Chinese "instructors" to Obenemasi in order to "acquaint them with the general surroundings of this camp, buildings, terrain, etc., and to give their expert recommendations as to whether the camp was an ideal place for the type of training envisaged by the President…the training of potential guerrilla officer cadets."[406] Obenemasi would be one of the largest camps in Ghana, and in January 1965 it was estimated that there were 210 students from countries throughout sub-Saharan Africa and 17 Chinese instructors present. The curriculum consisted of classes in "guerilla warfare, explosives and weapons, the use of telecommunications equipment and battlefield first aid."[407]

The presence of guerrilla training camps and Chinese instructors did not remain a secret for too long and in the fall of 1964 the Ghanaian government came under intense criticism from neighbouring countries and the media. A public statement from several West African leaders appeared on 14 February 1965 in *Le Monde* condemning "the actions of certain states, notably Ghana, which welcomes agents of subversion and organizes training camps on their national territory."[408] The Chinese presence in Ghana caused officials from the Ivory Coast to publicly add that the "peril threatening Africa," was now "yellow-tainted Peking Communism."[409]

The existence of the training camps in Ghana was also a subject of the Fifth Extraordinary Session of the Council of Ministers of the OAU in

Lagos from 10-13 June 1965. During the conference, Adamou Mayaki, Niger's foreign minister, spoke to the delegates about the frequent incursions of Ghanaian-trained commandos into his country. Fifteen, he said, had been recently captured and it was clear "they were trained, organized, and armed in Ghana with a view to coming to kill in my country. At the present time, training camps and death camps exist…in the following places: Mampong, Hasi, Osini, Aksim, Konongo, and Siniani."[410] Besides the training camps, Nkrumah, aided by East Germany, had also formed a "Special African Service" in 1965 specifically to spy on African delegates to the OAU Conference in Accra in October 1965. Nkrumah, said Thompson, "possessed an infinite capacity for mischief."[411]

As relations between Accra and Washington faltered, the United States began plotting Nkrumah's downfall in early 1964. The President of Ghana, noted the Director of the Office of West African Affairs in the State Department to a colleague, was "living in a state of fear induced by the several assassination attempts and an overriding sense of insecurity, and consequently is increasingly irrational and irresponsible." Time, added the Director, was not on the side of the United States as:

> The Parliament, judiciary and police have been emasculated; a purge of the universities is now under way and one of the civil service imminent. Although moderate elements still exert a slight influence on Nkrumah, he increasingly depends for advice and counsel on the small group of leftists in his immediate entourage. Nkrumah is consciously and deliberately creating a police state based on national Marxist principles.[412]

However, with substantial aid programs totalling $350 million underway in Ghana in 1964, including the funding and building of the Volta Dam project and the construction of a major aluminum smelter by the Kaiser-Reynolds Syndicate, the United States was not keen to depart Ghana and potentially facilitate Russia's growing influence in the country. Thus, discussions began in Washington on the possible ways and means to limit Nkrumah's influence or remove him from power altogether. The Director of the Office of West African Affairs, under the heading of "Psychological Warfare" suggested that the United States could undertake an intensive effort to convince the Ghanaian people that their future welfare and independence necessitated Nkrumah's removal. He also recommended the Ghanaian people be told Nkrumah's policies would result in the "Soviet bloc domination of Ghana, thereby substituting one form of colonialism for another."[413]

As Washington considered what to do with Nkrumah, it was clear his plans to become a central figure in Africa's future were already beginning to unravel without the need for any American intervention. To arrest the tide that was now turning against him, Nkrumah hosted the October 1965 OAU annual conference. To demonstrate that all was well in Ghana nothing was spared even though the Ghanaian economy was near collapse. To this end, Nkrumah would spend £10 million to build sixty-five self-contained presidential villas "that would have satisfied the demands of millionaires," a banqueting hall for two thousand guests and elaborate fountains operated by seventy-two jets that propelled water sixty feet into the air."[414] The conference, nevertheless, was a failure, as a significant number of African leaders, concerned with Nkrumah's support for subversive activities across the continent, did not attend. "There is a certain madness in Ghana at present," Nigeria's Sir Abubakar Tafawa Balewa told a press conference in mid-March 1965, "we should not boycott the conference because of Ghana's puerile attitude but rather because it is difficult for the heads of state to meet in Accra, where the undesirable elements of their own countries are harbored by the Ghanaian government."[415]

The clock was now ticking against Nkrumah. "Foreign reserves," noted Thompson, "were all but depleted, as wines, eggs, and consumer goods were flown in from Europe to convince [OAU] delegates that all was well in Ghana."[416] However, things were not well. Government run businesses were poorly managed and inefficient. Government debt had also risen. Pegged at £184 million in 1963, by 1964 the debt had grown to £349 million. Even these amounts were suspect and likely low as record keeping was very poor. "From being one of the most prosperous countries in the tropical world at the time of independence in 1957," said Meredith, "Ghana by 1965 had become virtually bankrupt."[417]

The road to bankruptcy in Ghana, had, in actual fact, begun well before Nkrumah launched his ambitious plan to host the OAU in Accra.

Ghana, as previously mentioned, boasted upon independence "the most advanced infrastructure of any independent country in sub-Saharan Africa."[418] Then, and in order to attract foreign investment, the Ghanaian Government continued making major infrastructure investments. This drive to continue improving infrastructure, as a means to stimulate economic growth, stemmed from the work carried out by Professor W.A. Lewis, a professor at the University of Manchester in England. Lewis had been invited by Nkrumah's National Government in 1951 to examine and report on Ghana's economic prospects and his final report, published in 1953, would become "a major policy guide for the next decade."[419]

In the report, Lewis wrote that improving agricultural output and productivity was the number one priority for the government as doing so would, amongst other matters, free up labour for industry. More important though, was his recommendation that Ghana make major investments in its infrastructure in order to attract foreign private investment. However, many of the infrastructure investments Nkrumah would approve were often inappropriate for Ghana's emerging economy and often too expensive given the resources available. As A.W. Seidman would later write in *Ghana's Development Experience*, development plans were frequently hampered by poor planning, poor management and the employment of too many workers than necessary. New manufacturing plants were habitually built in already developed locations "reinforcing patterns of growth and congestion in already developed areas rather than spreading their effects throughout the country."[420]

For all the investment made, the manufacturing sector hardly grew between 1961 and 1965. In 1961, for example, 29,300 workers were employed in the public and private manufacturing sector. By 1965, the number of workers engaged in manufacturing had barely grown by 1,000 to 30,300. Manufacturing, as a percentage of Gross Domestic Product, was only 4.4% in 1964.[421] By 1965, and with world cocoa prices falling, Ghana was in an economic crisis. "Its financial resources," said Seidman, "had almost vanished, it was deeply in debt to foreign creditors, and continued government expenditures and local food shortages combined to contribute to inflationary pressures that pushed prices up rapidly."[422] Nkrumah, said Mazrui, had surrounded himself with "presidential flatterers" for advisors.[423] "His last year in power," continued Jon Kraus, revealed "numerous illustrations of his failure to respond to the regime's most pressing economic and political problems, in contrast to many M.P.s, ministers, and bureaucrats who regularly attempted to alert him to the current crises and to take measures to stem them."[424]

By 1965, the Ghanaian government was forced to renegotiate its foreign debts and to seek a more reasonable repayment schedule and in early 1966, several Eastern European countries did agree to reschedule Ghana's debts. However, Western governments and companies, the holders of approximately 80% of Ghana's debts, were less inclined to rescue Nkrumah until Ghana had agreed to measures laid out by the International Monetary Fund. In particular, the International Monetary Fund recommended, in addition to some foreign and domestic trade amendments, that Ghana limit recurrent and capital expenditures, halt the launching of new projects, reduce the price paid to the cocoa farmers, end budget subsidies for state enterprises, and control public spending.[425] Nkrumah immediately acted on the recommendation to reduce the production price paid to cocoa farmers by two-thirds of the 1963-1964 level. On 21 February 1966, Finance Minister Amoako-Atta outlined further budget restrictions to Parliament, including restrictions on the expenditure of funds by ministers and public officials. As it was, given the overthrow of the government that would occur two days later, Nkrumah's institutional restructuring plans were never put into effect.

The decision to cut the price paid to cocoa farmers was not at all popular in a region of the country that had largely been opposed to Nkrumah from the outset. Besides economic woes, Nkrumah also faced growing opposition to his rule. In January 1964, a policeman had fired several rifle shots at him. The assassin, wrestled to the ground by his intended target, was taken away, but not before one of the President's bodyguards had been shot and killed. There was some evidence, wrote Baynham, that the policeman, Seth Ametewee, had been paid by senior police officers to carry out the assassination. Certainly, Nkrumah was suspicious of the police force and following the assassination attempt purged senior staff and appointed the head of the Criminal Investigation Department, Mr. J.W.K. Harlley, as Commissioner. As it would turn out, said Baynham, Harlley would inspire and organize the army-police coup in 1966 and while they could not have launched events on their own, in the end the police were the "driving force" in ending Nkrumah's rule.[426]

A growing distrust of the armed forces and the police had led Nkrumah to introduce *The Security Service Act of 1963* that grouped special intelligence units and the President's Own Guard Regiment (POGR) into a single National Security Service composed of three departments reporting directly to his office. The First Department, the Presidential Detail Department, had three sections, including a Cuban-trained and supervised civilian presidential bodyguard, a counter-intelligence section and the POGR. The Second Department included a Soviet-trained special intelligence unit used to spy on the civilian population, while the Third Department was a Military Intelligence section that kept a close watch on the armed forces for any signs of subversion.[427]

No doubt worried about the loyalty of the Ghana Army, Nkrumah turned to the Soviet Union and East Germany to build-up the POGR. The POGR, itself, had been initially intended as a ceremonial guard manned by older soldiers unfit for field duty. However, Nkrumah began restructuring and re-equipping the unit and by 1963-64 it had 50 officers and 1,142 men. A second battalion began forming in 1965 and a substantial arms deal was reached with the Soviet Union – 24 light artillery guns, 21 medium mortars, 15 anti-aircraft guns, 20 heavy machine-guns and ammunition were purchased.[428] Draft plans discovered after the February 1966 coup envisioned a POGR of between three and five battalions. Garrisoned around the presidential residence in Accra, the POGR would eventually become a direct and potentially potent rival to the Canadian trained Ghana Army.[429]

It is clear that in Ottawa the situation developing in Ghana was now well understood, yet, there was never any serious discussion around withdrawing the Canadian training team.[430] On the other hand, there was little desire in Cabinet to provide Nkrumah with advanced weaponry. The Secretary of State advised Cabinet in June 1963 that the Ghanaian government was interested in purchasing six, and perhaps more, CL-41G *Tutor* aircraft. The 'G' version had a ground support capability but as Mr. Martin pointed out, there was no real reason to deny the sale of aircraft for this reason. There was, he added, a Canadian military assistance mission in the country and Canada had friendly relations with Ghana. Not all Ministers were convinced. The situation in Africa, they noted, was explosive and "in view of the leading role adopted by Mr. Nkrumah in the campaign of African countries against South Africa, it would be unwise to sell these aircraft to Ghana, especially in the light of the decision to deny the sale of similar aircraft to South Africa."[431]

In July 1963, Cabinet obtained, via a Memorandum to Cabinet, additional information on the proposed demonstration of the *Tutor* in Ghana. "There are certain reasons," Cabinet was advised, "why the Canadian Government might consider it inadvisable to sell military equipment to Ghana," including:

- The armed forces of Ghana might be used with those of other African states in a war of "liberation" against Portugal, South Africa and, conceivably, Southern Rhodesia;[432]

- Ghana might use its armed forces against its nearest neighbour, Togo, on which it has territorial claims;

- The authoritarian regime of President Nkrumah might use its armed forces to maintain itself in power, against the wishes of the people of Ghana; and

- In his extreme anti-colonialism, his verbal attacks on "neo-colonialism" and imperialism, President Nkrumah sometimes appears to support the communist line and there has been concern that Ghana might be used by the Communists as a base for their penetration of Africa.[433]

Despite these issues, Ministers were nevertheless advised that there were other factors that actually might outweigh objections to selling jet aircraft to Ghana. For one, Ghana was described as the most advanced of the newly independent African states, with a high standard of living. It was therefore understandable for the Ghanaian government to desire well-equipped armed forces. Besides, Cabinet was told the British and Italians were willing to sell their jets and even if they declined to do so, the Communist bloc would step in. Furthermore, "it would seem illogical to train the Ghanaian Army to become a modern and efficient fighting force and yet to refuse to sell them modern conventional weapons."[434] The

Memorandum to Cabinet, as a result, recommended the government support the demonstration of the *Tutor* in Ghana. In addition, it was suggested that requests from Ghana for additional items such as anti-personnel mines, rifles and machine-guns be considered favourably. However, in this latter issue, care would have to be exercised not to "supply large consignments of weapons which might find their way to insurgent forces in the Portuguese territories and South Africa.[435] In the end, commercial matters put a close to any sales of jet aircraft as the $60,000 needed to send one *Tutor* to Ghana proved too costly for Canadair.[436]

To have painted a picture in the Memorandum to Cabinet of Ghana being a potential source of serious trouble in Africa but then conclude that selling jet fighters to Nkrumah made good business sense was indicative of the view in some quarters that Defence Production was more interested in selling aircraft than worrying about the potential effects such sales might have. Also, if the Ghana Army, as it was suggested, might be used to further Nkrumah's political aims, it made little sense to keep the Canadian training team in the country. That is unless the Canadian government believed that in time a well-trained, professional Ghana Army might soon remove Nkrumah. If they did believe this, Colonel James Bond, the Canadian military attaché, likely dampened expectations in late 1965:

> If any conclusions can be drawn, I would say that the President, as C-in-C Armed Forces, has their full support. Although they may be critical of the Party and resent incursions by it into the Armed Forces, I am doubtful if this would cause any serious thought of revolt. For such a revolt to develop, would require a strong leader from within the Armed Forces and I just do not see anyone who might provide it, either now or in the immediate future.[437]

As it would come to pass, the assessment provided in the annual intelligence report was wrong. In fact, in Washington, the American government was well aware that a coup would likely occur in 1965 or 1966 and as early as 10 February 1965, it had been noted that plotting was "actively underway to oust Nkrumah in the very near future. Plans are incomplete, and this, like previous plots, may collapse before execution."[438] In March

1965, the United States ambassador to Ghana, William P. Mahoney, spoke with the Director of the Central Intelligence Agency on the situation in Ghana, and although the ambassador believed that popular opinion was running strongly against Nkrumah, he remained unconvinced that a coup led by Major-General Otu and Brigadier-General Ankrah would take place soon. He did believe, nonetheless, that Nkrumah would be gone within a year but because of a tendency of the coup plotters to procrastinate he could not provide a specific date.[439] Certainly, speculation about the possibility of a coup in Ghana was rife. In May 1965, a memorandum from the National Security Council to the President's Special Assistant for National Security Affairs noted that:

> We may have a *pro-Western coup in Ghana* soon. Certain key military and police figures have been planning one for some time, and Ghana's deteriorating economic condition may provide the spark. The plotters are keeping us briefed, and State thinks we're more on the inside than the British. While we're not directly involved (I'm told), we and other Western countries (including France) have been helping to set up the situation by ignoring Nkrumah's pleas for economic aid. The new OCAM (Francophone) group's refusal to attend any OAU meeting in Accra (because of Nkrumah's plotting) will further isolate him. All in all, looks good.[440]

In July 1965, likely suspecting the Ghana Army might be plotting a coup, Nkrumah had Major-General Otu and the newly promoted Major-General Ankrah dismissed from the army and placed under house arrest. "There is some evidence to suggest," wrote Baynham, that Otu and Ankrah were in fact "involved in conspiratorial conversations against the regime in 1965." Indeed, Baynham continued, Ghanaian officers later told him that "Commissioner of Police Harlley, in collaboration with Lieutenant-Colonel Kotoka, had twice approached Otu and Ankrah with plans to oust Nkrumah" in April 1965 and then in May 1965. In the latter instance, Nkrumah's decision to attend the Commonwealth Prime Ministers' Conference in London in June 1965 acted as a catalyst for the coup plotters who planned to arrest the CPP leadership. At the last moment, however, Otu allegedly "lost his nerve" and Nkrumah survived another day.[441]

Thus, another eight months would pass before the Ghana Army was ready to move against the President. Their plans had been made easier by Nkrumah's decision to leave Ghana for an extended trip to Egypt, Pakistan, China and North Vietnam in a one-man effort to broker several peace deals. Nkrumah departed Accra on 21 February 1966 bound initially for Egypt, where he met President Nasser. He then flew on to Pakistan and presented his peace plan for Kashmir to President Ayub. Nkrumah's staff had tried to dissuade him from leaving the country repeatedly as rumours abounded that a military coup had been planned. At the airport as Nkrumah's plane left the tarmac, Thompson noted that he himself had overheard several diplomats "placing bets on the possibilities (and time) of a coup."[442]

The bettors did not have long to wait. "Operation Cold Chop" began at 0400 hrs on 23 February 1966 when 600 men of the Third Battalion, Second Brigade, led by Colonel Kotoka from the Tamale Garrison began moving South. To deceive the government's intelligence organization, the troop movement had been billed as a "test exercise" for a pending deployment to Rhodesia.[443] Several hours later most government ministers had been taken into custody and resistance from POGR soldiers deployed around Flagstaff House had crumbled. The Ghana Army and its newly formed National Liberation Council (NLC) was now in charge and Colonel Afrifa was ready to justify the coup by charging that Nkrumah's party and ideology:

> ...was based on deceit; its manifesto was a hotch-potch of political slogans and half digested political theories snatched from discredited political philosophers. Its ideology, supposedly based on Marxism, was a confusion of half-truths about Africa, worship of the personality, and the blurred vision of a socialist paradise, unrelated in any way to the specific conditions of our country and our time. Its leader was a man…who claimed that his policies were based on scientific truth, and yet consulted every day with fetish men and magicians. A man who claimed the highest moral virtue, yet was corrupt, a thief, and a liar.[444]

In the days following the 1966 coup, it was somewhat surprising that the army and police did not face a public backlash. In 1965, for example, the CPP claimed to have two million members organized in 2,000 branches.

Even conservative estimates put the party membership at 400,000 in 1966, far more people than a few battalions of troops.[445] Yet the CPP would turn out to be a shell as Dennis Cohen noted in his assessment of the CPP following the coup:

> Examination of the structure of the CPP reveals two main points. First, the CPP was not a unified, monolithic party with a clear chain of command and smoothly-working articulation. It was a disjointed, sporadically functioning, fragmented party dominated by local and regional bosses and including groups of younger, more ideologically-oriented members. The latter were largely confined to the press, functional organizations, and party apparatus posts, while the former filled roles in both party and government. Secondly, the CPP had no real powers of policy implementation of its own, or final powers, of decision-making, for important decisions were taken at the top in the President's office where impulses from the party, the civil service, the chiefs, etc., were received.[446]

The ease in which Nkrumah was overthrown and the absence of any public or CPP opposition to the coup resulted in C.E. McGaughey, the Canadian High Commissioner, urging Ottawa to recognize the new government as quickly as possible. The NLC, he wrote, was in firm control and "all here welcome this development except party functionaries and communist diplomatic missions."[447] McGaughey was also keen to give an account of events before and after the coup – no doubt to allay fears in External Affairs that the coup had been overly violent. Nkrumah's reaction in Peking upon learning of the coup, he said, was one of "incredulity," and since the coup his key ministers had deserted him one by one.[448] Furthermore, the Russians, Chinese and East Germans were now leaving the country in droves, the first major airlift of Russians having occurred on 1 March 1966. "As to the rumours," it was added, "of Russian elements in what little resistance there was, these are largely false although there were Russians instructors for Nkrumah's security forces. We have been able to substantiate only one Russian death in military hospital. It was of dysentery. Some Chinese instructors were at subversive training camp near Konongo but there was… no resistance."[449]

The next day, in a follow-on message, the full flight of Soviet and Chinese advisors from Ghana was reported to Ottawa. All told, Soviet advisors involved in the following activities were sent home (numbers of advisors are indicated in brackets): Ministry of Defence (54), Geology (47), Agriculture (36), Ghana Airways (20), Nuclear Research (27), Bui Dam (18), Fisheries (75), Tamale air base project (200), Teachers and Educational advisors (125), Housing advisors (15), and miscellaneous advisors (48).[450] Chinese advisors and technicians suffered a similar fate and China closed its embassy on 5 November 1966.

A few weeks after the coup, the High Commission continued its efforts to ensure Canada would support the military regime. The NLC, noted a message, had "destroyed Nkrumah's machinery for domestic political control, dismantled his contrivances for subversion abroad, disbanded the President's Own Guard Regiment [and] thrown the Russian and Chinese rascals out."[451] Tumultuous as the coup was, and despite a general disdain for military intervention in the developing world, the High Commission could not help admitting that "a wonderful thing has happened for the West in Ghana and Canada has played a worthy part."[452] In fact, the High Commissioner was full of praise for the Canadian military assistance team and in particular the Canadian presence at the Ghanaian Defence College where they were conducting the junior officer staff course. In a personal letter to the Under Secretary of State for External Affairs, he noted with pride how "all the chief participants of the coup were graduates of this course."[453]

With the coup over and the NLC running affairs in Ghana, the Canadian training team now had to adjust to the post-coup period where the best officers were taken away to oversee other government departments and money for operations and spare parts had all but run out. In April 1966, the High Commission in Ghana, responding to the dire operational needs of the Ghana Air Force, wrote directly to de Havilland. The issue surrounded a lack of critical spare parts for *Caribou* aircraft – only one of eight available was in service. Air Vice Marshal Michael Otu's chief concern was Nkrumah attempting a counter-coup from Guinea or at the very least endeavouring to undermine the NLC by blowing up key infrastructure using small raiding teams. The fact the Soviet Union had recently supplied two transport aircraft to Guinea, each capable of carrying

50 troops, was a factor in his assessment. In his view, the Ghana Army needed to have all eight *Caribou* so that troops could deploy anywhere in the country on a moment's notice.[454]

In July 1967, Colonel Bond was tasked by the Department of National Defence to write an assessment of the Ghana Armed Forces and what new measures Canada could take to provide military assistance. According to him, in 1961, the Ghana Army had been reasonably well equipped but in the following years had been neglected. The coup, he added, had done little to turn matters around. Indeed, "during 1966 the preoccupation of the senior officers with their civilian duties as members of the National Liberation Council and as regional administrators, resulted in an unconscious neglect of the welfare of the Army."[455] Any able intermediate level officer, which included senior captains, majors and lieutenant-colonels, he noted, had been assigned regional or district administrative duties leaving the Army short. The poor economic situation also meant that hard cash was in limited supply and therefore no short-term re-equipment effort was possible. The list of problems he identified was lengthy:

- Senior officers who are members of the National Liberation Council have not devoted sufficient time to their military jobs, thus getting out of touch with the morale situation in the Army;

- The equipment state of the Armed Forces remains woefully bad. This is partly due to lack of money to buy equipment, partly due to poor repair organizations, and partly due to failure of senior officers to face facts and take appropriate action even when recommended to them;

- Officers at all levels are too "nice" and indecisive. They do not follow through and enforce orders and regulations. This is particularly true of unpopular orders;

- Senior and intermediate level officers are posted and re-posted too frequently. There is a lack of continuity in jobs, including important ones such as senior staff appointments in the Ghana Armed Forces Headquarters HQ);

- Intermediate level officers are too inexperienced, and lack decisiveness. In general, leadership qualities are low;

- Over the past four years the standards for acceptance of candidates for officer training have been relaxed for political and family reasons, and to ensure full quotas on courses. Military Academy (GMA) recommendations for retarding or failing of candidates have been over-ruled and the product of the GMA has not been maintained at a qualitative level;

- Junior officers, on leaving GMA do not have proper training in units. Their relationship with the NCOs has been poor and the standards of man-management and leadership are very low;

- Junior officers, or at least a great many of them are not interested in their responsibilities, but are interested primarily in their privileges and prestige; and

- There is a widening rift between officers and men. The majority of the officers are southern (Ewe or Ga) and the majority of the other ranks (particularly the NCOs) are northern (Ashanti, Moshi, Gonja, Dagomba and Mamprusi).[456]

The level of frustration the Canadian team experienced in 1967 was readily apparent in the discussion paper. Canadians, it was noted, had been "individually effective" but a greater, more focused effort was needed if the Ghanaian military was to be re-built in the post-coup period. The discussion paper also concluded that: "CAFTTG, as a working body with a strength of just under twenty all ranks can NOT be an effective force in re-building the Ghana Army."[457]

In fact, the discussion paper implied that the Ghanaian military, even though the foundations were still firm, would have to be extensively re-built, and quickly, as the situation was deteriorating day by day. The *raison d'être* of having a military in Ghana, it was concluded, was the first question in need of an answer. Second, it was asked, "can the Ghana

Armed Forces (really the Ghana Army) be reclaimed, reorganized and reanimated to perform their role."[458] These two questions were not so easily answered when "the aims and/or roles of the Ghana Armed Forces are not clear even in the mind of the C-in-C,"[459] the then recently promoted Lieutenant-General Ankrah. Nevertheless, the discussion paper did provide three roles for the Ghanaian military: The Defence of Ghana; Support to the Ghana Police for internal security matters; and the provision of "unsophisticated" forces to UN or OAU peacekeeping missions.[460]

To begin re-building the military in Ghana, the discussion paper suggested, would require a number of significant decisions to be taken. Foremost, the organization, size and equipment of the armed forces needed review. Was it essential to have two brigades of infantry or jet aircraft? Did the Navy need frigate type vessels for coastal and fisheries patrols and anti-smuggling duties? Certainly, under Nkrumah the armed forces had acquired expensive capabilities with limited utility. Headquarters had also grown in size and needed trimming. Lastly, the Ghana Military Academy, it was suggested, required a total overhaul and the introduction of a three-year entry course for officer cadets. The discussion paper further posited that the "continual pruning of deadwood in all ranks," was essential for an effective military.[461]

To bring about a more relevant, efficient and effective Ghana Army, the discussion paper proposed expanding the CAFTTG back to its original thirty all ranks. While this assessment was likely an accurate estimation of the number of Canadians needed, fulfilling this demand would have created additional personnel and financial demands on the Canadian Forces. For example, it was proposed in the discussion paper that while the five officers involved in procurement efforts in Ghana had done a reasonable job, to be effective, eight more majors were required. Another six or seven majors for the military academy and other training schools was also suggested. Having three officers, embedded as brigade-training advisors was another key recommendation.[462]

Certainly, in the post-coup period, training requests from Ghana began to mount just when the Canadian Forces were being told by the government to reduce military assistance training and expenditures. For example, on-the-job training spots for Financial Control Officers had been requested by Ghana in early 1968 along with permission for a second officer from the Ghanaian Judge Advocate General Branch to be posted for six months in Canada. The Ghanaian government also asked that two Canadian military doctors be sent to front-line positions in the Accra Military Hospital and then presented a "shopping list" of military equipment they were interested in having or buying.[463]

By October 1968, 12 Ghanaian officers were in Canada undergoing training – one at the Army Staff College, three at staff school, six at Canadian Forces Base (CFB) Borden on an intelligence course, one attached to the Judge Advocate General Branch and one officer on an equipment course. Four additional officers had just returned to Ghana after attending an Electrical Mechanical Engineering (EME) course run by Mobile Command. The training team in Ghana, though small in size, had conducted numerous courses, even though recruiting had been considerably reduced. The Ghana Military Academy, for example, had a fresh intake while the Training School was running cook and clerk serials plus physical education courses. The school of infantry also completed several courses in mid-1968, including senior non-commissioned officer tactics, platoon weapons, 81mm mortar and drill. Approximately 125 students went through these courses from 20 May to 28 September 1968.[464]

In March 1969, Brigadier-General Henri Tellier, Director General Plans, traveled to Ghana to visit the Canadian training team. The team in Ghana, he said, was "doing a superb professional job in instructing the Ghanaians to manage and train themselves. This was confirmed by every Ghanaian to whom I spoke including General Ankrah."[465] However, a lack of money for military assistance following the election of Trudeau, and the slowness of obtaining permission to spend what money was available, was beginning to have a direct impact on how Canada was now being viewed by developing states like Ghana. Exasperated by a lack of response from Ottawa on several key military assistance questions, Colonel J.V. Watts, the senior Canadian officer in Accra, wrote to Ottawa in August 1970 that:

> The request for the extension of the CAFTTG until 1973 is
> still outstanding as is the provision of a project engineer
> for the static communications project. The long delays

> which have been experienced on these items, and on oth-
> ers such as the familiarization visit for Cols Agyekum
> and Gbagonah, have resulted in comments progressing
> from the humorous finally to the caustic and have become
> somewhat embarrassing at times. It is not a case of right
> or wrong or of complaint; it is considered that we can and
> should do better.[466]

By 1970, however, the Canadian government was quickly trimming its
military assistance funding. There was simply not enough money to do
any better. Besides, noted the High Commissioner three years earlier,
"for some African and Asian diplomats stationed in Accra, I gather that
there is a tendency to identify our aid policies particularly where military
assistance is concerned with the aims of American and British policies.
American and British objectives are unfortunately not regarded by such
observers as being above criticism or suspicion."[467] Yet Ghana continued
to receive great attention from the United States in particular. "From the
very moment I stepped off the plane," said Vice President Hubert Humphrey to the President in 1968, "I got the strong impression that Ghana
was a reflection of its top leadership: efficient, bustling, forward-looking,
pragmatic and intensely aware of the need to progress during the years
immediately ahead." Furthermore, Humphrey said, "if any country de-
serves our support, if any people merit our help, Ghana stands high on
such a list."[468]

And, there was good reason to be optimistic regarding Ghana's future
when, in October 1969, the Ghana Armed Forces went back to their barracks following national elections and the installation of a civilian government led by Dr. Kofi Busia. The handing back of power to a civilian
government was seen as a major achievement by Ghana's military leadership: "The recent return to civilian rule in Ghana with the complete
support of the Defence Forces," noted a Memorandum to Cabinet in June
1970, "has demonstrated that they share the Canadian view of the position of the military in a democratic society."[469]

However, Dr. Busia had a difficult road ahead as Ghana's economic
situation continued to decline. While in power, the NLC tried to run
the country responsibly but Gross National Product had been stagnant

since 1960 and economic growth was practically non-existent. Foreign debt also continued to be an issue prompting economist Douglas Scott to observe that "Ghana's foreign debt servicing structure was among the worst in the world at the time."[470]   When world prices for cocoa fell from $825 per ton in 1970 to just $487.50 per ton one year later the Ghanaian government had no choice but to adopt severe austerity measures, banning the import of automobiles and televisions. The national currency was also devalued by 44%.[471] Lastly, the 1971 budget reduced defence spending by ten per cent – a decision the armed forces were not at all pleased about. But, as the Minister of Finance said at the time, the current level of defence expenditures "was clearly onerous for a small country such as ours."[472] Without a doubt, Ghana was in need of Canadian military assistance, however meager. In this regard, Dr. Busia travelled to Canada in 1970, asking that the CAFTTG continue its operations until 1974. The challenge for the Canadian government, however, was that Ghana already consumed two-thirds of the available funds allocated for military assistance.[473]

In April 1971, the High Commission in Ghana reported to External Affairs that the Ghanaian government had now come forward with their complete military assistance requirements. It may have been, with the winding up of the Canadian effort in Tanzania, that they perceived an opportunity to increase the support to their country. Certainly, their demands were extensive, including a desire to increase the number of training spots for naval and air force personnel requiring technical training and the extension of the CAFTTG for what was described as an indefinite period.[474] The basic fact, noted the High Commissioner, was that if the request from Ghana were to be approved, Canada would become the major provider of military assistance to that country. Furthermore, he cautiously added that:

> While the civil regime appears to be in control, there is growing dissatisfaction in the country with the present government. There are also rumours, probably not unfounded, that corruption in high places is as rife now as it ever was. If over the next number of years the economy worsened and dissatisfaction were to become greater, their might either be (a) an effort by the government to use the armed forces to

> maintain civil control or (b) a decision by the armed forces
> in what seems to be an African tradition to assume control.[475]

The worsening political situation in Ghana was of great concern in Ottawa and during the 25th meeting of the Military Assistance Committee on 14 October 1971, a decision was taken to phase out the Ghana program by summer 1973.[476] As it would turn out though, the Ghana Army was preparing to act well before summer 1973 and on 13 January 1972 Dr. Busia was overthrown. He had left Ghana on 11 January to receive treatment for an eye condition in London. Lieutenant-Colonel I. K. Acheampong, commander of Ghana's first army brigade, led the coup. Major Norman Graham, part of the Canadian team in Ghana, knew matters were deteriorating in Ghana and the coup came as no surprise:

> Within two years of its inauguration, the government of the second republic was floundering. I picked up faint signals of discontent at cocktail parties and some grumbling by officers at defense headquarters. Several perks enjoyed by the army were withdrawn and the local currency, the cedi, was devalued. The government, which relied on the army for stability, was pulling the tiger's tail. It should have known it would turn and bite them."[477]

Less than two weeks after the coup, on 24 January 1972, J.C.G. Brown the Under Secretary of State for External Affairs, sent a letter to the High Commissioner in Ghana regarding the CBC television program *Viewpoint*. On 17 January 1972, *Globe and Mail* reporter Hugh Winsor had been interviewed on the subject of Canada's military assistance to Ghana during the show. In his letter, Brown provided the High Commissioner with a copy of Winsor's opening remarks:

> A military coup in Africa can hardly be considered a remarkable event. Indeed there was a period in the mid-sixties when news of a military takeover in some African country was almost a part of breakfast as bacon and eggs. But the coup last week in Ghana was different than most – you and I were involved. Oh, I don't mean that the Canadian soldiers we had stationed in Ghana actually participated in the putsch. Our sins in this case were more of omission.

But it is rather interesting that Canada has had military training teams in Ghana since 1961 and in that period the officers they were training have taken over the Government, not once but twice. If we start from the preposition that the replacement of an elected government by a military regime is an undesirable development, where does that leave Canadians? It might be argued that Ghana's first Prime Minister Kwame Nkrumah had so corrupted the democratic process that the soldiers were the only means available of getting him out. The same can't be said for the government of Dr. Busia, the Prime Minister who just lost his job. Even though the Canadian officers in Ghana were not directly involved in the overthrow, leaving them there on a business as usual basis amounts to a tacit approval of their students' action.[478]

In the same program, Winsor criticized a lack of Canadian involvement in Ghana prior to the coup. Help of any kind had not been forthcoming from Ottawa he said. This was especially upsetting for him as he viewed Canadians as having a key role to play in Africa as the "black man's friend in the Commonwealth."[479] Winsor, himself, had a special attachment to Africa having taught journalism at the Institute of Adult Education in Dar es Salaam from 1966 to 1969. Winsor concluded the broadcast by admitting that Ghana's civilian government didn't do such a good job after all. Then again, he added, there was "no evidence that the soldiers can do any better and it is a good opportunity to ask again why armies are encouraged in the developing countries at all and to ask again why Canada is overseas training [them]."[480]

The second coup in Ghana spelled the end of Canada's commitment to provide extensive military assistance to Accra. There was already little appetite in Ottawa for funding military assistance programs to begin with. By February 1974, the CAFTTG team leader, Lieutenant-Colonel R.P.L. de Gobeo was down to one person – him. And on his shoulders fell the last remaining vestiges of possible future Canadian support to Ghana, the construction and operation of a brand new staff college. According to de Gobeo, the need for a mid-level staff college was acute as only six overseas vacancies were available for 150 officers.[481]

The Ghanaian government, noted de Gobeo, were likely to ask Canada support the running of their new staff college vice requesting British help. "The Ghana authorities," he wrote, "are not anxious to take the step of virtually re-activating the British Joint Services Training Team in Ghana and probably feel that to do so would lay them open to charges from other African nations that they are encouraging a resurgence of co-lonialism and imperialism in Ghana."[482] To adequately staff the college, he believed the Ghanaians would ask Canada to provide the Deputy Commandant in the rank of colonel, four lieutenant-colonels to act as Directing Staff (one being an air force officer) and a major to look after administrative matters. The establishment of a national staff college, he concluded, was the "most essential training requirement."[483]

Despite two military coups, there was still a desire in External Affairs to continue supporting the Ghanaian military-led government by establish-ing the new staff college. The Canadian Forces, for example, had already drawn up plans for the staff college, and its establishment of personnel. The only reason why these plans had not been implemented was due to the Ghanaian military being unable to agree on its final location. The Military Academy and Training School in Teshie had enough land avail-able but some Ghanaian officers wanted the staff college elsewhere. As for the Canadian High Commissioner in Ghana, he was eager to secure support for building the staff college wherever it might be located. "One factor," he wrote in a message to External Affairs, "counselling our par-ticipation in the project, if sufficient funds are available is a familiar argu-ment, which we have refrained from using hitherto, of not/not opening door to Soviet bloc influence. Although we are not/not attracted to Com-munists under the bed syndrome, recent events are worth brief mention in this connection."[484]

The pressure applied by the High Commissioner had its intended effect and in June 1975 a memorandum was prepared by External Affairs for the Secretary of State, Allan MacEachen, in order to obtain his "reaction to the request that Canada assist in the establishment of a military staff college in Ghana."[485] In the memorandum, the Minister was advised that the Canadian contribution would be significant, potentially involv-ing eleven officers and a financial commitment of between $400,000 and $500,000 per year for a minimum of five years. The Minister was also reminded, however, that the entire military assistance allocation was just $440,000 per year. Therefore, if the staff college project was supported in the absence of additional funding, all other military aid efforts would have to end affecting 12 other developing countries. The Minister was also advised that not helping establish the staff college might cause the military government in Accra to think Canada was undermining their rule. The military government, it was further suggested to the Minister, "would not be able to accept that a country as apparently as wealthy as Canada could not find the relatively small amount of money required, particularly when we are expending substantial resources in other forms of aid to Ghana through CIDA."[486] In fact, the additional funding proposed for the staff college was approximately one-thirtieth of the aid supplied annually to Ghana through CIDA.[487]

Based on the June 1975 memorandum, MacEachen directed his staff to prepare a Memorandum to Cabinet outlining the proposal and the associated costs in manpower and funds. The draft Memorandum to Cabinet was completed in October and forwarded to the Minister for review with a covering letter. The Minister had visited Ghana in early 1974 and met with the High Commissioner and officials from the Ghanaian government and discussed a number of topics. Believing, therefore, that he would be supportive of establishing the staff college, the covering letter was, as expected, sympathetic to the whole idea of moving forward with the project.

The Memorandum to Cabinet itself had taken time to prepare as the Department of National Defence wanted to ensure enough officers were available. However, the success of the Staff College project still rested on the Canadian government providing an additional $400,000 to $500,000 in military assistance funding each year, mostly for salaries and allowances for the eleven Canadian military officers destined for Ghana.[488] For proponents of the staff college program, however, the news was grim. The Minister, while supporting the general concept, knew the financial circumstances facing the government would prevent approval. Margin notes on the Memorandum to Cabinet noted that the "Minister has decided not to put this forward at this time. He will be prepared to look at it again later, perhaps a year from now, in light of the circumstances at that time."[489] This note was a delaying tactic if ever, as MacEachen was well aware that the prime minister would not support any more money for military assistance.

MacEachen's decision meant an end to Canada's major role in Ghana. The High Commissioner met with officials from the Ghanaian government to break the news and offer what little help he could. Ghana subsequently withdrew its request for Canadian assistance and the British were invited to take the lead, which they did. The British High Commission in Ottawa also informed External Affairs that the British Government was moving forward with the staff college project in Ghana, while the British Military Advisor in Ottawa, Colonel T.W. Tilbrook, wished to know when the Canadian government might approve a request for three Canadian lieutenant-colonels as Directing Staff.[490] Subsequently, in 1976, the British and Canadian training teams in Ghana did come together to form the Commonwealth Military Advisory Team and three Canadian officers were assigned to Ghana. The assignment of even three senior Canadian officers to Ghana, given the previous political upheavals in that country, was an extraordinary decision. Two military coups and a worsening economy, it seems, were not enough to make Ottawa reconsider its Ghanaian commitments, military or economic.

Looking back, few would have predicted how events in Ghana would eventually turnout. Certainly, when Nkrumah first asked Diefenbaker to provide his country with military assistance, the prime minister had been undoubtedly pleased. Although some in Cabinet were concerned about the future political motives of the Ghanaian President, Nkrumah was a symbol of African independence and many developed countries, Canada included, wanted him, and Ghana, to succeed. No doubt Colonel Cooper's positive report on the Ghanaian military and political situation also helped overcome fears in Ottawa that military support to Accra might be misused in some fashion. No doubt also that Gutteridge's study carried a lot of weight in Ottawa, convincing as it was that providing military assistance to Ghana was a relatively safe proposition with good political returns. In fact, Gutteridge concluded that a military coup was simply "hard to envisage," adding that Ghana appeared to have a "better than average chance of establishing professional armed forces."[491]

Yet Nkrumah's abandonment of democracy, his increasingly radical nationalism, and his cooperation with China and the Soviet Union could not help but spark suspicion in the United States. As early as 1960, Nkrumah had effectively begun to stifle any sort of internal political opposition while he continued focusing his efforts on becoming a leading African political figure and proponent of black independence. Central to his plans to rid the continent of the last remaining colonial powers and white-led governments, wrote Baynham, was going to be the armed forces and, in particular, the Ghana Army. However, his rapid expansion plans coupled with the dismissal of British officers in 1961, Baynham continued, had almost resulted in "wholesale shambles," which was, in his opinion, only avoided by the arrival of the Canadian training team.

It is likely the case that the Canadian personnel assigned to Ghana were initially unaware of Nkrumah's long-range plans to use his military for more than just internal security. However, an early indication of Ghana's eagerness to take on a proactive role in African affairs had been demonstrated by the deployment to the Congo, which involved a substantial part of the Ghana Army for a three-year period ending in 1963. Looking back on the early days of the Congo mission, Gutteridge remarked that the deployment had brought a new sense of solidarity and unity to the Ghana Army that it did not possess before. On the other hand, and more ominously, many of the soldiers and officers had also been, he added, exposed "to the schemes and intrigues of the poorer quality of politicians."[492]

It did not take long for the Canadians charged with assisting the Ghanaian military to grasp the difficult political situation the country was in when Nkrumah was in power. There were few "party officers" in the Army in 1962, said Hunt, but nevertheless no one would openly criticize the President or the CPP. The training team fathomed almost immediately upon arrival that Nkrumah's plans to politicize the Army would likely create a backlash amongst the troops:

> The question was: would the officer corps – still largely British trained, moderate and Western-oriented – defend itself, or would it continue to support the legally elected regime and thus bring about its own destruction. To see the Ghanaian

officers with whom we worked struggling to deal with this situation was not only a wrenching experience to the Canadian officers, but an education in the futility of judging affairs in another culture by our standards. We at the Military Academy continued to give lectures about an Army's responsibility to be loyal to the duly elected civilian government, to which the cadets listened respectfully but, I'm sure, with inner amusement at this white man's fairy tale.[493]

That the political situation in Ghana in the early 1960s could be described as tumultuous is an understatement. Nkrumah had been targeted for assassination on several occasions. The Central Intelligence Agency (CIA), the KGB, East Germany, and others were all, in some fashion, mixed up in the country while the Chinese operated several guerilla training camps. Nkrumah's *Security Service Act* had also created a powerful, separate security apparatus from the police and army. Plans to ensure the POGR would become an effective counterweight to the Ghana Army had also been developed and it is not difficult to imagine that Nkrumah, once the POGR had reached sufficient strength, would have disbanded the Ghana Army. Still, if the writing was on the wall for all to see regarding an eventual coup, Colonel Bond was not convinced. Mistakenly, as it would turn out, he believed the Ghana Army was in no condition to lead a coup.

When the coup did happen, the military-dominated NLC took charge of the country's affairs. Yet, the new government had little to no money. First of all, Nkrumah's previous expansion plans for the military had to be halted and anyway, competent senior officers were soon given administrative roles in the new government, meaning that few were left over to manage military affairs. The Canadian training team, as a result, quickly grasped that if the Ghana Army were to have any chance of becoming a professional force they would have to start their training efforts all over again. However, the post-coup period was a time when requests for military assistance would be frowned upon by the government. When Dr. Busia came to Canada in 1970 and asked the Canadian government to extend the CAFTTG mission until 1974, his appeal fell on deaf ears. As it was, military assistance to Ghana was already consuming two-thirds of the limited funds allocated for military assistance in 1970 and additional help for Ghana would have necessitated an end to all other foreign military assistance programs. Ottawa was also well aware by now that becoming involved militarily in Africa was laden with risk.

Before the second coup took place in January 1972, the Military Assistance Committee had already decided to phase out military assistance to Ghana in 1973. Yet, surprisingly, External Affairs was still eager to maintain a Canadian military presence. The result was a last ditch effort on their part to obtain funds for a staff college and the military personnel to staff it. However, the Secretary of State was certainly aware that Trudeau would be averse to Canada propping up a military regime with a new, substantial, military assistance effort and by 1976, the CAFTTG mission was over.

CHAPTER 9

CANADA'S MILITARY ASSISTANCE TO TANZANIA

What is Tanzaphilia? It is neither a disease nor an exotic flower. It is a political phenomenon. I would define "Tanzaphilia" as the romantic spell that Tanzania casts on so many of those who have been closely associated with her. Perhaps no African country has commanded greater affection outside its borders than has Tanzania. Many of the most prosaic Western pragmatists have been known to acquire that dreamy look under the spell of Tanzania. Perhaps Easterners too, have known moments of weakness.

Ali. A. Mazrui, 1967

Although it is clear from Tanzania's decision to terminate our military assistance program that we have not succeeded in preventing the swing to virtual full reliance on China, we did succeed in postponing this development until the Tanzanian forces were basically organized and had acquired their own internal cohesion, which should leave them in a much better position to deal with possible Chinese subversion.

Interdepartmental Military Assistance Committee,
9 July 1969

An exploratory request for Canadian military training assistance had been received from Tanganyika as early as 1962, mainly due to the Tanganyikan government being well aware of Canada's military support to Ghana.[494] A more formal request for military assistance was then sent to Ottawa in April 1963, but Paul Hellyer, in the midst of a departmental re-structuring exercise, was adamant that nothing could be done.[495] Even when President Nyerere subsequently raised the issue of Canadian military assistance with the prime minister during a state visit to Canada in July 1963, the Department of National Defence insisted the government not make any commitment to provide a training team similar to the one in Ghana. It was not until summer 1964, therefore, that the Canadian Forces were finally directed by Pearson to send a survey team to Dar es Salaam.

The question, though, is why, as was asked in the previous chapter regarding Ghana, did Canada become involved, militarily, in East Africa? There was no compelling reason to send Canadian military personnel into a region few in Ottawa knew much about. Moreover, the Tanganyikan army had staged a mutiny in January 1964 that forced Nyerere to go into hiding until his government, with the help of British, then Nigerian troops, could restore order. Tanganyika was also home to many African liberation movements, including the Front for the Liberation of Mozambique (FRELIMO) that was busily fighting the Portuguese, a NATO partner, in Mozambique. In fact, having amassed enough combat strength, FRELIMO units crossed the Rovuma River, separating southern Tanzania from Mozambique, for the first time on 24 September 1964 – one day after the Canadian survey team arrived in Dar es Salaam.[496] So, why did the Canadian government offer military training assistance to Dar es Salaam?

To begin, it is not intended to delve in to the complete colonial history of Tanganyika, but after 1945, suffice to say, the colony remained under British control with a government that "pursued a political strategy in Tanganyika… profoundly hostile to the aspirations of the African nationalists."[497] In particular, the Tanganyikan government sought to entrench, in disproportionate numbers, Asian and European representation in government, while turning to Tanganyikan chiefs as a means to influence and control the African community.[498] Against this backdrop, Nyerere formed the Tanganyikan African National Union (TANU) in 1954.

As a new political movement, TANU was very successful. In July 1954, membership was just 15,000, but by September 1957 the number of card carrying members had increased to over 200,000. The reaction of the government was to do all it could to prevent Nyerere from gaining further ground, for example, banning him in 1957 from making speeches for four months.[499] Nevertheless, it was apparent that TANU, as a political force, was gaining momentum in the period 1957-1958 and as a result the British decided in December 1959 to transfer full power to a new Tanganyikan government as fast as they could. The elections that followed on 30 August 1960 led to an overwhelming victory for TANU and the British Governor appointed Nyerere as Chief Minister. Talks leading to full internal self-government began soon after and Tanganyika became independent on 9 December 1961.[500] Then, in elections held on 9 December 1962, Nyerere became the country's first President.

Compared to other colonies such as Nigeria and Ghana, said Cranford Pratt, "Tanganyika's advance to independence had occurred at a prodigious pace."[501] There was good reason to expect, therefore, that given the inexperience of his government, Nyerere would face many challenges in the post-independence period. However, and fortunately for him, Tanganyika was reasonably stable, the mutiny aside, with few ethic differences and no regional separatist movements, unlike the situation that had faced Nkrumah in Ghana. Moreover, as Catherine Hoskyns noted, few countries had any economic interests in Tanganyika:

> With the exception of diamond mines in the northwest, Tanganyika had no significant mineral resources to exploit, and her varied agricultural resources had been developed without extensive foreign investment in the economy. Here again her situation was in marked contrast to that of her neighbours and if this had left her poorer in terms of infrastructure and revenue, it at least meant that there were fewer assets which foreign interests might manoeuvre to protect. At the same time, virtually no African middle class had emerged which might be tempted to espouse foreign rather than local interests.[502]

From a military perspective, in 1961, Tanganyika had little in the way of armed forces to protect its sovereignty. Prior to independence, two infantry battalions of the King's African Rifles (KAR), part of the British East African Command's 11th Division, were stationed in Tanganyika. But both the 6th and 26th battalions were, said Nestor Launda, "more or less a superior police force organised for rapid deployment to quell tax revolts, labour disputes or nationalist demonstrations," especially in Mauritius where they often did garrison duty.[503] At independence, the 6th Battalion became the First Battalion Tanganyika Rifles (at Colito Barracks in Dar es Salaam), the 26th Battalion was designated the Second Battalion Tanganyika Rifles (at Kalewa Barracks in Tabora) and an additional infantry company was located at Nachingwea in Southern Tanganyika. Name changes aside, all key command positions were held by British officers and non-commissioned officers.[504]

Nyerere, it appears, seemed unconcerned that his army was commanded by British officers. Indeed, upon independence there would only be three Tanganyikan officers, one of whom was of Asian background. He had even considered disbanding the army prior to independence but in the end settled for a conservative ten-year schedule for their eventual Africanization.[505] Defence, commented Luanda, was not a high priority for the President given other challenges facing the country:

> Most parliamentary debates in early independent Tanganyika concerned issues of political, economic and social development. Those few debates that focused on foreign and defence policy issues were quite controversial and instructive. Two opposite, broad propositions were taken on the question of defence: the pro-army position was that Tanganyika needed a sizeable professional army which would be responsible for defending its national borders and which could also make a contribution to the liberation struggle in Southern Africa. The anti-army position held that Tanganyika had no external enemies and thus did not need a large army. It was argued that the nominal force inherited at independence should be deployed to undertake nation-building activities. The most extreme version of this argument was that Tanganyika should dissolve even the small force inherited at independence and place the country's defence in the hands of the United Nations, in order to demonstrate its peaceful intentions.[506]

When both battalions of the Tanganyikan Rifles mutinied on 20 January 1964, there were probably many in the TANU leadership who wished they had disbanded the army. Certainly, Nyerere had tried to move away from the concept of having a standing army that just sat in its barracks

consuming limited resources. Prior to the mutiny, for example, he undertook plans to integrate the army into the economic life of the country by assigning soldiers to public works projects and ordering them to
grow their own food. In 1963, the British army commander took issue
with this, telling the Minister of Defence that the Public Works Department was better suited to development work, not the armed forces. Soldiers were also aggrieved by the low pay they received and that after
almost three years of independence there were still only 35 Tanzanian
officers, and half of these were non-commissioned officers. Furthermore,
Nyerere had taken the unusual step of turning down all the officer candidate nominations put forth by the Minister of National Defence two
weeks before the mutiny took place.[507]

Although the Tanganyikan army was small, the mutiny took its toll. Loot-
ing resulted in the death of 20 people in Dar es Salaam and Nyerere and
Vice President Rashidi Kawawa fled the capital. Order was not established for several days and only after a major British intervention by 600
Royal Marines. Relieved that his grip on power remained intact, Nyerere
was nevertheless aware that he would now appear a puppet of the British. The result was a decision to order the British out while a Nigerian
Battalion moved in to Dar es Salaam to provide security. Fortunately, for
Nyerere, the mutineers were disorganized and had no plan to overtake
the state. "The mutiny," noted Andrew Coulson, "was over thirty minutes after sixty British marines landed by helicopter on the [field] hockey
pitch at Lugalo barrack outside Dar es Salaam."[508]

The events of January 1964 were a shock for the Tanganyikan government and in the aftermath, Nyerere immediately took steps to disband
the army. In its place, he called on the youth of TANU to create a new
armed forces based on a limited national service program. The idea was
that recruits would engage in three months of nation-building activities, such as bush clearing and road building, followed by six months of
training in the army or police.[509] As a matter of fact, one could not join
the army without first passing through national service and becoming a
member of TANU. As Luanda noted, the most important consideration
for Nyerere was to ensure the new army would be well-trained and highly professional, but, more importantly, politically loyal.[510] To this end,
TANU political officers were posted throughout the army.

Nyerere's new army, with 1,300 soldiers and its TANU political officers, was officially inaugurated on 1 September 1964, shortly before Brigadier Love arrived in Dar es Salaam. The Canadian High Commissioner, present at the inauguration ceremony, sent a message on developments, to Ottawa, the following day:

> Yesterday, we saw the President together with second Vice Presidents Karume and Kawawa [review] the passing out of some 1,300 new troops including thirty women. These troops form the nucleus of the new post-mutiny army. Many were selected in June from among members of the national service in which they had already spent three months on quote nation building projects unquote. Since June they have had a further three months of intensive basic training. After they had passed by smartly in review order to the tune of African and British marches the troops stood and took an oath of allegiance to the united republic. The consensus of observers present yesterday was that the troops had put on a good show and that the President had every reason to be pleased with the performance of this completely African force which had been entirely trained by African officers.[511]

While Nyerere might have been skeptical on the need for Tanzania to maintain an army prior to independence, he was not, however, against the use of military force to overthrow white-dominated regimes in southern Africa. In fact, soon after independence his government had refused landing rights in Tanzania for any commercial aircraft destined for South Africa and introduced a boycott on South African goods. The Portuguese Consul-General's office in Dar es Salaam was also closed.[512] Then, in 1961, political refugees from southern Africa began turning up in Dar es Salaam. The first to arrive were members of the Zimbabwe African People's Union (ZAPU), outlawed in 1961 by the Southern Rhodesian government. In 1961, the African National Congress (ANC) and the Pan-African Congress (PAC) had also been banned in South Africa and by 1963 the authorities had infiltrated and broken up both groups. This led to a small-scale exodus of ANC and PAC members who also concentrated in Dar es Salaam and London.[513]

It was not surprising that liberation movements found a second home in Tanganyika as Nyerere had sought to lead the movement for African self-government well before independence. For instance, his government took on the leadership of the Pan-African Freedom Movement of East and Central Africa (PAFMECA) founded on 17 September 1958. The aim of this organization was to develop a common, non-violent strategy for the different national movements in British East and Central Africa seeking self-government. However, militant black nationalists in South Africa, Southern Rhodesia, and the Portuguese territories were not convinced the principle of non-violence would succeed and in time their influence would grow. As a result, Tanganyika, Mazrui said, would eventually cease to be the leader of the "neo-Ghandian (sic) movement of PAFMECA" and become the main coordinator of liberation movements in southern Africa employing insurgency methods to gain political power.[514]

In 1963, Dar es Salaam became the headquarters of the OAU Liberation Committee, chaired by Oscar Kambona, the Tanganyikan Foreign Minister. Clearly, noted Pratt, both before and after independence, Nyerere had committed himself to the liberation struggle in southern Africa:

> Many African states, though strongly condemning South African racism and Portuguese colonialism, had not wished to complicate their internal politics nor to compromise their relationships with the Western powers by facilitating such activities within their own country. Nyerere's answer, however, was never really in doubt. He would not engage in the moral gymnastics which would have been required simultaneously to condemn Portugal, South Africa and Rhodesia and then to obstruct the efforts of African nationalists to secure training and arms after they had turned in despair to armed struggle.[515]

It was towards ending the Portuguese presence in Mozambique that Nyerere directed much of his energy. Unlike the British, French, and other colonial powers in Africa, the Portuguese government had expressed no desire to grant independence to Angola, Guinea-Bissau or Mozambique. Lisbon, instead, would fight tenaciously to hold on to its territories despite increasing casualties and spiraling costs. Why was this? John S. Saul identified two reasons. The first was that Portugal itself was economically weak and if its African territories had been voluntarily granted independence, it would have been highly unlikely the Portuguese government would have had any continuing influence in them. Second, the situation was complicated by the fact that Portugal was a dictatorship. Any move on the part of Lisbon, therefore, to promote democracy in Africa would have called in to question why Portugal itself was not democratic.[516]

The support offered by Nyerere to FRELIMO was wide-ranging. Most important, Tanganyika [hereafter Tanzania] became a sanctuary for FRELIMO and several of their bases were located in the southern areas of the country, along the border of Mozambique – a border the Portuguese military were reluctant, at least initially, to cross. The Tanzanian government and its army also coordinated the delivery of weapons and supplies to the liberation movement including small arms, mines, mortars, light anti-aircraft guns, and shoulder launched surface to air missiles.[517] As a result of having a sanctuary and a steady source of supplies, FRELIMO was able to organize and equip a guerrilla army of between 5,000 and 10,000 soldiers "that maintained considerable military pressure at various times and places on Portuguese defences [in Mozambique] through ambushes, mining operations, and attacks on small, lightly defended *postos administrativos* and military installations."[518] In fact, the military pressure FRELIMO was able to generate against the Portuguese was reported on in 1965 by Lord Kilbracken who had been sent to Mozambique by the *Evening Standard* of London to write an account of the war. "The battle zone," he wrote:

> ...stretches some 20 to 40 miles inland along all Mozambique's lake shore from the Tanzanian to the Malawi border. In 3,000 terrorized square miles the Portuguese, both civilian and military, are now confined to five isolated garrisons: Metangula, Maniamba, Cobue, Olivenca, and Nova Coimbra...not one white settler...remains in all the area. Their once neat holdings are today silent and abandoned. And most of the Africans – they belong to the Nyanja tribe – have fled to the mountains and islands or to Tanzania or Malawi.[519]

In response to FRELIMO's attacks, Portugal steadily increased the size of its military presence. In 1964, there were approximately 25,000 troops in Mozambique and by the end of 1965 this figure had increased to about 40,000. At the beginning of 1970 another 20,000 troops were added, bringing the total number to 60,000 personnel. Besides the regular army, navy and air force personnel, many of whom were conscripts, the Portuguese also deployed elite commando units trained in counter-insurgency warfare.[520]

The export of Canadian arms to Portugal, a NATO ally, was often complicated by their significant military presence in Africa. Ottawa, while agreeing to supply arms to Lisbon for NATO purposes, was not at all interested in seeing its weapons used to suppress FRELIMO and other guerilla groups. Furthermore, the UN Security Council had passed a resolution in 1963 asking member countries not to provide Portugal with military equipment or assistance that would allow the continued "repression of colonial peoples."[521] As far as Cabinet was concerned "in the absence of satisfactory Portuguese assurances that military items would not be used outside the NATO area, applications for export permits relating to the export of arms and military equipment to Portugal or its territories should not be approved."[522]

However, the United States, noted Richard Leonard continued to supply Portugal with military assistance. In particular, he made reference to a "bizarre covert operation involving CIA connections to smuggle twenty B-26 bombers to Portugal that was halted by U.S. Customs after seven had been delivered." Moreover, he added, Portugal also obtained aircraft, helicopters, and naval vessels from other NATO allies that ended up in Portugal's African colonies.[523] Certainly, in late 1967, the Cabinet was aware that other countries were continuing to supply Portugal with arms that were ending up in Africa. The Secretary of State for External Affairs reported to his colleagues in December that Canada was, in effect, losing business to countries that did not take their "international obligations" seriously. The Minister of Trade and Commerce added, in the case of arms sales to Portugal, that it was "unrealistic to refuse orders when they would quickly be taken up by the United States or the United Kingdom. Portugal has bought many piston-engine aircraft from us and expected to get them serviced at the large United Aircraft Company factory established in Longueil for the purpose."[524]

The support provided by Tanzania to various southern African liberation movements annoyed many. "In Britain at least [Tanzania] had replaced Ghana as the *bête noire* of the right-wing press," wrote Hoskyns in 1968. However, she continued, the "low-keyed, undogmatic approach of Tanzania's leaders, and especially the President, made it difficult to make extremist labels stick."[525] Nyerere was also opposed, unlike Nkrumah, to assisting African revolutionary movements directed against countries governed by Africans. He was also not inclined to promote a pan-African view, noting in a speech on Mozambique's post-colonial future that:

> What comes after freedom is an affair of the people of these territories…It is not for us to decide what sort of government they will have or what sort of system they will adopt. Tanzania must support the struggle for freedom in these areas regardless of the political philosophy of those who are conducting the struggle…Our own commitment to socialism in Tanzania is irrelevant to the right of the people of Mozambique to choose their own government and their own political system.[526]

While Tanzania might have been the *bête noire* of the British right-wing press, Nyerere, nevertheless, continued to command great respect in his country and around the world. In Tanzania, said Pratt, the population had no doubt that "they had in their midst a leader of unquestionable integrity, who, whatever his policy errors, was profoundly committed to their welfare."[527] In 1967, for example, Nyerere announced that Tanzania would embark on the path of "African socialism" based on the concept that prior to colonialism Africans had lived in a caring, cooperative environment of equals.[528] Indeed, in his 1967 Arusha Declaration (Nyerere's vehicle to introduce his socialist plans) he directed the nationalization of all private banks, major food processors, and the eight largest foreign export trading companies.[529] He then spoke about the need for Tanzania to become "self reliant" and less dependent on foreign aid. An agrarian program was also presented based on communal farms that would become known as "ujamaa" villages.

Finally, to combat what he perceived to be the creation of a privileged political class in Tanzania and growing corruption, he laid down a leadership code which prohibited senior government and TANU party members from holding more than one job, engaging in private business ventures and having more than one house.[530] Achieving 100 per cent compliance with his plans, of course, would have been too much to ask for any leader. However, Nyerere recognized that he and his government had to change course. On the other hand, in Ghana, said Cohen, "socialist ideology was regarded as at best a useless encumbrance, and at worst a positive evil by most of the highest-ranking members of the CPP. They tolerated it and even paid lip service to it in order to please Nkrumah, but for few did their commitment go beyond this perfunctory level."[531]

Two years prior to the Arusha Declaration, Tanzania had also experimented with competitive elections in a one-party structure. Western liberals who had become disenchanted with the growth of democracy in Africa, wrote Mazrui, had been very pleased. "To some Western liberals," he continued, "Nyerere was almost the last hope. Could he save a little of their old pride? Could he vindicate at least a little of their old faith in the feasibility of new democratic forms in Africa?"[532] It appears he did. In particular, Welch, contrasting the political situation in Ghana and Tanzania, observed that:

> Elections in Ghana became near-meaningless illustrations of the untrammeled role of the C.P.P. and its leader. Ghanaians were not called to the polls in 1965, following ratification of the amendment formalising single-party rule; the President simply proclaimed all C.P.P. candidates elected without the fuss, bother, expense, and legitimization that a national ballot might have provided. Elections in Tanzania took on a far different character. T.A.N.U. nominated two candidates in most constituencies in the 1965, 1970, and 1975 elections, and voters enjoyed a choice, often made clear by their distaste for incumbent M.P.s. The circulation of the parliamentary elite continued. T.A.N.U. remained a vital party, and did not become an empty shell, as had the C.P.P. There was thus little need for members of the armed forces to intrude into the political process, in an attempt to restore electoral choice.[533]

CHAPTER 9

Welch might have added that the Tanzanian armed forces were also unlikely to become involved in unseating the government simply due to
the support they were providing to FRELIMO. Their focus, besides the
re-building of their numbers and capabilities, was elsewhere.

Despite Nyerere's support to liberation movements in southern Africa
and the nationalization program that followed the Arusha Declaration,
Western governments, said Coulson, were so impressed with Nyerere's
focus on self-reliance, "that they were willing to overlook the nationaliza-
tions that followed the Arusha Declaration, with the result that Tanzania
became a major recipient of Western capital, much of it on concession-
ary terms."[534] Moreover, continued P.F. Nursey-Bray, on the subject of
Nyerere's African socialism plans:

> Only in Tanzania, was there a genuine attempt to imple-
> ment the precepts of this political theory. It is this fact that
> accounts for the hold that Tanzania has exercised over the
> minds of intellectuals with a sympathetic interest in Africa.
> Tanzania under the leadership of Nyerere has embarked
> on a set of policies that, whatever scepticism may be enter-
> tained regarding their effectiveness, appear to have been
> motivated by a genuine desire for social change in the di-
> rection of greater equality, an attempt at development with-
> out undue reliance on external resources, and a desire to
> create institutions based on an African model of a commu-
> nitarian village society.[535]

Canada, its government and its intellectuals, were indeed sympathetic to
the needs of Tanzania, despite Nyerere's support to national liberation
movements and his nationalization program. In fact, Ottawa's military,
technical and economic aid to Tanzania would increase throughout the
1960s. In particular, military assistance to the Tanzanian government
was based on the following factors:

- Tanzania's requirements were sufficiently modest that Canada could make a meaningful contribution towards meeting them without placing an undue strain on the Canadian
  Forces;

- Tanzania was one of the poorest countries in East Africa and it was clear the development of the armed forces to a sufficient level to provide internal stability could not be carried out without some kind of outside assistance;

- President Nyerere was recognized around the world as a pro-Western, highly capable leader. Thus, it was important to provide him with a serious alternative to communist assistance in carrying through a modest defence program; and

- A well-trained, well-led armed forces was seen as a prerequisite for successful social and economic development in Tanzania and therefore the maintenance of President Nyerere in power.[536]

Despite the altruistic nature of the objectives outlined above, it was widely accepted at the time, said Clyde Sanger in 1969, "that Canada reluctantly offered [military] help after Britain and the United States urged Ottawa to step forward and level the political balance."[537] Sanger's assessment was, in fact, correct as the Military Assistance Committee had also noted in a 1969 review of Canadian military assistance commitments that the decision to assist Tanzania came about under "considerable urging" from the British and American governments.[538] The concern in London and Washington at the time was based on the ever-increasing presence of the Chinese in Tanzania and in this regard Canada was seen in both capitals as one of the few potentially effective counter-weights to Beijing's aggressive African foreign policy.

Chinese military assistance was first offered to Tanzania in early 1964 and in June 1964 the Vice-President of Tanzania traveled to Beijing to discuss matters further. Tanzania then opened an embassy in the Chinese capital in October and in February 1965 Nyerere traveled to China. Chou En-lai, on a reciprocal visit, arrived in Dar es Salaam four months later. Of more importance to the West was the arrival of the first Chinese military instructors in Tanzania – their arrival reported in the British newspaper, the *Observer*, in late August 1964. The article generated such media interest in Tanzania that Nyerere had little choice but to call a press conference on 31 August to explain his decision to request Chinese military support. V.G. Turner, the Canadian High Commissioner, reported to Ottawa that the President had "expressed resentment at Western warnings of the risks he was taking by allowing Chinese instructors to come here. He noted that the maximum risk was that the army might revolt, and pointed out that when it had revolted in January it had not repeat not been trained by the Chinese."[539] The President further remarked that the entire concept of being non-aligned meant that one could ask for help from anyone.[540] Furthermore, he said, the Chinese presence was limited to six months.

Without doubt, the Chinese were far quicker to respond to calls for military assistance than the West. For example, in September 1964, Turner spoke with Brigadier-General Sam Sarakikya, the Tanzanian Chief of Defence Forces, about the recent arrival of Chinese instructors and equipment, including rifles, machine guns and mortars. Sarakikya, said the High Commissioner, had told him the Chinese would only be allowed to train Tanzanian trainers and there would be no contact with the troops. However, the General also pointed out how "astonished" he was that the Chinese could respond to requests for aid so rapidly, usually within a month, while it took six months or more when dealing with western countries.

The main reason for the Chinese presence, remarked the High Commissioner, was President Nyerere's desire to buildup his armed forces as rapidly as possible and to take assistance from wherever he could. Nonetheless, said Turner, the Chinese had gained a significant foothold, militarily and economically, from which, he added, they would not be "easily dislodged."[541] What's more, the Chinese government offered significant economic and technical support to Tanzania. For example, President Nyerere and Kenneth Kaunda of Zambia were eager to build a railway link between their two countries that would also provide the Zambians with a route to the sea, bypassing white-controlled South Africa and Rhodesia. When financing for the project was not forthcoming from the West, China stepped up and a technical team arrived in Tanzania in August 1965.

There were two key motives surrounding China's interest in Tanzania. The first was economic and in 1971, China became the principal source of imports for Tanzania, displacing the British. In fact, the growth of Chinese imports to Tanzania was striking. In 1962, trade was nonexistent between the two countries but by 1967 Tanzania was importing 74 million Shillings of Chinese goods and exporting 62 million Shillings in return. By 1973 though, matters had changed dramatically. Tanzanians were now importing 682 million Shillings of Chinese goods while exports had only risen to 98 million Shillings.[542] The balance of trade was clearly in China's favour.

However, it is likely the central focus behind the Chinese presence in Tanzania was driven by the desire in Beijing to promote revolutionary movements throughout sub-Saharan Africa. Chou En-lai, as previously noted, had said as much in June 1965, telling his Tanzanian hosts that Africa was, in his view, "ripe for revolution."[543] Yet, despite the numerous liberation groups and the formidable Chinese presence in Tanzania, the Canadian Government was still willing to send a Brigadier with a survey team to Dar es Salaam in September 1964 to obtain a better idea of what role the Canadian Forces could play, in particular through the establishment of a military academy.

The survey team that arrived in Tanzania on 23 September 1964 did so comfortable in the knowledge that the Canadian Forces now knew more about training African militaries than it had in 1961 when the CAFTTG was dispatched to Ghana. The team, led by Brigadier Love, also included Colonel Deane-Freeman, the Canadian military attaché in Ghana. They were joined by Lieutenant-Colonel J.P. Francis, Lieutenant-Colonel J.C. Gardner, Squadron Leader W.I. Butchart, Mr. A.J. Darling from the Department of Finance and Mr. A. Kroeger from External Affairs. To ensure the arrival of the survey team would be well covered in the Tanzanian Press, the High Commission in Dar es Salaam issued a press release the day prior to their arrival:

> The Canadian Government has over the period of several months been actively considering, in consultation with His Excellency Mwalimu Julius Nyerere and the members of his Government, requests for assistance in the training and equipping of the armed forces of the United Republic of Tanganyika and Zanzibar. The Canadian Government has now agreed to a request made by President Nyerere to send a military survey team to look into these matters. The team is expected to arrive in the United Republic on September 23. In light of the survey team's report and recommendations

> the Canadian government will consider as a matter of
> urgency what assistance it would be possible and appro-
> priate to offer to the United Republic taking into account
> Canada's capabilities and various other commitments.
> Recently, the United Republic Government accepted a
> Canadian offer of training places for Army officer cadets.
> Twelve cadets arrived in Canada by Royal Canadian Air
> Force transport on September 16.[544]

The press release had its effect and both the Tanzanian and Kenyan press reported on the arrival of the survey team.[545] However, the survey team itself had little time to read the local newspapers, as the day after their arrival the entire group was in front of President Nyerere, his Vice President, the Minister of State and the Defence Permanent Secretary. The President told Brigadier Love that besides looking into the creation of a military training centre he also wanted him to provide advice on the overall force structure of the Tanzanian military. Under questioning from Brigadier Love, the President added that he needed military forces that could assist the police with internal security issues and allow for a minimum level of defence from external threats. Additionally, the President believed his armed forces should assist in development projects including road construction. Finally, the desire by the President to have a tactical squadron for the air force was discussed. The main concern for the High Commissioner was that the terms of reference provided to the survey team did not include a requirement to furnish the Tanzanian Government with a complete force structure review. External Affairs was consulted and permission was quickly given to do as President Nyerere asked.[546]

When the survey team arrived in Tanzania, the Tanzanian military was in the process of slowly re-building after the 1964 mutiny and it consisted of three battalions of infantry. One battalion was located in Nachingwea (between Songea and Mtwara) in the south and was responsible for the border with Mozambique. A second battalion was based at Tabora, available for operations in the north and west, including responsibility for the borders with Kenya, Uganda, Rwanda, Burundi, and the Congo. The third infantry battalion was garrisoned in the capital while a planned battalion for Zanzibar had yet to form. However, there was no provision for logistics, engineer, ordinance or signals units, and therefore battalion field operations were not possible beyond a few days. Moreover, there were only 53 officers, half the number needed not including officers for the planned fourth battalion.[547]

As a starting point for the examination of Tanzania's defence requirements, and in consultation with the High Commissioner, the survey team discussed amongst themselves why Tanzania needed an armed forces and what roles it might have. Tanzania was a large country, bigger than France and West Germany combined. Its roads and railways were few and just moving around the country, above all during the rainy season, was very difficult. There was also the contentious issue of integrating the communist trained Zanzibar People's Liberation Army into the regular army, following the amalgamation of Zanzibar and Tanzania in April 1964. The consensus was that the military, given a lack of resources to grow much beyond its present size, would have to have as its primary role the maintenance of internal order, supporting the police forces when necessary. Border protection was deemed to be of secondary importance.

Brigadier Love delivered the survey team report verbally to President Nyerere just before the team departed Dar es Salaam on 8 October 1964. Given the presence of Mr. Darling and Mr. Kroeger, it was also possible to provide the President with an economic and financial assessment of the Tanzanian economy, and an estimation of the funds needed to support the armed forces. As for the military recommendations, President Nyerere was told that if a Canadian military assistance team were to deploy to Tanzania the priority of effort would need to be given over to:

- The establishment of bases, a military academy, plus a service battalion, an engineer and a signals unit. Upon completion of this step, sub-units of the aforementioned units would be deployed with the battalions creating self-sufficient battalion groups able to operate independently;

- The development of an integrated force, with the air element (and perhaps eventually a naval element) sharing with the Army the various services, headquarters and base installations. All personnel, regardless of service, would go through the same basic military training. With regard to the civilian component of the defence establishment, the idea was to closely follow the basic organization of the Canadian Department of National Defence; and

- The development of a Field Force Headquarters, which would be separate from National Military Headquarters so as to separate policy and planning more clearly from day-to-day operations.[548]

When the survey team arrived back in Canada, Brigadier Love laid out the resources needed to support the Tanzanian military in far more detail. He suggested a training team of 26 all ranks and one civilian be phased into Tanzania over a year or possibly longer. However, he highly recommended that the team leader and a small advance party be sent as soon as possible. Furthermore, Love was firm that up to 20 places for officer training in Canada had to be set aside for Tanzanian cadets and that Canada should definitely fund a military academy, which in his view, would become an "identifiably Canadian project." Given the time required to build this facility he suggested 50 surplus military huts be sent as an interim solution. Finally, given the presence of a robust West German air force training team in Tanzania, there was no need, he concluded, for Canada to provide any additional assistance for the air force.[549]

Not having to provide military assistance to the Tanzanian air force was likely met with a degree of relief in Ottawa as, according to a separate Canadian report on the Tanzanian air force and general civilian air operations, Tanzania "had no military air capability whatsoever, no aircraft or associated equipment, no military airfield facilities and no trained personnel, either aircrew or ground crew."[550] Furthermore, airfield lighting was almost non-existent and most flying in the country, civilian and military was done during the day. Nevertheless, President Nyerere had been eager to establish an air force to move his army internally and to have a small jet fighter force that could act as a deterrent to incursions by Portuguese and Rhodesian aircraft. However, the report suggested that while an air transport component of one or two small squadrons would be a realistic undertaking, any effort to create a tactical fighter squadron of between six and ten aircraft was not. President Nyerere, noted the report, clearly did not appreciate the complexity or expense of keeping up such a capability.[551]

Despite the challenges of creating an air force from the ground up, West Germany had nevertheless signed a five-year aircrew and technician training program agreement with the Tanzanian government in 1964. Along with training, the West Germans also planned to supply aircraft including eight *Piaggio* trainers, eight DC-27 trainers, four DO-28 liaison/communication aircraft and six to 12 *Noratlas* transport aircraft. In fact, the training program, described as "well-supported" and "comprehensive" was already underway by the time the Canadian survey team arrived in Dar es Salaam, with ten Tanzanians in West Germany for pilot training.[552] Colonel Treppe, the senior West German officer, was also acting as the Air Advisor in the Tanzanian Ministry of Defence and therefore it was not "considered necessary or desirable that Canada provide additional aid at this time."[553] However, the West German government was not so inclined to support the creation of a fighter squadron even if the aircraft were propeller driven as, by African standards, this capability would still be significant.

Characteristically, the Department of Finance, even if Canada's role was to be limited to training the Tanzanian army, was not enthusiastic about matters. The Deputy Minister of Finance, for example, wrote to External Affairs in early October to say that the team would undoubtedly encounter serious difficulties and that sooner or later tens of millions of dollars would have be spent by Canada equipping the Tanzanian military. The Deputy Minister also questioned why Canada would agree to help Tanzania, echoing a view in his department that the entire effort was nothing more than a concession to British and American pressure with no definable strategy. In a six-page detailed reply, Cadieux disagreed with the assessment made by the Department of Finance, noting the survey team had estimated only $7 million was needed. Furthermore, he added, "rather than encouraging an inflation of Tanzania's military programme, I believe the presence of a Canadian advisory team would encourage a concentration upon modest and practical projects consistent with Tanzania's real needs and the resources it may reasonably expect to have available."[554]

Besides the intervention by the Deputy Minister of Finance, the issue of financing the Tanzanian mission was also central at the second meeting of the Military Assistance Committee on 27 October 1964. The aim of the meeting was to review the report prepared by Brigadier Love, following his visit to Tanzania, and to ensure a planned Memorandum to Cabinet on Canada's military assistance to the Tanzanian government would address why the Canadian government should become engaged. Mr. Hudon, representing the Department of Finance, and no doubt his Deputy Minister, suggested that the committee should ask itself what the basis of an engagement with the Tanzanians really was. Is one of Canada's objectives, he asked, "merely to provide a Western presence to offset East Germans and Red Chinese or are we aiming for the complete exclusion of the communists?"[555] Mr. Menzies, the chair, replied that Canada's aim was to ensure Tanzania had a military force capable of guaranteeing its internal security and independence and, as reported by Brigadier Love, this would require a minimum of four infantry battalions and a five-year program.[556] The other Committee members agreed with this assessment and that a five-year military assistance program should be recommended to Cabinet. The Memorandum to Cabinet would also spell out in detail the expected scope and costs of military assistance to Tanzania for fiscal year 1965-1966:

- Costs associated with the Training and Advisory Team of up to 35 personnel – $400,000;

- Training in Canada for 25 Tanzanian personnel – $132,500;

- Engineering Survey for the future Military Training Centre – $32,500;

- Fifty Pre-fabricated huts (built in 1953) as an interim solution for the Military Academy – $182,500;

- Construction costs for a new Military Academy – $1 million spread over three years;

- Surplus Canadian military equipment – $500,000; and

- Recurring support after 31 March 1966 – estimated at $700,000.[557]

With the Memorandum to Cabinet now tabled, Cadieux recommended to Cabinet that Canada approve a military assistance program for Tanzania consisting of no more than 33 personnel. The prime minister was in agreement even though in his final opinion Canada's efforts would likely not "have a substantial impact on developments in that part of Africa where the Chinese were very active."[558] Space was also made available for 25 Tanzanian trainees in Canada and the High Commissioner in Dar es Salaam was authorized to negotiate an agreement covering military assistance over the five-year period.[559] Then, with a fair degree of fanfare, Pearson issued a statement concerning the provision of Canadian military training and advisory assistance to Tanzania, on 8 December 1964:

> On September 22, 1964, the Secretary of State for External Affairs stated in the House of Commons that the Government was actively considering a request for military assistance which had been received from Tanzania, and that a Military Survey Team had been sent to that country. The Team have since submitted their report, and the Government has, after careful consideration, concurred in their recommendation that the most valuable contribution Canada could make to the development of the Tanzanian defence and security forces would be in the field of military training and advice concerning defence organization.
>
> It is a source of great personal satisfaction to me that suitable means have been found for Canada to cooperate with the United Republic of Tanzania in the development of the defence and internal security forces of that important member of the Commonwealth. We respect the desire of the Tanzanian Government to follow a policy of non-alignment, and the programme which has been agreed in principle between our two Governments is in no way intended to interfere with that policy. However, experience has shown that the assurance of stability is an essential prerequisite for the implementation of effective programmes of economic and social development, and such stability cannot be assured without adequate security forces. That Canada should assist Tanzania in the training and organization of such forces is entirely appropriate, particularly in the view of the contributions we are already making to Tanzania's development programme.[560]

CHAPTER 9

The provision of a training team to Tanzania meant that Canada was fast becoming an important supplier of military assistance in sub-Saharan Africa. And, as was previously noted, the Canadian government and military had learned a good deal from their experiences in Ghana and to a lesser extent with Nigeria. Thus, before the Canadian contingent left for Tanzania, the Commander of what would be known as the Canadian Armed Forces Advisory Training Team Tanzania (CAFATTT) was provided with "political guidance" to assist him in the conduct of the mission. The political guidance opened with an assessment of the country, its leader and Canadian economic and technical development activities. Tanzania was described as "one of the poorest countries in Africa" facing a massive development problem but nevertheless led by a "highly capable leader of moderate political views with a distinct pro-western orientation."[561] As far as economic and technical aid was concerned there were 22 Canadian teachers and teacher trainers plus 10 technical advisors in the country. Twenty-six Tanzanian students were on training programs in Canada and Canada had agreed to engage in a $1 million aerial mapping project in south-eastern Tanzania. Another $200,000 in equipment had been provided to the Dar es Salaam Technical College.[562] More importantly, Dar es Salaam was identified as the home of several African liberation movements. The Tanzanian Foreign Minister, as previously mentioned, was also indentified in the political guidance as the Chairman of the OAU Liberation Committee.

The reasons for providing aid to Tanzania were also given in the political guidance. First, military assistance was deemed to be a cost-effective means for the West to support President Nyerere in the maintenance of order in Tanzania – a condition deemed essential for economic and social progress. Second, the President wanted modest armed forces and therefore it was well within the means of Canada to support his efforts, even though most of the military infrastructure developed by the British in Eastern Africa was in Kenya. Canada had also maintained good relations with Tanzania since its independence and was a viable western alternative to a continuing British military mission. The "urgings" of the British and Americans on Canada to help offset the communist presence was also noted as key reason for the military assistance mission.[563] Finally, the new Commander was advised that, "political discussions, although unavoidable at times, should not be indulged in or carried to great lengths.

Although the possibility of communist military help was an important reason for the decision to send the team to Tanzania, experience has shown that attempts by Westerners to point out the evils of communism are often not productive and hence should normally be avoided."[564]

Armed with their political guidance, the training team advance party, commanded by Colonel H.E.C. Price from the Regiment of Canadian Guards, arrived in Dar es Salaam on 23 January 1965. They were soon joined by Lieutenant-Colonel J.C. Gardner from the Fort Garry Horse who became the senior training advisor while Major John Rozee, with the Royal Canadian Army Service Corps, acted as the senior logistics officer. Besides these three officers, the initial team that arrived in Tanzania included six additional Majors, three Captains and 12 Sergeants.[565]

Their first task was to confirm the actual strength of the Tanzanian military, the state of training and the types and serviceability of weapons, vehicles and general equipment. Based on their assessment a training plan was drawn up and steps undertaken to establish a military academy. The team also wrote detailed policy papers on the future establishment of the Tanzanian People's Defence Force and the organization and equipment of infantry battalions, which were both subsequently approved and implemented by the Tanzanian authorities. Colonel Price also noted in his first quarterly report the challenges the team would face given the diversity of training being offered to the Tanzanians. For instance, he mentioned that of the 91 Tanzanian officer candidates in training, 11 were in Canada, 61 in the United Kingdom, eight in Egypt and 11 more in the Soviet Union. Furthermore, a Chinese military assistance team was in Dar es Salaam training 500 reserve force personnel on the use of small arms – the Chinese, he noted, were expected to leave in May 1965.

However, the Chinese had also taken over the training of the Tanzanian Marine Police in 1965 and they would provide the Tanzanians with four patrol boats the following year – a move leading to the eventual stand-up of a Chinese-trained navy. Russian instructors had also been spotted in Arusha training with one of the battalions.[566] Still, the presence of the Chinese and Russians would be soon overshadowed in a series of events that would result in Canada making its largest military training commitment ever to a developing country. The catalyst for what followed began in Bonn, West Germany and would lead to the RCAF replacing the German air force training mission that Brigadier Love had mentioned in his visit report.

In March 1965, Norman Berlis, Canada's new High Commissioner in Tanzania, provided External Affairs with the details of a meeting he had held with President Nyerere regarding Tanzania's relations with East and West Germany. Problems with the two German states had arisen following the union between Tanganyika and Zanzibar – Tanganyika had developed good relations with West Germany and Zanzibar with East Germany. President Nyerere knew that if his government recognized East Germany that the West Germans would likely cut off military and economic assistance. The most the West Germans would accept, said the President, was an East German trade mission in Dar es Salaam.

In the end, the Tanzanian government permitted the move of the East German "embassy" in Zanzibar to Dar es Salaam, but their new offices would only be allowed the designation "Consulate General." Furthermore, the President determined that the Tanzanian government, in order to soothe relations with Bonn, would not officially recognize East Germany. Nevertheless, the West Germans were not mollified, withdrawing their military aid immediately. Additionally, Nyerere was warned that all other West German programs, economic and technical, would likely be eliminated as well – essentially a threat that if the East Germans were allowed to re-locate to Dar es Salaam there would be further consequences for the Tanzanian government. The West German position, Nyerere had told the High Commissioner had "really made him angry."[567] Thus, and as soon as the West Germans began pulling out their military training team, he ordered all other West German aid programs to end immediately. In need of another country to help build his air force, Nyerere turned to Canada. Indeed, he may have been indirectly influenced by Brigadier Love, who, in his final briefing to the President had said, "from a soldier's point of view, military training and advice is best supplied from a single source so that one plan is followed, one military philosophy is developed, one set of standards is established."[568]

Love, at the time, was undoubtedly making reference to the growing Chinese presence in Tanzania and not the West German military assistance team. Nevertheless, the Canadian High Commissioner in Dar es Salaam was eager to embrace Love's way of thinking and have Canada take the place of West Germany. As he wrote in a letter to External Affairs, there might also be scope for aircraft sales provided the repayment terms were generous and no doubt "some of our people would very much like to sell Canadian aircraft to Tanzania." Moreover, he continued:

> It stands to reason that Nyerere would want as quickly as possible to find some other source for air force assistance. Not only is this a project which has a goodly prestige element attached to it, but I think Nyerere will feel the need to show his own people that Tanzania has other friends and does not depend on Germany. I am flattered that Nyerere has turned first to Canada, for this is further evidence of his faith in us – even though I am well aware of the complications which this will pose.
>
> One complication will surely be that we would not want to have any misunderstandings with the Germans if we should pick up a project abandoned for sensitive political reasons. But I imagine the Germans will understand that, even though they felt impelled to make the gesture, it would be better for Canada to pick up the pieces than China or Yugoslavia or one of the other "friends" who will doubtless be willing to help. We went into the business of military training with the expectation that we would be able to work closely with the Germans. It might well affect the success of our military training programme if we should now find that an unfriendly country was taking over the German Air Force role. If Canada does not agree, I assume that Nyerere will feel that he must continue to approach other countries until he finds a taker – I can't think of other western countries likely to have the facilities for taking this on, and thus it seems to me that a real danger has arisen of a communist country being given this golden opportunity to increase very substantially its influence in East Africa.[569]

A program to support the Tanzanian air force, by building up a transport air wing of approximately 450 personnel, was therefore announced by Ottawa in September 1965 and the RCAF training team, led by Group Captain G.H. Currie arrived soon after.[570] As Colonel Price wrote, "the air force contingent also has its work cut out for it. They are, in fact, building a small air wing from scratch."[571] While basic flight and trades training for the Tanzanian air force were to be conducted in Canada, the plan called for advanced training to be carried out in Tanzania by the Canadian team. This latter requirement would necessitate the establishment of a supply section, a ground school, an avionic section and a training group to provide advanced aero engine, airframe, instrument, electrical, and telecommunications trades training. Conversion training to *Otter* and *Caribou* aircraft for Tanzanian pilots returning from Canada would also have to be done. Fortunately, the West Germans did leave some of their equipment behind including stands, benches, generators, starters and four vans.[572]

With the arrival of the RCAF, the training team assigned to Tanzania was divided into two groups – advisory and training. The key difference was that the advisory team, at the defence headquarters in Dar es Salaam, was posted to Tanzania for two years and therefore could bring their families. Those assigned to the training group were on a one-year unaccompanied tour at Colito Barracks outside Dar es Salaam. At the new military academy, with its staff of 250, 18 Canadian officers were given key positions in the academy's five wings: administrative, basic training, officer training, battalion training and technical training. In 1966, 47 courses were planned at the academy while two-man Canadian training teams were also sent out to assist units develop training plans and exercises.[573]

In all, the assistance program in Tanzania would consist of the following: up to 25 personnel training the army and up to 57 personnel to create and train the air wing. Up to 25 positions had also been authorized on an annual basis for officer cadet training in Canada beginning in 1964 until 1969 – the course conducted between September 1965 and September 1966, had 17 of 25 vacancies filled. By January 1966, 24 Tanzanian pilot trainees were also in Canada, while at Camp Borden 63 air force technical trainees were on various courses.[574] Canadian officers were also asked to assist their Tanzanian counterparts in other ways. For example,

Colonel Price became a key advisor to Brigadier-General Sarakikya. A new Tanzanian Defence Act and a Pension and Superannuation Act were drafted by the training team and published by the government. Given the Tanzanian Army had Chinese weapons but no drill manuals in English, the Canadians wrote these as well. Lastly, Colonel Price reported to Ottawa on a visit by two of his officers to a Tanzanian run, FRELIMO supply depot:

> Large holdings of various types of stores and foodstuffs held at former Prison Services training compound Kienduchi near Colito Barracks were reviewed by Lt Col Rozee and Maj Chaln at the request of the TPDF officers charged with their care. Recommendations were made for improvement and disposal of unserviceable and unidentifiable items. These stores are held for FRELIMO and are gradually being issued presumably to training camps in various parts of Tanzania. Although food including Russian canned pork in rusted and blown cans and rat infested flour and rice, appeared to be dangerous to health and the lowest quality, the issuing officers stated that "there had been no complaints" which would indicate that the users must be fairly dedicated fighters or awfully hungry.[575]

Along with training assistance in Tanzania and Canada, the building of a new military academy in Tanzania was a high priority for the Canadian Government, and the entire cost of the project was estimated to be $5.2 million, of which Canada would contribute half the funds. This was a considerable sum, considering the 1964 Memorandum to Cabinet said construction costs would amount to just $1 million spread over three years. However, the Military Assistance Committee was convinced the money would be well spent and that "it would be desirable for Canada to leave in Tanzania at the end of the five year army programme a creditable reminder of its military assistance contribution."[576] Cabinet agreed with this assessment, indicating also that Canada should assume control of the entire construction effort and that a team could head to Tanzania in late January or early February 1968 to begin working out the details so that construction could begin.[577]

CHAPTER 9

In 1968, with almost 90 Canadian military advisors now working in Tanzania and the overall program developing very well, there was every expectation in Ottawa that Tanzania would ask for an extension of Canada's military assistance mission for several more years to come. As it was, the Tanzanian government would have a change of heart and little by little, the Chinese would also chip away at Canada's military assistance efforts. The beginning of the end to Canada's military presence in Tanzania commenced with the 1966-1967 Tanzanian defence budget in which a need for tanks and artillery was identified. Up until now, the Tanzanian battalions had only been equipped with light weapons, mostly of Chinese origin. If Western countries were unwilling to provide Tanzania with tanks, however, the Chinese position was exactly the opposite.[578]

In due course a tank squadron was organized and 14 Chinese T-62 light tanks, along with maintenance support were provided to the Tanzanians as a gift.[579] In addition to heavy weapons, the Tanzanian Government was also eager to acquire fighter aircraft and training, which "they felt they needed to deal with the Portuguese."[580] However, it was fear of being drawn into a regional conflict that resulted in Cabinet rebuffing a Tanzanian request for Canadian fighter aircraft and this decision would soon set the conditions for an end to Canada's military assistance to Tanzania in January 1970. As for the fighters, the Chinese readily filled the gap, building an air base at Ngeregere near Dar es Salaam, training jet fighter pilots in China and supplying a squadron of 12 MIG-17 jets for the air force in 1974.[581]

Another contentious issue for the Military Assistance Committee in 1969, concerned the future of the yet to be built military academy and Canada's agreement to pay $2.6 million or 50% of the construction costs. There had already been considerable procrastination regarding this file for a variety of reasons. Now that the Canadian training team would leave Tanzania there was apprehension that a new Academy could fall into communist hands. As Brigadier-General Tellier noted in his report after visiting Tanzania in March 1969, "the Commander of our military assistance team and his principal advisors all very strongly recommended against our becoming involved in any way, shape or form in the building of this academy in the light of recent events. We would, in fact, be involved in building an academy to be used by instructors of the Chinese People's Republic."[582] That was more than enough reason for an already cashed strapped Military Assistance Committee to pull its support.[583]

As for Prime Minister Trudeau, the end of the Canadian military assistance mission in Tanzania, more than likely, was a relief as he would have wanted to avoid any diplomatic problems arising from potential disagreements between Canadian and Chinese military advisors given his desire to establish formal relations with mainland China as quickly as possible. He had turned his attention to the issue of recognizing Beijing soon after coming into office and Canada's ambassador in Sweden made his first contact with the People's Republic chargé d'affaires in February 1969. From there, negotiations proceeded at a "desultory pace" but relations were eventually established in October 1970 with almost immediate economic benefits.[584] Canada had begun wheat shipments to China in May 1961, but in 1970-1971, Canada's share of the Chinese import wheat market climbed from 65% to 100%.[585]

As Canadian military assistance to Tanzania began winding down in late 1969, Ottawa's economic assistance and general aid, on the other hand, increased. In fact, by 1970, Tanzania was Canada's top recipient of foreign aid.[586] However, the aid supplied was not necessarily provided for purely selfless reasons. As Linda Freeman noted, more than 80 per cent of the aid Canada sent was "tied aid" requiring the Tanzanian government to purchase goods and services from Canadian businesses. This proved very lucrative for companies such as International Harvester, a major supplier of farm machinery for a joint Canadian-Tanzanian wheat-growing program, the first phase that began in 1970.[587]

Because of his reliance on Canadian aid, and the need for Canadian military assistance of some sort after 1970, Nyerere did not wish to damage relations with Ottawa too much over the fighter issue. During a four-day visit to Canada in September 1969 he went out of his way, during a lunch given by Trudeau, to recognize Canada's military assistance efforts. He began his speech by praising Pearson's efforts to resolve the Suez Crisis of 1956 and Canada's position on Rhodesia and South Africa. "Small and poor countries like mine," he added, "have warm respect for Canada; we do not find your comparative power intimidating, but rather a reassurance in world affairs." It was this reciprocal respect between the two countries, Nyerere explained that:

> Tanzania appealed to Canada in 1964, when it became necessary for us to ask for assistance in military training. The Canadian Government was reluctant to respond to this appeal because of the very understandable, and indeed very good reason that this country did not wish even to appear to be involved in the military affairs of other nations. These scruples Tanzania respects, but I am glad to say that our two countries were able to agree on practical assistance which reduced this danger to a minimum. It was agreed that we should not have 'military advisors'; these are rather discredited in the modern world. But Canada did undertake to help us with the training of officers and with the establishment of an Air Transport Wing for the People's Defence Forces.

> Mr. Prime Minister, I wish to take this opportunity to say that we appreciate the assistance. The work has been extremely well done and the officers and men of the Canadian Forces have been helpful and very correct. They have enhanced the reputation of this country as one which respects others even while helping them.

> The fact that Tanzania has now given notice that we shall not ask for a renewal of this five-year contract is thus a tribute to Canada. It does not mark a deterioration in relations, nor the growth of any suspicions or hostilities between us. We are able to allow this agreement to come to its natural end because most of the things which were agreed upon will have been completed by the due date. Mr. Prime Minister – thanks to the work of Canadians in Tanzania and in this country – we believe that, for the most part, we shall be able to take over officer training ourselves next year. We shall also be able to maintain the Air Transport Wing which you have helped us establish.[588]

In Ottawa there was a sense of relief that the Tanzanian mission was about to end given the number of politically contentious issues that had occurred in East Africa.[589] Certainly, the Chinese presence in the country was cause for ongoing unease. However, foremost amongst the concerns in External Affairs with the Tanzanian mission had been the arrival of the air force training team in December 1965, shortly after Rhodesia's Unilateral Declaration of Independence on 11 November 1965. The issue with the deployment was that External Affairs believed Rhodesia might view the arrival of the Canadian team as a hostile move given their aim was to create a new Tanzanian air force and therefore a potential future threat. The same assessment equally applied to the Portuguese in Mozambique who would have also regarded the formation of a Tanzanian air force as a danger.

Nevertheless, the final estimation was that withdrawing Canadian training teams from Ghana, Tanzania and Nigeria wholesale would be counterproductive as their departure would likely be interpreted "by Africans (however mistakenly) as an indication that not only did we not propose to take what the Africans regarded as the necessary measures to bring down the Smith regime, but that we also wished to stand in the way of Africans taking such measures."[590] To ensure Canadian Forces personnel did not become involved in operations, directly or indirectly, External Affairs had issued, in 1965, instructions "to all our teams in Africa reminding them of their non operational status with reference to the Rhodesian situation. Our team in Tanzania in particular has been instructed not to provide advice or participate in planning of any kind with regard to any military measures which Tanzania may consider or adopt in the Rhodesian crisis."[591]

Besides the Rhodesian issue, the Canadian Government was also well aware that Tanzania was home to many liberation movements. This was no secret. Indeed, in October 1964, the Canadian government had already noted that "in recent weeks, an armed struggle for the "liberation" of Mozambique [had] been launched."[592] President Nyerere, during a speech at the University of Toronto almost exactly five years later said quite clearly that his country had been and was "naturally and inevitably allies of the freedom fighters."[593] The problem for Canada was that the majority of these "freedom fighters" were in FRELIMO fighting a NATO ally, Portugal. Furthermore, the Tanzanian military was aiding FRELIMO and the Tanzanian army, trained and mentored by the Canadian Forces, likely caused the Portuguese to think twice before crossing the Rovuma River on hot pursuit missions.[594]   Additionally, both South Africa and Rhodesia were claiming, at a time when the Russian and Chinese presence in Africa was considerable, that they were the last two bastions of anti-communism in sub-Saharan Africa.

In fact, Nyerere was clear with his audience in Toronto that since Western countries were not willing to secure peaceful change in sub-Saharan Africa by stopping their support for the Portuguese, Rhodesians and South Africa, the only choice left was for African countries to ask the Soviet Union and the Chinese for military assistance. However, he was quick to point out that African states were not blind. "We do not imagine," he told his listeners, "that communism makes great powers less subject to the temptations of greatness." Nor, Nyerere wished to point out, were Tanzanians communist. Communist supplies of arms and training were welcome, he said, out of pure necessity. As for the threat communism posed, he recognized "the possibility that those who are helping us may have different motives. That is what we are told and we have no proof that it is not so. But we do have proof of our existing need and of practical offers of help."[595]

With the Canadian training team out of Tanzania, External Affairs was, however, not willing to abandon Nyerere completely as there were compelling reasons for keeping a small military presence in Tanzania. Monitoring the Chinese was one factor but it was also clear in Ottawa that the Tanzanian air wing needed some form of continuing help. Certainly, noted an External Affairs memorandum written in December 1970:

> It has become quite apparent to the Tanzanian air wing since the termination of our training agreement, that they must institute a training programme for pilots and technicians if they are going to maintain themselves. The Canadian officer, Major Joy, who is still in Tanzania, has become involved in Tanzanian efforts to set up the necessary courses. As all previous courses were run in Canada or by Canadians the training publications and films were Canadian.[596]

It was then recommended that Canada provide $15,000 (a one time gift) to help the Tanzanians produce the publications they needed. Furthermore, the Military Assistance Committee decided that Major Joy would remain in Tanzania for two more years and if a Pilot Training Advisor were to be available then this already running position would be re-staffed.[597] The provision of training courses in Canada for Tanzanian students would also continue well past 1970 with vacancies offered at the Army Staff College, on air traffic controller and terminal equipment technician courses.

Regarding the overall effort to support Tanzania, the Military Assistance Committee concluded that although Canada had not succeeded in keeping the Chinese military out of Tanzania, the CAFATTT had succeeded in postponing this development until the Tanzanian forces were basically organized and "in a much better position to deal with possible Chinese subversion."[598] That the mission itself even lasted for five years without any major incidents, said Sanger, was, in his view, "a remarkable record in a country where there are few friends of NATO."[599] That the mission ever started, however, is perhaps even more remarkable. An initial request for Canadian military assistance had arrived in Ottawa in 1962, but a more direct appeal came in July 1963 when Nyerere visited Ottawa. Yet, at the time of the second request, Pearson's Liberals had only been in power a few short months and the Department of National Defence was preoccupied with the possibility of re-structuring. Plus, Canada already had a training team in Ghana and the UN missions in the Congo and Egypt were ongoing. Consequently, no help for Tanzania was forthcoming and six months after Nyerere left Ottawa empty-handed his military mutinied. While it is impossible to determine if a decision to support Tanzania in 1963 might have prevented the mutiny, the Canadian government was prepared, in December 1965, to sign an agreement to establish a Canadian training mission that would re-build the Tanzanian army over a five-year period.

The Government's stated reasons for providing military assistance to Tanzania, on the surface at least, made perfect sense. Nyerere was considered pro-Western and the needs of the Tanzanian army were described as "sufficiently modest" allowing Canada to make "a meaningful contribution" towards the future security of the country. Establishing a good degree of internal stability was also described as a necessary precursor to any other development work. Yet, it is doubtful that the Canadian government would have ever sent a training team to Tanzania if not for the presence of the Chinese. Indeed, Brigadier Love arrived in Dar es Salaam just one month after the *Observer* reported on the arrival of Chinese military instructors in August 1964. Brigadier-General Sarakikya may have been quite right to criticize a lack of response from Western nations to Tanzania's military assistance prior to August 1964. How surprised he must have been though, to see the prompt arrival of the Canadian survey team in September 1964.

The good news, from a Canadian perspective, was the survey team could count on several years worth of experience in Ghana to guide them in their planning. Including Colonel Deane-Freeman, the Canadian military attaché in Ghana as part of the team, was also a clever decision as his experiences were invaluable when President Nyerere asked Love to furnish him with a complete force structure review. When Love returned to Ottawa and completed his final report, the inclusion of an assessment of the Tanzanian economy served as a fine example of a Canadian government approaching its offer of military assistance with great care and consideration, instead of just doing whatever the Tanzanian government wanted. The political guidance given to the CAFATTT prior to deployment was also another example of capturing, for the team leader, Canada's complete development efforts in Tanzania to better improve his situational awareness.

As for the growth of the CAFATTT mission to encompass the training of the air force – there was no expectation of having to provide a team to build the Tanzanian air force in late 1964 as the West Germans had already established a program for this express purpose. When Canada did find itself accepting responsibility for providing additional assistance, concern then arose over the possibility that Rhodesia and the Portuguese authorities in Mozambique might construe a modern Tanzanian air force as a threat. What is again noteworthy is the speed at which the Canadian air force training team assembled. Trouble between the Tanzanian and West German governments had arisen in early 1965 over the future of their military assistance team, but once a decision was taken in Bonn to pull out of Tanzania it did not take long for the Canadian government to respond. No doubt urged on by their allies, and perhaps enthusiastic over the possibility of future aircraft sales, the Canadians tasked with building up the Tanzanian air force were firmly in place by January 1966.

As the CAFATTT established itself and began the process of building up the Tanzanian army and air force the Military Assistance Committee believed Nyerere would ask Pearson to maintain the team past the agreed upon five-year program. However, the 1966-1967 Tanzanian defence budget in which the government identified a need for tanks and artillery marked a turning point. It will be recalled that Cadieux had said early on in response to the Deputy Minister of Finance that the presence of a Canadian advisory team "would encourage a concentration upon modest and practical projects consistent with Tanzania's real needs and the resources it may reasonably expect to have available." Tanks, artillery and later a desire to obtain fighter jets could hardly now be considered as consistent with Tanzania's real needs – at least from a Canadian perspective.

There was, in Ottawa, also a genuine fear of being drawn into a regional conflict and the Canadian government was well aware that their Canadian-trained Tanzanian army was aiding the various rebel groups based in Tanzania. As Martin Bailey observed, it was simply, for the Canadian government, becoming "too dangerous to allow Canada, a NATO member, to train an army that was almost in a state of war with Portuguese troops in Mozambique."[600] However, there was great care taken not to irrevocably damage relations with Dar es Salaam over the withdrawal of the CAFATTT. Even when the Military Assistance Committee had very limited funds in its budget, a small program of military assistance for Tanzania continued well beyond the official CAFATTT mandate.

CHAPTER 10

TRUDEAU AND THE CESSATION OF CANADA'S MILITARY ASSISTANCE

> *Our enemies are the political profiteers, the swindlers, the men in the high and low places that seek bribes and demand 10 percent; those that seek to keep the country divided permanently so that they can remain in office as ministers and VIPs of waste; the tribalists, the nepotists; those that made the country look big-for-nothing before the international circles; those that have corrupted our society and put the Nigerian political calendar back by their words and deeds.*

> Major Chukwuma Nzeogwu, Nigeria, 15 January 1966

> *I think the people who are in the armed forces have a right to know where we are going…many people in our universities, many people in our financial circles, many people in our provincial governments are saying we are spending too much on defence.*

> Prime Minister Pierre Trudeau, 12 April 1969

On 25 June 1968, Canadians went to the polls and elected a majority Liberal government. Pierre Elliot Trudeau, who had taken over from Lester Pearson that same year, was affirmed as Canada's prime minister.[601] Trudeau had entered politics in 1965, winning his seat in Mount Royal, Quebec. Then, just two years later, Pearson appointed him Minister of Justice. Pearson, however, was ready to leave politics in 1967 after failing to win a majority government after two attempts. He announced his retirement in December 1967, paving the way for the Liberal Party to choose a new leader, which they did on 5 April 1968.

At the beginning of his term in office, Trudeau was hampered by a lack of funds brought on by the immense cost of sustaining social programs introduced by his predecessor. In an interview held in early 1969 he spoke of how his government could not support any new programs and that continuing with the old ones would be difficult. "Since we've been in power," he said, "we've cut a number of things, for instance winter works, the causeway to Prince Edward Island, the telescope in British Columbia… Despite all these cuts, you see that spending forecasts keep increasing because all the plans we have embarked on for health, hospitals, education etc.… the costs are climbing at a frightening pace. We've cut a lot everywhere, and we're still short of money."[602]

A lack of money for social programs coupled with a relatively healthy defence budget was obviously on the mind of the prime minister when he spoke at a dinner given by the Liberal Association of Alberta in April 1969. The topic was his government's planned reorientation of foreign policy away from NATO. The changes Canada was making, he said, would be far reaching, affect all Canadians and last a generation:

> Our foreign policy, the one we are defining for Canada, is also very important for another reason. Our defence budget as you know is one-sixth of the total budget. That's a lot of money – $1,800 million for defence. And it's a lot of money especially when you realize that it's accompanied by a great deal of uncertainty by Canadians. There is a tendency in the past few years, when more money is needed for housing or more money is needed for anti-pollution schemes or more money is needed for social welfare legislation, for every form of expenditure in Canada (a project here, a research grant there), on the part of individuals, on the part of institutions and on the part of provincial governments, to say to the Federal government "Spend less on defence, you'll have more for this other worthwhile project" – whether it be education or health or housing or urban growth. There is a tendency on the part of all Canadians to say "Take it away from defence, you will have more money for the worthwhile things" – implying, I suppose (and this comes, as I say, from many institutions, and even from provincial governments), that the money we spend on defence is not well spent.[603]

Trudeau's April 1969 speech was likely not a surprise for the bureaucracy in Ottawa who would have been well aware the prime minister strongly believed that Canada's foreign and defence policies were outdated. During the months preceding the 1968 election, Trudeau had already issued "Canada and the World," his major foreign policy statement, in which he announced that his government, if elected, would immediately undertake an all-encompassing review of Canada's foreign and defence policies. For him, defence policy had led foreign policy for far too long, and in particular, Canada's role in NATO dominated both, leaving little room for imagination and change. In fact, Trudeau believed that the emergence of the developing world and the need for a better distribution of wealth between the have and the have-not nations was of far greater importance for Canada's long-term security than spending money on defence. In a 1968 speech he remarked: "that in the long run the overwhelming threat to Canada will not come from foreign investments or foreign ideologies, or even – with good fortune – foreign nuclear weapons. It will come instead from two-thirds of the people of the world who are steadily falling farther and farther behind in their search for a decent standard of living."[604] Thus, Canada's Overseas Development Aid (ODA) contributions grew dramatically when he was first in power and by 1974 had increased to 0.51% of GNP. In fact, ODA was one of the few budgetary allocations not cut back by the government at the time.[605]

While economic and technical aid was a high priority for Trudeau, he was not at all content to have the Canadian Forces continue providing military assistance to the developing world. Nor was he eager to sell weapons to countries that could not afford them. In November 1968, he made his arms sales policy clear in a memorandum circulated in Cabinet on aid policies and arms purchases. If a country receiving Canadian aid, he noted, embarked upon major purchases of sophisticated weapons when no real threat existed to its security, overall assistance to that country would need to be carefully reviewed to determine whether its continuation was justified. Simply put, Trudeau was not at all convinced that military aid of any kind to the developing world was useful and he would ultimately stop the Canadian Forces from having any meaningful role in doing so.[606] Trudeau was also adamant that Canada would not become entangled in Cold War intrigues in the developing world or anywhere else for that matter and the substantial Canadian military assistance missions in Ghana and Tanzania had certainly left plenty of cause for concern in Ottawa. Thus, when the 1971 Defence White Paper was published it was clear the government's defence priorities had changed. Certainly, military assistance was no longer a priority.

Well before the 1971 Defence White Paper, the fact was that Trudeau had already determined the Canadian Forces were too expensive, overextended and "simply incapable of assuming seriously the additional and alternative tasks that the new government expected would be necessary."[607] More to the point, he did not agree that Canada's presence in NATO, at a cost of $120 million per year, was at all politically influential. He also believed the Soviet Union no longer constituted a major threat and the underlying basis of Canadian defence policy was, therefore, completely mistaken. Instead, Trudeau wanted alternatives to foreign and defence policies that were being driven by membership in NATO and NORAD and by increasing yet inconclusive UN missions. Trudeau, said Radwanski, essentially regarded foreign policy as being mainly concerned with the pursuit of domestic policy abroad and was unconvinced that assigning the country a broader international role served any purpose. "We shouldn't be trying to run the world. We should be trying to make our own country a good place," Trudeau told CTV in 1968. That same year he was quoted in the *Toronto Star* as saying "We're perhaps more the largest of the small powers than the smallest of the large powers."[608]

In the lead up to the 1971 Defence White Paper, Trudeau took the decision on 15 May 1968 to launch a formal defence review. This was followed by a Cabinet decision on 19 July 1968 to conduct a global foreign policy assessment. However, when the first, draft defence review was presented to Cabinet in August 1968 it was rejected "on the grounds that it amounted to nothing more than a reaffirmation of current policy."[609] What Trudeau wanted were options – including the potential impact of what might happen if Canada withdrew from NATO altogether. He was also focused on domestic defence, stemming from separatist bombings that had occurred in Quebec throughout the 1960s and a major riot in Montreal just before the 1968 general election. Two years later, attacks on Canada by the Front for the Liberation of Quebec (FLQ), had resulted in the deployment of 12,500 troops in Montreal (Operation Essay) and Ottawa (Operation Ginger) under the 1970 War Measures Act. "Except for one infantry battalion and an armoured regiment held in Calgary," noted Dan Loomis, "the entire army and tactical airforce in Canada was deployed in a massive show of force."[610] Barney Danson, a member of Trudeau's Liberal government also recorded how, "the atmosphere in Ottawa, and particularly on the Hill, was bunker like. There were armed military personnel at all critical points in the city [and] each minister and each embassy was assigned guards on a twenty-four hour basis. Parliament Hill was virtually an armed camp."[611] Jack Granatstein, summarizing the situation at the time, added that:

> The idea of Canada as an ordered conservative society had been severely shaken. For the government, the lesson of 1970 seemed to be that the barrel of available, reliable military force had been scraped. Just enough troops for the task had been available. If more had been necessary, Ottawa might have been forced to bring the boys home from NATO duty or from Cyprus peacekeeping.[612]

For Trudeau, the simple fact of maintaining troops in NATO, supporting NORAD and deploying on UN missions had become impossible to sustain. A potentially larger role at home just complicated matters, as there was simply not enough money to do everything. Between the 1968-69 and the 1972-73 fiscal years, for example, defence spending had grown from just $1.761 billion to $1.932 billion – a $171 million increase that could not even keep the defence budget ahead of inflation. As a result, the money for capital expenditures decreased to just 8.0% of the budget while personnel levels fell from 98,473 in 1968 to 81,626 in 1972.[613] Compared to the 120,871 men and women in the military in 1963 this was a dramatic decline in fortune.[614]

Given the prime minister's reluctance to support NATO and the need to respond to domestic crises, the 1971 Defence White Paper was a major departure from its 1964 predecessor that stressed peacekeeping and international obligations. For the foreseeable future, the Canadian Forces would have the following priorities:

- The surveillance of Canadian territory and coastlines;

- The defence of North America in cooperation with the United States;

- The fulfillment of such NATO commitments as may be agreed upon; and

- The performance of such international peacekeeping roles as from time to time might be assumed by the government."[615]

With regards to Canada's military role in NATO, the document went on to say that the Canadian government would intend, "in consultation with Canada's allies, to take early steps to bring about a planned and phased reduction of the size of the Canadian Forces in Europe."[616] These eventual reductions were significant. The 10,000 personnel assigned to NATO were reduced by 50 per cent. What remained amounted to a 2,800 man ground force and three squadrons of F-104 *Starfighter* aircraft whose nuclear strike role was replaced by ground support and reconnaissance missions. As for the rest of the military, the government decided to sell the last navy aircraft carrier, the *Bonaventure*, decrease the Reserves from 23,000 to 19,000 personnel and close several bases.[617] Besides manpower reductions, the funds allocated towards military assistance also fell considerably under the new prime minister who was keen to phase out all such efforts as soon as possible. Indeed, Canada's military assistance was almost completely terminated in July 1969, when Cabinet decided that military assistance to developing countries would be phased out over a three-year period beginning in fiscal year 1970-71.

There were several reasons behind the decision to stop providing military assistance to the developing world. For one, Trudeau did not want developing countries to squander their meager resources buying weapons, but he was also very concerned that Canada might become mixed up in a proxy conflict in the developing world between the United States and the Soviet Union or even China. Then again, Trudeau was not convinced that a developing country asking the Soviets or Chinese for economic or military help was really of strategic importance to the West. In the lead up to the Cabinet decision to end military assistance, the Military Assistance Committee had gone to great lengths to convince the government that maintaining a modest program was in Canada's best interests. In summer 1969, the Committee went to work on a review of military assistance efforts so far. The aim was "to consider whether Canadian aid to developing countries should or should not continue to include a small program of military assistance in selected instances; and to discuss the nature and extent of future Canadian military assistance."[618] The review was certainly extensive and divided into five sections with four supporting Annexes as noted below:

- Section I – Introduction;

- Section II – Future Military Trends in Developing Countries;

- Section III – The Role of Canadian Military Assistance in Canadian Policy;

- Section IV – Possible Form, Location, and Size of Canadian Military Assistance;

- Section V – Summary of Recommendations;

- Annex A – Past and Present Canadian Military Assistance: Details and Assessment;

- Annex B – Military Assistance Committee Terms of Reference;

- Annex C – Select Bibliography on Military Aspects of the Developing World; and

- Annex D – Costing Criteria for Military Assistance.

The review began, likely acknowledging the fact that the prime minister regarded military assistance as a waste of time and money, by noting that there were, indeed, a large number of countries where the provision of Canadian military assistance would not be wise. In particular, it was deemed inadvisable to offer military assistance to:

- Countries which, although perhaps normally uncommitted, are openly Communist-oriented and the exclusive preserve of Communist countries in regard to military assistance;

- Countries which are a focus of confrontation between Communist and Western powers and which are receiving an abundance of military assistance from both;[619]

- Generally, parties to a conflict in which it is well established Canadian policy to remain uncommitted to either side;

- Countries which are considered to have aggressive or potentially aggressive intentions;

- Countries which have armed forces clearly in excess of legitimate defensive requirements;

- Countries in which military assistance on a significant scale might be interpreted as an implied Canadian commitment or willingness to help safeguard the security of the country in question (unless the Government wished to imply such a willingness, as a deterrent to the countries' neighbours);

- Latin America. Most Latin American countries have few external defensive needs and ample U.S. assistance; they have long been independent, and their military usually constitutes a deeply entrenched political element unlikely to be responsive to the Canadian approach to military problems; and

- Dependent territories (e.g. the Associated States in the Caribbean for which Britain retains responsibility for external affairs and defence).[620]

As a result of the guidelines, it was suggested future Canadian military assistance efforts would likely be best directed toward Southeast and South Asia, Commonwealth and Francophone countries in sub-Saharan Africa and the Caribbean. It was also suggested Canada not concentrate its military assistance efforts in any one country from now on. "The high concentration of Canadian military assistance in Tanzania in recent years," noted the report, "made for a particularly effective program but posed certain political risks at the same time." In retrospect, concluded the authors, "perhaps too many eggs were placed in the Tanzanian basket."[621] Of course, the real question the Military Assistance Committee needed to address is which countries Canada should support with military assistance.

To this end, the review suggested that limited military assistance for Malaysia, Singapore, Burma, Indonesia, Thailand, South Korea, Ceylon, Tanzania, Ghana, Zambia, Kenya, Uganda, Nigeria (post civil war), Cameroon, Congo (Kinshasa), Jamaica, Barbados, Trinidad, and Guyana would be useful from a foreign policy perspective. However, many of the countries on the list would likely have been of concern to the prime minister and nor did it make much sense to include, for example, Tanzania, which had already been technically ruled out by the Committee's own recognition that those countries with a strong communist presence were off limits for Canadian military assistance. Not only that, Tanzania had also become much more involved with supporting FRELIMO fighting the Portuguese in Mozambique. Shubi Ishemo observed, for example, that it was the Tanzanian army who had secured the border with Mozambique and provided security for FRELIMO camps inside Tanzania. As a matter of fact, an acknowledgement of the vital support obtained from Nyerere was offered by Samora Machel, the new President of an independent Mozambique, in a speech given in 1975:

> When in Mozambique we speak of Nyerere, we remember the names that are landmarks of our history. When we invoke the name of Julius Nyerere, we remember Kongwa, the military camp where we trained the guerrillas that purified the liberation struggle; we remember Tunduru, where our children learned a new life that we are building; we remember Bagamoyo, our education centre that prepared the cadres for victory which we knew was certain; we remember Mtwara, our rearguard hospital, where we treated our war wounded, and where we formed new cadres for our health services. With the name of Nyerere we remember with profound emotion, Nachingwea, the laboratory of our struggle, the camp where we trained our best soldiers and where, in our day to day work, a New Man was constructed.[622]

In Burma, democratic rule had come to end in 1962 when General Ne Win led a military *coup d'état*. In Indonesia, an attempted coup on 30 September 1965 resulted in a violent anti-communist purge, during which some 500,000 to one million people were killed. The situation was no better in

Thailand where, since 1932, the military continued to play a central role in politics. Why South Korea was on the list of potential countries for military assistance was a mystery, given that the Committee itself concluded in their review that military assistance to Seoul, in the end, would likely "not be in the Canadian interest as it could create an impression that Canada might back the South Koreans militarily in the event of a new conflict with the North."[623] Then there was Ceylon, a country facing a growing Tamil insurgency that would break out in full in April 1971. Jamaica was also plagued by civil disorder for which the Jamaica Defence Force (JDF) had to deploy for internal security purposes on more than one occasion. In South America it was recognized that Venezuela would probably continue to resort to force to settle its ongoing border dispute with Guyana.[624] As for Uganda, Idi Amin would overthrow its civilian government in 1971. Even offering token amounts of military assistance to former French colonies in Africa was problematic. "Military assistance to former French African colonies," the review noted, "would have to be provided in such a manner that the French did not feel compelled to take steps to prevent it."[625]

Obviously, the Military Assistance Committee could not predict how events would unfold in Ceylon and Uganda two years hence. Nevertheless, it is not difficult to imagine that Trudeau would have regarded the list of "acceptable" countries for Canadian military assistance, as proposed by the Military Assistance Committee, with a great deal of skepticism. For a prime minister who had done his utmost not to become embroiled in the Nigerian civil war, or to send a peacekeeping contingent afterwards, it was also unlikely he found the Committee's conclusion that "Canada might be virtually the only possible source of [military] assistance trusted by all Nigerian factions," as particularly encouraging news.[626]

In the review, the Military Assistance Committee did its best to convince Trudeau, however, that providing military assistance, although potentially not risk free, was worth the effort. Military assistance, they suggested, could help preserve internal stability so that economic development efforts could proceed without interference. Military assistance would also help the recipient country better judge their real defence needs and help developing countries focus their resources on economic development. Furthermore, Canadian military assistance could increase Canada's influence in the developing world. Modest contributions, it was pointed out, had considerable symbolic effect – the provision of transport aircraft in 1963 to India during the border war with China being a case in point. Military aid, coupled with economic and other assistance, the authors of the review concluded, would also demonstrate that Canada was concerned about all aspects of a country's development. A more comprehensive approach, it was determined, would likely result in "better receptivity" to Canadian advice in general and thus "a more effective Canadian policy in the country."[627] Economically speaking, Canadian military assistance and military sales, chiefly aircraft sales, it was correctly suggested, had provided Canadians with jobs. Still, there was general recognition that carelessly selling military equipment to developing countries was not politically prudent, as "Canadians have no wish to be thought of by anyone as merchants of death."[628]

The overall conclusion of the review was that while a major reduction in the level of military assistance was now being contemplated, the Committee believed that maintaining a limited program would be politically advantageous. "It is considered," noted the review, "that a small, selective program of military assistance can increase the effectiveness of Canadian policy in the developing world, and can contribute to Canadian efforts to promote economic and social progress, provided that such a program remains minor in scale, and is made complementary to the much larger Canadian economic aid program."[629] The review, therefore, recommended the amount of money allocated for military assistance only be reduced from $3-4 million each year to $1.5 million for fiscal year 1970-71, an amount equal to 1% of the economic aid budget. The Committee also proposed the government might wish to further reconsider this budgetary reduction in subsequent years. "A theoretical upper limit for the future," it was suggested, "could be a maximum of 2% of the economic aid budget."[630]

Trudeau, however, was not convinced that giving the Military Assistance Committee any money was money well spent. Nor was he alone in not wanting to continue providing military assistance to the developing world. For example, when the Kenyan government faced an internal security issue in the northeast along the Somali border in 1966-67, Nairobi

requested Canada provide them with a *Caribou* aircraft for use by the Kenyan Police, either as a gift or with financial assistance. The request had
not been received favourably in Canada although the Military Assistance
Committee was willing to offer the Kenyan military two *Caribou* aircraft,
thinking that future sales might result. However, the High Commissioner
in Nairobi was very concerned Kenya might end up acquiring unnecessary
and unaffordable aircraft for the Kenyan air force. "I am still doubtful,"
he wrote to External Affairs in April 1967, "that we should embark upon
a military assistance programme for Kenya." In his view, he continued,
"the Kenyan Government has shown admirable judgment and restraint
in refraining from large expenditures on unnecessary military equipment
and in giving priority to development needs. Unlike the governments of
many other new nations, the Kenyan authorities have resisted the prestige
appeal of building up their Armed Forces on a scale out of proportion to
their real requirements."[631] It would, he concluded, be irresponsible to
offer the Kenyan Government aircraft via military assistance.

In a last ditch attempt to reverse the 29 July 1969 Cabinet decision to do
away with all military assistance by 1974, External Affairs and the Department of National Defence, working through the Military Assistance
Committee, prepared a new Memorandum to Cabinet in March 1970, on
why maintaining a military assistance program was important for Canada's long-term interests. In a covering letter to the Memorandum to
Cabinet, Ministers were advised:

> Since the Cabinet Directive was issued in the context of a
> comprehensive programme designed to curb government
> expenditures, the Committee has not been in a position to
> judge whether it was based on considerations other than
> financial ones. That is, officials are unaware whether min-
> isters, in deciding to phase out military assistance, weighed
> the longer term foreign policy and economic arguments for
> and against the provision by Canada of this type of aid to
> developing countries.[632]

Ministers were also reminded of the efforts that the Canadian military
had made to support military training assistance and why Canadian help
was often sought. The reasons provided included cultural and linguistic

affinity and having well-established general aid programs often with a Commonwealth connection. Politically, Ministers were then advised that an emphasis on training foreign military officers was important as "military leaders in many developing countries, if they do not actually form the government, frequently wield much more power and influence domestically than is the case in the majority of western domestic nations."[633] It was also mentioned that it "would seem in Canada's general interest on broad foreign policy grounds to keep open the possibility of exercising a constructive influence on the men who often will form the political elite in developing countries, by continuing to provide training places for officers in our military institutions where they receive not only technical military training but are also exposed to Canadian values and attitudes."[634] Furthermore, the Memorandum to Cabinet suggested that military assistance would have a wider modernizing effect in a recipient country even though the view that modernization could be achieved through militarization had largely been dismissed by 1970. Nevertheless, the authors of the Memorandum to Cabinet relied upon William Gutteridge's *Armed Forces in New States* (1962) and John Johnson's, *The Role of the Military in Underdeveloped Countries* (1962) for inspiration, noting that:

> Military assistance may be seen as a means of insuring Canada's investment in the developing country's economic growth. Secondly, in many developing countries the military is employed in a civil role, providing essential communication, transportation and supply services to remote areas, and in the construction of public facilities. Again, strengthening the developing country's capacities in this respect can make a direct contribution to economic development. Thirdly, the shortage of skilled workers is an endemic problem in the economy of most developing countries. The pool of technically trained personnel, essential to any military establishment, provides an important economic resource. Assistance in military trades training can, therefore, make a long-term contribution to a developing country's effort to build an adequate skilled labour force.[635]

Canada, it was further noted, "had also appeared an attractive choice from a developing countries' standpoint because, while the quality of our military training and technology compare favourably with those of major nations, we are free of the stigma attaching to ex-colonial powers; nor does acceptance of military help from us have the political connotations which co-operation in this field with the great powers might carry."[636] Commercially, the Memorandum to Cabinet continued, "there can be no doubt that our ability to offer military assistance has been a significant factor in promoting the export of Canadian defence equipment."[637]

The intent of the Memorandum to Cabinet, in light of a Cabinet decision to end military assistance activities, was "to seek the Cabinet's approval for continuing military assistance on a modest scale to developing nations," past 1973-74 to an amount not exceeding $500,000 a year.[638] But before Cabinet was approached, the subject of continuing with a military assistance program was referred to the Cabinet Committee on External Affairs and Defence in November 1970. Both the Minister of National Defence, Donald Macdonald and the Secretary of State for External Affairs, Mitchell Sharp, were eager to continue with a military assistance program, but others on the Committee were not. In fact, some Ministers believed that the proposal to continue with a program of military assistance, which was an attempt to reverse an earlier Cabinet decision, was simply not a good idea. They believed, noted an External Affairs memorandum, that "the continuation of a programme, however small, might draw us into a Vietnam-type situation." Furthermore, noted the memorandum, there was a "feeling (unstated perhaps) that Canada should confine its aid to civilian projects and stay out of the military assistance business entirely."[639]

To ensure the Secretary of State was armed with the best information possible to convince his colleagues of the wisdom of continuing to assist select militaries in the developing world, his staff did their utmost to provide him with good ammunition. They suggested that he might wish to remind his colleagues that the entire recommended military assistance program was only $500,000 per year, $100,000 of which was dedicated to supporting Malaysia and Singapore following a recent foreign policy paper on the Pacific that had clearly stated Canada's intention "to provide on request some modest, carefully evaluated advisory training assistance to Malaysia and Singapore."[640] Finally, if his colleagues were concerned that Canada might become involved in a Vietnam-like situation (where military advice had escalated over time to America becoming fully engaged in the war) the Minister was advised that this was unlikely from a Canadian perspective. In particular, he was reminded "none of the twenty-four Canadian officers serving with our training team were involved in any way in the local revolution leading to the overthrow of President Nkrumah."[641] "In some cases," the Minister was advised, "certain projects have been discouraged in order to avoid any possibility of Canadian involvement in a sensitive local situation or one which could have wider international repercussions. Our discouragement of Tanzanian efforts to involve us in a jet air force programme, and our withdrawal of military assistance from Nigeria at the beginning of the Civil War are cases in point."[642]

It was not until late December 1970 that the Cabinet finally received for their consideration a Memorandum to Cabinet drafted by the Secretary of State, the Minister of National Defence and the Minister for Industry, Trade and Commerce regarding plans for a modest resumption of military assistance for developing countries including Malaysia and Singapore. Even though the amount of aid suggested, $500,000 in total, was very modest compared to Canada's former military assistance program, Prime Minister Trudeau remained unconvinced the proposal had any merit. During the discussion, following tabling of the Memorandum, he noted that on 29 July 1969, Cabinet "had decided to phase out military assistance on the grounds that such a program did not have the emphasis the government wished to see placed on such foreign policy themes as social justice."[643] Furthermore, said Trudeau, the program of military assistance being proposed "appeared to him to be particularly illiberal," and he asked his Cabinet colleagues if it were really necessary for the "Canadian government to be involved in the training of military officers of the military regimes of underdeveloped countries."[644]

In reply, Sharp stressed the importance of maintaining close ties with both Malaysia and Singapore and offered the possibility that arms sales might follow any resumption in military aid. The Minister of National Defence suggested that Canada's political influence in the region might be enhanced through closer military ties and act as a "counterweight to Chinese, British and United States involvement."[645] At the end of the discussion, there was what could be construed as a small victory for the pro-military assistance members of Cabinet as it was agreed that approximately $100,000 per year for two years would be set aside for Malaysia and Singapore. In addition, Cabinet acquiesced to a continuation of military assistance past 1974, albeit on a reduced scale. Furthermore, the Military Assistance Committee was provided with new direction:

- Funds, subject to a limit of $500,000, should be provided from the Department of External Affairs' annual budgetary allocations to cover the costs of continuing general military training programs for the armed forces of non-NATO countries;

- The funds should be applied to cover the costs of general military training programs and not for general military assistance in the supply or sale of military arms or equipment;

- The Military Assistance Committee should continue to exercise supervision over the carrying out of programs approved by the Cabinet and such other programs of military training as might in future be approved; and

- The Military Assistance Committee should refer to Cabinet for approval any proposals for the undertaking of a new program of military training assistance.[646]

For the Military Assistance Committee, the December 1970 Cabinet decision was good news. However, there was no doubt a degree of disappointment amongst the members when they were told by the Department of Finance that only $440,000 would be available for fiscal year 1971-72.[647] As it was, the Committee had been hard pressed to manage military assistance programs with the $500,000 allocated in fiscal year 1970-71, the first year of the three-year draw down period. As Table 9 demonstrates, every penny had to be managed carefully.

Country	Detail	Cost in $	Balance in $
	**1970-71 Already Approved**		
	Opening Balance		500,000
Tanzania	Team cost	30,000	470,000
	Spare parts (local purchase)	10,000	460,000
	ROTP (see endnote)	28,759	431,241
	Staff training	2,800	428,441
	Caribou engine overhaul	12,000	416,441
	Book donation	5,000	411,441
Ghana	Team cost	200,000	211,441
	Staff training	5,600	205,841
	Communications survey	1,500	204,341
Zambia	OCTP from 1969/1970	6,000	198,341
	New OCTP (see end-note)	3,400	194,941
Malaysia	Air Advisor	10,000	184,941
	Projector	141	184,800
	Visits	1,342	183,458
Jamaica	Staff training	2,800	180,658
	Pilot check team	3,200	177,458
Kenya	Staff training	2,800	174,658
Uganda	Staff training	2,350	172,308
Korea	Staff training	1,875	170,433
Trinidad and Tobago	Miscellaneous courses	15,620	154,813
	OCTP	570	154,243
Singapore	Midshipmen	19,200	135,043
Nigeria	Staff training	950	134,093
	**1970-71 Costs of Items Before Committee for Approval**		
Tanzania	New ROTP	2,500	
	Attachment Major Nkwera	525	
	Extension Major Joy	---	
Malaysia	Extension Captain Wood	10,000	Final cost for scientists depends on deploy-ment date
	Defence Research Scientists	Less than 23,000	
Singapore	Naval Training Team	Less than 103,789	Final cost for team depends on deploy-ment date
Nigeria	Liaison Visit	3,000	
	Total Cost if all ap-proved	142,814	Debit 8,721

Table 9 – Military Assistance Committee Estimate of Financial Position at 29 July 1970 for Fiscal Year 1970/71[648]

The financial situation facing the Military Assistance Committee was in stark contrast to that experienced by those responsible for Canada's ODA budget. Indeed, amongst the widespread financial cuts across government, the overall decline of the defence budget and the almost complete wrapping up of military assistance following the election of Trudeau in 1968, there was at least one bright spot and this was the amount of money allocated by the government to ODA. Trudeau's interest in bridging the gap between rich and poor nations meant money for development would increase considerably during his first four years as prime minister.

In recognition of the growing influence of CIDA, a representative of the Agency was invited to the 18th meeting of the Military Assistance Committee on 10 April 1969. The minutes of the meeting recorded that "the Chairman introduced Mr. Ingalls of CIDA to the meeting and stated that he had been invited to sit in with a view to offering any comments which he saw fit because of the related activities sponsored by CIDA in countries to which we give military assistance."[649] It is possible that the members of the Military Assistance Committee believed that partnering with CIDA might be one way to overcome their financial crisis. However, it appears that it was not until the 26th meeting held on 29 March 1972 that serious consideration was given to some sort of collaboration when a representative from External Affairs, the minutes noted, asked if it:

> Might be desirable to maintain some parallelism between CIDA programmes and the military assistance programmes in the countries of Anglophone Africa with a view to ensuring priorities were roughly similar. Mr. Wilson (CIDA) noted, however, that the CIDA programme [was] an amalgamation of a number of distinct projects and that for any given country it might differ substantially from the military assistance allotment.[650]

The potential of leveraging CIDA funds for military assistance efforts came up once more at the 27th meeting of the Military Assistance Committee held on 27 November 1972. In particular, it was suggested that if the Jamaican military were engaged in development activities then perhaps CIDA should fund them. However, Mr. Whittelton from External Affairs, observed that, "CIDA had consistently refused requests for projects where the military were directly involved." Mr. Wilson, the CIDA representative, replied that while CIDA would not rule out joint civilian and military projects, funding from the Military Assistance Committee would have to be considered first.[651]

However, with just $440,000 per year for the foreseeable future, the Military Assistance Committee must have been envious of the money flowing into the ODA budget and frustrated that they were unable to foster closer cooperation with CIDA. As External Affairs and DND suffered through budget cuts, CIDA was relatively unscathed. In fact, the total CIDA budget was overseen by a growing staff that went from 363 employees and a $223 million budget in 1968 to 937 employees in 1974 with a budget of $522 million to administer. Overseas development aid then reached a significant $903.5 million in 1975-76.[652] Thus, as military assistance funds dried up in the early 1970s, CIDA money continued to flow, with two-thirds of its ODA allocation going to 10 countries in the world, four of which were Ghana, Niger, Nigeria and Tanzania – all of which, except Niger, that had benefited from Canadian military assistance.[653]

As far as military assistance to Francophone countries in Africa was concerned, such help was practically non-existent while the Military Assistance Committee functioned. But this was not unique between 1960 and 1968 when total Canadian aid to Francophone Africa only amounted to $300,000. By 1973 though, one-fifth, or $80 million, of the CIDA budget was now being funneled to these countries.[654] New bi-lateral programs resulted in road building projects in Niger, geological surveys in Niger and Upper Volta (now Burkina Faso), electrical projects in Togo and Dahomey (now Benin) and numerous other activities across the continent. The only activity absent from the list was military assistance of any kind, no doubt partly due to the inability of the Canadian Forces to even provide French language training for their own personnel at the time.[655]

With less than $500,000, the Military Assistance Committee concentrated on managing its existing, limited programs with little room to take on any additional tasks. A request from the Iranian government to have Canada train 50 pilots a year for five years, while carefully considered by Ottawa, was eventually turned down.[656] In June 1971, the Government of Ceylon (Sri Lanka) also requested Canada help build up their armed forces. The High Commissioner in Colombo had originally suggested that a serving or retired senior officer of at least brigadier-general rank, on a short term assignment, would be helpful and this officer could provide advice on the future composition, training and equipping of the Ceylonese military. Furthermore, he had recommended the former CDS, Frank Miller, "would suit Ceylon's requirements admirably."[657]

The request for help by the Government of Ceylon had largely been driven by a Tamil insurgency that broke out in full force on 5 July 1971. Shortly afterwards, Prime Minister Sirimavo Bandaranaike had asked the Canadian government to send troops to restore order but Trudeau declined to intervene, indicating that the Canadian government would only be willing to offer non-military aid. The request for a military advisor, however, was strongly supported by External Affairs and the Under-Secretary requested the Department of National Defence assist them in convincing Cabinet that the temporary provision of a Canadian military advisor to Ceylon for at least three months would be to Canada's advantage."[658] However, the Minister of National Defence (MND) was not inclined to support the request, informing the CDS that in his view "it would not be in the Canadian interest to so involve ourselves in Ceylonese domestic affairs."[659]

Through the period 1970-73, the Military Assistance Committee was therefore limited to managing individual Canadians on specific missions and looking after foreign military students training in Canada. With regard to vacancies at the Army Staff College course in Kingston, as an example, it was believed in 1970-71 that 14 vacancies for foreign students would be available. But, as the Chairman of the Committee noted, it had been "a yearly struggle with CFHQ [Canadian Forces Headquarters] to obtain sufficient places at Staff College for the number of military assistances requests we have for this valuable training."[660] At a meeting in April 1971, the Chairman expressed his concern that the Committee would certainly not meet all its tasks with the planned 1971-72 budget of $440,000. Cameroon had requested four officer candidate places and *Buffalo* conversion training for two pilots; Jamaica needed a helicopter pilot vacancy; Kenya had asked for two pilot spots for *Chipmunk* training; Zambia wanted seven officer cadet training positions in 1971 and an additional four spots for training transport officers. Fiji had also requested two officer cadet vacancies.[661]

In 1972, new requests for assistance from Barbados and Burma would arrive in Ottawa, along with a Nigerian appeal for Canada to train 20 jet fighter pilots. Most of these requests could simply not be fulfilled due to a lack of funds. Then, in 1973, it looked as if the Military Assistance Committee's work would come to an abrupt end when the Chairman postponed a meeting in September 1973 due to an ongoing cost-cutting exercise in External Affairs that had essentially removed what money there was for military assistance work.[662] By December, the crisis had passed. The military assistance budget would be funded again to a maximum of $440,000, but not a penny more.[663]

That Canada's military assistance efforts were largely at an end was undoubtedly due to the personal influence of the prime minister. Speaking in 1969 at the National Press Club in Washington, he had told his audience how pleased Canada had been and would continue to be when its views on international matters were requested. However, he added, "we may be excused, I hope, if we fail to take seriously the suggestion from some of our friends from time to time that our acts or failure to act in this way or that way will have profound international consequences or will lead to wide-scale undesirable results."[664]

The foreign policy document *Foreign Policy for Canadians* that came out the year before the 1971 Defence White Paper provided additional proof that the prime minister would not follow in the footsteps of Pearson. Inside the document, it was not difficult to discern that when speaking of international institutions and "their continuing relevance in new world situations," that NATO and the UN were targets.[665] Furthermore, the document indicated that it would not be wise to predict what kind of role Canada would play internationally in future. Most certainly, foreign policy would no longer be based on the assumption that Canada would continue to be seen as the "helpful fixer" in international affairs.[666] In essence, the message to the rest of the world was that Canada's economic, political and social interests would now come first.

In part, however, Trudeau had little choice but to adopt a Canada first policy. For one, he had quickly realized that the country could barely afford its social programs and domestic security issues were at the forefront when he came to power. Thus, it was likely difficult for him to justify the expense of having troops in Europe, on UN missions and carrying out military assistance work in light of the economic and political situation at home. On the other hand, Trudeau was also devoted to breaking the Cold War impasse that was siphoning off money for armaments while people in the developing world were struggling to establish themselves. If elected, he said, his government would immediately undertake an all-encompassing review of Canada's foreign and defence policies.

The outcome of the review was alarming for many in Ottawa. Indeed, "the onset of the Trudeau years," was described as "a traumatic time for the old guard, both politicians and bureaucrats."[667] One could have easily added the military leadership as a third group in this "old guard." The fact was that Trudeau was unconvinced that Canada assuming a broader international role via the Canadian Forces served any useful purpose. Furthermore, he did not wish to see Canada become entwined in Cold War intrigues and the Canadian military assistance mission in Tanzania was problematic in this regard. In early 1969, for example, his government had already planned to officially recognize the People's Republic of China, which it finally did on 13 October 1970. However, if the Canadian military assistance effort in Tanzania had continued, and political issues with the Chinese arisen, Trudeau's foreign policy plans might have been easily spoiled very early on.

The decision by the government to end military assistance efforts in the developing world did not sit well with External Affairs especially as there was recognition that offering such aid was useful for political and economic reasons. Twice, in 1969 and then again in 1970, the Military Assistance Committee did their best to convince Trudeau that continuing a modest program was a worthy endeavour. The problem for the Committee was that it was difficult to identify developing countries with untarnished political records that Trudeau might agree to continue working with. No doubt the 1969 list of "acceptable" countries for Canadian military assistance, proposed by the Military Assistance Committee, would have been a non-starter with Trudeau, likely from his very first glance. Nor would he have been open to spending $1.5 million or, as was suggested, 2% of the economic aid budget or $3 million when he had called for a complete end to all military assistance work.[668]

Nevertheless, it is not difficult to imagine the frustration experienced by the Military Assistance Committee soon after securing a Cabinet decision to continue with their work. First of all, the Committee never obtained the full $500,000 they had fought hard for. Instead, the Department of Finance could only allocate $440,000 and even this amount appeared in jeopardy at one point. Although a difference of $60,000 may seem trivial today, based on inflation, the Committee was looking at a reduction of almost $350,000. Second of all, there must have been a degree of envy given the money flowing into the ODA budget and frustration that a whole-of-government aid approach, at least in a handful of countries, could not be arranged with CIDA.

As it was, however, the 1970 Memorandum to Cabinet on the importance of continuing Canada's military assistance efforts did achieve the desired effect – the maintenance of a small program funded yearly, at least on paper, at $500,000. Ministers had been told that combining military assistance with other development work would allow for a more comprehensive and effective development policy and this was in Canada's best interests. In many developing countries, they were also reminded that the military was in charge, either directly or indirectly, and so exposing them to Canadian values and attitudes would allow the Canadian government to have a "constructive influence" on the political elite in developing countries. There was, as always, a final reminder that military assistance often resulted in jobs for Canadians. Still, there was no escaping the fact that Canada was giving up on any serious attempt to keep its military assistance efforts going. And while a modest program would continue, its funding was never certain. Moreover, thirty years would pass before the funds allocated for military assistance even came close to the amount spent in the 1960s.

CHAPTER 11

CONCLUSION

During the 1960s, abundant coups and political intrigues, especially in Africa, provided British film studios and Hollywood with ample material for use in films and television. In 1964, Twentieth Century-Fox filmed the *Guns at Batasi* at Pinewood Studios in Great Britain. The movie stared Richard Attenborough in the role of Regimental Sergeant Major Lauderdale while Jack Hawkins played Colonel John Deal. The two, along with a contingent of British military advisors, found themselves in the midst of a coup in an unnamed East African country where they had been engaged in a military assistance role.

Meanwhile, on television, *Danger Man* featured actor Patrick McGoohan as John Drake, a NATO special operative. A popular 1960s series, *Danger Man* frequently addressed contemporary political issues and the Middle East and Africa were often the source of many program plots. The November 1964 episode, *The Galloping Major*, concerned the prime minister of a new African nation who feared the opposition was about to topple his government. In October 1965, in *Loyalty Always Pays*, Drake's mission was to confirm if "the rumour that an African nation [had] accepted British financial aid while also signing an agreement with the Red Chinese," was true or not. One month later, *The Mercenaries*, featured the actor on the trail of a commando army preparing to overthrow the ruler of an African nation.[669]

If Prime Ministers St. Laurent, Diefenbaker, Pearson, or Trudeau, their Cabinets or even the members of the Interdepartmental Military Assistance Committee ever watched the *Guns at Batasi* or *Danger Man*, it is difficult to say. But even if they did not, it would have been almost impossible to miss the stories of coups, counter-coups, aborted coups and military mutinies in the post-war developing world that were featured regularly in newspapers, magazines and on radio at the time. Yet, despite what they may have read or heard, St. Laurent, Diefenbaker and Pearson were more than willing to assist the developing world by whatever means they could, including the provision of military assistance.

CHAPTER 11

Supplying NATO allies with surplus military equipment and training NATO personnel in Canada in the post-war period was expected of Canada as an alliance member. However, selling demilitarized frigates, which were more than likely to be remilitarized by their recipients, plus small and heavy arms to developing countries at war, for the most part, was voluntary. There is no escaping the fact, though, that successive post-war Canadian governments did sell substantial amounts of weaponry to, in particular, India, Israel, the Nationalist Chinese and Pakistan. There was, to be sure, a certain amount of hand-wringing that took place in Ottawa each time a deal was contemplated – selling arms, it seems, was considered by many in Cabinet as un-Canadian and "incompatible with the sort of image Canada should project abroad."[670] When Trudeau was in power, selling arms or offering military assistance was simply seen, in his view, as illiberal. But faced with pressure from domestic arms and aircraft manufacturers to permit sales, seldom did Canadian governments say no. Indeed, it was difficult to say no when arms sales meant preserving jobs. Sales also meant that Canadian arms industries could re-invest profits and keep pace with the latest technology – in effect, arms sales allowed Canadian industry to modernize. Egypt's Ali or the Japanese leadership at the turn of the 19th century would have all recognized the business model, although from the evidence available it can be concluded that there was no master plan to offer Canadian military assistance to foreign countries as a means to boost domestic armaments production.

As for the military coups that had crisscrossed the developing world, their significance did not prevent post-war Canadian governments, at least prior to the election of Trudeau, from offering military assistance to newly independent countries in Asia, the Middle East and Africa. And even though the number of Canadian military personnel involved in training and advising foreign militaries in places such as Ghana and Tanzania were few in number, they were highly trained and able to get to work quickly. These men were in Africa for several reasons. The overarching aim, certainly for London and Washington, was to have Canada take a leading role in countering Soviet and Chinese influence in post-colonial sub-Saharan Africa. Both the British and Americans had little choice but to ask Canada to intervene on their behalf as there were few countries, especially within NATO, that did not have some sort of colonial baggage in one form or another.

Doubts amongst members of the Canadian government regarding the wisdom of providing countries in the developing world with military assistance were likely dispelled by the popular belief, certainly amongst some academics in the early 1960s, that well-trained, professional militaries had an important modernization role to play. British officers, who remained behind on secondment in Africa during the immediate post-colonial period, in-turn, probably influenced the academics. Major-General Alexander, for example, made sure his readers understood that in a county like Ghana one could not establish political stability and ensure economic development if the "soldiery" was to function unrestrained – for him, military assistance could never be considered a "waste of money."[671] On the other hand there were plenty of examples, historical and contemporary, of militaries from Latin America to the Far East interfering in politics.

There was little evidence to show that leaders in the post-colonial developing world, in particular in sub-Saharan Africa during the early years of the independence drive, ever worried about their chances of being toppled in a military coup. Neither did many outside observers, including academics and politicians, believe militaries in the post-colonial period had any significant political role to play. The Canadian High Commissioner in Accra observed in 1964 that there was no evidence, in his opinion, of the Ghanaian military wanting to play an active role in politics. Quite the reverse was the case, he had written to External Affairs. Colonel Bond, the Canadian military attaché, shared the High Commissioner's point of view. Both likely believed that a well-trained, non-politicized, professional military force in Ghana would help secure the country and promote economic development. However, the Ghanaian military, one of the more professional military forces in Africa upon independence, staged its first coup in 1966.

There was also little evidence to show that post-colonial developing countries, again in sub-Saharan Africa, spent any time considering what type of military they really needed for their particular circumstances. The situation was different in the rest of the world in the post-war period where countries such as Malaysia, India, Pakistan and Israel faced substantial conventional military threats. But circumstances in the former African colonies were far different as few, if any, were threatened by their neighbours. Nevertheless and often for prestige purposes, new armies, navies and air forces were created and equipped with unneeded and expensive weapons that most could not afford. As Gutteridge later concluded, sub-Saharan countries would have been better off with just having more police – although, in Ghana at least, the police had played a significant role in the overthrow of Nkrumah.

In the end, the high hopes that militaries, especially in sub-Saharan Africa, might contribute to overall development activities were undoubtedly misplaced. The armed forces in almost every sub-Saharan country were just too small, often divided along ethnic lines, not well trained and therefore unable to act as agents of modernization or change. They were in no position to lead development activities by building economic infrastructure or offering managerial expertise to their civilian counterparts. When a coup did take place, and the military themselves became corrupt, it was also a double blow for African societies who believed a professional military leadership espousing higher values than their civilian counterparts would wipe out corruption and raise the standard of living for the entire population. "Their fall from grace," said Odetola, referring to military led governments, had "the compounding effect of ensuring, in the minds of the public, that the last hope [had] gone."[672]

As for the Canadian Forces, its leadership was never really interested in military assistance missions. Requests from External Affairs to the Canadian Forces to provide help to several developing countries in the early 1950s were almost always turned down. These undertakings, as far as Foulkes was concerned, took time and effort and appeared to have little in the way of easily foreseeable results. "Mindful that there are brush-fires on the periphery of NATO which cannot be ignored," he said, "we must ensure that in dealing with such situations nothing is done to in any way weaken the determination to defend the NATO area."[673] It was true that the military preferred NATO and NORAD where real enemies and friends existed and where defeat would be decisive. Pursuing wider strategic aims with diplomatic and development overtones was not really what military leaders considered prudent or affordable in the circumstances. Indeed, said Canadian diplomat Arthur Andrew, perhaps a little too unkindly, "the self-styled simple soldier man [liked] to know with some certainty where people stood."[674]

Yet, when finally obliged by the Canadian government to undertake military missions in faraway places, the Canadian Forces had little choice but to act decisively and quickly. The survey teams that went to Ghana, Nigeria, Malaysia and Tanzania came up with reasonable plans that were generally well received by their hosts. When the need to coordinate the number of requests for Canadian military assistance increased, the rest of government also responded well, leading to the establishment of the Interdepartmental Military Assistance Committee in August 1964.

On the one hand, the Committee was established in order to ensure Canada's military assistance efforts were properly coordinated and designed to help recipient governments achieve internal stability and focus on, among other aspects, economic growth. On the other hand, the aim of sending Canadian Forces personnel to countries such as Ghana and Tanzania was often based on entirely different reasons – the perceived need to stop the Soviet Union and China from gaining too much influence. In this regard, Walter Laqueur wrote in 1961 that Africa would continue to be the main area of contest "between West and East for many years to come."[675] Peter Snow, again in 1961, said Africa would be the "last battlefield" on which the West and East would fight it out.[676] Two years later, G. Mennen Williams, the United States Assistant Secretary of State for African Affairs, wrote that the main thrust of worldwide communist activity, from his vantage point, continued to be the "destruction of the Western position in Africa."[677] The perceived need to combat communism in Africa continued when Douglas-Home informed Pearson in August 1964 of "how immensely valuable" it would be if Canada could find a way to prevent the Chinese from "gaining virtual control of the local training" of Tanzania's army.[678]

Principally, then, the focus of Canada's military assistance efforts, particularly in the post-colonial period, was to check the spread of communism in sub-Saharan Africa. In the matter of Ghana, this was certainly the case after the Canadian-trained Ghana Army overthrew Nkrumah's government in 1966. As the High Commission in Accra reported to Ottawa in the days following the military takeover, the coup leaders had destroyed Nkrumah's political apparatus, dismantled the Chinese-run guerrilla training camps, disbanded the Soviet trained POGR and "thrown the Russian and Chinese rascals out."[679] On the other hand, the Canadian

Forces did not embark for Ghana in 1961 with the intent of fostering a coup. No Canadians, based on the evidence available, played a direct role in the events that unfolded in 1966. In Tanzania, the Canadian presence was less successful in keeping the Chinese military from gaining overall control. Nevertheless, the belief in Ottawa was that the five years spent in training the army and air force would have a lasting effect and this was reason enough to ensure a modest Tanzanian military assistance program continued after 1970. In addition, President Nyerere seemed more intent on utilizing Chinese military assistance efforts to his own ends – the liberation of Mozambique and an end to white rule in Rhodesia. He was not about to turn his country over to Beijing.

When it did come to combating communism in places such as Tanzania, Canadian diplomat John Holmes was not convinced, however, that offering military assistance was really worth the effort. In his view, the Canadian government should have simply told countries in the developing world that, "we no longer cared about their alignment. If they wanted to turn to Communists for help…that was their business… such a policy…would clear the air of charges of neocolonialism, and we might begin to enjoy the plight of Moscow and Peking trying to cope with too many clients."[680]

Besides attempting to nip the spread of communism in the bud and seeking commercial opportunities whenever possible, there is no doubt that both Diefenbaker and Pearson held the Commonwealth in high regard and thus supporting developing countries, in particular with ODA and military assistance was important for them and to the many Canadians who shared in their idealism. As Paul Martin Sr. observed, the decision to provide military assistance to Tanzania had also been based on a genuine desire to assist the Tanzanian government provide the necessary "conditions of security and stability in which economic and social development programs [could] be carried out."[681]

In retrospect, could the Canadian Forces have contributed more to Canada's overall development activities in Africa following Trudeau's election in 1968? Could they have taken advantage of his plans to increase the ODA budget to put forth a wider strategy? There were some in National Defence who saw the utility of such ideas but they were in the minority, and as defence budgets contracted, preserving Canada's NATO and NORAD contributions remained the priority. Still, there might have been an opportunity to offer up a new diplomatic, development and defence strategy when Trudeau first called on his Ministers to examine what they were doing and why. Then again, it is more than likely Trudeau would not have been pleased to see any fresh plans, no matter how well coordinated with External Affairs or CIDA that involved Canada providing military assistance, in any substantial way, after 1968. Trudeau understood that becoming involved militarily with developing countries had been, and would likely continue to be, a source of political problems for his government. As Windle observed, the United States military, through its military assistance programs, had assumed major political responsibilities in the developing world, a role that Trudeau clearly did not want Canada to have.[682] His desire to end Canada's military assistance efforts, it can be concluded, was certainly prudent given the domestic and international political situation at the time.

Indeed, internationally, Trudeau was more focused on pursuing his own foreign policy agenda that involved recognizing mainland China for example, and seeking to distance himself from the United States. However, his attention was focused, more so, on pressing domestic security issues resulting from the FLQ Crisis. "I am speaking to you," he had said to Canadians during a television broadcast on 16 October 1970, "at a moment of grave crisis, when violent and fanatical men are attempting to destroy the unity and freedom of Canada."[683] His government was also searching for any means to finance social programs established by his predecessor while having to introduce new ones following the 1972 election. Therefore, defence spending, and certainly the funds allocated for military assistance, was no longer a priority for the government. If money was to be spent on defence, Canada's own security needs would come first, not those in the developing world.

ENDNOTES

1   Although utilizing the term "Canadian Armed Forces" or "Canadian Forces" to describe Canada's armed forces did not come into use until 1968, for the purposes of this book the term "Canadian Forces" is used to describe the Canadian military before 1968 as well.

2   Sean M. Maloney, *The Roots of Soft Power – The Trudeau Government, De-NATOization and Denuclearization, 1967-1970* (Kingston: Queen's Centre for International Relations, 2005), 43.

3   Maloney, 21.

4   Donald Stoker, "The History and Evolution of Foreign Military Advising and Assistance, 1815-2007," *Military Advising and Assistance – From Mercenaries to Privatization, 1815-2007*, ed. by Donald Stoker (London: Routledge, 2008), 1.

5   Edward Mead Earle, "Adam Smith, Alexander Hamilton, Friedrich List: The Economic Foundations of Military Power," *Makers of Modern Strategy: From Machiavelli to the Nuclear Age*, ed. by Peter Paret, (Princeton: Princeton University Press, 1986), 218.

6   Ibid., 219.

7   Ibid., 220.

8   Ibid., 224.

9   Jacob E. Cooke, "Tench Coxe, Alexander Hamilton, and the Encouragement of American Manufactures," *The William and Mary Quarterly*, 3rd Ser. Vol. 32, No. 3, July 1975, 371.

10 M.P. Cowen and R.W. Shenton, *Doctrines of Development* (London: Routledge, 1996), 154.

11 Cooke, 373.

12 Karl Walling, "Was Alexander Hamilton a Machiavellian Statesman?" *The Review of Politics*, Vol. 57, No. 3, Summer, 1995, 420.

13 Ibid., 439.

14 John P. Dunn, "Egypt's Nineteenth-Century Armaments Industry," *The Journal of Military History*, Vol. 61, No. 2, April 1997, 232.

15 John P. Dunn, "Missions or Mercenaries? European Military Advisors in Mehmed Ali's Egypt, 1815-1848," *Military Advising and Assistance – From Mercenaries to Privatization, 1815-2007*, ed. by Donald Stoker (London: Routledge, 2008), 17.

16 Dunn, "Egypt's Nineteenth-Century Armaments Industry," 244.

17 Ibid., 235-236.

18 F. S. Rodkey, "Colonel Campbell's Report on Egypt in 1840, with Lord Palmerston's Comments," *Cambridge Historical Journal*, Vol. 3, No. 1, 1929, 111.

19 Ibid., 112.

20 Dunn, "Egypt's Nineteenth-Century Armaments Industry," 242.

21 Gwyn Campbell, "An Industrial Experiment in Pre-Colonial Africa: The Case of Imperial Madagascar 1825-1861," *Journal of Southern African Studies*, Vol. 17, No. 3, September 1991, 526.

22 Ibid., 546-547.

23 Ibid., 531. $2.5 million in potential slave export earnings were lost between 1820 and 1826.

24 Ibid., 538.

25 Ibid., 552.

ENDNOTES

26   L.S. Stavrianos, *Global Rift: The Third World Comes of Age* (New York: William Morrow and Company, Inc., 1981), 349.

27   Ibid., 355.

28   Kozo Yamamura, "Success Illgotten? The Role of Meiji Militarism in Japan's Technological Progress," *The Journal of Economic History*, Vol. 37, No. 1, March 1977, 124-125.

29   Stavrianos, 356.

30   Barton C. Hacker, "The Weapons of the West: Military Technology and Modernization in 19th-Century China and Japan," *Technology and Culture*, Vol. 18, No. 1, January 1977, 52.

31   Yamamura, 114.

32   Ibid., 117.

33   Hyman Kublin, "The "Modern" Army of Early Meiji Japan," *The Far Eastern Quarterly*, Vol. 9, No. 1, November 1949, 23. By agreement with the Japanese government, a French military mission arrived in Japan in late 1866. A military school was established in Yokohama but little was achieved before fighting broke out in Japan and the French mission was forced to depart. See: Kublin, 25. A second French military mission arrived in May 1872 and continued its work until 1880. However, from 1874, French influence began to wane and the Japanese eventually turned to the Germans for military training assistance. See: Kublin, 33.

34   Ibid., 30. By the end of the Sino-Japanese war the Japanese Army had grown to approximately 400,000 men.

35   Mary C. Wright, "The Adaptability of Ching Diplomacy: The Case of Korea," *The Journal of Asian Studies*, Vol. 17, No. 3, May, 1958, 364.

36   Ibid., 368.

37   George M. McCune, "Russian Policy in Korea: 1895-1898," *Far Eastern Survey*, Vol. 14, No. 19, September 26, 1945, 272. The Japanese felt it was their mission to civilize Korea. The Queen's murder, nevertheless, came as a surprise in Tokyo. Those involved with the plot were returned to Japan and stood trial, however, they were not convicted. See: Hilary Conroy, "Chosen Mondai: The Korean Problem in Meiji Japan," *Proceedings of the American Philosophical Society*, Vol. 100, No. 5, October 15, 1956.

38   Ibid., 274.

39   Hilary Conroy, "Chosen Mondai: The Korean Problem in Meiji Japan," *Proceedings of the American Philosophical Society*, Vol. 100, No. 5, October 15, 1956, 453.

40   Stavrianos, 361.

41   Dunn, "Egypt's Nineteenth-Century Armaments Industry," 254.

42   Earle, 247.

43   Ibid., 247.

44   Cowen and Shenton, 162.

45   Charles Windle and T.R. Vallance, "Optimizing Military Assistance Training," *World Politics*, Vol. 15, No. 1, October 1962, 96.

46   Henry Bienen wrote in "Armed Forces and National Modernization: Continuing the Debate," that what actually constituted modernization – its very definition – remained "highly contentious" amongst researchers. Some academics and analysts, he noted, preferred quantifiable variables to judge if a country was becoming more or less modernized. In this category fell, as examples, rates of economic growth, levels of literacy and life expectancy, trends toward urbanization and the distribution of income – categories, that for the most part, were relatively simple for researchers to begin collecting data. Others, Bienen pointed out, chose to define modernization along different lines that were less easy to quantify such as measuring societal stability and

coherence. Further, based on the study of individuals in society, some researchers sought signs of societal modernization by examining personality or measuring the presence of democratic traits. "Unless," concluded Bienen, "we have at least a common understanding of the dependent variable, modernization, it is rather difficult to ascertain what are the militaries' impacts." See: Henry Bienen, "Armed Forces and National Modernization: Continuing the Debate," *Comparative Politics*, Vol. 16, No. 1, October 1983, 1.

47   Edward Shils, "The Military in the Political Development of the New States," *The Role of the Military in Underdeveloped Countries*, ed. by John J. Johnson (Princeton, New Jersey: Princeton University Press, 1962), 9.

48   Ibid., 8.

49   Morris Janowitz, *Military Institutions and Coercion in the Developing Nations* (Chicago: The University of Chicago Press, 1977), 176.

50   A.F. Mullins, Jr., *Born Arming – Development and Military Power in New States* (Stanford, California: Stanford University Press, 1987), 1.

51   Daniel Lerner and Richard D. Robinson, "Swords and Ploughshares: The Turkish Army as a Modernizing Force," *The Military Intervenes – Case Studies in Political Development*, ed. by Henry Bienen (Hartford, Connecticut: Connecticut Printers, 1968), 128. However, the modernizing influence that conscription could bring to a developing country had been recognized long before the Turkish example. Olavio Bilac, writing on the introduction of conscription in Brazil in 1916, noted that compulsory military service would result, positively, in "obligatory civic education, cleanliness, and hygiene, as well as psychological and physical regeneration. The cities are full of idle men, shoeless and in rags, who do not know the alphabet or the bathtub, animals who have only the appearance of human beings. For those dregs of society, the barracks will be their salvation." See: Alain Rouquié, *The Military and the State in Latin America*, translated by Paul E. Sigmund (Berkeley: University of California Press, 1987), 95.

52   Henry Bienen, *The Military and Modernization* (Chicago: Aldine–Atherton, Inc, 1971), 8. In November 1958, President Eisenhower created the *President's Committee to Study the Military Assistance Program* under the chairmanship of William Henry Draper, Jr., a former Under Secretary of the Army. The Committee was tasked with conducting an independent analysis of the United States military assistance portion of the Mutual Security Program. An initial report was sent to Eisenhower on 17 March 1959 and the final report followed on 17 August 1959. In summary, the *Draper Report* recommended increased funding for military assistance and improvements to the administration and planning of military assistance efforts. In addition, the report recommended that more emphasis needed to be placed on the selected development of foreign officers clearly destined for higher command. For an overview of the *Draper Report* See: the *Papers of Dwight David Eisenhower*. Internet: <http://www.eisenhowermemorial.org/presidential-papers/second-term/documents/1191.cfm>. Accessed: 5 March 2009.

53   John Johnson, *The Role of the Military in Underdeveloped Countries* (Princeton, New Jersey: Princeton University Press, 1962), v.

54   John P. Lovell and C. I. Eugene Kim, "The Military and Political Change in Asia," *Pacific Affairs*, Vol. 40, No. 1 / 2, Spring – Summer, 1967, 118.

55   Ibid., 118.

56   James S. Coleman, and Belmont Brice Jr., "The Role of the Military in Sub-Saharan Africa," *The Role of the Military in Underdeveloped Countries*, ed. by John J. Johnson (Princeton, New Jersey: Princeton University Press, 1962), 396-397. An alternative view

of the African experience during the war was provided by Michael Crowder in his 1968 book *West Africa under Colonial Rule*: "Africans had fought alongside white men, killed white men, seen brave Africans and white cowards, slept with white women, met white soldiers who treated them as equals, or who were, like themselves, hardly educated. They had visited new countries, seen people like the Indians living in squalor and poverty such as they had never seen at home. Above all, having fought in the defence of freedom, they considered it their right that they should have some share in the government of their land." Quoted in: Simon Baynham, *The Military and Politics in Nkrumah's Ghana* (Boulder, Colorado: Westview Press, 1988), 28.

57   Olatunde Odetola, *Military Regimes and Development – A Comparative Analysis in African Societies* (London: George Allen & Unwin, 1982), 21.

58   Shils, 33. The truth, in reality, was frequently quite different and colonial powers were keen to create ethnic imbalances within their colonial forces to ensure political stability. Enlisted personnel were, in fact, frequently recruited from minorities with little to no affiliation with larger tribes who might have greater aspirations for independence. In Morocco, the French generally recruited amongst the Berbers while in mainly Moslem Indonesia the Dutch relied upon Christians from the North Celebes and Ambon Islands to furnish manpower. In 1961, the Kamba and Kalenjin tribes in Kenya, which represented between 9 and 11% of the population, made up 34% of the army. In Ghana, 62% of the soldiers and non-commissioned officers came from the far north while in Nigeria two-thirds of the officers were Ibos. Even amongst the leadership of the South Korean Army, which relied heavily on support from the United States, there was a tendency "for Christian officers to rise to prominent positions." See: Janowitz, *Military Institutions and Coercion in the Developing Nations*, 128-129.

59   Odetola, 21.

60   Bienen, *The Military and Modernization*, 16.

61   Ibid., 9.

62   Janowitz, *Military Institutions and Coercion in the Developing Nations*, 11.

63   Ibid., 13 and 22.

64   J.D.C. Boulakia, "Military Expenditures and African Economic Development," *Canadian Journal of African Studies*, Vol. 2, No. 2, Autumn 1968, 200.

65   Ibid., 199.

66   W.F. Gutteridge, *The Place of the Army in Society in Commonwealth African Territories* (R.M.A. Sandhurst: Unpublished Study, 1961-62, 12. RG 24, National Defence, Vol. 21490, CSC 2137.6 Part 2 – Military Assistance to Nigeria.

67   Canada, Library and Archives Canada (hereafter LAC), "Sale of Arms to India and Pakistan," 1 September 1948, 1. RG 2, Privy Council Office, Series A-5-a, Vol. 2642, Reel T-2365.

68   Canada, LAC, "Sale of Arms; Pakistan," 24 November 1948, 1. RG 2, Privy Council Office, Series A-5-a, Vol. 2642, Reel T-2366. The security situation in India and Pakistan following partition, and on going fighting in Kashmir, were cause for concern in Cabinet that Canada might in fact end up fuelling the crisis.

69   Julius K. Nyerere, *Freedom and Development – A Selection from Writings and Speeches 1968-1973* (London: Oxford University Press, 1974), 116.

70   Tim Shaw, "South Africa's Military Capability and the Future of Race Relations," revised version of his paper presented at the Conference on Africa in World Affairs, December 1969. As quoted in *Arms and Development – Proceedings of the First Pan-African Citizens' Conference*, ed. by Frederick S. Arkhurst (New York: Praeger Publishers, 1972), 33.

71 Canada, LAC, "Canadian Military Assistance to Developing Countries – A Review by the Interdepartmental Military Assistance Committee, 9 July 1969," 2-3. RG 24, National Defence, Series B-1, Volume 21834, File FMC 4760-1 (Parts 10 and 11).

72 Ibid., 3. The authors of the report, however, were eager to acknowledge that the wasteful use of limited resources by developing countries was not exclusive to military assistance. "The same is often true of development expenditures," noted the report, as "many countries have a "steel mill syndrome" leading them to also expend resources on grandiose projects of limited utility. See: 3.

73 In the case of Guyana, armed forces would prove a necessity. In 1962, four years prior to Guyana's independence, the Venezuelan government declared an 1899 decision between Great Britain and Venezuela on the delineation of borders between Venezuela and Guyana, null and void. The government in Caracas subsequently claimed five-eights of Guyana's territory while Suriname and Brazil both raised their own territorial claims on Guyana. In October 1966, and despite the on-going work of the Guyana-Venezuela Mixed Boundary Commission to "find satisfactory solutions for the practical settlement of the controversy," the Venezuelan army invaded Guyana and occupied the eastern half of Ankokko Island. See: George K. Danns, "The Role of the Military in the National Security of Guyana," *Militarization in the Non-Hispanic Caribbean*. Edited by Alma H. Young & Dion E. Phillips (Boulder, Colorado: Lynne Rienner Publishers, Inc., 1986), 121.

74 Boulakia, 195.

75 Coleman and Brice, 394.

76 Claude E. Welch, Jr., "Praetorianism in Commonwealth West Africa," *The Journal of Modern African Studies*, Vol. 10, No. 2, July 1972, 206.

77 Mullins, 3.

78 Ibid., 3.

79 Baynham, 84.

80 Ibid., 84.

81 Claude E. Welch, Jr., "African Military and Political Development: Reflections on a Score of Years, and Several Score of Studies," *A Journal of Opinion*, Vol. 13, 1984, 41.

82 Ibid., 41.

83 Baynham, 84.

84 John J. Johnson, *The Military and Society in Latin America* (Stanford, California: Stanford University Press, 1964), 1.

85 Brian Loveman, *For la Patria: Politics and the Armed Forces in Latin America* (Wilmington, Delaware: Scholarly Resources Inc., 1999), 69.

86 Edwin Lieuwen, "Militarism and Politics in Latin America," *The Role of the Military in Underdeveloped Countries*, ed. by John J. Johnson (Princeton, New Jersey: Princeton University Press, 1962), 157. Large militaries also came with other hidden costs. In 1959 there were 20,000 *generals de pijamas* or retired officers drawing a pension in Argentina. Next door, pensions for 1,500 Brazilian generals and 38 field marshals also consumed a significant portion of the national budget. See: Johnson, 7 and 259.

87 It was Samuel Huntington, Janowitz pointed out, who had mistakenly concluded that the professionalization of the military would also ensure political neutrality. Rather optimistically, Johnson also believed that "greater professionalization can be predicted with considerable assurance. As it occurs there will be a tendency for officers to rise in rank and reach senior positions so late in life that they will have lost their political ambitions and will have learned to obey as well as to command." See: Johnson, *The Role of the Military in Underdeveloped Countries*, 257.

ENDNOTES

88   Gutteridge, *The Place of the Army in Society in Commonwealth African Territories*, 17.

89   Shils, 17.

90   Canada, LAC, "Canadian Military Assistance to Developing Countries – A Review by the Interdepartmental Military Assistance Committee," 9 July 1969, 4.

91   Ibid., 3.

92   Janowitz, *Military Institutions and Coercion in the Developing Nations*, 52.

93   Gutteridge, *The Place of the Army in Society in Commonwealth African Territories*, 2.

94   Aristide R. Zolberg, *Military Intervention in the New States of Tropical Africa: Elements of Comparative Analysis*, "The Military Intervenes – Case Studies in Political Development," ed. by Henry Bienen (Hartford, Connecticut: Connecticut Printers, 1968), 81.

95   Canada, LAC, "Memorandum for the Minister," 26 August 1964, 1. RG 25, External Affairs, Vol. 10403, File: 27-20-1-2, Part 1. Military Assistance – Canada – Military Assistance Committee.

96   Ibid., 1.

97   Canada, LAC, "Canadian Military Assistance to Developing Countries," 25 June 1970, 6. RG 25, External Affairs, Vol. 10403, File: 27-20-1-2, Part 2. Military Assistance – Canada – Military Assistance Committee.

98   In Chile, for example, a German training mission was established in 1886 and more than 30 German officers were employed training the Chilean military by 1899-1900. In 1906, noted Alain Rouquié, "a program of reform of the army's organization and internal regulations was completed that transformed the Chilean military into a veritable reflection of the German army." See: Rouquié, 78.

99   Chester Pach, *Arming the Free World: The Origins of the United States Military Assistance Program, 1945-1950* (Chapel Hill: University of North Carolina Press, 1991), 5.

100   American Rhetoric, the *Truman Doctrine*. Speech delivered on 12 March 1947 before a Joint Session of Congress. Internet: <http://www.americanrhetoric.com/speeches/harrystrumantrumandoctrine.html>. Accessed: 20 July 2007.

101   Pach, 10.

102   Ibid., 15.

103   Ibid., 12.

104   Windle, 91.

105   Ibid., 92.

106   Pach, 232.

107   Bienen, *The Military and Modernization*, xiii.

108   Pach, 6.

109   Ibid., 4.

110   Augusto Varas, *Militarization and the International Arms Race in Latin America* (Boulder, Colorado: Westview Press, 1985), 45.

111   Ibid., 46.

112   Daniel S. Papp, "Communist Military Assistance," *Communist Nations' Military Assistance*, ed. by John F. Cooper and Daniel S. Papp (Boulder, Colorado: Westview Press, Inc, 1983), 2. In the post-colonial period, new players also entered the arms sales market. In 1970, Austria and Switzerland had little to no share of the global arms sales market. In 1978, they exported $120 million and $200 million of arms respectively. See: Papp, 10.

113   Varas, 43.

114   Nyerere, 210.

115   Varas, 46-47.

116   Odd Arne Westad, *The Global Cold War* (Cambridge: Cambridge University Press, 2005), 135-143.

117 Ibid., 134-135.

118 Roger E. Kanat, "Soviet Military Assistance to the Third World," *Communist Nations' Military Assistance*, ed. by John F. Cooper and Daniel S. Papp (Boulder, Colorado: Westview Press, Inc, 1983), 61.

119 Ibid., 49-50. The information in Table 3 has been extracted from Kanat's *Table 3.3 – Deliveries of Soviet Armaments to Noncommunist Developing Countries, 1967-1978.*

120 Thomas P. Melady, *Western Policy and the Third World* (New York: Hawthorn Books, Inc, 1967), 59.

121 Ibid., 27.

122 Robert Legvold, *Soviet Policy in West Africa* (Cambridge, Massachusetts: Harvard University Press, 1970), 60.

123 Ibid., 64.

124 Melady, 56.

125 Legvold, 65.

126 John F. Cooper, "Chinese Military Assistance," *Communist Nations' Military Assistance*, ed. by John F. Cooper and Daniel S. Papp (Boulder, Colorado: Westview Press, Inc, 1983), 97.

127 Peter A. Poole, "Communist China's Aid Diplomacy," *Asian Survey*, Vol. 6, No. 11, November 1966, 622.

128 Ibid., 627.

129 Melady, 63.

130 Phillip Snow, "China and Africa," *Chinese Foreign Policy – Theory and Practice*, ed. by Thomas W. Robinson and David Shambaugh (Oxford: Oxford University Press, 1994), 307.

131 Uri Ra'anan, *The USSR Arms the Third World: Case Studies in Soviet Foreign Policy* (Cambridge, Massachusetts: The M.I.T. Press, 1969), 191-192 and 216-217.

132 Ibid., 231.

133 Sunday Abogonye Ochoche, "The Military and National Security in Africa," *The Military and Militarism in Africa*, ed. by Eboe Hutchful and Abdoulaye Bathily (Dakar, Senegal: Codesiria Book Series, 1998), 115.

134 Legvold, 63.

135 C.P Stacey, *A Date with History – Memoirs of a Canadian Historian* (Ottawa: Deneau, 1983), 2.

136 Ibid., 27.

137 D.W. Middlemiss and J.J. Sokolsky, *Canadian Defence – Decisions and Determinants* (Toronto: Harcourt Brace Jovanovich, 1989), 20.

138 J.L. Granatstein, "Canada and Peacekeeping: Image and Reality," *Canadian Foreign Policy – Historical Readings* (Toronto: Copp Clark Pitman Ltd., 1986), 238.

139 Canada, DND, *Canada's Defence Programme 1949-50* (Ottawa: Queen's Printer and Controller of Stationery, 1954), 17.

140 James Eayrs, *In Defence of Canada – Peacemaking and Deterrence* (Toronto: University of Toronto Press, 1972), 92.

141 Ibid., 94.

142 Canada, DND, *Canada's Defence Programme 1949-50*, 8.

143 Eayrs, 101.

144 Ibid., 101.

145 As a result of the Canada's military role in Korea, the army increased in size by 112% in one year alone – from 20,369 to 43,250 personnel. See: Canada, Department of National Defence (hereafter DND), "Canada's Defence Programme 1951-52," (Ottawa:

Printer to the King's Most Excellent Majesty, 1949), 17. In addition, the defence budget rose from $385 million in fiscal year 1949-50 to almost $1.9 billion in fiscal year 1952-53. See: Ross Fetterly, "The Influence of the Environment on the 1964 White Paper," *Canadian Military Journal* (Ottawa: Department of National Defence, Winter 2004-2005), 51.

146 Canada, DND, *Canada's Defence Programme, 1954-55* (Ottawa: Queen's Printer and Controller of Stationary, 1954), 11-12. The brigade was just a portion of a larger army contribution built around the 1st Canadian Infantry Division in Canada with two additional brigades and supporting troops.

147 Canada, DND, *Canada's Defence Programme, 1953-54* (Ottawa: Queen's Printer and Controller of Stationery, 1953), 11-12.

148 Canada, DND, *Canada's Defence Programme, 1954-55*, 14.

149 Canada, DND, *Canada's Defence Programme, 1956-57* (Ottawa: Queen's Printer and Controller of Stationery, 1956), 13.

150 John English, *The Worldly Years – The Life of Lester Pearson, 1949-1972* (Toronto: Alfred A. Knopf, 1992), 139.

151 Lester B. Pearson, *Mike – The Memoirs of the Right Honourable Lester B. Pearson – Vol. II, 1948-1957* (Toronto: University of Toronto Press, 1973), 261.

152 Ibid., 262.

153 Canada, DND, *Canada's Defence Programme, 1957-58* (Ottawa: Queen's Printer and Controller of Stationery, 1957), 8.

154 Canada, DND, *The Canadian Defence Budget – Prepared by the Ad Hoc Committee on Defence Policy* (Ottawa: DND, 4 September 1963), 2-3.

155 Canada, DND, *Report of the Ad Hoc Committee on Defence Policy* (Ottawa: DND, 30 September 1963), 28.

156 Canada, DND, *The Canadian Defence Budget – Prepared by the Ad Hoc Committee on Defence Policy*, iii.

157 Canada, DND, *Report of the Ad Hoc Committee on Defence Policy*, 29.

158 Desmond Morton, *A Military History of Canada – From Champlain to Kosovo* (Toronto: McClelland & Stewart Inc., 1999), 254.

159 Diefenbaker was Canada's 13th Prime Minister and served in this capacity from 21 June 1957 until 22 April 1963.

160 John G. Diefenbaker, *One Canada – Memoirs of the Right Honourable John G. Diefenbaker: The Years of Achievement, 1957-1962, Vol. 2* (Toronto: Macmillan of Canada, 1976), 187.

161 Sean M. Maloney, *Canada and UN Peacekeeping – Cold War by Other Means, 1945-1970* (St. Catharines, Ontario: Vanwell Publishing Limited, 2002), 83.

162 Ibid., 83.

163 Jack Granatstein and Douglas Lavender, *Shadows of War, Faces of Peace* (Toronto: Key Porter Books, 1992), 100.

164 Ibid., 100.

165 Diefenbaker, 127.

166 Granatstein and Lavender, 110. The Canadian contingent was cut in half in 1969, but brought back up to strength in 1974 when the Turkish government ordered their military to invade the island.

167 J.L. Granatstein, "Canada: Peacekeeper – A Survey of Canada's Participation in Peacekeeping Operations" *Peacekeeping – International Challenge and Canadian Response* (Lindsay, Ontario: Canadian Institute of International Affairs, Contemporary Affairs No. 39: 1968), 165.

168 Sutherland, 20 and 21.

169 Maloney, *Canada and UN Peacekeeping – Cold War by Other Means, 1945-1970*, 83. General Foulkes was appointed Chairman of the General Staff (Army) in August 1945. He served in this role until 1951 when he became Chairman of the newly created Chiefs of Staff Committee, a position equal in nature to the Chief of Defence Staff today. As James Eayrs noted, Foulkes, from August 1945 until his retirement in 1960, was "the government's principal military advisor." See: Eayrs, 62.

170 Granatstein, "Canada: Peacekeeper – A Survey of Canada's Participation in Peace-keeping Operations," 176.

171 Ibid., 176.

172 Paul Hellyer, *Damn the Torpedoes: My Fight to Unify Canada's Armed Forces* (Toronto: McClelland & Stewart, 1990), 33.

173 Granatstein, "Canada and Peacekeeping: Image and Reality," 236.

174 Sean Maloney, *War Without Battles – Canada's NATO Brigade in Germany, 1951-1993* (Whitby, Ontario: McGraw-Hill Ryerson Limited, 1997), 190.

175 The table is based on data from: (1) L.A. Willner, S. Maloney, and Sandy Babcock, *Canadian Forces Operations 1945-1969 – ORD Project Report PR 2002/11.* (Ottawa: Operational Research Division: October 2002; (2) J.L. Granatstein, *Canada: Peacekeeper – A Survey of Canada's Participation in Peacekeeping Operations*; (3) Canada, LAC, "Review of International Commitments (V-3185-3 DI Plans)," 8 September 1966. RG 24, National Defence, Series B-2, Vol. 21577, File S-2-5040-12 (4), Annex A; 3. UN Peacekeeping website. Internet: <http://www.un.org/Depts/dpko/dpko/index.asp>. Accessed: 3 March 2008.

176 Canada, DND, *Report of the Ad Hoc Committee on Defence Policy*, 58.

177 Granatstein, "Canada: Peacekeeper – A Survey of Canada's Participation in Peace-keeping Operations," 187.

178 Canada, DND, "Panel on the Economic Aspects of Defence," 1 December 1958, 1 (Ottawa, DND, Department of History and Heritage (hereafter DHH), Box 7, File 124, Equipment – Mutual Aid.

179 Morton, 233.

180 Canada, Department of Foreign Affairs and International Trade (hereafter DFAIT), "Under-Secretary of State for External Affairs to the Secretary of State for External Affairs," 10 November 1954, 1. Documents on Canadian External Relations, Vol. 20 – 262, Chapter III (NATO), Part 1 – Annual Review and Mutual Aid Policy. Internet: <http://www.dfait-maeci.gc.ca/department/history/dcer/details-en.asp?intRefId=273>. Accessed: 28 February 2008.

181 Canada, DFAIT, "Under-Secretary of State for External Affairs to the Secretary of State for External Affairs," 19 June 1959. Documents on Canadian External Relations, Vol. 26 – 100, Chapter II (NATO), Part 6 – Annual Review, Mutual Aid and Infrastructure. Internet: <http://www.international.gc.ca/hist/dcer/details-en.asp?intRefid=10918>. Accessed: 28 February 2008. In 1959, it was recommended to Cabinet that in future Canada should refer to the Military Assistance Program as "contributions to infrastructure and military costs of NATO and other assistance."

182 Canada, LAC, "Training of Foreign Aircrew in Canada," 1 March 1967, 1. RG 24, National Defence, Series B-2, Vol. 21577, File S-2-5040-12 (3). Thirty additional Norwegian pilots obtained *Sabre* operational training in 1964.

183 Canada, DFAIT, "Under-Secretary of State for External Affairs to the Secretary of State for External Affairs," 19 June 1959. Documents on Canadian External Relations, Vol. 26 – 100, Chapter II (NATO), Part 6 – Annual Review, Mutual Aid and Infrasturcture. Internet: <http://www.international.gc.ca/hist/dcer/details-en.asp?intRefid=10918>. Accessed: 28 February 2008.

ENDNOTES

184   Canada, DND, "Panel on the Economic Aspects of Defence," 1 December 1958, 2 (Ottawa, DND, DHH, Box 7, File 124, Equipment – Mutual Aid).

185   Time Magazine, "For Tomorrow," 17 January 1944. Internet: <http://www.time.com/time/magazine/article/0,9171,796313,00.html>. Accessed: 28 February 2008. When Ottawa created the War Assets Corporation on 29 November 1943, John Ballantyne Carswell, President of the Corporation, explained that the aim of the organization, at the end of the war, was to: "impound all war-material surpluses – machinery, tools, raw materials, even military and naval camps, barracks and flying fields – in one tremendous reservoir. Sales will be controlled. The trick will be to release material slowly enough to avoid a market glut and unemployment, fast enough to prevent equipment's becoming obsolete."

186   Canada, DFAIT, "Under-Secretary of State for External Affairs to the Prime Minister, Sale of Armaments (including ammunition and implements of war) to Foreign Governments," 30 April 1946, 1. Documents on Canadian External Relations, Vol. 12 – 1186, Chapter 12 (Relations with Individual Countries), Part 11 (Latin America – Sale of Arms). Internet: <http://www.dfait-maeci.gc.ca/department/history/dcer/details-en.asp?intRefid=12342>. Accessed: 14 February 2008.

187   Sandy McClearn, *The Canadian Navy of Yesterday & Today – World War II Canadian Ship Listing 1931-1945*. Internet: <http://www.hazegray.org/navhist/canada/ww2/>. Accessed: 6 August 2008.

188   Martin Gilbert, *Israel – A History* (New York: William Morrow and Company, Inc., 1998), 254.

189   The Canadian Commercial Corporation (CCC), Corporate Profile. Internet: <http://www.ccc.ca/eng/abo_whoWeAre_corporateProfile.cfm>. Accessed: 28 February 2008. The CCC was established "to assist in the development of trade between Canada and other nations and to assist persons in Canada to obtain goods or commodities from outside Canada and to dispose of goods and commodities that are available for export from Canada."

190   Canada, DFAIT, "Acting Under-Secretary of State for External Affairs to the Acting Secretary of State for External Affairs," 8 November 1948, 1. Documents on Canadian External Relations, Vol. 14 – 736, Chapter VII (International Economic Relations), Part 11 (Production and Export of Arms). Internet: <http://www.dfait-maeci.gc.ca/department/history/dcer/details-en.asp?intRefid=10476>. Accessed: 29 February 2008.

191   Canada, DFAIT, "Secretary of State for External Affairs to Heads of Post Abroad," 1 May 1948, 1. Documents on Canadian External Relations, Vol. 14 – 729, Chapter VII (International Economic Relations), Part 11 (Production and Export of Arms). Internet: <http://www.dfait-maeci.gc.ca/department/history/dcer/details-en.asp?intRefid=10469>. Accessed: 29 February 2008. It should also be noted that on 1 January 1948, Canada had taken its seat in the Security Council for a two-year term. Pearson would also serve as the President of the UN General Assembly in 1952-53.

192   Canada, DFAIT, "Assistant Under-Secretary of State for External Affairs to the Economic Division, Manufacture of Arms in Canada for Export, 12 February 1948," 1. Documents on Canadian External Relations, Vol. 14 – 727, Chapter VII (International Economic Relations), Part 11 (Production and Export of Arms). Internet: <http://www.dfait-maeci.gc.ca/department/history/dcer/details-en.asp?intRefid=10467>. Accessed: 29 February 2008. The first request to obtain arms from a current production line had actually occurred in June 1946. However, the request from the Netherlands was withdrawn over issues of price.

193 Government of Canada, *Special Committee on Defence – Minutes of Proceedings and Evidence, 24 November 1964* (Ottawa: Queen's Printer and Controller of Stationary, 1964), 898.

194 Ibid., 899.

195 Canada, DFAIT, "Assistant Under-Secretary of State for External Affairs to the Economic Division, Manufacture of Arms in Canada for Export," 12 February 1948, 1.

196 Canada, DFAIT, "Secretary of State for External Affairs to the Cabinet, Export of Arms from Current Production," 25 March 1948, 1. Documents on Canadian External Relations, Vol. 14 – 728, Chapter VII (International Economic Relations), Part 11 (Production and Export of Arms). Internet: <http://www.dfait-maeci.gc.ca/department/history/dcer/details-en.asp?intRefid=10467>. Accessed: 29 February 2008.

197 Ibid., 1.

198 Canada, DFAIT, "Minister of Finance to the Prime Minister," 6 December 1948, 1. Documents on Canadian External Relations, Vol. 14 – 1113, Chapter XIII (Far East), Part 1 (China), Section C (Trade Credits to China). Internet: <http://www.dfait.gc.ca/department/history/dcer/details-en.asp?intRefid=10801>. Accessed: 3 March 2008.

199 Stavrianos, 602.

200 Ibid., 602.

201 Canada, DFAIT, "Secretary of State for External Affairs to Cabinet, Sale of Arms to China," 7 October 1948, 1. Documents on Canadian External Relations, Vol. 14 – 734, Chapter VII (International Economic Relations), Part 11 (Production and Export of Arms). Internet: <http://www.dfait-maeci.gc.ca/department/history/dcer/details-en.asp?intRefid=10475>. Accessed: 29 February 2008.

202 Ibid., 1.

203 Time Magazine, "Left at the Pier," 5 January 1948. Internet: <http://www.time.com/time/magazine/article/0,9171,794096,00.html?iid=chix-sphere>. Accessed: 10 March 2008. Retired Canadian fighter ace, Wing Commander Robert Fumerton, helped train *Mosquito* pilots in China in 1948. See: <http://www.thestar.com/Obituary/AtoG/article/108225>.

204 Canada, DFAIT, "Under-Secretary of State for External Affairs to the Secretary of State for External Affairs," 29 June 1948, 1. Documents on Canadian External Relations, Vol. 14 – 730, Chapter VII (International Economic Relations), Part 11 (Production and Export of Arms). Internet: <http://www.dfait-maeci.gc.ca/department/history/dcer/details-en.asp?intRefid=10470>. Accessed: 29 February 2008.

205 Canada, DFAIT, "Secretary of State for External Affairs to Cabinet, Sale of Arms to China," 7 October 1948, 1. Documents on Canadian External Relations, Vol. 14 – 734, Chapter VII (International Economic Relations), Part 11 (Production and Export of Arms). Internet: <http://www.dfait-maeci.gc.ca/department/history/dcer/details-en.asp?intRefid=10475>. Accessed: 29 February 2008.

206 Canada, DFAIT, "Acting Under-Secretary of State for External Affairs to the Acting Secretary of State for External Affairs," 16 November 1948, 1. Documents on Canadian External Relations, Vol. 14 – 1109, Chapter VIII (Far East), Part 1 (China), Section B (Evacuation of Canadians from China). Internet: <http://www.dfait.gc.ca/department/history/dcer/details-en.asp?intRefid=10797>. Accessed: 3 March 2008.

207 Canada, DFAIT, "Acting Under-Secretary of State for External Affairs to the Acting Secretary of State for External Affairs," 15 December 1948, 1. Documents on Canadian External Relations, Vol. 14 – 1115, Chapter XIII (Far East), Part 1 (China), Section C (Trade Credits to China). Internet: <http://www.dfait.gc.ca/department/history/dcer/details-en.asp?intRefid=10803>. Accessed: 3 March 2008.

208   Canada, LAC, "Sale of Arms to India and Pakistan," 1 September 1948, 4. RG 2, Privy Council Office, Series A-5-a, Vol. 2642, Reel T-2365.

209   Canada, LAC, "Export of Arms and Ammunition; China; India; Pakistan," 12 October 1948, 5-6. RG 2, Privy Council Office, Series A-5-a, Vol. 2642, Reel T-2365.

210   Canada, LAC, "Sale of Munitions to India and Pakistan," 8 December 1948, 9. RG 2, Privy Council Office, Series A-5-a, Vol. 2642, Reel T-2366.

211   Ibid., 9.

212   Canada, LAC, "Export of Military Equipment; India; Pakistan," 5 January 1949, 12. RG 2, Privy Council Office, Series A-5-a, Vol. 2643, Reel T-2366.

213   Canada, LAC, "Export of Arms to Pakistan," 5 April 1950, 3. RG 2, Privy Council Office, Series A-5-a, Vol. 2645, Reel T-2366.

214   Canada, LAC, "Export of Military Equipment to Pakistan," 19 May 1960, 8-9. RG 2, Privy Council Office, Series A-5-a, Vol. 2746.

215   The information in Table 5 is mainly based on Cabinet records in the RG 2, Privy Council series. The dollar amounts are not, taken in isolation, that large. The sale of field artillery ammunition in June 1952, for example, would amount to approximately $39 million in 2009 dollars after adjustments for inflation (using the Bank of Canada inflation calculator). Nevertheless, with orders originating from other countries the arms industry was tossed a lifeline.

216   Canada, DND, "463rd Meeting of the Chiefs of Staff Committee," 16 May 1950, Item VII, Paragraph 29, extract, no page number. (Ottawa: DND, DHH, Series XIV: Chiefs of Staff Committee Meetings, Box 76, File 4-5). The Joint Intelligence Bureau (JIB), part of the Defence Research Board, dealt with economic and technical intelligence analysis.

217   Canada, DND, "455th Meeting of the Chiefs of Staff Committee," 11 January 1950, Item IX, Paragraph 31, extract, no page number. (Ottawa: DND, DHH, Series XIV: Chiefs of Staff Committee Meetings, Box 70, File 9). Previously, External Affairs had forwarded requests for arms export permits to the Secretary of the Chiefs of Staff Committee and the Secretary would then send the request to the most appropriate Chief of Staff for assessment.   The Secretary would then send the Service recommendation, approved by the Service Chief, to External Affairs. The Chief of the General Staff (Army) did not agree with the proposal to involve the JIB in coordinating and assessing export requests. He was concerned that Service Chiefs might not be advised or aware of export requests and that the new system would not be any more efficient than the current. The Army was also concerned that they might miss out on opportunities to export old stocks of arms and ammunition that could then be replaced or replenished with new equipment or stocks. As it was, it appears the involvement of the JIB simply relieved the Secretary of the coordination function as the JIB essentially reported their findings to him for onward consideration by the Chiefs of the General Staff and eventually External Affairs.

218   Canada, DFAIT, "Deputy Under-Secretary of State for External Affairs to the Secretary of State for External Affairs," 28 May 1953, 1. Documents on Canadian External Relations, Vol. 19 – 983, Chapter IX (Western Europe and the Middle East), Part 3 (Middle East), Section B (Israel), Sub-Section I (Export of Arms). Internet: <http://www.dfait-maeci.gc.ca/department/history/dcer/details-en.asp?intRefId=2614> Accessed: 22 February 2008.

219   Ibid., 1.

220   Canada, LAC, "Sale of Guns to Israel," 19 October 1954, 8. RG 2, Privy Council Office, Series A-5-a, Vol. 2656, Reel T-2369.

221 Ibid., 9. In July 1955, another contentious arms order arrived in Ottawa. This time, the Israeli government asked Canada to supply 800 *Browning* machine guns. However, not wanting to be seen fuelling an arms race, the Canadian government decided to limit the sale to just 200 machine guns at a rate of 20 per month. The decision to limit sales would later be overturned following pressure from the Israeli government but the 1956 Suez Crises halted all sales.

222 Canada, LAC, "Arms Shipments to the Middle East," 8 March 1956, 19. RG 2, Privy Council Office, Series A-5-a, Vol. 5775, Reel T-12185. The actual order from Canada had been for 15 aircraft of which six had already been delivered.

223 Canada, LAC, "Export of Arms to the Middle East; Policy," 15 March 1956, 8. RG 2, Privy Council Office, Series A-5-a, Vol. 5775, Reel T-12185.

224 Canada, DFAIT, "Assistant Under-Secretary of State for External Affairs to the Secretary of State for External Affairs, Export of Arms to Israel," 29 August 1958, 1. Documents on External Relations, Vol. 25 – 235, Chapter 2 (Middle East), Part 2 (Export of Arms to the Middle East). Internet: <http://www.dfait-maeci.gc.ca/department/history/dcer/details-en.asp?intRefid=8322>. Accessed: 14 February 2008.

225 Ibid., 1.

226 Canada, DFAIT, "Head, Commonwealth and Middle East Division, to the Under-Secretary of State for External Affairs," 5 November 1956. Documents on External Relations, Vol. 22 – 70, Chapter 1 (The Middle East and the Suez Crisis), Part 1 (Middle East), Section C (Export of F-86 Interceptors to Israel). Internet: <http://www.international.gc.ca/department/history/dcer/details-en.asp?intRefid=2816>. Accessed: 3 March 2008. The cancellation of the export permit created a fair degree of friction between the Canadian and Israeli governments. As far as the Israeli government was concerned they had bought and paid for the eight aircraft and although the aircraft were still in Canada they were, in their opinion, their legal property. However, this was not a view shared by the Canadian Government, which resisted pressure to release the aircraft. Indeed, the Israeli Government was advised that if they wished to have their money returned they should take the matter up with Canadair not Ottawa.

227 Canada, DFAIT, "Assistant Under-Secretary of State for External Affairs to the Secretary of State for External Affairs," 4 April 1956, 1. Documents on External Relations, Vol. 22 – 33, Chapter 1 (The Middle East and the Suez Crisis), Part 1 (Middle East), Section C (Export of F-86 Interceptors to Israel), Internet: <http://www.international.gc.ca/department/history/dcer/details-en.asp?intRefid=2779>. Accessed: 3 March 2008.

228 Canada, LAC, "Export of Arms and Military Equipment to the Middle East," 12 December 1963. RG 2, Privy Council Office, Export of Arms and Military Equipment to the Middle East, Series A-5-a, Vol. 6254.

229 Canada, LAC, "Military Assistance to India," 19 December 1963, Annex A, 1. (Annex A – Military Assistance to India, is dated 9 May 1963). RG 58, Auditor General, Vol. 278, File: S-2-5070-85/335-1. National Defence – India – Military Training Assistance (1963-1964).

230 The information in Table 6 is based on: T.F.J. Leversedge, *Canadian Combat and Support Aircraft: A Military Compendium* (St. Catharines, Ontario: Vanwell Publishing, 2007).

231 Canada, LAC, "Canadian Military Assistance to Developing Countries," 25 June 1970, Appendix 1 to Annex A. RG 25, External Affairs, Vol. 10403, File: 27-20-1-2, Part 2. Military Assistance – Canada – Military Assistance Committee. The transport

and general shipping details surrounding the support to India were worked out at a meeting held in Ottawa in February 1963. Air Commodore Latif, the Indian Air Advisor based in Washington, attended the meeting. The Indian government had originally asked for 45 *Caribou* aircraft.

232   The Department of Defence Production was created in 1951 to better coordinate Canada's defence industrial output during the Korean War.

233   Canada, LAC, "Export of Arms; Purchase of F86 Aircraft by Columbia," 15 March 1956, 9. RG 2, Privy Council Office, Series A-5-a, Vol. 5775, Reel T-12185. A total of 390 Mk. 6s *Sabre* jets went to the RCAF with the majority going to the Air Division squadrons in Germany and France. Another 225 were exported to the West German Luftwaffe, six were sold to the Colombian Air Force and 34 went to the South African Air Force in 1956. In January 1966, Germany sold 90 of its *Sabre* aircraft to Iran but they were quickly transferred to Pakistan and became the main day fighter of the Pakistan Air Force. Internet: <http://www.aviation.technomuses.ca/pdf/SabreMk6.pdf>. Accessed: 2 October 2007

234   Canada, LAC, "Export of Military Aircraft; General Policy," 2 August 1956, 3. RG2, Privy Council Office, Series A-5-a, Volume 5775, Reel T-12185.

235   Canada, LAC, "Export of Military Equipment to the Dominican Republic," 30 July 1970, 5-6. RG 2, Privy Council Office, Series A-5-a, Vol. 2745.

236   Canada, LAC, "Export of Military Equipment to Venezuela," 28 September 1959, 8. RG 2, Privy Council Office, Series A-5-a, Vol. 2745.

237   Canada, LAC, "Export of Military Trucks to Venezuela," 3 February 1960, 5. RG 2, Privy Council Office, Series A-5-a, Vol. 2745.

238   Canadian Institute of Strategic Studies Proceedings, *Canada, the Caribbean and Central America*, ed. by Brian MacDonald, Fall 1985, 103.

239   Ibid., 104.

240   Canada, LAC, "Establishment of Canadian Diplomatic Missions in Dar es Salaam, Tanganyika and the Republic of Cameroon," 20 November 1961, 4. RG 2, Privy Council Office, Series A-5-a, Vol. 6176.

241   Ibid., 4.

242   Diefenbaker, 110-111.

243   Canada, LAC, "Control of Export of Military Equipment – Policy and Procedures," 14 September 1960, 8. RG 2, Privy Council Office, Series A-5-a, Vol. 2747.

244   Ibid., 8-9.

245   Canada, LAC, "South Africa – Canadian Policy," 2 November 1961, 2-3. RG 2, Privy Council Office, Series A-5-a, Vol. 6176.

246   Ibid., 3.

247   Canada, LAC, "Export of Military Equipment to South Africa," 12 October 1962, 5. RG 2, Privy Council Office, Series A-5-a, Vol. 6193.

248   Canada, LAC, "Proposal of Sales Promotion of Jet Trainer Aircraft to South Africa," 25 June 1963, 10. RG 2, Privy Council Office, Series A-5-a, Vol. 6253.

249   Ibid., 2.

250   Ibid., 3.

251   Canada, DFAIT, "Under-Secretary of State for External Affairs to the Secretary of State for External Affairs," 10 November 1954, 1. Documents on Canadian External Relations, Vol. 20 – 262, Chapter III (NATO), Part 1 – Annual Review and Mutual Aid Policy. Internet: <http://www.dfait-maeci.gc.ca/department/history/dcer/details-en.asp?intRefId=273>. Accessed: 28 February 2008. To ensure the right defence production investments would be made, the Departments of Defence Production and

National Defence undertook a study in 1954 to determine the long term equipment deficiencies of the Canadian Forces and, in particular, deficiencies that would exist following mobilization.

252 Canada, DFAIT, "Head, Defence Liaison (1) Division, to the European Division," 4 November 1955, 1. Documents on Canadian External Relations, Vol. 21 – 149, Chapter II (NATO), Part 1 – Annual Review and Mutual Aid, Section A – General Policy. Internet: <http://www.dfait-maeci.gc.ca/department/history/dcer/details-en.asp?intRefId=266>. Accessed: 22 February 2008.

253 Greg Donaghy, "The Rise and Fall of Canadian Military Assistance in the Developing World, 1952-1971," *Canadian Military History*, Vol. 4, No. 1, 1995, 76.

254 Canada, DND, "Training of Foreign Service Personnel in Canada," 2 October 1953, 1. (Ottawa, DND, DHH, Series XIV: Chiefs of Staff Committee Meetings, 560th Meeting of the Chiefs of Staff Committee, 16 March 1954, Box 79, File 21). Besides the ten NATO students, the Army Staff College also had one Australian, one Pakistani and one Indian student on course.

255 Canada, DND, "Requests from Other Countries for the Training of Service Personnel in Canadian Defence Establishments," 26 January 1953, 5. (Ottawa, DND, DHH, Series XIV: Chiefs of Staff Committee Meetings, 560th Meeting of the Chiefs of Staff Committee, 16 March 1954, Box 79, File 21).

256 Donaghy, 76.

257 Table 7 was compiled from: "Requests from Other Countries for the Training of Service Personnel in Canadian Defence Establishments," 26 January 1953 and "Training of Foreign Service Personnel in Canada," 2 October 1953. Both documents can be found at: (Ottawa, DND, DHH, Series XIV: Chiefs of Staff Committee Meetings, 560th Meeting of the Chiefs of Staff Committee, 16 March 1954, Box 79, File 21).

258 Donaghy, 77.

259 Ibid., 77.

260 Canada, DEA, "Visit of the Prime Minister to Ottawa," July 24-27 1958, 1. (Ottawa: Documents on External Relations, Vol. 24 – 468, Chapter 3 (Commonwealth Relations), Part 7, Section F). Internet: <http://www.dfait-maeci.gc.ca/department/history/dcer/details-en.asp?intRefId=6890>. Accessed: 14 February 2008.

261 Canada, DEA, "Movement for Independence of African Territories," no date (Ottawa: DEA 11253 – B – 40, Vol. #26 454, Chapter IX, Africa, 1959), 1. Internet: <http://www.dfait-maeci.gc.ca/department/history/dcer/details-en.asp?intRefid=11272>. Accessed: 24 February 2007.

262 Ibid., 1.

263 Walter Laqueur, "Communism and Nationalism in Tropical Africa," *Foreign Affairs*, Vol. 39, No. 4 (July 1961), 610.

264 Snow, 290.

265 Canada, DEA, "Movement for Independence of African Territories," no date, 1.

266 Ibid., 1.

267 Canada, CIDA, *Ghana and Tanzania – Facts at a Glance* (Ottawa: Canadian International Development Agency, 2006), 1. Internet: <http://www.acdi-cida.gc.ca>. Accessed: 24 February 2007.

268 Canada, LAC, "Request from Ghana for Canadian Military Instructors," 2 March 1961, 1. Privy Council Office, RG 2, Series A-5-a, Vol. 6176. Ghana also purchased 14 *Beaver* aircraft.

269 Keith Hopkins, "Civil-Military Relations in Developing Countries," *The British Journal of Sociology*. Vol. 17, No. 2, June 1966, 167. Ghana's population was 7 million in

1965-66, of which 22.5% of the population was literate. However, this statistic compared rather favourably with other African countries such as Nigeria with just 10% of 55.6 million people able to read and write.

270 Canada, DND, "Colonel P.S. Cooper to Air Marshall F.R. Miller, Chairman Chiefs of Staff," 8 April 1961, 2. (Ottawa, DND, DHH, Box 133, File 3232, Possible Canadian Military Assistance to Ghana, Raymont Fonds (73/1223)).

271 Ibid., Annex A, 1.

272 Ibid., 3.

273 Canada, LAC, "Provision of Canadian Military Training Assistance to Ghana," 1 June 1961, 7. RG 2, Privy Council Office, Series A-5-a, Vol. 6176.

274 Canada, Canada Treaty Information, "Technical Assistance Agreement on Military Training between the Government of Canada and the Government of the Republic of Ghana," 8 January 1962 (modified on 14 February 1978). Internet: <http://www.accord-treaty.gc.ca/ViewTreaty.asp?Treaty_ID=100915>. Accessed: 14 February 2008.

275 Canada, DND, "Visit of Nigerian Defence Minister," 13 September 1961, 1. (Ottawa: DND, DHH, Box 28, File 489, Raymont Fonds (73/1223)).

276 Canada, DND, "Visit to Canada of Nigerian Minister of National Defence," 18 September 1961, 1-2. (Ottawa: DND, DHH, Box 28, File 489, Raymont Fonds (73/1223)).

277 Donaghy, 79.

278 Canada, LAC, "Progress Report – Selection of Nigerian Pilot Trainees," 21 January 1963, 1. RG 25, External Affairs, Vol. 5448, File 11384-B-40-Part 4.

279 Canada, LAC, "Ministry of Industry," 11 May 1964, 1. RG 24, National Defence, Vol. 21491, File 2137.7V1 – Military Assistance to the UN – General.

280 Canada, LAC, "T. LeM. Cater (High Commissioner) to Vice Admiral H.S. Rayner (Chief of Naval Staff)", 27 February 1963, 1. RG 25, Vol. 5448, File 11384-B-40-Part 4. Two lieutenant-commanders were eventually sent to Nigeria in April 1964 to teach naval subjects but they returned to Canada on commencement of the Nigerian Civil War.

281 Canada, LAC, "Aide-Memoire for the Chairman Chiefs of Staff – Military Assistance to Nigeria," 5 July 1962, 1-3. RG 24, National Defence, Vol. 21490, CSC 2137.6, Part 2.

282 Canada, LAC, "Discussions with Nigerian Defence Officials," 17 April 1964, 1. RG 24, National Defence, Vol. 21491, File 2137.6V5 – Military Assistance to Nigeria.

283 Canada, LAC, "Military Training Assistance for the Congo," 13 March 1962, 4. RG 2, Privy Council Office, Series A-5-a, Vol. 6192.

284 Ibid., 5.

285 J.M. Lee, *African Armies and Civil Order* (London: Chatto & Windus, 1969), 85.

286 Donaghy, 80.

287 Canada, DND, "Request for Military Training and Equipment," 18 March 1963, 1. (Ottawa: DND, DHH, Series XIV: Chiefs of Staff Committee Meetings, 738th Meeting of the Chiefs of Staff Committee, 2 May 1963, Box 72, File 3).

288 Canada, DND, "DEA to Air Chief Marshal Miller," 9 April 1963, 1. (Ottawa: DND, DHH, Series XIV: Chiefs of Staff Committee Meetings, 738th Meeting of the Chiefs of Staff Committee, 2 May 1963, Box 72, File 3).

289 Ibid., 1.

290 Canada, DND, "Request for Military Assistance – Tanganyika," 23 April 1963, 1. (Ottawa: DND, DHH, Series XIV: Chiefs of Staff Committee Meetings, 738th Meeting of the Chiefs of Staff Committee, 2 May 1963, Box 72, File 3).

291 Ibid., 1.

292   Canada, LAC, "Right Honourable Lester B. Pearson from the Right Honourable Sir Alexander Douglas-Home," 21 August 1964, 1-2. RG 19, Department of Finance, Vol. 3871, File 8382/T171-1, Part 1. International Programmes and International Finance – Military Assistance Programmes – Tanzania – United Republic of – Generally.

293   Canada, LAC, "Under Secretary of State for External Affairs to Air Chief Marshall Miller," 10 June 1964, 1. RG 24, National Defence, Vol. 21491, File 2137.7V1 – Military Assistance to the United Nations.

294   Ibid., 1.

295   Ibid., 8.

296   Canada, LAC, Memorandum, "Military Assistance Requests – Summary by Country as of 10 May 1963," 1. RG 24, National Defence, Vol. 21491, File 2137.8V – Military Assistance to Trinidad and Tobago.

297   Canada, LAC, "Memorandum for the Minister," 26 August 1964, 1. RG 25, External Affairs, Vol. 10403, File: 27-20-1-2, Part 1. Military Assistance – Canada – Military Assistance Committee.

298   Donaghy, 81.

299   Ibid., 78.

300   Canada, LAC, "Military Assistance to non-NATO Countries," 27 August 1964, 8-9. RG 2, Privy Council Office, Series A-5-a, Vol. 6265.

301   Ibid., 7.

302   Ibid., 7.

303   Ibid., 7.

304   Ibid., 7.

305   Ibid., 8.

306   Ibid., 8.

307   Mr. Menzies was the head of the Defence Liaison (1) Division in External Affairs. The Division was formed in 1952 in order to improve coordination between External Affairs and the Department of National Defence. The head of the Defence Liaison (1) Division was a senior post and after a year as Chair of the Interdepartmental Military Assistance Committee, Menzies became Canada's High Commissioner to Australia. In 1968, the Defence Liaison (1) Division was renamed and became the Office of Politico-Military Affairs with a NATO and North American Defence Division and a Peacekeeping and Military Assistance Division. Mr. J.S. Nutt, who replaced Menzies, recommended to the Under Secretary of State in September 1968, that from September 1968 onwards, Mr. M. Shenstone, head of the Peacekeeping and Military Assistance Division, now chair the Committee. The Under Secretary approved. See: Canada, LAC, "Chairmanship of Military Assistance Committee," 11 September 1968 1. RG 25 External Affairs, Vol. 10403, File 27-20-12, Part 1. Military Assistance – Canada – Military Assistance Committee.

308   Canada, LAC, "Record of Decisions, First Meeting of the Military Assistance Committee," 15 September 1964, 1. RG 25, External Affairs, Vol. 10403, File: 27-20-1-2, Part 1. Military Assistance – Canada – Military Assistance Committee.

309   Canada, LAC, Letter, "Venezuelan Enquiry Regarding Military Training in Canada," 15 September 1964, 1. RG 25, External Affairs, Vol. 10409, File 27-20-5 (Part 1).

310   Canada, LAC, "Military Assistance to URTZ," 16 September 1964, 1. RG 19, Department of Finance, Vol. 3871, File 8382/T171-1, Part 1. International Programmes and International Finance – Military Assistance Programmes – Tanzania – United Republic of – Generally.

ENDNOTES

311 Ibid., 1. Interestingly, relations between Tanganyika and the United States took a turn for the worse in November 1964. As Bienen wrote: "In November, 1964, the [Tanzanian] Minister of External Affairs, Mr. Kambona produced some letters in bad French purporting to stem from the American embassy in Leopoldville which told of an American plot to overthrow the Tanzanian Government and to bomb Chinese places of interest in Tanzania." Although the letters were likely fakes, the resulting rift in relations led to a round of high level expulsions by both governments of senior diplomatic staff. See: Henry Bienen, "National Security in Tanganyika After the Mutiny," *Transition*, No. 21 (1965), 40.

312 Canada, LAC, "Military Assistance to Tanganyika, 23 September 1964," 1-2. RG 19, Department of Finance, Vol. 3871, File 8382/T171-1, Part 1. International Programmes and International Finance – Military Assistance Programmes – Tanzania – United Republic of – Generally.

313 Canada, LAC, "Military Assistance to the United Republic of Tanganyika and Zanzibar," 2 October 1964, 1. RG 19, Department of Finance, Vol. 3871, File 8382/T171-1, Part 1. International Programmes and International Finance – Military Assistance Programmes – Tanzania – United Republic of – Generally.

314 Canada, LAC, "Military Survey Team to the United Republic of Tanganyika and Zanzibar – Confidential Instructions," undated but likely issued in September 1964. RG 19, Department of Finance, Vol. 3871, File 8382/T171-1, Part 1. International Programmes and International Finance – Military Assistance Programmes – Tanzania – United Republic of – Generally.

315 Canada, LAC, "Military Assistance for Malaysia," 22 January 1965, 3. RG 2, Privy Council Office, Series A-5-a, Vol. 6271.

316 Ibid., 3. See: Canada, LAC, "Sale of Canadair CL-41 Aircraft to Malaysia," 30 March 1965, 9. RG 2, Privy Council Office, Series A-5-a, Vol. 6271.

317 Canada, LAC, "Military Assistance to non-NATO Countries," 10 February 1965, 5. RG 2, Privy Council Office, Series A-5-a, Vol. 6321.

318 Canada, LAC, "Military Assistance Committee Meeting, Notes by External Affairs prepared on 26 January 1966," 1 February 1966, 1. RG 25, External Affairs, Vol. 10403, File: 27-20-1-2, Part 1. Military Assistance – Canada – Military Assistance Committee.

319 Ibid., 2. The Canadian senior naval officer in Nigeria had noted that the Nigerian navy was in need of "a small ship of about the size of a minesweeper... for general training." A ship, it was noted, such as the mothballed HMCS *Resolute*, built in 1954 at a cost of $4.5 million, could be provided as aid although according to the High Commissioner in Lagos, the Nigerians "might well expect Canada to pay for refit, armament and even maintenance." See: Canada, LAC, Military Assistance Committee Meeting, "Notes by External Affairs prepared on 27 January 1966," 1 February 1966 – Agenda Items, 3. RG 25, External Affairs, Vol. 10403, File: 27-20-1-2, Part 1. Military Assistance – Canada – Military Assistance Committee.

320 Canada, LAC, "De Havilland Sales of Caribou Aircraft," 7 May 1966, 1. RG 25, External Affairs, Vol. 10409, File 27-20-5 Ghana (Part 3).

321 Ibid., Appendix II.

322 Canada, DND, "54th Meeting of the Vice Chiefs of Staff Committee," 23 May 1961, 2. (Ottawa: DND, DHH, Series V: Vice Chiefs of Staff Committee, Box 26, File 8).

323 Ibid., 2.

324 Canada, LAC, "Military Assistance," 18 August 1964, 2. RG 19, Department of Finance, Vol. 3871, File 8382/T171-1, Part 1. International Programmes and International Finance – Military Assistance Programmes – Tanzania – United Republic of – Generally.

325   Canada, LAC, "Record of Decisions, Eighth Meeting of the Military Assistance Committee," 20 July 1966, 2. RG 25, External Affairs, Vol. 10403, File: 27-20-1-2, Part 1. Military Assistance – Canada – Military Assistance Committee.

326   Canada, LAC, "High Commission Accra to External Affairs, the Role of the Canadian Military Training Team in Ghana," 30 January 1964, 1. RG 24, National Defence, Vol. 21578, File S-2-5010-12-85/280/0.

327   Canada, LAC, "Report on Visit to Ghana by Major-General W.A.B. Anderson," 20-25 January 1964, 1. RG 25, External Affairs, Vol. 10415, File 27-20-5 Ghana (Part 2). That the Ghanaian military were eager for Canada's continued military support, however, was in stark contrast to the position taken by the Defence Minister, Kofi Bazko. Anderson described the then Defence Minister as "obviously a Nkrumah man." He had been friendly and courteous, reported Anderson, but at no time did he wish to discuss Canada's military assistance efforts. "Nothing could have been more marked," he continued, "than to go from the Chiefs of Staff where I was being implored to continue and increase our assistance, to the office of the Minister where the subject never arose." What Anderson did not likely know in 1965 was that the Ghana Army intended to overthrow Nkrumah's government, which they did in 1966. The tension between the Ghana Army and the Government was no doubt the reason why the Defence Minister was not keen to discuss Canada's military assistance with Anderson. Anderson, with promotion, would go on to command Force Mobile Command (the Army) in December 1966.

328   Ibid., 2.

329   Canada, LAC, "Review of International Commitments (V-3185-3 DI Plans)," 8 September 1966, 1. RG 24, National Defence, Series B-2, Vol. 21577, File S-2-5040-12 (3).

330   Ibid., 2.

331   Ibid., 5.

332   Ibid., 4.

333   Canada, LAC, "Review of International Commitments," 12 September 1966, 1. RG 24, National Defence, Series B-2, Vol. 21577, File S-2-5040-12 (3). The Topsey reference was likely referring to Topsey, the little slave girl in Harriet Beecher Stowe's *Uncle Tom's Cabin* (1852) who being young had grown rapidly in size. In essence, he was probably inferring that UN and military assistance missions had begun to increase with wild abandon.

334   Canada, LAC, "Review of International Commitments," 21 September 1966, 1. RG 24, National Defence, Series B-2, Vol. 21577, File S-2-5040-12 (3).

335   Canada, LAC, "Training of Foreign Nationals," 6 October 1966, 1. RG 24, National Defence, Series B-2, Vol. 21577, File S-2-5040-12 (3).

336   Ibid., 3.

337   Ibid., 3.

338   In the United States, the Joint Chiefs of Staff recommended the establishment of a central Pan-African Military School either in Ethiopia or Nigeria, supported by the United States and other pro-Western nations, to the Secretary of Defence in 1964. The attendance of students from African nations, they noted, would hopefully "spread Western philosophy and ideals, and would contribute to offsetting the training and political orientation offered by the Sino-Soviet Bloc." The intent was to provide instruction to junior military leaders using a program similar to the one conducted at the Officer Leadership Training Course in Fort Knox, Kentucky that featured "military concepts, fundamental tactics, weapons instruction, counterinsurgency, civic action, discipline, and moral responsibility." United States, Department of State.

Foreign Relations of the United States, 1964-1968, Volume XXIV, Africa Region. Entry 189, "Memorandum from the Joint Chiefs of Staff to Secretary of Defense McNamara," 24 December 1964. Internet at: <http://www.state.gov/www/about_state/history/vol_xxiv/r.html>. Accessed: 13 February 2008.

339 Canada, LAC, "Military Training Foreign Nationals," 9 June 1967, 1. RG 24, National Defence, Series B-1, Vol. 21834, File FMC 4760-1, Parts 10 and 11. The report may have been in response to a Planning Guidance Paper 1967-1973, dated 23 March 1967, in which the Minister of National Defence had directed the Canadian Forces to "assume a continuance of training assistance at present levels." Ibid., 15.

340 Canada, LAC, "Military Paper on the Conduct of Military Training of Foreign Military Personnel by the Canadian Armed Forces," 31 May 1967, 1-2. RG 24, National Defence, Series B-1, Vol. 21834, File FMC 4760-1, Parts 10 and 11.

341 Ibid., 5.

342 Canada, DND, Speech, "Ending the Arms Race, Speech by the Honourable Paul Martin, Secretary of State for External Affairs, to the Amherstburg Rotary Club, Bob-lo Island, Ontario," 31 August, 1967, 3. (Ottawa, DND, DHH, Box 46, File 848, Canadian Policy – Foreign and Domestic (1964-1970)).

343 Robert O. Matthews, "Canada and Anglophone Africa," *Canada and the Third World*, ed. by Peyton Lyon and Tareq Y. Ismael (Toronto: Macmillan of Canada: 1976), 109.

344 Pierre Elliot Trudeau, *Memoirs* (Toronto: McClelland & Stewart Inc., 1993), 281.

345 Canada, DND, "Conditions for Peace in Africa and the World," 17 June 1966, 3. Notes used by the Secretary of State for External Affairs, the Honourable Paul Martin at the Consultation "Focus on Africa" sponsored by the Canadian Council of Churches, Queen's University, Kingston, June 17, 1966. (Ottawa, DND, DHH, Box 46, File 848, Canadian Policy – Foreign and Domestic (1964-1970)).

346 Canada, DND, "Colonel P.S. Cooper to Air Marshall F.R. Miller, Chairman Chiefs of Staff," 8 April 1961, Annex 2, 2.

347 University of Pennsylvania, University Archives and Records Center (African Studies Center). Internet: <http://www.archives.upenn.edu/people/notables/nkrumah/nkrumah_exhibit.html>. Accessed : 23 February 2009. The website notes that Nkrumah had passed his preliminary exams for a doctorate in 1944.

348 Ali A. Mazrui, "Nkrumah: The Leninist Czar," *Transition*, No. 75/76, The Anniversary Issue: Selections from *Transition*, 1961-1976, 1997, 108. Wanting to involve French West African countries in the Secretariat's work, Nkrumah had also traveled to Paris where he met several African members of the French National Assembly including Sourou Apithy, Léopold Senghor and Houphouët-Boigny.

349 Dennis L. Cohen, "The Convention People's Party of Ghana: Representational or Solidarity Party?" *Canadian Journal of African Studies*, Vol. 4, No. 2, Spring, 1970, 176.

350 Henry L. Bretton, "Current Political Thought and Practice in Ghana," *The American Political Science Review*, Vol. 52, No. 1, March 1958, 46.

351 Robert M. Price, "Neo-Colonialism and Ghana's Economic Decline: A Critical Assessment," *Canadian Journal of African Studies*, Vol. 18, No. 1, 1984, 164-165.

352 Bretton, 57.

353 Ibid., 58.

354 Mazrui, "Nkrumah: The Leninist Czar," 111.

355 Bretton, 56-57.

356 Nkrumah had good reason to be concerned that Ghana might break apart if regional or special interest political parties gained ground. Ghana, upon independence was actually a grouping of four territories. The Gold Coast, as Ghana was previously

known, contained three territorial groupings – the Gold Coast colony, the Asante and the Northern Territories. Then, in May 1956, British Mandated Togoland voted to join Ghana.

357   Price, "Neo-Colonialism and Ghana's Economic Decline: A Critical Assessment," 191.

358   William Gutteridge, "Undoing Military Coups in Africa," *Third World Quarterly*, Vol. 7, No. 1, January 1985, 80.

359   Bretton, 58.

360   Claude E. Welch Jr., "The Right of Association in Ghana and Tanzania," *The Journal of Modern African Studies*, Vol. 16, No. 4, December 1978, 648.

361   Ibid., 649.

362   Fritz Schatten, *Communism in Africa* (London: George Allen & Unwin Ltd, 1966), 147.

363   Martin Meredith, *The Fate of Africa* (New York: Public Affairs, 2005), 180.

364   Ibid., 180.

365   Mazrui, "Nkrumah: The Leninist Czar," 123.

366   W.F. Gutteridge, "The Armed Forces in Ghana Today," *Canadian Army Journal*, Vol. 15, No. 3, 1961, 46.

367   Zach Levey, "The Rise and Decline of a Special Relationship: Israel and Ghana, 1957-1966," *African Studies Review*, Vol. 46, No. 1, April 2003, 161.

368   Meredith, 180.

369   Christopher Andrew and Vasili Mitrokhin, *The World Was Going Our Way – The KGB and the Battle for the Third World* (New York: Basic Books, 2005), 435.

370   Kwame Nkrumah, *The Autobiography of Kwame Nkrumah*, (London: Thomas Nelson and Sons Ltd., 1957), 163.

371   Baynham, 68.

372   Ibid., 68.

373   Garry Hunt, "Recollections of the Canadian Armed Forces Training Team in Ghana, 1961-1968, *Canadian Defence Quarterly*, April 1989, 44.

374   The West African Frontier Force was given legal recognition in 1901. King George V granted the prefix "Royal" in 1928. See: Baynham, 21 and 41.

375   Mullins, 18. French colonial policy in Africa differed considerably from the British when it came to Africans serving in the military. From the outset, colonies were seen in Paris as having vast pools of young men available for military service. Senegalese troops, for example, served in the Napoleonic wars, in the Crimea, in Mexico, and in the Franco-Prussian War of 1870. In particular, the French began drafting Africans for military service in 1912 and in 1917 there were thirty-one Senegalese battalions serving on the Somme. However, by November 1918, there were ninety-two Senegalese battalions serving in the French Army. Permanent conscription in French West and Equatorial Africa was then introduced in 1919 with a view of maintaining an African military of 100,000 personnel. From 1919 onwards, based on territorial quotas, 10,000 men were drafted for service in the French military. During the Second World War, over 100,000 men were mobilized from French West and Equatorial Africa while another 80,000, at the commencement of fighting, found themselves deployed in France. Africans could also be promoted up to Captain in the French military, although this was rare.

376   Baynham, 23. In 1960 just 25 per cent of the officers in the Nigerian military were actually Nigerians. However, the situation in the Sudan was completely different. In 1953, the British, realizing that the Sudan was approaching independence, embarked upon a crash training program that resulted in nearly 400 officers obtaining their

commission. "When independence was achieved in 1956, the Sudanization of the officer corps was virtually complete." See: Coleman and Brice, 368-370.

377   Ibid., 33. In the *Ghana Armed Forces Magazine* in February 1967, Lieutenant A. Enninful, wrote that in post-war Ghana, recruitment had continued to be very difficult as the military was seen as a "haven for criminals and illiterates." Similar thoughts applied to the Nigerian military. N.J. Miners quoted in his book, *The Nigerian Army 1956-60*, an officer who recalled the Nigerian Army as simply "a place for the illiterates and criminals whose duties were to kill and be generally brutal." Cited in Baynham, 39 and 44.

378   Ibid., 25.

379   Ibid., 27.

380   Ibid., 32.

381   Ibid., 67-68.

382   W.F. Gutteridge, *The Place of the Army in Society in Commonwealth African Territories*, 15. Gutteridge was the Senior Lecturer on Modern Subjects at the Royal Military Academy Sandhurst and the Commonwealth Relations Office had passed his study to the Canadian High Commission in London. Major-General George Kitching, Chairman of the Canadian Joint Staff in London subsequently forwarded the study to the Chairman, Chiefs of Staff noting "the Gutteridge Report is for official use only and that distribution is limited to Canadian and British eyes only." See: Canada, LAC, "Requirement for Defence Organization in Commonwealth African Territories," 8 June 1962, 1. RG 24, National Defence, Vol. 21490, CSC 2137.6 Part 2 – Military Assistance to Nigeria.

383   Baynham, 45.

384   Gutteridge, *The Place of the Army in Society in Commonwealth African Territories*, 16. Captain John L. Sharpe served with the Canadian training team in Ghana between 1966 and 1968. He noted that most of the junior Ghanaian officers had the equivalent of a Grade X education. Soldiers, he wrote, "were lucky if they had a few years of schooling" and the majority of officers, while showing "an excellent ability to memorize written texts and subsequently give it back to you almost verbatim," lacked initiative. He had also assumed the Ghanaians officers would naturally be accustomed to traveling in the open bush or jungle. To his surprise, he found the officers, to be "city boys" who were not at all comfortable going "into the bush" for training and field exercises. John L. Sharpe, Major-General (retired), *Two Years in Ghana West Africa 1966-68* (Ottawa: Unpublished Memoir, 2007), 4.

385   Levey, 161.

386   According to Baynham, the four Soviet fast patrol boats were not actually attached to the Navy. Crewed by Russians, they came under the control of Ghana's Border Guard, and were used to ferry arms and ammunition to opposition groups in countries bordering the Gulf of Guinea. See: 150.

387   Baynham, 74.

388   Canada, LAC, "Annual Intelligence Report Ghana (Military Attaché 75/65)," 23 November 1965, 1. RG 25, External Affairs, Vol. 10415, File 27-20-5 Ghana (Part 2).

389   Ibid., 7. See: Baynham, 75.

390   A.K. Ocran, *A Myth is Broken* (Harlow: Longmans, 1968), 6-7.

391   Ibid., 95.

392   Baynham, 125.

393   Hunt, 44.

394　Anton Bebler, *Military Rule in Africa – Dahomey, Ghana, Sierra Leone and Mali* (New York: Praeger Publishers, 1973), 35. The military equipment provided to Ghana came from a wide variety of sources. In 1967, Israel sent 100 jeeps for use by the Ghanaian army but without any spare parts. Meanwhile, 60% of the heavy vehicle fleet was already unusable due to the same problem. See: Lee, 96. Besides an expansion of the Ghana Army, the Police Force also increased in size from 6,000 in 1957 to 13,500 personnel in 1966.

395　Canada, LAC, "Annual Intelligence Report Ghana (Military Attaché 75/65)," 23 November 1965, 8.

396　Ibid., 8.

397　Canada, LAC, "Colonel Deane-Freeman, Commander CAFTTG to the Canadian High Commissioner," Ghana, 28 July 1965, 1. RG 25, External Affairs, Vol. 10415, File 27-20-5 Ghana (Part 2).

398　Ibid., 1. At the time of his writing, the Canadian team in Ghana had been reduced from 26 to just 16 officers and men. However, the Colonel was keen to see: the number of Canadians reduced even further by replacing them with trained Ghanaian officers as they became available. Prior to 1965, a one for one replacement program had not been possible due to the rapid expansion of the Ghanaian military and the need for every trained officer in front-line units. However, by 1965, expansion plans had been curtailed as the economy began to collapse. As a result, more staff college trained Ghanaian officers were now ready to takeover previously Canadian held roles. The Military Academy and Training Schools (MATS) was located just outside Accra. In 1967, MATS comprised the Defence College, the Ghana Military Academy and five other training schools: School of Infantry, School of Physical Education, Education School, Clerks Training Wing, and the Cooks Training Wing.

399　Ibid., 4.

400　Canada, LAC, "Replacement of Commander of the CAFTTG," 4 August 1965, 1. RG 25, External Affairs, Vol. 10415, File 27-20-5 Ghana (Part 2).

401　Scott W. Thompson, *Ghana's Foreign Policy, 1957-1966 – Diplomacy, Ideology and the New State* (Princeton, New Jersey: Princeton University Press, 1969), 272. During the assassination attempt Nkrumah narrowly missed being killed. A grenade, thrown towards his party, killed a bodyguard and left the President with minor shrapnel wounds in his back.

402　Ibid., 301.

403　Ibid., 302.

404　Donovan C. Chau, "Assistance of a Different Kind: Chinese Political Warfare in Ghana, 1958-1966," *Comparative Strategy*, Vol. 26, No. 2, March 2007, 144.

405　Thompson, 359. In April 1964, Barden proposed that Ghanaian trained and financed militants from the camps be fanned out across Africa because, as he said: "Ghana has made it clear that the stage is reached where imperialism, apartheid, and neocolonialism must be fought by armed revolution. As the leading African nation fighting against these evils Ghana must make available to the freedom fighters greater facilities for training." See: Thompson, 359.

406　Legvold, 252.

407　Chau, 149. In addition to training support, Chau noted that the Chinese had also planned on building two weapons factories in Ghana to make grenades and mines but the factories were never built. However, he did note that in March 1965, a shipment of Chinese small arms – 40 truckloads in all – had been off-loaded in Ghana, likely destined for the training camps. See: 146 and 150. The camps conceived by

Nkrumah for training "freedom fighters" had been partially staffed by Soviet advisors for a short period. When a new camp opened in December 1961 at Mampong, the Soviet Union readily supplied two teaching staff but for just six months. The Russians wrote Legvold, had been "disconcerted by a totally inept operation, [and] found this kind of activity of diminishing value. See: 162.

408 Legvold, 253.
409 Ibid., 254.
410 Thompson, 379.
411 Ibid., 388.
412 United States, Department of State, Foreign Relations of the United States, 1964-1968, Volume XXIV, Africa. Entry 237, *Memorandum from the Director of the Office of West African Affairs to the Assistant Secretary of State for African Affairs*, 11 February 1964. Internet: <http://www.state.gov/www/about_state/history/vol_xxiv/x.html>. Accessed: 1 January 2008.
413 Ibid. Accessed: 1 January 2008.
414 Meredith, 190.
415 Time Magazine, "Revolutionaries Adrift," 26 March 1965. Internet: <http://www.time.com/time/magazine/article/0,9171,841756,00.html?promoid=googlep>. Accessed: 1 June 2008.
416 Thompson, 383.
417 Meredith, 187.
418 A.W. Seidman, *Ghana's Development Experience* (Nairobi: East African Publishing House, 1978), 142.
419 Ibid., 81.
420 Ibid., 218.
421 Ibid., 214-215.
422 Ibid., 141.
423 Mazrui, "Nkrumah: The Leninist Czar," 125.
424 Jon Kraus, "On the Politics of Nationalism and Social Change in Ghana," *The Journal of Modern African Studies*, Vol. 7, No. 1, April 1969, 129.
425 Ibid., 242.
426 Baynham, 135.
427 Ibid., 136.
428 Ibid., 78.
429 One of the key issues leading to the coup in February 1966 had been Nkrumah's decision in July 1965 to remove the POGR from the regular army's command structure. The unit, reporting directly to the President, was trained and equipped by the Soviet Union who ran a special POGR training camp at Shia Hills. See: A.A. Afrifa, *The Ghana Coup – 24 February 1964* (London: Frank Cass & Co. Ltd.), 1966, 244-245.
430 The only time serious consideration seems to have been given to bringing the Canadian training team in Ghana back to Canada was in the aftermath of the Rhodesian government's Unilateral Declaration of Independence in November 1965. In Ottawa, the fear was that the training team in Ghana might become indirectly involved in the crisis as some African countries, such as Ghana, were considering taking military action against the white regime. "Ghana has shown itself," noted an External Affairs memorandum, to be "one of the most militant African states and would probably be most eager to contribute a substantial contingent to any African force established to confront Rhodesia." Therefore, and "since Ghana would in all likelihood spearhead any extreme African military measure against Rhodesia, withdrawal of our team

from Ghana may at one point be deemed essential by the Canadian Government."
Canada, LAC, "Implications of Rhodesian Crisis for Canadian Military Assistance to
African States," 15 December 1965, 2-4. RG 25, External Affairs, Vol. 10415, File 27-20-
5 Ghana (Part 2).

431   Canada, LAC, "Promotion of Sales of Jet Trainer Aircraft to Ghana," 25 June 1963, 11.
RG 2, Privy Council Office, Series A-5-a, Vol. 6254.

432   During the Rhodesian crisis of late 1965, and according to Colonel Afrifa, Nkrumah
was prepared to use the Ghanaian military in an attack on the white regime. This
initiative, Colonel Afrifa wrote, was one of the key reasons the military decided to
overthrow the government in February 1966: "From concern of my troops," he said,
"I felt it would be criminal and purposeless to lead such an army of excellent soldiers,
ill-equipped, to fight in an unnecessary war." See: Afrifa, 104.

433   Canada, LAC, "Memorandum to Cabinet, Export of Military Equipment to Ghana,"
17 July 1963, 1. RG 20, Industry, Trade and Commerce, Series A-3, Vol. 1657, File
20-242-G11, Military Equipment – Supplies for Armed Services of Foreign Countries
– Trade Relations – Ghana (1963-1968).

434   Ibid., 2.

435   Ibid., 3.

436   Canada, LAC, "Demonstration of Canadair CL-41 Aircraft in Ghana," 30 December
1963, 1. RG 20, Industry, Trade and Commerce, Series A-3, Vol. 1657, File 20-242-G11,
Military Equipment – Supplies for Armed Services of Foreign Countries – Trade Relations – Ghana (1963-1968).

437   Canada, LAC, "Annual Intelligence Report Ghana (Military Attaché 75/65)," 23 November 1965, 1.

438   United States, Department of State, Foreign Relations of the United States, 1964-1968,
Vol. XXIV, Africa. Entry 257, "Memorandum for the Deputy Director Central Intelligence on recent OCI Reporting on Ghana," 25 February 1966. Internet:<http://www.
state.gov/www/about_state/history/vol_xxiv/y.html>. Accessed: 1 January 2008.

439   United States, Department of State, Foreign Relations of the United States, 1964-1968,
Volume XXIV, Africa. Entry 251, "Memorandum of Conversation, 11 March 1965 between the Director Central Intelligence Agency and the United States Ambassador to
Ghana." Internet: <http://www.state.gov/www/about_state/history/vol_xxiv/y.
html>. Accessed: 1 January 2008.

440   United States, Department of State, Foreign Relations of the United States, 1964-1968,
Volume XXIV, Africa. Entry 253, "Memorandum from Robert W. Komer of the National Security Council Staff to the President's Special Assistant for National Security Affairs," 27 May 1965. Internet: <http://www.state.gov/www/about_state/history/
vol_xxiv/y.html>. Accessed: 11 February 2008. In August 1965, President Johnson
met with Ghana's Foreign Minister Alex Quaison-Sackey, and the Ambassador of
Ghana in Washington. The purpose of the visit was to advise President Johnson
that Nkrumah planned to visit Hanoi to broker a peace deal between North Vietnam
and the United States: "The Foreign Minister said that he brought the President the
very warm greetings of President Nkrumah, and a letter. As soon as he had finished
reading the letter, the President gave the Foreign Minister a categorical assurance
that no U.S. military operations would interfere with any visit to Hanoi by President
Nkrumah. The President, said Komer, had said (1) we are not bombing Hanoi, (2) we
have not intensified our bombing of North Vietnam, and (3) the President will be in
no danger. Komer then added a line in reference to (3) saying "who is he kidding?
(probably referring to Ho, not Nkrumah)." See: United States, Department of State.

ENDNOTES

Foreign Relations of the United States, 1964-1968, Volume XXIV, Africa. Entry 254, "Memorandum of Conversation, 6 August 1965." Internet: <http://www.state.gov/www/about_state/history/vol_xxiv/y.html>. Accessed: 11 February 2008.

441 Baynham, 143.

442 Thompson, 194. According to John Stockwell, the CIA station in Accra maintained "intimate" contact with elements in the Ghana Army planning to oust Nkrumah and was given unofficial credit for the coup. During the coup, the CIA station was able to put their hands on classified Soviet equipment and had plans to storm the Chinese embassy – plans that were turned down by Washington. Stockwell also reported that eight Soviet advisors were killed during the coup, which both the Russians and the Canadian High Commissioner in Ghana correctly denied had happened. See: John Stockwell, *In Search of Enemies: A CIA Story* (New York: W.W. Norton & Company, Inc., 1978), 201.

443 Afrifa, 32.

444 Ibid., 98.

445 Cohen, 179.

446 Ibid., 179.

447 Canada, LAC, "New Government Ghana," 2 March 1966, 1. RG 25, External Affairs, Vol. 10415, File 27-20-5 Ghana (Part 2).

448 Canada, LAC, "Ghana – New Regime Consolidates," 2 March 1966, 1. RG 25, External Affairs, Vol. 10415, File 27-20-5 Ghana (Part 2).

449 Ibid., 3. Rumours that eleven Soviet advisors with the POGR had been shot during the coup were quickly dispelled by Moscow. On 9 March 1966 the Soviet newspaper *TASS* printed an article in which the deaths were deemed "a fabrication from beginning to end." See: Legvold, 267.

450 Canada, LAC, "Ghana Coup – Expulsion of Soviet and Chinese Technical Assistance Personnel," 3 March 1966, 3. RG 25, External Affairs, Vol. 10415, File 27-20-5 Ghana (Part 2). Thompson noted that the Polish government had worked hard to support the Ghanaian government through their aid efforts. "Polish technical experts were always quick to assure their Ghanaian counterparts that they came to Ghana as professionals, not as ideologues, which was appreciated. After the 1966 coup, they were excepted from the anti-Communist fervor generated by the new regime." See: Thompson, 277. The Tamale airfield project had been a significant undertaking. Major Norman Graham visited the site in northern Ghana during his posting (1970-72) and "was totally unprepared for the sight" that greeted him. There were huge piles of steel reinforcing rods for the planned concrete runways and six hundred houses for construction workers plus a partially completed officers' mess. Workshop buildings, untouched since the 1966 coup, contained crates of equipment including drill presses, lathes, hand-tools and so on. "Heavy earth-moving equipment, bulldozers, road graders and trucks of various sizes," he added, "were left where they stood when the Russians left." He had been told in Accra that the Tamale airfield would have been the largest airfield in Africa. See: Norman A. Graham, *From the Barrack Room to the Boardroom, The Memoirs Of A Self-Made Man* (New York, iUniverse Inc, 2007), 165.

451 Canada, LAC, "Canadian Training Team," 8 March 1966, 1. RG 25, External Affairs, Vol. 10415, File 27-20-5 Ghana (Part 2).

452 Ibid., 1.

453 Canada, LAC, "Personal Letter High Commissioner in Ghana to the Assistant Under Secretary Department of External Affairs," 10 March 1966, 2. RG 25, External Affairs, Vol. 10415, File 27-20-5 Ghana (Part 2). The military coup in 1966 was followed by

an abortive counter-coup on 17 April 1967. Given the name "Operation Guitar Boy," 120 troops from B Squadron of the Reconnaissance Regiment attempted to overthrow the NLC. Although the coup was unsuccessful, largely due to the intervention of the police, Lt Benjamin Arthur (and his accomplices, Lt Yeboah and 2Lt Osei-Poku) did assassinate General Kotoka. The coup led the British and Canadian training teams in Ghana to formulate evacuation plans in the event of another emergency. See: Baynham, 241.

454 Canada, LAC, "High Commission Ghana (Commercial Division) to De Havilland Aircraft of Canada Ltd," 6 April 1966, 1. RG 20, Industry, Trade and Commerce, Series A-3, Vol. 1657, File 20-242-G11, Military Equipment – Supplies for Armed Services of Foreign Countries – Trade Relations – Ghana (1963-1968). After the coup, Nkrumah went into exile in Guinea. He died of cancer in a Romanian hospital in 1972.

455 Canada, LAC, "Discussion Paper – Canadian Forces Attaché – Ghana Armed Forces and Canadian Military Assistance," 12 July 1967, 2. RG 25, External Affairs, Vol. 10415, File 27-20-5 Ghana (Part 4).

456 Ibid., 2-3.

457 Ibid., 10.

458 Ibid., 3.

459 Ibid., 3.

460 Ibid., 4.

461 Ibid., 5.

462 Ibid., 10. It is important to note that Canada was not the sole source of military assistance to Ghana in the post-coup period. The Royal Air Force contingent, often up to 100 officers and men, supported the Ghana Air Force while the Royal Navy provided some 80 officers and men in support of the Ghanaian Navy. In late 1967, the British completed a survey of the Ghana Air Force. "The technical side of the Air Force operation," was identified as "a large problem – the technicians receive good training from the British, but while they can learn from rote, the application of technical knowledge is difficult for them. This is due to a complete lack of any mechanical involvement during childhood." See: Canada, LAC, "Survey of Ghana Air Force," 20 November 1967, 1. RG 25, External Affairs, Vol. 10415, File 27-20-5 Ghana (Part 4).

463 Canada, LAC, "Record of Decisions, Fifteenth Meeting of the Military Assistance Committee," 5 January 1968, 3. RG 25, External Affairs, Vol. 10403, File: 27-20-1-2, Part 1. Military Assistance – Canada – Military Assistance Committee. The shopping list of equipment included, among several requirements, 2,000 blankets, five portable water purification plants, and 3,188 pairs of boots. The Department of National Defence was able to provide these items but at a cost to the Military Assistance Committee of $43,000. See: Canada, LAC, "Military Assistance to Ghana – Ghanaian Requirement for Equipment," 23 May 1968, 1. RG 25, External Affairs, Vol. 10415, File 27-20-5 Ghana (Part 5).

464 Canada, LAC, "Report of the Commander, Canadian Armed Forces Training Team Ghana Third Quarter," 1968, 11 October 1968, 1 and Annex A. RG 25, External Affairs, Vol. 10415, File 27-20-5 Ghana (Part 4).

465 Canada, LAC, "Tour Report – Visit by DGP to Ghana and Tanzania 3-14 March 1969," 21 March 1969, 6. RG 24, National Defence, Vol. 21834, File FMC 4760-1 (Parts 10 and 11).

466 Canada, LAC, "Report of the Commander, Canadian Armed Forces Training Team Ghana, Third Quarter 1970," 3 August 1970, 1. RG 25, External Affairs, Vol. 10416, File 27-20-5 Ghana (Part 8).

ENDNOTES

467 Canada, LAC, "Ghana Armed Forces and Canadian Military Assistance," 18 July 1967, 4. RG 25, External Affairs, Vol. 10415, File 27-20-5 Ghana (Part 4).

468 United States, Department of State, Foreign Relations of the United States, 1964-1968, Volume XXIV, Africa Region. Entry 231, "Report From Vice President Humphrey to President Johnson on the Vice President's Visit to Africa," 30 December 1967 to 11 January 1968, 12 January 1968. Internet: <http://www.state.gov/www/about_state/history/vol_xxiv/w.html>. Accessed: 13 February 2008.

469 Canada, LAC, "Memorandum to the Cabinet, Canadian Military Assistance to Developing Countries," 25 June 1970, (Secret), 2.

470 Robert M. Price, "Military Officers and Political Leadership: The Ghanaian Case," *Comparative Politics*. Vol. 3, No. 3, April 1971, 361.

471 Welch, "Praetorianism in Commonwealth West Africa," 213.

472 Ibid., 213.

473 Canada, LAC, "Military Assistance – Ghana," 11 December 1970, 1. RG 25, External Affairs, Vol. 10416, File 27-20-5 Ghana (Part 8).

474 Canada, LAC, "Military Assistance – Ghana," 6 April 1971, 1. RG 25, External Affairs, Vol. 10416, File 27-20-5 Ghana (Part 8). The amount of money budgeted for military assistance to Ghana in 1971-72 was $206,038.

475 Ibid., 2.

476 Canada, LAC, "Summary Record of Decisions and Discussion, 25th Meeting of the Military Assistance Committee Meeting," 14 October 1971, Agenda, 15. RG 25, External Affairs, Vol. 10403, File: 27-20-1-2, Part 3. Military Assistance – Canada – Military Assistance Committee.

477 Graham, 203.

478 Canada, LAC, "Military Assistance to Ghana," 24 January 1972, 1. RG 25, External Affairs, Vol. 10416, File 27-20-5 Ghana (Part 9).

479 Ibid., 1.

480 Ibid., 2.

481 Canada, LAC, "Report of the Commanding Officer, Canadian Armed Forces Training Team, Ghana. First Quarter, 1973," 30 March 1973, 2. RG 25, External Affairs, Vol. 10416, File 27-20-5 Ghana (Part 10). In addition to the need for a staff college, de Gobeo noted that the Ghanaian military would soon begin teaching a series of courses for junior, intermediate and senior civil servants. The aim behind the new courses was to develop a better understanding between the military and civil service. The officer cadet training program was also being extended from 12 to 18 months so that the principles of civilian management could be incorporated. The idea, added de Gobeo, was "to cater for the future needs of the military government in providing military officer's to supervise civil aspects of administration, local industry, and Regional appointments." See: 2.

482 Canada, LAC, "Report of the Commanding Officer, Canadian Armed Forces Training Team, Ghana. Fourth Quarter, 1973," 14 January 1974, 2. RG 25, External Affairs, Vol. 10416, File 27-20-5 Ghana (Part 10).

483 Ibid., 2.

484 Canada, LAC, "High Commission Accra to External Affairs," 13 May 1975, 1. RG 25, External Affairs, Vol. 10416, File 27-20-5 Ghana (Part 13).

485 Canada, LAC, "Memorandum for the Minister, Ghana Staff College Project," 13 June 1975, 1. RG 25, External Affairs, Vol. 10416, File 27-20-5 Ghana (Part 14).

486 Ibid., 2.

487 Canada, LAC, "Memorandum for the Minister, Establishment of Military Staff College Ghana," 21 October 1975, 3. RG 25, External Affairs, Vol. 10416, File 27-20-5 Ghana (Part 14).

488 Ibid., 1.

489 Ibid., 2.

490 Canada, LAC, "British High Commission Ottawa to External Affairs (Defence Relations), Ghana Staff College – Feasibility Study," 3 March 1976, 1. RG 25, External Affairs, Vol. 10416, File 27-20-5 Ghana (Part 15).

491 Gutteridge, *The Place of the Army in Society in Commonwealth African Territories*, 27.

492 Ibid., 26.

493 Hunt, 46.

494 Tanzania has had several official names since 1961. It was Tanganyika until 26 April 1964, then the United Republic of Tanganyika and Zanzibar and after the passing of the 1965 constitution, Tanzania.

495 Donaghy, 80.

496 Walter C. Opello, Jr., "Guerilla War in Portuguese Africa: An Assessment of the Balance of Force in Mozambique," *A Journal of Opinion*, Vol. 4, No. 2, Summer, 1974, 30. A surprise raid, FRELIMO managed to successfully attack a Portuguese administrative post in the town of Mueda, 100 kilometers inside Mozambique. In June 1963, 200 FRELIMO members had travelled to Algeria where they received training in the use of small arms and sabotage methods. On their return to Tanganyika in early 1964, they became trainers in FRELIMO camps located in southern Tanganyika.

497 Cranford Pratt, *The Critical Phase in Tanzania, 1945-1968: Nyerere and the Emergence of a Socialist Strategy* (Cambridge: Cambridge University Press, 1976), 12. Tanganyika, prior to the First World War, had been a German colony. Following the Treaty of Versailles in 1919, Britain received a League of Nations mandate to administer the colony. In 1947, the British government then decided to place Tanganyika under UN trusteeship and as part of the trusteeship agreement Britain was given the responsibility to develop the political life of the territory in preparation for eventual full independence.

498 Ibid., 12. Pratt noted that there were, in 1961, 10,450,000 Africans, 102,400 Asians, and 22,300 Europeans living in Tanganyika.

499 Ibid., 35-37.

500 Ibid., 55.

501 Ibid., 56.

502 Catherine Hoskyns, "Africa's Foreign Relations: The Case of Tanzania," *International Affairs*, Vol. 44, No. 3 July 1968, 449.

503 Nestor Luanda, "A Changing Conception of Defence: A Historical Perspective of the Military in Tanzania," *Evolutions and Revolutions: A Contemporary History of Militaries in Southern Africa* (Pretoria: Institute for Security Studies, 2005), 297.

504 Ibid., 299.

505 Elise Forbes Pachter, "Contra-Coup: Civilian Control of the Military in Guinea, Tanzania, and Mozambique," *The Journal of Modern African Studies*, Vol. 20, No. 4, December 1982, 598.

506 Luanda, "A Changing Conception of Defence: A Historical Perspective of the Military in Tanzania," 300. Mazrui added that Nyerere's regime was "perhaps the only nationalist regime in Africa that seems to have had a genuine crisis of conscience as to whether to have an army at all on attainment of independence." See: Ali A. Mazrui, "Anti-Militarism and Political Militancy in Tanzania," *The Journal of Conflict Resolution*, Vol. 12, No. 3, September 1968, 270.

ENDNOTES

507   Pachter, 599.

508   Andrew Coulson, *Tanzania – A Political Economy* (Oxford: Claredon Press, 1982), 140. The mutiny was not a spontaneous event and clearly had been well planned. Troops from the first battalion in Dar es Salaam, for example, entered the capital on a Sunday evening (19 January) and quickly gained control of the radio station and all police stations. The main airport and President Nyerere's home and office were also occupied. As Bienen noted, however, no members of government took advantage of the situation to unseat Nyerere and the "mutiny leaders insisted they wanted no coup but reiterated demands for a more than double wage increase for most ranks e.g. from Shs.105 a month for privates to Shs.260 a month." See: Henry Bienen, "National Security in Tanganyika After the Mutiny," 41.

509   Henry Bienen, "Military and Society in East Africa: Thinking Again about Praetorianism," *Comparative Politics*, Vol. 6, No. 4 July 1974, 512.

510   Nestor Luanda, "A Historical Perspective on Civil-Military Relations: 1964-1990," *Civil Security Relations in Tanzania: Investigating the Relationship Between the State, Security Services and Civil Society*, edited by Martin Rupiya, Jonathan Lwehabura and Len le Roux, (Pretoria: Institute for Security Studies, 2006), 17.

511   Canada, LAC, "Military Assistance," 2 September 1964, 2-3. RG 19, Department of Finance, Volume 3871, File 8382/T171-1, Part 1. International Programmes and International Finance – Military Assistance Programmes – Tanzania – United Republic of – Generally. The High Commissioner added that in his view, if the Canadian government did decide, following the planned visit of the survey team, to provide military assistance to Tanganyika, there would be "some good soldierly material to work with."

512   Pratt, *The Critical Phase in Tanzania*, 128.

513   Ibid., 135.

514   Mazrui, "Anti-Militarism and Political Militancy in Tanzania," 277.

515   Pratt, *The Critical Phase in Tanzania, 1945-1968*, 136.

516   John S. Saul, "The Revolution in Portugal's African Colonies: A Review Essay," *Canadian Journal of African Studies*, Vol. 9, No. 2, 1975, 321.

517   L. H. Gann, "Portugal, Africa, and the Future," *The Journal of Modern African Studies*, Vol. 13, No. 1, March 1975, 8.

518   Opello, 35. The number of FRELIMO soldiers varies amongst sources. According to Gann, Portugal estimated in 1974 that FRELIMO had 1,000 men operating in Mozambique, with another 1,000 recruits in Tanzania. However, the small numbers reported might have been for domestic consumption, demonstrating the Portuguese military had the upper hand when in fact their hold on the country was tenuous at best.

519   Ibid., 30.

520   Ibid., 33. Richard Leonard, quoting a 1974 UN report, noted that the Portuguese had 80,000 troops in Mozambique. See: Richard W. Leonard, "Frelimo's Victories in Mozambique," *A Journal of Opinion*, Vol. 4, No. 2, Summer, 1974, 38. In the period 1969-70, when Canada was drawing down its military presence in Tanzania, the Portuguese launched Operation *Gordian Knot*, an offensive campaign led by Brigadier-General Kaulza de Arriaga. Arriaga believed that the defensive strategy of previous years had been ineffective and as one of Portugal's leading counterinsurgency experts he was able to turn the tide, for a while, by launching direct attacks on FRELIMO bases and sanctuaries. See: Opello, 32.

521   Canada, LAC, "Export of Arms to Portugal," 17 October 1963, 4. RG 2, Privy Council Office, Series A-5-a, Vol. 6254, 4.

522   Ibid., 4.

523 Leonard, 44.

524 Canada, LAC, "Export of Military Equipment to Portugal," 18 December 1967, 8. RG
2, Privy Council Office, Series A-5-a, Vol. 6323, 8.

525 Hoskyns, 454-455.

526 Pratt, *The Critical Phase in Tanzania, 1945-1968*, 155.

527 Cranford Pratt, "Julius Nyerere: Reflections on the Legacy of His Socialism," *Canadian
Journal of African Studies*, Vol. 33, No. 1, 1999, 138.

528 P. F. Nursey-Bray, "Tanzania: The Development Debate," *African Affairs*, Vol. 79, No.
314, January 1980, 55.

529 Pratt, *The Critical Phase in Tanzania, 1945-1968*, 238.

530 Susanne D. Mueller, "The Historical Origins of Tanzania's Ruling Class," *Canadian
Journal of African Studies*, Vol. 15, No. 3, 1981, 484. As Pratt noted, one prime example
of what was happening in Dar es Salaam was the building of large houses by the elite
that were then rented out to foreigners. See: Pratt, *The Critical Phase in Tanzania, 1945-
1968*, 235.

531 Cohen, 187.

532 Ali A. Mazrui, "Tanzaphilia," *Transition*, No. 75/76. The Anniversary Issue: Selections from *Transition*, 1961-1976, 1997, 167.

533 Welch, "The Right of Association in Ghana and Tanzania," 654.

534 Coulson, 2.

535 Nursey-Bray, 56.

536 Canada, LAC, "Military Assistance to the United Republic of Tanganyika and Zanzibar," 27 October 1964, Annex A, 4-5. RG 19, Department of Finance, Volume 3871, File
8382/T171-1, Part 1. International Programmes and International Finance – Military
Assistance Programmes – Tanzania – United Republic of – Generally. Also: Canada,
LAC, *Canadian Military Assistance to Developing Countries – A Review by the Interdepartmental Military Assistance Committee*, 9 July 1969, Annex A, 6.

537 Clyde Sanger, *Half a Loaf – Canada's Semi-Role Among Developing Countries* (Toronto:
The Ryerson Press, 1969), 61-62.

538 Canada, LAC, "Canadian Military Assistance to Developing Countries – A Review by
the Interdepartmental Military Assistance Committee," 9 July 1969, Annex A, 6.

539 Canada, LAC, "Military Assistance," 2 September 1964, 6. RG 19, Department of Finance, Volume 3871, File 8382/T171-1, Part 1. International Programmes and International Finance – Military Assistance Programmes – Tanzania – United Republic
of – Generally.

540 In fact, Tanzania obtained considerable help from Israel during the period 1964-66,
and almost 500 Tanzanians were sent to Israel for military and police training. The Israeli government had also agreed to train the paramilitary Tanzanian National Youth
Service beginning in 1963. Following the 1964 mutiny, 800, National Youth Service
soldiers were drafted and became the nucleus of Tanzania's new army. See: Abel Jacob, "Israel's Military Aid to Tanzania, 1960-66," *The Journal of Modern African Studies*,
Vol. 9, No. 2, August 1971, 174-178.

541 Canada, LAC, "Communist China Military Assistance," 9 September 1964, 1-3. RG
19, Department of Finance, Volume 3871, File 8382/T171-1, Part 1. International Programmes and International Finance – Military Assistance Programmes – Tanzania
– United Republic of – Generally. After lengthy negotiations, the Chinese formally
committed to building the 1,600 kilometer railway line in September 1967 and construction commenced in April 1970 with some 45,000 African workers employed during the planned five-year construction project. As a demonstration of the importance

ENDNOTES

China placed on the project and to assert its presence in Tanzania, almost 15,000 Chinese technical experts and railway workers assisted with construction efforts – a feat that the Canadian government, and every other Western nation for that matter, could simply not match. The cost to build the Tanzam railway was estimated to be £300 (UK) million at the time. See: Martin Bailey, "Tanzania and China," *African Affairs*, Vol. 74, No. 294, January 1975, 48.

542 Ibid., 50.

543 Poole, 627. Not all went China's way in sub-Saharan Africa. Hastings Banda, President of Malawi, accused the Chinese of corrupting African leaders while other African statesmen "expressed their disillusionment over China's goals and methods of intervening in the continent's affairs." See: Poole, 627.

544 Canada, LAC, "Canadian Military Survey Team to Visit the United Republic," 22 September 1964, 1. RG 19, Department of Finance, Volume 3871, File 8382/T171-1, Part 1. International Programmes and International Finance – Military Assistance Programmes – Tanzania – United Republic of – Generally.

545 Canada, LAC, "Visit of Canadian Military Survey Team: Publicity," 30 September 1964, 1. RG 19, Department of Finance, Volume 3871, File 8382/T171-1, Part 1. International Programmes and International Finance – Military Assistance Programmes – Tanzania – United Republic of – Generally. A group photograph of the survey team and an article appeared on 24 September 1964 in the *Tanganyikan Standard* and the *Nationalist* (both English language newspapers) and the *Ngurumo* (Swahili and only the article). *The East African Standard*, in Nairobi, Kenya, also ran the story. The Tanganyika Broadcast Organization also mentioned the arrival of the survey team in radio broadcasts on both 23 and 24 September 1964.

546 Canada, LAC, "Military Survey Team," 24 September 1964, 2-3. RG 19, Department of Finance, Volume 3871, File 8382/T171-1, Part 1. International Programmes and International Finance – Military Assistance Programmes – Tanzania – United Republic of – Generally.

547 Canada, LAC, DND, "Canadian Military Survey Team Report, United Republic of Tanzania and Zanzibar," October 1964, 9. RG 19, Department of Finance, Volume 3871, File 8382/T171-1, Part 1. International Programmes and International Finance – Military Assistance Programmes – Tanzania – United Republic of – Generally.

548 Canada, LAC, DND, "Canadian Military Survey Team Report, United Republic of Tanzania and Zanzibar," October 1964, 21.

549 Ibid., 24.

550 Canada, LAC, "Report on the Provision of an Air Component for the Military Forces of the United Republic of Tanganyika and Zanzibar," undated, 1. It is possible that Squadron Leader Butchart, who accompanied Brigadier Love to Tanzania, wrote this report but it was not included in the final report submitted by the team. RG 19, Department of Finance, Volume 3871, File 8382/T171-1, Part 1. International Programmes and International Finance – Military Assistance Programmes – Tanzania – United Republic of – Generally.

551 Ibid., 4.

552 Ibid., 6.

553 Ibid., 7.

554 Canada, LAC, "Military Assistance to Tanzania," 10 November 1964, 1. RG 19, Department of Finance, Volume 3871, File 8382/T171-1, Part 1. International Programmes and International Finance – Military Assistance Programmes – Tanzania – United Republic of – Generally.

555 Canada, LAC, "Record of Decisions, Second Meeting of the Military Assistance Committee," 17 November 1964, 1. RG 25, External Affairs, Volume 10403, File: 27-20-1-2,
Part 1. Military Assistance – Canada – Military Assistance Committee.

556 Menzies also proposed that Canada should "make effective use of surplus DND
equipment and facilitate the sale of new Canadian equipment." See: Canada, LAC,
"Record of Decisions, Second Meeting of the Military Assistance Committee," 17 November 1964, 2.

557 Canada, LAC, "Memorandum to the Cabinet, Military Assistance to the United Republic of Tanganyika and Zanzibar," 6 November 1964, 3. RG 19, Department of
Finance, Volume 3871, File 8382/T171-1, Part 1. International Programmes and International Finance – Military Assistance Programmes – Tanzania – United Republic
of – Generally. The recurring (annual) support in 2008 dollars would be equal to $4.7
million based on the Bank of Canada inflation calculator. However, the cost of the
entire effort to support the Tanzanian military (army and air force) between 1965 and
1970 was estimated to be $12,600,000. Using the Bank of Canada inflation calculator
this amount would be equal to Canada spending $80,000,000 in 2008 dollars or about
$16 million per year over the five years the program was in operation.

558 Canada, LAC, "Military Assistance to the United Republic of Tanganyika and Zanzibar," 1 December 1964, 1. RG 2, Privy Council Office, Series A-5-a, Volume 6265.

559 Ibid., 8.

560 Canada, DND, "Tanzanians Train in Canada," *Canadian Army Journal*, Vol. 19, No. 1,
1965, 29-31.

561 Canada, LAC, DND, "Preliminary Draft, Political Guidance for the Commander of
the Canadian Military Training Team, Tanzania," 11 January 1965, 1. RG 19, Department of Finance, Volume 3871, File 8382/T171-1, Part 1. International Programmes
and International Finance – Military Assistance Programmes – Tanzania – United
Republic of – Generally.

562 Ibid., 2. In 1961-1968, Pratt noted that Canadian development aid to Tanzania was
only $24,000. In 1967-68, this amount had increased to $3.5 million. In addition, he
reported that in 1967-68 that there were, in Tanzania, a total of 33 Canadian secondary
school teachers, 11 teacher trainers and five professors provided by Canada. Another
16 Canadians were involved in other non-education related roles that included three
wildlife and conservation advisors, two forestry advisors, three social service planners, two in development planning and one in cooperative planning. Another 30
to 40 Canadians, recruited for international service under the Canadian University
Service Overseas program, were employed by the Tanzanian government in various
roles. See: Pratt, "The Critical Phase in Tanzania," 157 and 281.

563 Ibid., 5.

564 Ibid., 7. Team members were also advised that while social contact with Soviet military advisors was acceptable, in keeping with the practice in Ottawa and foreign
capitals, contacts with Chinese and East German officers was not as Canada did not
recognize these countries. Lastly, it was noted that "Canadian advisors and technicians in other parts of Africa have found that in order to perform their duties as efficiently as possible endless patience and good humour are required."

565 Canada, DND, "Canadian Team for Tanzania," *Canadian Army Journal*, Vol. 19, No.
1, 1965, 27. Besides the Colonel, the advance party included Major A.M. Potts (the
Administrative Officer) and Sergeant P.L. Magaloe (the Administrative Clerk). All
three had flown from Ottawa to London on 15 January 1965 and then to Accra where
they met with Colonel Deane-Freeman and members from the Ghana training team

between 19-22 January. See: Canada, LAC, "Team Report No. 1 – Period 15-31 January 1965," February 1965, 1. RG 19, Department of Finance, Volume 3871, File 8382/T171-4, Part 1. International Programmes and International Finance – Military Assistance Programmes – Tanzania – United Republic of – Generally.

566 Canada, LAC, "Canadian Armed Forces Advisory and Training Team, Tanzania, Quarterly Report, January-March 1965," 31 March 1965, 2. RG 19, Department of Finance, Volume 3871, File 8382/T171-1, Part 1. International Programmes and International Finance – Military Assistance Programmes – Tanzania – United Republic of – Generally.

567 Canada, LAC, "German Relations with Tanzania," 12 March 1965, 3. RG 19, Department of Finance, Volume 3871, File 8382/T171-1, Part 1. International Programmes and International Finance – Military Assistance Programmes – Tanzania – United Republic of – Generally. The West German decision to end its foreign aid to Tanzania was largely based on the Hallstein Doctrine – a Doctrine that derived its name from Walter Hallstein, the head of the West German Foreign Office. In essence, the Doctrine, implemented from 1955 onwards, said that Bonn would neither establish or maintain diplomatic relations with countries that recognized the German Democratic Republic (East Germany).

568 Canada, LAC, DND, "Canadian Military Survey Team Report, United Republic of Tanzania and Zanzibar, October 1964," Appendix I, 12. Before the survey team arrived in Tanzania, in September 1964, there were already concerns being expressed by Canada's Embassy in Bonn, West Germany regarding the German commitment to train the air force. In a letter to External Affairs it was noted that the West German Foreign Office was considering the suspension of all aid given the deterioration of relations between the two countries. See: Canada, LAC, "Military Assistance to Tanganyika," 19 August 1964, 1. RG 19, Department of Finance, Volume 3871, File 8382/T171-1, Part 1. International Programmes and International Finance – Military Assistance Programmes – Tanzania – United Republic of – Generally.

569 Canada, LAC, "N.F. Berlis (High Commissioner Tanzania) to A.R. Menzies," 28 February 1965, 2. RG 19, Department of Finance, Volume 3871, File 8382/T171-1, Part 1. International Programmes and International Finance – Military Assistance Programmes – Tanzania – United Republic of – Generally.

570 The RCAF training team advance party led by Squadron Leader Mackenzie (with 14 personnel) arrived in Dar es Salaam on 4 January 1966. See: Canada, LAC, "Team Report No. 13 – Period 1-31 January 1966," 1. RG 19, Department of Finance, Volume 3871, File 8382/T171-4, Part 1. International Programmes and International Finance – Military Assistance Programmes – Tanzania – United Republic of – Generally.

571 Canada, DND, "Tanzania Tale," *Sentinel*, Vol. 2, No. 2, March 1966, 24-25.

572 Canada, LAC, "Team Report No. 13 – Period 1-31 January 1966," 2.

573 Canada, DND, "Tanzania Tale," 25.

574 Canada, LAC, Programme, "United Nations Commitments, and Control Commissions as of 25 January 1966," 5. RG 25, External Affairs, Volume 10409, File 27-20-5 (Part 2). From what can be ascertained from several sources, a total of 32 Tanzanian pilots, 8 maintenance officers and 150 ground crew/technicians were actually trained in Canada. Pilot training, it should be noted, was a two-year commitment for the trainees.

575 Canada, LAC, "Team Report No. 13 – Period 1-31 January 1966," 5-7.

576 Canada, LAC, "Record of Decisions, Eighth Meeting of the Military Assistance Committee," 20 July 1966, 2. RG 25, External Affairs, Volume 10403, File: 27-20-1-2, Part 1. Military Assistance – Canada – Military Assistance Committee.

577 Canada, LAC, "Provision of Canadian Military Training Assistance to Tanzania," 27 September 1966, 1. RG 2, Privy Council Office, Series A-5-a, Volume 6321. Also: Canada, LAC, "Record of Decisions, Fifteenth Meeting of the Military Assistance Committee," 5 January 1968, 3. RG 25, External Affairs, Volume 10403, File: 27-20-1-2, Part 1. Military Assistance – Canada – Military Assistance Committee.

578 The risk that the Tanzanian government might embark on an expansion of their military forces beyond a level that Ottawa was comfortable with, was well understood in External Affairs before the decision to provide Nyerere with military assistance was made. In November 1964, the Under Secretary of State, had written to the Deputy Minister of Finance, noting that "if Tanzania were to decide as some stage to develop more expensive force components such as artillery, armoured reconnaissance or a tactical air force, and if these items were to be offered by communist countries a much more difficult situation would exist. This is a problem which the West will have to face when and if it arises." See: Canada, LAC, "Military Assistance to Tanzania," 10 November 1964, 4. RG 19, Department of Finance, Volume 3871, File 8382/T171-1, Part 2. International Programmes and International Finance – Military Assistance Programmes – Tanzania – United Republic of – Generally.

579 Andrew B. Godefroy, "The Canadian Armed Forces Advisory and Training Team Tanzania 1965-1970," *Canadian Military History*, Vol. 3, No. 2, 2002, 44. In addition, 20 T-59 medium tanks were also delivered to the Tanzanian military. See: Bailey, 44.

580 Canada, LAC, "Canadian Military Assistance to Developing Countries – A Review by the Interdepartmental Military Assistance Committee," 9 July 1969, 6.

581 Bailey, 44.

582 Canada, LAC, "Visit by DGP to Ghana and Tanzania 3-14 March 1969," 21 March 1969, 9. RG 24, National Defence, Volume 21834, File FMC 4760-1 (Parts 10 and 11). When Tellier visited the training team in March 1969, he noted that there were 89 Canadian Forces personnel, and many of their families, now deployed in Tanzania.

583 The Monduli Military Academy eventually opened in 1974 and the curriculum catered for both military commanders and TANU party leaders. Graduates from the Academy could be posted to the military, the party or the government. The Academy, said Luanda, fulfilled the desire by Nyerere to have a small, professional regular army but one that was, nevertheless, decidedly political. See: Luanda, "A Historical Perspective on Civil-Military Relations: 1964-1990," 20.

584 Ivan Head and Pierre Trudeau, *The Canadian Way: Shaping Canada's Foreign Policy, 1968-1984* (Toronto: McClelland and Stewart, 1995), 224.

585 Ronald C. Keith, "China and Canada's 'Pacific 2000 Strategy,'" *Pacific Affairs*, Vol. 65, No. 3, Autumn, 1992, 323.

586 Canadian aid to Tanzania was characterized in the early 1960s by support for education. In Canada, Tanzanian secondary school teachers were trained at the University of Calgary and Brock University. In Tanzania, aid was concentrated on improving the Tanzanian Railway Corporation's railway network. After 1969, when military aid began winding down, general aid efforts grew considerably. Canadian teachers flocked to Tanzania while road building and forestry studies were launched. Canadian advisors were also assigned to several government ministries. To improve wheat production, agricultural experts were also sent from Canada. Finally, electricity generation and the building of transmission networks was a key focus for Canadian aid. See: Roger Young, *Canadian Development Assistance to Tanzania* (Ottawa: The North South Institute, 1983), 45-46.

587 Linda Freeman, "CIDA, Wheat, and Rural Development in Tanzania," *Canadian Journal of African Studies*, Vol. 16, No. 3, (1982), 479-504.

588 Nyerere, 105-106.

589 For example, in June 1970, a treason trial was held in Dar es Salaam following the arrest of several politicians and military officers who had been accused of plotting a coup the year prior. The coup leader was alleged to have been Oscar Kambona, who had resigned from the Tanzanian government in June 1967 after disagreeing with Nyerere's Arusha Declaration. Kambona left Tanzania in 1967 and moved, initially, to London. He was tried in absentia. Chief amongst the military officers accused were Colonel William Makori Chacha and Captain Elia Dustan Lifa Chipka. The planned coup was to have taken place between 10-15 October 1969 when Nyerere and Major-General Sarakikya were out of the country. Following a 127 day trial, Colonel Chacha received a ten-year sentence while Captain Chipka, thought to be one of the ringleaders was given life imprisonment. See: Godfrey Mwakikagile, *Nyerere and Africa: End of an Era* (Las Vegas, Nevada: Protea Publishing Co., 2005), 360-366.

590 Canada, LAC, "Implications of Rhodesian Crisis for Canadian Military Assistance to African States," 15 December 1965, 4. RG 25, External Affairs, Volume 10409, File 27-20-5 (Part 2).

591 Ibid., 2.

592 Canada, LAC, "Military Assistance to the United Republic of Tanganyika and Zanzibar," 27 October 1964, Annex A, 5.

593 Nyerere, 116.

594 In October 1964, it was noted that "the armed forces of the United Republic are not now and will not for some years to come be capable of mounting any sort of effective military campaign, least of all against the 18,000 troops which Portugal is reportedly maintaining in Mozambique. Moreover, if the United Republic Government is to receive outside advice concerning the organization, training and capabilities of its forces, it is much to be preferred that such advice come from Canada rather than a country with more adventurist inclinations." See: Canada, LAC, "Military Assistance to the United Republic of Tanganyika and Zanzibar," 27 October 1964, Annex A, 5. However, Godefroy notes that three years later, in November 1967, the anti-tank and machine gun sections from the 3rd Battalion had been sent to Lake Nyasa following a border incident and that these two sections may have played a role in the sinking of two small Portuguese gunboats. See: Godefroy, 43.

595 Ibid., 121.

596 Canada, LAC, "External Affairs, Military Assistance Committee Meeting to be held on 18 December 1970," 16 December 1970, 1-2. RG 25, External Affairs, Volume 10403, File: 27-20-1-2, Part 3. Military Assistance – Canada – Military Assistance Committee.

597 Canada, LAC, "Summary Record of Decisions and Discussion, 27th Meeting of the Military Assistance Committee Meeting," 27 November 1972, 1. RG 25, External Affairs, Volume 10403, File: 27-20-1-2, Part 4. Military Assistance – Canada – Military Assistance Committee.

598 Canada, LAC, "Canadian Military Assistance to Developing Countries – A Review by the Interdepartmental Military Assistance Committee," 9 July 1969, 7.

599 Sanger, *Half a Loaf – Canada's Semi-Role Among Developing Countries*, 74. Pratt also acknowledged the important role the Canadian Forces had played in Tanzania in his book, *The Critical Phase in Tanzania, 1945-1968*. "For five years a strong team of Canadian officers and senior non-commissioned officers, numbering at its peak nearly

ninety men," he wrote, "played a most important role in the re-creation of an effective Tanzanian military force after the 1964 mutiny." See: Pratt, 158.

600   Bailey, 44.

601   In 1968 the Liberals won 155 of 264 seats in the House of Commons – the first majority since 1962.

602   George Radwanski, *Trudeau* (Toronto: Macmillan Company of Canada, 1978), 238-239.

603   Canada, DND, "The Relation of Defence Policy to Foreign Policy," Excerpts from an Address by Prime Minister Trudeau to a Dinner of the Alberta Liberal Association, Calgary, 12 April 1969, 1. (Ottawa, DND, DHH, Box 121, File 3067, Evolution of Canadian Defence Policy, Raymont Fonds (73/1223)).

604   Peyton Lyon, *Canada and the Third World* (Toronto: Macmillan of Canada: 1976), xxxv.

605   Ibid., 25. In 1961 for example, Canadian foreign aid had amounted to only 0.19% of gross national product (GNP) compared to the United States at 0.73% and West Germany at 0.83%. In 1971-1972 aid to India alone was over $100 million – no small sum at the time.

606   Trudeau, *Memoirs*, 107.

607   Head and Trudeau, 76. The Canadian contribution to NATO was not regarded by the Prime Minister as militarily significant at all. In his book he specifically referred to a British Institute of Strategic Studies account completed at the time noted that Canadian aircraft in Europe represented just 4 per cent of the available fighters, while the brigade, with its 60 *Centurion* tanks, amounted to only 1.5 per cent of the ground troops available on the north and central fronts. See: 78.

608   Radwanski, 183.

609   Head and Trudeau, 66.

610   Dan Loomis, *Not Much Glory – Quelling the F.L.Q.* (Toronto: Deneau Publishers, 1984), 142.

611   Barney Danson, *Not Bad for a Sergeant – The Memoirs of Barney Danson* (Toronto: Dundurn Press, 2002), 110. The shock of this period, and the challenge to Canadian sovereignty when the United States oil tanker *Manhattan* sailed through the Northwest Passage was enough to propel domestic defence to the top priority for the military in the White Paper of 1971 – it had been the last priority in 1964.

612   Granatstein, "Canada and Peacekeeping: Image and Reality," 239.

613   Middlemiss and Sokolsky, 35.

614   Morton, 254.

615   Ibid., 255.

616   Canada, Department of External Affairs, *A Defence Policy for Canada*, 3 April 1969 (Ottawa: Department of External Affairs, Statements and Speeches, 1969), 2.

617   Morton, 255 and Middlemiss, 32.

618   Canada, LAC, "Canadian Military Assistance to Developing Countries – A Review by the Interdepartmental Military Assistance Committee," 9 July 1969, 1.

619   Someone, it should be noted, had written "Tanzania" in the margin.

620   Canada, LAC, "Canadian Military Assistance to Developing Countries – A Review by the Interdepartmental Military Assistance Committee," 9 July 1969, 13-14.

621   Ibid., 15.

622   Shubi L. Ishemo, "Symbol That Cannot Be Substituted: The Role of Mwalimu J. K. Nyerere in the Liberation of Southern Africa, 1955-1990," *Review of African Political Economy*, Vol. 27, No. 83, March 2000, 87.

623 Canada, LAC, "Canadian Military Assistance to Developing Countries – A Review by the Interdepartmental Military Assistance Committee," 9 July 1969, 13.

624 Ibid., 20.

625 Ibid., 20.

626 Ibid., 19.

627 Ibid., 7.

628 Ibid., 9.

629 Ibid., 5.

630 Ibid., 23.

631 Canada, LAC, "Kenya Request for Caribou Aircraft," 28 April 1967, 1. RG 25, External Affairs, Volume 10409, File 27-20-5.

632 Canada, LAC, "Canadian Military Assistance to Developing Countries," 19 March 1970, 1.

633 Ibid., 4.

634 Ibid., 4.

635 Ibid., 5-6.

636 Ibid., 3.

637 Ibid., 4.

638 Canada, LAC, "Memorandum to the Cabinet – Canadian Military Assistance to Developing Countries," 25 June 1970, 1.

639 Canada, LAC, "Memorandum for the Minister – Military Assistance Review, 19 November 1970," 1. RG 25, External Affairs, Volume 10403, File: 27-20-1-2, Part 3. Military Assistance – Canada – Military Assistance Committee.

640 Ibid., 2.

641 Ibid., Annex A, 2. It was true that Canadian military personnel engaged in military assistance work had kept themselves, and the country, away from politically embarrassing situations. Still, Canadian officers in Ghana were placed in challenging situations likely not envisioned when first planning the mission. For example, Major Robert Frost arrived in Ghana in September 1961, just before Nkrumah dismissed Alexander. Major-General Otu, the new Chief of Defence Staff, had little military staff experience. As a result, the Canadian High Commissioner asked Frost to help Otu choose three new heads of service, organize his personal staff and suggest who might fill other key staff appointments. Canadians also came into contact with high-level political delegations, especially from the Soviet Union. In November 1961, the First Deputy Chairman of the USSR, Anastas I. Mikoyan, escorted by Frost, toured the Military Academy. Finally, some Canadian officers, in 1966, were aware the day before that a coup would take place. From: private correspondence, Mr. Robert Frost to the author, 5 February 2008.

642 Ibid., Annex A, 2-3.

643 Canada, LAC, "Military Assistance for Developing Countries," 23 December 1970, 8. RG 2, Privy Council Office, Series A-5-a, Volume 6359.

644 Ibid., 8. Trudeau, according to Radwanski, was always well prepared for Cabinet meetings, the Privy Council Office having provided him with a two page memorandum on each substantive issue to be discussed outlining the positions that would be taken by Ministers and offering a recommended position to take. However, as Mitchell Sharp (Secretary of State for External Affairs from 1968-74) noted, Trudeau "never came into the Cabinet and said, 'This is what we will do.' But at the same time, we recognized that we were the majority party in 1968 because Trudeau had been the leader. We all had this sort of feeling that we were there because Trudeau was the

prime minister. It wasn't as if he laid down any policy approach, but we realized he was the man who brought us where we were. Pearson was merely one of us, whereas Trudeau was not – he was someone extraordinary." See: Radwanski, 173.

645   Ibid., 8.

646   Ibid., 8-9.

647   Canada, LAC, *Summary Record of Decisions and Discussion, 24th Meeting of the Military Assistance Committee Meeting*, 7 April 1971, 1. RG 25, External Affairs, Volume 10403, File: 27-20-1-2, Part 3. Military Assistance – Canada – Military Assistance Committee.

648   Canada, LAC, "Military Assistance Committee Meeting Agenda," 31 July 1970. RG 24, Vol. 21578, File S-2-5040-12 (Part 5), Annex A. Table 9 has been adapted from the Annex. ROTP is short for the Regular Officer Training Plan, which involved the candidate obtaining a bachelor's degree over an extended period in Canada. OCTP is short for the Officer Candidate Training Plan, which provided basic officer training to candidates without attendance at university.

649   Canada, LAC, "Summary Record of Discussions and Decisions, at a Meeting of the Military Assistance Committee on 10 April 1969," 16 April 1969, 1. RG 24, National Defence, Volume 21834, File FMC 4760-1 (Parts 10 and 11).

650   Canada, LAC, "Summary Record of Decisions and Discussion – 26th Meeting of the Military Assistance Committee Meeting," 29 March 1972, 14. Present at the 26th meeting was the Director General Bureau of Defence and Arms Control, External Affairs and Mr. Wilson from CIDA. There were nine representatives from External Affairs (compared to nine in total from everyone else). Mr. J.M. Knowles, from Industry, Trade and Commerce, noted that as a result of the training assistance offered to Malaysia, Canada had sold over $25 million of defence equipment. $17.6 million had been spent on training and equipping the Tanzanian military.

651   Canada, LAC, "Summary Record of Decisions and Discussion – 27th Meeting of the Military Assistance Committee Meeting," 27 November 1972, 12.

652   David R. Morrison, *Aid and Ebb Tide – A History of CIDA and Canadian Development Assistance* (Waterloo: Wilfrid Laurier Press, 1998), 121.

653   Clyde Sanger, "Canada and Development in the Third World," *Canada and the Third World*, ed. by Peyton Lyon and Tareq Y. Ismael (Toronto: Macmillan of Canada: 1976), 285. The 1968-69 CIDA annual review stated that the organization would begin to concentrate its efforts in ten countries grouped into four regions in order to achieve better effects on the ground. These groupings were: India, Pakistan, Ceylon, and Malaysia (the Colombo Plan region), Nigeria and Ghana (Anglophone Africa), Tunisia, Cameroon, and Senegal (Francophone Africa) and the Commonwealth Caribbean as a whole. See: David Morrison, 80.

654   Louis Sabourn, "Canada and Francophone Africa," *Canada and the Third World*, ed. by Peyton Lyon and Tareq Y. Ismael (Toronto: Macmillan of Canada: 1976), 150.

655   Ibid., 151-152. The Military Assistance Committee discussed the issue of training Francophone students from Africa in Canada in November 1972. There appeared to be a general reluctance to do so or to attach African officers to units in Quebec. In particular, the Committee was told that much of the training information was only available in English. Mr. Tardif, the desk officer in External Affairs for Francophone Africa, would go on to say: "While several countries of Francophone Africa are favourable areas for the reception of military assistance, current Canadian training capabilities in the French language precludes a substantial programme at this time." See: Canada, LAC, "Summary Record of Decisions and Discussion, 27th Meeting of the Military Assistance Committee Meeting," 27 November 1972, 11.

656   Canada, LAC, "Summary Report, Meeting with the Iranian Ambassador," 27 November 1970, 1. RG 25, External Affairs, Volume 10417, File: 27-20-5-IRAN, Part 1. Defence – Military Assistance – Training Assistance – Iran (1964-1979).

657   Canada, DND, Message, "Request for Canadian Advice on Make-up of Ceylon Armed Forces," 3 June 1971, 1. (Ottawa, DND, DHH, Box 58, File 1112, Aid to Foreign Countries, Raymont Fonds (73/1223)).

658   Canada, DND, "Ceylonese Request to Provide a Canadian Forces Advisor," 28 June 1971, 1. (Ottawa, DND, DHH, Box 58, File 1112, Aid to Foreign Countries, Raymont Fonds (73/1223)).

659   Ibid., 1.

660   Canada, LAC, "External Affairs, Military Assistance Committee Meeting to be held on 18 December 1970," 16 December 1970, 4.

661   Canada, LAC, "Summary Record of Decisions and Discussion – 24th Meeting of the Military Assistance Committee Meeting," 7 April 1971, 1. RG 25, External Affairs, Volume 10403, File: 27-20-1-2, Part 3. Military Assistance – Canada – Military Assistance Committee.

662   That funding for military assistance was in doubt was probably attributable to new government social spending following the Federal election on 30 October 1972. After the votes had been counted, the Liberal Party had 109 seats compared to the Conservatives with 107. As a minority government, Trudeau was forced to forge an alliance with David Lewis, leader of the New Democratic Party. The price for his cooperation, however, "pushed the Liberal minority government into cutting personal income taxes, raising old-age pensions, and trebling family allowances." See: Christina McCall and Stephen Clarkson, *Trudeau and Our Times: Volume 2: The Heroic Delusion* (Toronto: McClelland & Stewart Inc., 1994), 110.

663   Canada, LAC, "Summary Record of Decisions and Discussion – 29th Meeting of the Military Assistance Committee Meeting," 18 December 1973, Agenda, 1. RG 25, External Affairs, Volume 10403, File: 27-20-1-2, Part 4. Military Assistance – Canada – Military Assistance Committee.

664   Trudeau, 79.

665   Government of Canada, *Foreign Policy for Canadians* (Ottawa: 1970), 6.

666   Ibid., 7.

667   Canada, DFAIT, *Canada and the World: A History - 1968 - 1984: The Trudeau Years*. Internet: <http://www.international.gc.ca/department/history-histoire/canada9-en.asp>. Accessed: 8 July 2008.

668   Based on the Bank of Canada inflation calculator, $3 million in 1970 would be equal to almost $17 million today.

669   *Danger Man – An Episode Guide*. Internet: <http://epguides.com/DangerMan/guide.shtml>. Accessed: 21 February 2008.

670   Canada, LAC, "Canadian Military Assistance to Developing Countries," 25 June 1970, 6.

671   H.T. Alexander (Major-General), *African Tightrope – My Two Years as Nkrumah's Chief of Staff* (London: Pall Mall Press, 1965), 120.

672   Odetola, 46.

673   Maloney, 83.

674   Arthur Andrew, *The Rise and Fall of a Middle Power – Canadian Diplomacy from King to Mulroney* (Toronto: James Lorimer & Company, Publishers, 1993), 141.

675   Laqueur, 610.

676   Snow, 290.

677   Melady, 59.

678   Canada, LAC, "Right Honourable Lester B. Pearson from the Right Honourable Sir Alexander Douglas-Home," 21 August 1964, 1-2.

679   Canada, LAC, "Canadian Training Team," 8 March 1966, 1.

680   Lyon, p. xxxix.

681   Matthews, 131.

682   Windle, 92.

683   Loomis, 138.

BIBLIOGRAPHY

PRIMARY SOURCES

LIBRARY AND ARCHIVES CANADA

RG 2, Privy Council Office

RG 19, Finance

RG 20, Industry, Trade and Commerce

RG 24, National Defence

RG 25, External Affairs

RG 58, Auditor General

RG 74, External Aid Office (CIDA)

DEPARTMENT OF HISTORY AND HERITAGE

Raymont Fonds

Series XIV, Chiefs of Staff Committee Meetings (Minutes)

CANADIAN GOVERNMENT PUBLICATIONS

Canadian Forces. *Canadian Forces Capstone Doctrine Manual.* Draft 2, January 2008.

Canadian International Development Agency. *Ghana and Tanzania – Facts at a Glance.* Ottawa: Canadian International Development Agency, 2006. Internet: http://www.acdi-cida.gc.ca.

Government of Canada. *Special Committee on Defence – Minutes of Proceedings and Evidence, 24 November 1964.* Ottawa: Queen's Printer and Controller of Stationary, 1964.

Department of External Affairs, *Foreign Policy for Canadians: International Development.* Ottawa: Queen's Printer, 1970.

Department of External Affairs. *Movement for Independence of African Territories.* Ottawa: DEA 11253 – B – 40, Vol. #26 454, Chapter IX, Africa,

BIBLIOGRAPHY

1959. Internet: http://www.dfait-maeci.gc.ca/department/history/dcer/details-en.asp?intRefid=11272.

Department of Foreign Affairs and International Trade. Documents on Canadian External Relations. Vol. 12 to Vol. 26 (1946-1959). Internet: http://www.dfait-maeci.gc.ca/department/history/dcer/browse-en.asp

Department of National Defence. *Canada's Defence – Information on Canada's Defence Achievements and Organization – 1947.* Ottawa: Reproduced in the Department of National Defence, 1947.

Department of National Defence. *Canada's Defence Programme 1949-50.* Ottawa: Printer to the King's Most Excellent Majesty, 1949.

Department of National Defence. *Canada's Defence Programme 1951-52.* Ottawa: Printer to the King's Most Excellent Majesty, 1951.

Department of National Defence. *Canada's Defence Programme, 1953-54.* Ottawa: Queen's Printer and Controller of Stationery, 1953.

Department of National Defence. *Canada's Defence Programme, 1954-55.* Ottawa: Queen's Printer and Controller of Stationery, 1954.

Department of National Defence. *Canada's Defence Programme, 1956-57.* Ottawa: Queen's Printer and Controller of Stationery, 1956.

Department of National Defence. *Canada's Defence Programme, 1957-58.* Ottawa: Queen's Printer and Controller of Stationery, 1957.

Department of National Defence. *Canadian Army Journal.* Vol. 19, No. 1, 1965.

Department of National Defence. *Directorate of Military Training Assistance Program – 2004-2005 Annual Report.* Ottawa: Department of National Defence, 2005.

Department of National Defence. *Directorate of Military Training Assistance Program – 2005-2006 Annual Report.* Ottawa: Department of National Defence, 2006.

Department of National Defence. *Report of the Ad Hoc Committee on Defence Policy.* Ottawa: Department of National Defence, September 30, 1963.

Department of National Defence. *Sentinel.* Vol. 2, No. 1, January-February. 1966.

Department of National Defence. *Sentinel*. Vol. 2, No. 2, March 1966.

Department of National Defence. *The Canadian Defence Budget – Prepared by the Ad Hoc Committee on Defence Policy, August 1963*. Ottawa: Department of National Defence, 4 September 1963.

Department of National Defence. *White Paper on Defence*. Ottawa: Queen's Printer: 1964.

Government of Canada. *International Policy Statement*. Ottawa: Department of Foreign Affairs and International Trade, 2005.

UNITED STATES GOVERNMENT

Department of State. *Foreign Relations of the United States, 1964-1968. Vol. XXIV, Africa.* Edited by Nina Davis Howland. United States Government Printing Office, Washington, 1999.

Presidential Papers. *The Papers of Dwight David Eisenhower, Volume XX - The Presidency: Keeping the Peace Part VII: Berlin and the Chance for a Summit; March 1959 to August 1959.* Internet: http://www.eisenhowermemorial.org/presidential-papers/second-term/documents/1191.cfm.

SECONDARY SOURCES

Afrifa, Akwasi. *The Ghana Coup, 24 February 1966*. London: Frank Cass & CO, Ltd, 1966.

Alba, Victor. "The Stages of Militarism in Latin America." *The Role of the Military in Underdeveloped Countries.* Edited by John J. Johnson. Princeton, New Jersey: Princeton University Press, 1962.

Alexander H.T. *African Tightrope – My Two Years as Nkrumah's Chief of Staff*. London: Pall Mall Press, 1965.

American Rhetoric. The Truman Doctrine. Speech delivered on 12 March 1947 before a Joint Session of Congress. Internet: http://www.americanrhetoric.com/speeches/harrystrumantrumandoctrine.html. Accessed: 20 July 07.

Andrew, Arthur. *The Rise and Fall of a Middle Power – Canadian Diplomacy from King to Mulroney*. Toronto: James Lorimer & Company, Publishers, 1993.

Andrew, Christopher and Vasili Mitrokhin. *The World Was Going Our Way – The KGB and the Battle for the Third World*. New York: Basic Books, 2005.

Anon. "Canadian Team for Tanzania." *Canadian Army Journal.* Vol. 19:1, 1965.

Arms and Development – Proceedings of the First Pan-African Citizens' Conference. Edited by Frederick S. Arkhurst. New York: Praeger Publishers, 1972.

Bailey, Martin. "Tanzania and China." *African Affairs*. Vol. 74, No. 294, January 1975.

Baynham, Simon, *The Military and Politics in Nkrumah's Ghana*. Boulder, Colorado: Westview Press, 1988.

Bebler, Anton. *Military Rule in Africa – Dahomey, Ghana, Sierra Leone and Mali*. New York: Praeger Publishers, 1973.

Bienen Henry. "Armed Forces and National Modernization: Continuing the Debate." *Comparative Politics*, Vol. 16, No. 1, October 1983.

Bienen, Henry. "Military and Society in East Africa: Thinking Again about Praetorianism." *Comparative Politics*. Vol. 6, No. 4 July 1974.

Bienen, Henry. "National Security in Tanganyika After the Mutiny." *Transition*. No. 21 (1965).

Bienen, Henry. *The Military Intervenes – Case Studies in Political Development*. Hartford, Connecticut: Connecticut Printers, 1968.

Bienen, Henry. *The Military and Modernization*. Chicago: Aldine-Atherton, Inc, 1971.

Bothwell, Robert, Ian Drummond, and John English. *Canada Since 1945*. Toronto, University of Toronto Press, 1989.

Boulakia, J.D.C. "Military Expenditures and African Economic Development." *Canadian Journal of African Studies*. Vol. 2, No. 2, Autumn 1968.

Bretton Henry L. "Current Political Thought and Practice in Ghana." *The American Political Science Review*. Vol. 52, No. 1, March 1958.

Campbell, Gwyn. "An Industrial Experiment in Pre-Colonial Africa: The Case of Imperial Madagascar 1825-1861." *Journal of Southern African Studies*, Vol. 17, No. 3, September 1991.

Canadian Institute of Strategic Studies. *Canada, the Caribbean and Central America*. Edited by Brian MacDonald. Proceedings, Fall 1985.

Chau, Donovan C. "Assistance of a Different Kind: Chinese Political Warfare in Ghana, 1958-1966." *Comparative Strategy*, Vol. 26, No. 2, March 2007.

Cohen, Dennis L. "The Convention People's Party of Ghana: Representational or Solidarity Party?" *Canadian Journal of African Studies*. Vol. 4, No. 2, Spring, 1970.

Coleman, James, S and Belmont Brice Jr. "The Role of the Military in Sub-Saharan Africa." *The Role of the Military in Underdeveloped Countries*. Edited by John J. Johnson. Princeton, New Jersey: Princeton University Press, 1962.

Conroy, Hilary. "Chosen Mondai: The Korean Problem in Meiji Japan." *Proceedings of the American Philosophical Society*, Vol. 100, No. 5, October 15, 1956.

Cooke, Jacob E. "Tench Coxe, Alexander Hamilton, and the Encouragement of American Manufactures." *The William and Mary Quarterly*, 3rd Ser. Vol. 32, No. 3, July 1975.

Cooper, John F. "Chinese Military Assistance." *Communist Nations' Military Assistance*. Edited by John F. Cooper and Daniel S. Papp. Boulder, Colorado: Westview Press, Inc, 1983.

Coulson, Andrew. *Tanzania – A Political Economy*. Oxford: Claredon Press, 1982.

Cowen, M.P. and R.W. Shenton. *Doctrines of Development*. London: Routledge, 1996.

Currie, G.H. "They Helped Build an Air Force." *Sentinel*. Vol. 3:4, April 1967.

Dallaire, Romeo. *Shake Hands with the Devil*. Toronto: Vintage Canada, 2004.

Danns, George K. "The Role of the Military in the National Security of Guyana." *Militarization in the Non-Hispanic Caribbean*. Edited by Alma H. Young & Dion E. Phillips. Boulder, Colorado: Lynne Rienner Publishers, Inc., 1986.

Danson, Barney. *Not Bad for a Sergeant – The Memoirs of Barney Danson*. Toronto: Dundurn Press, 2002.

BIBLIOGRAPHY

Diefenbaker, John G. *One Canada – Memoirs of the Right Honourable John G. Diefenbaker: The Years of Achievement 1957-1962*. Vol. 2. Toronto: Macmillan, 1976.

Donaghy, Greg. "Documenting the Diplomats: The Origins and Evolution of Documents on Canadian External Relations." *The Public Historian*, Vol. 25, No. 1, Winter, 2003.

Donaghy, Greg. "The Rise and Fall of Canadian Military Assistance in the Developing World, 1952-1971." *Canadian Military History*. Vol. 4, No. 1, 1995.

Dunn, John P. "Egypt's Nineteenth-Century Armaments Industry." *The Journal of Military History*. Vol. 61, No. 2, April 1997.

Dunn, John P, "Missions or Mercenaries? European Military Advisors in Mehmed Ali's Egypt, 1815-1848." *Military Advising and Assistance – From Mercenaries to Privatization, 1815-2007*. Edited by Donald Stoker. London: Routledge, 2008.

Earle, Edward Mead. "Adam Smith, Alexander Hamilton, Friedrich List: The Economic Foundations of Military Power." *Makers of Modern Strategy: From Machiavelli to the Nuclear Age*. Edited by Peter Paret. Princeton: Princeton University Press, 1986.

Eayrs, James. *In Defence of Canada – Peacemaking and Deterrence*. Toronto: University of Toronto Press, 1972.

English, John. *The Worldly Years – The Life of Lester Pearson, 1949-1972*. Toronto: Alfred A. Knopf, 1992.

Fetterly, Ross. "The Influence of the Environment on the 1964 White Paper." *Canadian Military Journal*. Winter 2004-2005.

Finer, S.E. *The Man on Horseback*: *The Role of the Military in Politics*. New York: Frederick A. Praeger, 1962.

Fitch, Robert and Mary Oppenheimer, *End of an Illusion*. New York: Monthly Review Press, 1966.

Fortmann, Michel and Martin Larose. "An Emerging Strategic Counter-Culture? Pierre Elliott Trudeau, Canadian Intellectuals and the Revision of Liberal Defence Policy Concerning NATO (1968-1969)." *International Journal*. Vol. 59, No. 3, Summer 2004.

Freeman, Linda. "CIDA, Wheat, and Rural Development in Tanzania," *Canadian Journal of African Studies*. Vol. 16, No. 3. 1982.

Gann, L. H. "Portugal, Africa, and the Future." *The Journal of Modern African Studies*. Vol. 13, No. 1, March 1975.

Gilbert, Martin. *Israel – A History*. New York: William Morrow and Company, Inc., 1998.

Global Militarization. Edited by Peter Wallensteen, Johan Galtung and Carlos Portales. Boulder, Colorado: Westview Press, Inc., 1985.

Godefroy, B. Andrew. "The Canadian Armed Forces Advisory and Training Team Tanzania 1965-1970." *Canadian Military History*. Vol. 3, No. 2, 2002.

Graham, Norman. *From the Barrack Room to the Boardroom: The Memoirs of a Self-Made Man*. New York, iUniverse Inc, 2007.

Granatstein, J.L. *Canada: Peacekeeper – A Survey of Canada's Participation in Peacekeeping Operations, Peacekeeping – International Challenge and Canadian Response*. Lindsay, Ontario: Canadian Institute of International Affairs, Contemporary Affairs No. 39: 1968.

Granatstein, J.L. *Canadian Foreign Policy – Historical Readings*. Toronto: Copp Clark Pitman Ltd., 1986.

Granatstein, J.L. "Canada and Peacekeeping: Image and Reality." *Canadian Forum*. August 1974.

Granatstein, J.L. and Douglas Lavender. *Shadows of War, Faces of Peace*. Toronto: Key Porter Books, 1992.

Great Falls/S.U.M. National Historic Landmark District. Internet: http://patersongreatfalls.org/0325pgf/00a.cgi?cr=01a00a00&hd=dhd&tl=dtl&tr=dtr&nl=dnl&bl=dbl&br=dbr&ft=dft&crx=00a. Accessed: 29 March 2008.

Green, Reginald H. and Ann Seidman. *Unity or Poverty – The Economics of Pan-Africanism*. Cambridge: Penguin Books, 1968.

Griffith, Lloyd, I. *The Quest for Security in the Caribbean – Problems and Promises in Subordinate States*. Armonk, New York: M.E. Sharpe, Inc., 1993.

Gutteridge, W.F. *Armed Forces in New States*. London: Oxford University Free Press for the Institute of Race Relations, 1962.

Gutteridge, W.F. "The Armed Forces in Ghana Today." *Canadian Army Journal*. Vol. 15, No. 3, 1961.

BIBLIOGRAPHY

Gutteridge, W.F. *The Place of the Army in Society in Commonwealth African Territories.* R.M.A. Sandhurst. Unpublished Study, 1960-61.

Gutteridge, W.F. "Undoing Military Coups in Africa." *Third World Quarterly.* Vol. 7, No. 1, January 1985.

Habron, John D. "Is there a Canadian Role in Regional Security?" *Canada, the Caribbean and Central America.* Edited by Brian MacDonald. Canadian Institute of Strategic Studies Proceedings, Fall 1985.

Hacker, Barton C. "The Weapons of the West: Military Technology and Modernization in 19th-Century China and Japan." *Technology and Culture.* Vol. 18, No. 1, January 1977.

Hale, William. *The Political and Economic Development of Modern Turkey.* London: Croom Helm, 1981.

Halpern, Manfred. "Middle Eastern Armies and the New Middle Class." *The Role of the Military in Underdeveloped Countries.* Edited by John J. Johnson. Princeton, New Jersey: Princeton University Press, 1962.

Head, Ivan and Pierre Trudeau. *The Canadian Way: Shaping Canada's Foreign Policy, 1968-1984.* Toronto: McClelland and Stewart, 1995.

Hellyer, Paul. *Damn the Torpedoes: My Fight to Unify Canada's Armed Forces.* Toronto: McClelland & Stewart, 1990.

Hettne, Bjorn. "The Ghanaian Experience with Military Rule." *Global Militarization.* Edited by Peter Wallensteen, Johan Galtung and Carlos Portales. Boulder, Colorado: Westview Press, Inc., 1986.

Hilliker, John and Donald Barry. *The Department of External Affairs, Vol. 2: Coming of Age, 1946-1968.* Montreal and Kingston: McGill-Queen's University Press, 1995.

Holmes, John W. "Canada's Role in the United Nations." *Air University Review.* May-June 1967.

Hopkins, Keith. "Civil-Military Relations in Developing Countries." *The British Journal of Sociology.* Vol. 17, No. 2, June 1966.

Hoskyns, Catherine. "Africa's Foreign Relations: The Case of Tanzania." *International Affairs.* Vol. 44, No. 3, July 1968.

Hunt, Garry, "Recollections of the Canadian Armed Forces Training Team in Ghana, 1961-1968." *Canadian Defence Quarterly.* April 1989.

Huntington, Samuel P. *Political Order in Changing Societies*. New Haven, Connecticut: Yale University Press, 1968.

Ishemo, Shubi L. "Symbol That Cannot Be Substituted: The Role of Mwalimu J. K. Nyerere in the Liberation of Southern Africa, 1955-1990." *Review of African Political Economy*. Vol. 27, No. 83, March 2000.

Jacob, Abel. "Israel's Military Aid to Tanzania, 1960-66." *The Journal of Modern African Studies*. Vol. 9, No. 2, August 1971.

Janowitz, Morris. *Military Institutions and Coercion in the Developing Nations*. Chicago: The University of Chicago Press, 1977.

Janowitz, Morris. *The Military in the Political Development of New Nations*. Chicago: The University of Chicago Press, 1967.

Johnson, John J. *The Military and Society in Latin America*. Stanford, California: Stanford University Press, 1964.

Johnson, John J. *The Role of the Military in Underdeveloped Countries*. Princeton, New Jersey: Princeton University Press, 1962.

Kanat, Roger E. "Soviet Military Assistance to the Third World." *Communist Nations' Military Assistance*. Edited by John F. Cooper and Daniel S. Papp. Boulder, Colorado: Westview Press, Inc, 1983.

Kaplan, Lawrence S. *A Community of Interests: NATO and the Military Assistance Program, 1948-1951*. Washington, D.C.: U.S. Government Printing Office, 1980.

Keith, Ronald C. "China and Canada's 'Pacific 2000 Strategy.'" *Pacific Affairs*. Vol. 65, No. 3, Autumn, 1992.

Kisanga, E.J. "Tanzania and the Organization of African Unity." *Foreign Policy of Tanzania 1961-1981: A Reader*. Edited by K. Mathews and S.S. Mushi. Dar es Salaam: Tanzania Publishing House, 1981.

Kposowa, Augustine J. and J. Craig Jenkins. "The Structural Sources of Military Coups in Postcolonial Africa, 1957-1984." *The American Journal of Sociology*. Vol. 99, No. 1, July 1993.

Kraus, Jon. "On the Politics of Nationalism and Social Change in Ghana." *The Journal of Modern African Studies*. Vol. 7, No. 1, April 1969.

Kublin, Hyman. "The "Modern" Army of Early Meiji Japan." *The Far Eastern Quarterly*. Vol. 9, No. 1, November 1949.

BIBLIOGRAPHY

Laqueur, Walter. "Communism and Nationalism in Tropical Africa." *Foreign Affairs*. Vol. 39, No. 4, July 1961.

Lee, J.M. *African Armies and Civil Order*. London: Chatto & Windus, 1970.

Legum, Colin. "Pan-Africanism, the Communists and the West." *African Affairs*. Vol. 63, No. 252, July 1964.

Legvold, Robert. *Soviet Policy in West Africa*. Cambridge, Massachusetts: Harvard University Press, 1970.

Leonard, Richard W. "Frelimo's Victories in Mozambique." *A Journal of Opinion*, Vol. 4, No. 2, Summer, 1974.

Lerner, Daniel and Richard D. Robinson. "Swords and Ploughshares: The Turkish Army as a Modernizing Force." *The Military Intervenes – Case Studies in Political Development*. Edited by Henry Bienen. Hartford, Connecticut: Connecticut Printers, 1968.

Leversedge, T.F.J. *Canadian Combat and Support Aircraft: A Military Compendium.* St. Catharines, Ontario: Vanwell Publishing, 2007.

Levey, Zach. "The Rise and Decline of a Special Relationship: Israel and Ghana, 1957-1966." *African Studies Review*. Vol. 46, No. 1, April 2003.

Library of Congress Country Studies, Ghana. Internet: http://lcweb2.loc.gov/cgi-bin/query/r?frd/cstdy:@field (DOCID+gh0160).

Lieuwen, Edwin. "Militarism and Politics in Latin America." *The Role of the Military in Underdeveloped Countries*. Edited by John J. Johnson. Princeton, New Jersey: Princeton University Press, 1962.

List, Friedrich. *The National System of Political Economy.* Translated by Sampson S. Lloyd, 1885. Internet: http://socserv.mcmaster.ca/econ/ugcm/3ll3/list/list1. Accessed: 31 March 2008.

Lockwood, Matthew. *The State They're In – An Agenda for International Action on Poverty in Africa*. Bourton Hall, Bourton-on Dunsmore, Warwickshire: ITDG Publishing, 2005.

Loomis, Dan G. *Not Much Glory – Quelling the F.L.Q.* Toronto: Deneau Publishers, 1984.

Lovell, John P and C. I. Eugene Kim. "The Military and Political Change in Asia." *Pacific Affairs*. Vol. 40, No. 1 / 2, Spring – Summer, 1967.

Loveman, Brian. *For la Patria: Politics and the Armed Forces in Latin America*. Wilmington, Delaware: Scholarly Resources Inc., 1999.

Luanda, Nestor. "A Changing Conception of Defence: A Historical Perspective of the Military in Tanzania." *Evolutions and Revolutions: A Contemporary History of Militaries in Southern Africa*. Pretoria: Institute for Security Studies, 2005.

Luanda, Nestor. "A Historical Perspective on Civil-Military Relations: 1964-1990." *Civil Security Relations in Tanzania: Investigating the Relationship Between the State, Security Services and Civil Society*. Edited by Martin Rupiya, Jonathan Lwehabura and Len le Roux. Pretoria: Institute for Security Studies, 2006.

Lyon, Peyton. *Canada and the Third World*. Toronto: Macmillan of Canada: 1976.

MacMillan, Margaret. *Nixon in China – The Week That Changed the World*. Toronto: Viking Canada, 2006.

Maloney, Sean M. *Canada and UN Peacekeeping – Cold War by Other Means, 1945-1970*. St. Catharines, Ontario: Vanwell Publishing Limited, 2002.

Maloney, Sean M. *The Roots of Soft Power – The Trudeau Government, De-NATOization and Denuclearization, 1967-1970*. Kingston, Queen's Centre for International Relations, 2005.

Maloney, Sean M. *War Without Battles – Canada's NATO Brigade in Germany, 1951-1993*. McGraw-Hill Ryerson Limited, 1997.

Matthews, Robert O. "Canada and Anglophone Africa." *Canada and the Third World*. Edited by Peyton Lyon and Tareq Y. Ismael. Toronto: Macmillan of Canada: 1976.

Mazrui, Ali A. "Anti-Militarism and Political Militancy in Tanzania." *The Journal of Conflict Resolution*. Vol. 12, No. 3, September 1968.

Mazrui, Ali A. "Nkrumah, Obote and Vietnam." *Transition*. No. 43, 1973.

Mazrui, Ali A. "Nkrumah: The Leninist Czar." *Transition*. No. 75/76. The Anniversary Issue: Selections from *Transition*, 1961-1976, 1997.

Mazrui, Ali A. "Tanzaphilia." *Transition*, No. 75/76. The Anniversary Issue: Selections from *Transition*, 1961-1976, 1997.

McCall, Christina and Stephen Clarkson. *Trudeau and Our Times: Volume 2: The Heroic Delusion*. Toronto: McClelland & Stewart Inc., 1994.

McClearn, Sandy. *The Canadian Navy of Yesterday & Today – World War II Canadian Ship Listing 1931-1945*. Internet: http://www.hazegray.org/navhist/canada/ww2/. Accessed: 6 August 2008.

McCune, George M. "Russian Policy in Korea: 1895-1898." *Far Eastern Survey*. Vol. 14, No. 19, September 26, 1945.

McGowan, Pat and Thomas H. Johnson. "Sixty Coups in Thirty Years – Further Evidence Regarding African Military Coups d'état." *The Journal of Modern African Studies*. Vol. 24, No. 3, September 1986.

Melady, Thomas Patrick. *Western Policy and the Third World*. New York: Hawthorn Books, Inc, 1967.

Meredith, Martin. *The Fate of Africa*. New York: Public Affairs, 2005.

Middlemiss, D.W., and Sokolsky, J.J. *Canadian Defence – Decisions and Determinants*. Toronto: Harcourt Brace Jovanovich, 1989.

Morrison. David R. *Aid and Ebb Tide – A History of CIDA and Canadian Development Assistance.* Waterloo: Wilfrid Laurier Press, 1998.

Morton, Desmond. *A Military History of Canada – From Champlain to Kosovo*. McClelland & Stewart Inc., 1999.

Mott, William H. *Military Assistance: An Operational Perspective*. Westport, Connecticut: Greenwood Publishing Group, 1999.

Mueller, Susanne D. "The Historical Origins of Tanzania's Ruling Class." *Canadian Journal of African Studies*. Vol. 15, No. 3, 1981.

Mullins, A.F., Jr. *Born Arming – Development and Military Power in New States*. Stanford, California: Stanford University Press, 1987.

Murray, Roger. "Second Thoughts on Ghana." *New Left Review*. 1/42, March-April 1967.

Mwakikagile, Godfrey. *Military Coups in West Africa since the Sixties*. Huntington, New York: Nova Science Publishers, Inc., 2001.

Mwakikagile, Godfrey. *Nyerere and Africa: End of an Era*. Las Vegas, Nevada: Protea Publishing Co., 2005.

Nelson, John R. Jr. "Alexander Hamilton and American Manufacturing: A Reexamination." *The Journal of American History*. Vol. 65, No. 4, March 1979.

Neuman, Stephanie G. "Arms Transfers, Military Assistance and Defence Industries: Socioeconomic Burden or Opportunity?" *Annals of the American Academy of Political and Social Science*. Vol. 535, September 1994.

Nkrumah, Kwame. *Neo-colonialism – The Last Stage of Imperialism*. London: Thomas Nelson and Sons Ltd., 1965.

Nkrumah, Kwame. *The Autobiography of Kwame Nkrumah*. London: Thomas Nelson and Sons Ltd., 1957.

Nun José. "The Middle Class Military Coup." *The Politics of Conformity in Latin America*. Edited by Claudio Veliz. New York: Oxford University Press, 1967.

Nunn, Frederick M. "Effects of European Military Training in Latin America: The Origins and Nature of Professional Militarism in Argentina, Brazil, Chile, and Peru, 1890-1940." *Military Affairs*. Vol. 39, No. 1, February 1975.

Nursey-Bray, P. F. "Tanzania: The Development Debate." *African Affairs*. Vol. 79, No. 314, January 1980.

Nyerere, Julius K. *Freedom and Development – A Selection from Writings and Speeches 1968-1973*. London: Oxford University Press, 1974.

Ochoche, Sunday, Abogonye. "The Military and National Security in Africa." *The Military and Militarism in Africa*. Edited by Eboe Hutchful and Abdoulaye Bathily. Dakar, Senegal: Codesiria Book Series, 1998.

Ocran, A.K. *A Myth is Broken*. Harlow: Longmans, 1968.

Odetola Olatunde. *Military Regimes and Development – A Comparative Analysis in African Societies*. London: George Allen & Unwin, 1982.

Opello, Walter C. Jr. "Guerrilla War in Portuguese Africa: An Assessment of the Balance of Force in Mozambique." *A Journal of Opinion*. Vol. 4, No. 2, Summer, 1974.

Pach, Chester, J. *Arming the Free World: The Origins of the United States Military Assistance Program, 1945-1950*. Chapel Hill: University of North Carolina Press, 1991.

BIBLIOGRAPHY

Pachter, Elise Forbes. "Contra-Coup: Civilian Control of the Military in Guinea, Tanzania, and Mozambique." *The Journal of Modern African Studies*. Vol. 20, No. 4, December 1982.

Packenham, Robert A. "Political-Development Doctrines in the American Foreign Aid Program." *World Politics*. Vol. 18, No. 2, January 1966.

Papp, Daniel S. "Communist Military Assistance." *Communist Nations' Military Assistance*. Edited by John F. Cooper and Daniel S. Papp. Boulder, Colorado: Westview Press, Inc, 1983.

Pearson, Geoffrey, A.H. *Seize the Day – Lester B. Pearson and Crisis Diplomacy*. Ottawa: Carleton University Press, 1993.

Pearson, Lester B. *Mike – The Memoirs of the Right Honourable Lester B. Pearson – Vol. II, 1948-1957*. Toronto: University of Toronto Press, 1973.

Phillips, Dion E., and Alma H. Young. "Toward and Understanding of Militarization in the Third World and the Caribbean." *Militarization in the Non-Hispanic Caribbean*. Edited by Alma H. Young & Dion E. Phillips. Boulder, Colorado: Lynne Rienner Publishers, Inc., 1986.

Pinkney, Robert. *Ghana Under Military Rule 1966-1969*. London: Methuen & Co Ltd., 1972.

Poole, Peter A. "Communist China's Aid Diplomacy." *Asian Survey*. Vol. 6, No. 11, November 1966.

Powell, John Duncan. "Military Assistance and Militarism in Latin America." *The Western Political Quarterly*. Vol. 18, No. 2, Part 1, June 1965.

Pratt, Cranford. "Julius Nyerere: Reflections on the Legacy of His Socialism." *Canadian Journal of African Studies*. Vol. 33, No. 1, 1999.

Pratt, Cranford. *The Critical Phase in Tanzania, 1945-1968: Nyerere and the Emergence of a Socialist Strategy*. Cambridge: Cambridge University Press, 1976.

Price, H.E.C. "Tanzania Tale…" *Sentinel*. Vol. 2:2, March 1966.

Price, Robert M. "Military Officers and Political Leadership: The Ghanaian Case." *Comparative Politics*. Vol. 3, No. 3, April 1971.

Price, Robert M. "Neo-Colonialism and Ghana's Economic Decline: A Critical Assessment." *Canadian Journal of African Studies*. Vol. 18, No. 1, 1984.

Pye, Lucian W. "Armies in the Process of Political Modernization." *The Role of the Military in Underdeveloped Countries*. Edited by John J. Johnson. Princeton, New Jersey: Princeton University Press, 1962.

Ra'anan, Uri. *Arms Transfers to the Third World: The Military Buildup in Less Industrialized Countries*. Boulder, Colorado: Westview Press Inc, 1978.

Ra'anan, Uri. *The USSR Arms the Third World: Case Studies in Soviet Foreign Policy*. Cambridge, Massachusetts: The M.I.T. Press, 1969.

Radwanski, George. *Trudeau*. Toronto: Macmillan Company of Canada, 1978.

Rasiulis, Andrew, P. "The Military Training Assistance Program (MTAP) – An Instrument of Military Diplomacy." *Canadian Military Journal*. Autumn 2001.

Reid, Escott. *Radical Mandarin, The Memoirs of Escott Reid*. Toronto: University of Toronto Press, 1989.

Rodkey, F. S. "Colonel Campbell's Report on Egypt in 1840, with Lord Palmerston's Comments." *Cambridge Historical Journal*. Vol. 3, No. 1, 1929.

Rouquié, Alain. *The Military and the State in Latin America*. Translated by Paul E. Sigmund. Berkeley: University of California Press, 1987.

Rupiah, Martin. "The 'Expanding Torrent': British Military Assistance to the Southern African Region." *African Security Review*. Vol. 5, No. 4, 1996.

Rustow, Dankwart A. *Politics and Westernization in the Near East*. Princeton: Center of International Studies, 1956.

Sabourn, Louis. "Canada and Francophone Africa." *Canada and the Third World*. Edited by Peyton Lyon and Tareq Y. Ismael. Toronto: Macmillan of Canada, 1976.

Sanger, Clyde. "Canada and Development in the Third World." *Canada and the Third World*. Edited by Peyton Lyon and Tareq Y. Ismael. Toronto: Macmillan of Canada, 1976.

Sanger, Clyde. *Half a Loaf – Canada's Semi-Role Among Developing Countries*. Toronto: The Ryerson Press, 1969.

Sater, William F. "The Impact of Foreign Advisors on Chile's Armed Forces, 1810-2005." *Military Advising and Assistance – From Mercenaries to Privatization, 1815-2007.* Edited by Donald Stoker. London: Routledge, 2008.

Saul, John S. "The Revolution in Portugal's African Colonies: A Review Essay." *Canadian Journal of African Studies.* Vol. 9, No. 2, 1975.

Schatten, Fritz. *Communism in Africa.* London: George Allen & Unwin Ltd, 1966.

Seidman, A.W. *Ghana's Development Experience.* Nairobi: East African Publishing House, 1978.

Sharpe, John L. *Two Years in Ghana West Africa 1966-68.* Ottawa: Unpublished Memoir, 2007.

Shaw, Tim. "South Africa's Military Capability and the Future of Race Relations." *Arms and Development – Proceedings of the First Pan-African Citizens' Conference.* Edited by Frederick S. Arkhurst. New York: Praeger Publishers, 1972.

Shils, Edward. "The Military in the Political Development of the New States." *The Role of the Military in Underdeveloped Countries.* Edited by John J. Johnson. Princeton, New Jersey: Princeton University Press, 1962.

Snow, Phillip. "China and Africa." *Chinese Foreign Policy – Theory and Practice.* Edited by Thomas W. Robinson and David Shambaugh. Oxford: Oxford University Press, 1994.

Spicer, Keith. *A Samaritan State? External Aid in Canada's Foreign Policy.* Toronto: Toronto University Press, 1966.

Stacey, C.P. *A Date with History – Memoirs of a Canadian Historian.* Ottawa: Deneau, 1983.

Stark, Frank M. "Theories of Contemporary State Formation in Africa: A Reassessment." *The Journal of Modern African Studies.* Vol. 24, No. 2, June 1986.

Stavrianos, L.S. *Global Rift – The Third World Comes of Age.* New York, William Morrow and Company, 1981.

Stigger, Phillip. "A Study in Confusion: Canadian Diplomatic Staffing Practices in Africa and the Middle East." *Canadian Journal of African Studies / Revue Canadienne des Études Africaines.* Vol. 5, No. 3, 1971.

Stockwell, John. *In Search of Enemies: A CIA Story*. New York: W.W. Norton & Company, Inc., 1978.

Stoker, Donald, *Military Advising and Assistance – From Mercenaries to Privatization*, 1815-2007. London: Routledge, 2008.

Sutherland R.J. "Canada's Long Term Strategic Situation." *International Journal*. Vol. 17, No. 3, Summer 1962.

Time Magazine, *Death at the Gate*, 25 January 1963. Internet: http://www.time.com/time/magazine/article/0,9171,940219,00.html Accessed: 18 November 2007.

Time Magazine, *For Tomorrow*, 17 January 1944. Internet: http://www.time.com/time/magazine/article/0,9171,796313,00.html. Accessed: 28 February 2008.

Thompson, Scott W. *Ghana's Foreign Policy, 1957-1966 – Diplomacy, Ideology and the New State*. Princeton, New Jersey: Princeton University Press, 1969.

Trudeau, Pierre Elliot. *Memoirs*. Toronto: McClelland & Stewart Inc., 1993.

University of Pennsylvania, University Archives and Records Center (African Studies Center). Internet: http://www.archives.upenn.edu/people/notables/nkrumah/nkrumah_exhibit.html. Accessed : 23 February 2009.

Varas, Augusto. *Militarization and the International Arms Race in Latin America*. Boulder, Colorado: Westview Press, 1985.

Walling, Karl. "Was Alexander Hamilton a Machiavellian Statesman?" *The Review of Politics*. Vol. 57, No. 3, Summer, 1995.

Welch, Claude E., Jr., "African Military and Political Development: Reflections on a Score of Years, and Several Score of Studies." *A Journal of Opinion*. Vol. 13, 1984.

Welch, Claude E., Jr. "Praetorianism in Commonwealth West Africa." *The Journal of Modern African Studies*. Vol. 10, No. 2, July 1972.

Welch, Claude E., Jr. *Soldier and State in Africa – a Comparative Analysis of Military Intervention and Political Change*. Evanston: Northwestern University Press, 1970.

BIBLIOGRAPHY

Welch, Claude E. Jr. "The Right of Association in Ghana and Tanzania." *The Journal of Modern African Studies*. Vol. 16, No. 4, December 1978.

Wesson, Robert G. *The Latin American Military Institution*. New York: Praeger, 1986.

Westad, Odd Arne. *The Global Cold War*. Cambridge: Cambridge University Press, 2005.

Whitaker, Reg and Steve Hewitt. *Canada and the Cold War*. Toronto: James Lorimer & Company Ltd., Publishers, 2003.

Willner, L.A., S. Maloney, and Sandy Babcock. *Canadian Forces Operations 1945-1969. ORD Project Report PR 2002/11*. Ottawa: Operational Research Division: October 2002.

Wilz, John Edward. "Did the United States Betray Korea in 1905?" *The Pacific Historical Review*. Vol. 54, No. 3, August 1985.

Windle, Charles and T.R. Vallance. "Optimizing Military Assistance Training." *World Politics*. Vol. 15, No. 1, October 1962.

Wolf, Charles Jr. "Defense and Development in Less Developed Countries." *Operations Research*. Vol. 10, No. 6, November – December 1962.

Wolf, Charles Jr. *Economic Impacts of Military Assistance*. Santa Monica: Rand Paper P4578, 1971.

Wolpin, Miles D. *Military Aid and Counterrevolution in the Third World*. Lexington, Massachusetts: Lexington Books, 1972.

Wright, Mary C. "The Adaptability of Ching Diplomacy: The Case of Korea." *The Journal of Asian Studies*. Vol. 17, No. 3, May, 1958.

Yamamura Kozo. "Success Illgotten? The Role of Meiji Militarism in Japan's Technological Progress." *The Journal of Economic History*. Vol. 37, No. 1, March 1977.

Young, Roger. *Canadian Development Assistance to Tanzania*. Ottawa: The North South Institute, 1983.

Yu, George T. "Africa in Chinese Foreign Policy." *Asian Survey*. Vol. 28, No. 8, August 1988.

Zolberg, Aristide R. *Military Intervention in the New States of Tropical Africa: Elements of Comparative Analysis*. "The Military Intervenes – Case Studies in Political Development." Edited by Henry Bienen. Hartford, Connecticut: Connecticut Printers, 1968.

ABOUT THE AUTHOR

Commissioned in 1982 as an artillery officer, Lieutenant-Colonel Christopher Richard Kilford has served throughout Canada, Germany and Afghanistan in various command, instructional and staff roles. More recently, he was the Military Liaison Officer to the Standing Senate Committee on National Security and Defence and has just completed a year-long tour in Afghanistan as the Deputy Military Attaché in the Canadian Embassy, Kabul. In 2011, upon completion of Turkish language training, Lieutenant-Colonel Kilford will then be posted to Ankara, Turkey as the Military Attaché in the Canadian Embassy. He has completed Army Staff College, the Canadian Land Forces Command and Staff Course, the Advanced Military Staff Course and was granted equivalency for the National Security Program in 2009.

In 1992, he obtained his Bachelor of Arts degree at the University of Manitoba in Political Science and now holds a Masters Degree in War Studies and a Masters Degree in Defence Studies, both from the Royal Military College. In 2009, he completed his Ph.D. at Queen's University in Kingston where his thesis focused on the subject of military training assistance in the developing world in the post-war period.

INDEX

C

INDEX

D

N

O

Observer 183, 204

Olatunde Odetola 30, *endnotes* **242**

Olympio, Sylvanus 28

Opello, Walter C., Jr. *endnotes* **267, 268**

Organization of African Unity 33, 34, 145-147, 152, 158, 177, 192

Organization of American States 87

Otu, Stephen, Major-General 121, 141, 152, 153, *endnotes* **276**

Otu, Michael, Air Vice Marshal 155

P

Pach, Chester 41, 43, 45, *endnotes* **244**

Pakistan vi, 6, 33, 39, 47, 56, 66, 72, 77-80, 85, 89, 90, 92, 96, 97, 153, 232, 233, *endnotes* **242, 250, 252, 277**

Pan-African Congress 176

Pan-African Freedom Movement of East and Central Africa 177

Panama 43, 71

Papp, Daniel, S. *endnotes* **244, 245**

Pasha, Ismail 17

Pearson, Lester 3, 59-61, 69, 72, 79, 107, 109, 172, 191, 199, 203, 205, 207, 227, 231, 235, 236, *endnotes* **246, 248, 255, 276, 278**

Peers, Roy 76

Pentagon, United States 44, 81

Perry, Matthew 19

Peru 43, 71

Philippines 43

S

T

U